The Splendor of Love

John Paul II's Vision for Marriage and Family

Walter Schu, L.C.

New Hope Publications

Nihil Obstat:
Msgr. David Q. Liptak, *Censor Librorum*

Imprimatur:
+Archbishop Daniel A. Cronin
(Hartford, CT)
April 29, 2002

The *Nihil Obstat* and *Imprimatur* are official declarations that a book or pamphlet is free from doctrinal or moral error. No implications are contained therein that those who have granted the *Nihil Obstat* or the *Imprimatur* agree with the contents, statements, or opinions expressed.

Cover Design: John Damelio; Peter Huynh, LC
Photo of John Paul II: Grzegorz Galazka (used with permission)
Family photo: Getty Images (used with permission)

ISBN #1-892875-18-7

For Father Marcial Maciel, L.C., Nuestro Padre. May this work help each one who reads it to love, live, and spread faithfully our Holy Father's teachings on marriage and the family. May it enable us to bring many others to know the truth that will set them free (cf. Jn. 8:32) — the One who is "the way, and the truth, and the life" (Jn. 14:6) — Jesus Christ.

Your Kingdom Come!

Contents

ACKNOWLEDGMENTS xvii

ABBREVIATIONS xix

INTRODUCTION: George Weigel xxi

PROLOGUE: A Gift to the Church and the World xxv

PART I MANKIND AND THE FAMILY

ONE   The Future of Humanity 3

TWO   Mankind's Future at Risk: Assaults on the Family 17

PART II DEFENDING MARRIAGE AND FAMILY: JOHN PAUL II's THEOLOGY OF THE BODY

THREE   The Exalted Dignity of Marriage:
        A Vision of the Human Person Born of Faith 51

FOUR   The Whole Human Person at a Glance 63

FIVE   The Three States of Man............................. 77

SIX   A Total Vision of Man: Three Applications 117

PART III NATURAL FAMILY PLANNING vs. CONTRACEPTION: TWO IRRECONCILABLE VIEWS OF THE HUMAN PERSON

SEVEN   "Love and All that is Opposed to Love": The Development
        of Natural Family Planning and Contraception.......... 157

EIGHT   Contraception's Ideological Roots:
        A Compelling Response 179

NINE   Contraception's View of Men and Women:
        Objects To Be Manipulated 213

TEN   What Lies Hidden Behind Contraception............... 251

ELEVEN   Natural Family Planning Views Men and Women: Free
        Personal Subjects in their Inviolable Mystery 275

TWELVE   "Through Him, With Him, In Him": Responsible
        Parenthood and the Spirituality of Marriage 329

CONCLUSION: Evangelizing the Family in
        the Third Christian Millennium 345

Select Bibliography 355

Index of Names 369

Index of Topics 373

Detailed Contents

ACKNOWLEDGMENTS xvii
ABBREVIATIONS xix
INTRODUCTION: George Weigel xxi
PROLOGUE: A Gift to the Church and the World xxv

PART I MANKIND AND THE FAMILY

ONE
THE FUTURE OF HUMANITY 3

I. Society's First and Vital Cell 5
  A. A Crucial Relationship 5
  B. The "First Society" 6
    1. A Communion of Persons 6
    2. Communion and Community 7
    3. The Community of the Family and Society 7
II. A Domestic Church: Humanity's Transcendent Destiny 8
  A. The Family's Prophetic Role:
    "A Believing and Evangelizing Community" 8
    1. A Gift that Lasts Forever 8
    2. "In the Image of God" 9
  B. The Family's Priestly Role:
    "A Community in Dialogue with God" 12
  C. The Family's Kingly Role:
    "A Community at the Service of Man" 14
  D. *Ecclesia Domestica*: Society's Best Ally 14

TWO
MANKIND'S FUTURE AT RISK: ASSAULTS ON THE FAMILY 17

I. Beyond Tears: The Rise of Planned Parenthood 19
II. "Male and Female He Created Them":
  The Threat of Same-Sex Partnerships 22
  A. A Question of "Tolerance" and Civil Rights? 22
  B. The Homosexual Agenda: To Destroy Marriage 22
    1. The Eradication of Marriage: An Overt Goal 22
    2. Why Same-Sex Partnerships Undermine Marriage 23
      a) Socially 23
      b) Legally 24
    3. Refuting "Same-Sex Partnership Status" as a Civil Right 24

4. The Ultimate Goal of Homosexual Activists: Redefine
Creation and Redemption 25
   a) "In the Beginning" 25
   b) Redeemed by Christ's Blood 26
   c) A Society that Would Oppose Christ's Redemption? 27
   d) True Compassion: "Go, and Sin No More" 27
C. "Clear and Present Danger":
Homosexual Advances Already Secured 28
   1. The Corporate Scene, Universities, and Municipalities 29
   2. The Courts 29
   3. The American Psychological Association 30
      a) Immoral Behavior as a Civil Right 30
      b) Just the Facts: A Quest for Young People 31
        (1) "Facts" or an Agenda? 31
        (2) Legal Threats and Academic Censorship 34
D. The Church's Liberating Teaching on Homosexuality 35
E. Our Duty as Christians and Citizens 36
III. Radical Feminism at the U. N.: "A Gender Perspective" 38
A. Dramas on the World Stage 38
B. The Overt Goal of Radical Feminism: Redefine Equality 39
C. A More Pernicious Goal: Redefine Gender Itself 40
D. Consequences of a Gender Perspective:
The Manipulation of Human Rights 41
E. How Did Radical Feminism Come About? 42
   1. The Early 1960s: Liberal Feminism 42
   2. The Late 1960s: Radical Feminists and Neo-Marxism 43
   3. Are Radical Feminists Really Marxists? 44
F. Really Radical Feminism: From Marxism to Deconstructionism 44
G. Cardinal Ratzinger Assesses U.N. Ideologies 45
H. Our Response to the U.N. as Christians 46

PART II DEFENDING MARRIAGE AND FAMILY:
JOHN PAUL II'S THEOLOGY OF THE BODY

THREE
THE EXALTED DIGNITY OF MARRIAGE:
A VISION OF THE HUMAN PERSON BORN OF FAITH 51
AN ADEQUATE ANTHROPOLOGY 53
I. The Only Creature God Willed for Itself 53
A. Why Are Persons So Unique? 54
   1. Only Persons Can *Love* 54
   2. Only Persons Are *Responsible* 55
B. Why Are Persons So Fragile?
Transcendent Greatness and Inescapable Dependence 55
C. Loving and Using: The Personalistic Norm 56
   1. Using 56

2. The Personalistic Norm 57
3. A Dilemma 57
4. A Response: Christ's New Commandment 58
5. Love and Marriage 59
II. Man Can Only Find Himself in the Sincere Gift of Self 59
III. Only Christ Fully Reveals Man to Himself 60

FOUR
THE WHOLE HUMAN PERSON AT A GLANCE 63

I. Between Two Worlds: The Rational Faculties 64
II. Where It All Begins: Sense Knowledge 68
III. Born To Obey Reason: The Emotions 69
A. Seeking Good and Avoiding Evil: The Concupiscible Passions 69
B. When Good is Difficult and Evil Threatens: The Irascible Passions . 70
C. The Emotions Among Themselves: How Should They Relate? 70
D. The Emotions Meet Reason and Will: What Should Happen? 71
IV. Fully Human Love: Will or Emotion? 73

FIVE
THE THREE STATES OF MAN 77

I. Original Man 79
A. Original Solitude 79
B. Original Unity 79
C. Original Nakedness 80
D. "Naked without Shame": The Nuptial Meaning of the Body 81
1. The Body Reveals Divine Mysteries 81
2. The Body Reveals Man 81
3. The Body Reveals Man and Woman as a Gift for Each Other 82
4. Creation Itself: A First and Fundamental Gift 82
5. Freedom: Condition for the Gift of Self 83
6. The Nuptial Meaning of the Body and Procreation 83
7. The Nuptial Meaning of the Body: A Final View 85
II. Historical Man 86
A. Tainted by Sin 86
1. The Appearance of Shame 87
2. Lust: The Source of Shame 88
3. The Nuptial Meaning of the Body in Peril 88
   a) From a Person to an Object 88
   b) From Free Self-Giving to Appropriation 89
4. "The Heart — A Battlefield between Love and Lust" 90
   a) "More Devious than Any Other Thing" 90
   b) A Quest for Love: The Twofold Meaning of Shame 91
   c) Shame and The Nature of the Human Person 92
B. Redeemed by Christ's Blood 95
1. An Appeal to the Heart: The Sermon on the Mount 95
2. The Redemption of the Body 96

3. Life According to the Spirit. 99
   a) A New Power at Work Within Us 99
   b) A New Freedom 100
   c) Purity: The Fruit of Life According to the Spirit 101
      (1) Twofold Dimension of Purity:
         Moral Virtue and Gift of the Holy Spirit 102
      (2) Twofold Dignity of the Body:
         Personal Spirit and Indwelling of the Holy Spirit 103
   d) Life According to the Spirit:
      Ethical Norm and Anthropological Truth. 104
   e) The Fruit of Purity in the Holy Spirit: Joy 105
III. Eschatological Man 107
  A. "He truly has risen! Alleluia!" 108
  B. What Will Heaven Be Like? Similarities and Differences. 109
  C. A Completely New State of Human Life 111
    1. Spiritualization of the Body 111
    2. Divinization of the Body. 112
    3. Face-to-Face Vision of God 112
    4. Communion of Saints 113
    5. Perfection of the Human Subject 113
    6. Fulfillment of the Nuptial Meaning of the Body 114

Six
A Total Vision of Man: Three Applications 117

I. "Virginity for the Kingdom of Heaven": The Celibate Vocation 118
  A. The Nature of the Call to Celibacy 119
  B. The Inner Meaning of Celibacy for the Kingdom 119
    1. A Charismatic Sign of Our Eternal Destiny 119
    2. A Decisive Turning Point in Revealing
      the Meaning of the Body 120
  C. What Moves Someone to Choose Celibacy? 121
  D. Celibacy and Marriage 122
    1. Two Complementary Vocations. 122
      a) How Marriage Sheds Light on Celibacy 123
      b) How Celibacy for the Kingdom Affirms Marriage 123
    2. Is the Celibate Vocation Superior? 124
    3. Only Charity is Supreme. 125
    4. Celibacy and Marriage: Living the Redemption of the Body . . . 126
II. "As Christ Loves the Church": The Vocation to Married Life 127
  A. Analogy and Mystery: To Glimpse the Transcendent 128
  B. Sacrament: The Hidden Mystery Made Visible 131
    1. From the Mystery of Creation and Redemption
      to the Seven Sacraments: A Fundamental Analogy 131
    2. The Keystone of Ephesians 5 133
  C. A Twofold Analogy: Understanding Marriage Itself 135
    1. "Out of Reverence for Christ" 135

2. A Sacrament of Hope 137
3. Marriage as a Sacrament:
   The Conjugal Union of Husband and Wife 140
   a) "I take you as my wife. . . . I take you as my husband":
      The Matter and Form of Marriage 140
   b) "Living in the Truth": The Language of the Body 142
   c) Speaking the Language of the Body in Truth:
      To Create a Culture of Life 145
III. "Love and Fruitfulness": Reflections on *Humanae Vitae* 147
   A. The Song of Songs:
      "Truth and Freedom — the Foundation of True Love" 147
      1. "My Sister, My Bride": Love Reveals the Person 149
      2. "A Garden Enclosed": The Freedom of the
         Gift and the Inviolable Mystery of the Person 150
   B. The Book of Tobit: Love as a "Test of Life and Death" 151
      1. A Struggle Between Good and Evil:
         The Objective Dimension of Human Love 151
      2. Conjugal Life as Liturgical:
         The Splendor of Redeemed Love 152

PART III NATURAL FAMILY PLANNING VS. CONTRACEPTION:
TWO IRRECONCILABLE VIEWS OF THE HUMAN PERSON

SEVEN
"LOVE AND ALL THAT IS OPPOSED TO LOVE":
   THE DEVELOPMENT OF NATURAL FAMILY PLANNING
   AND CONTRACEPTION 157
I. Contraception: Just What is at Stake? 158
II. The Development of Modern Forms of Contraception 160
   A. "Contraception": An Authoritative Definition 160
   B. Barrier Methods of Contraception 160
   C. Sterilization 162
   D. A Revolutionary Development: The Pill 164
      1. Is It Effective? 164
      2. Is It Safe? 165
      3. Is It Moral? 166
III. Is There a Reliable Alternative? — Natural Family Planning 167
   A. The Fertility Cycle 167
   B. Calendar Rhythm: A First, Ineffective Form of NFP 168
   C. Modern, Effective Methods of NFP 170
      1. The Sympto-Thermal Method 170
         —A Noble Sacrifice that Enriches Married Love 171
      2. The Ovulation or Billings Method 171
      3. A Little-Known Aspect of NFP: Ecological Breastfeeding 172
IV. Is Natural Family Planning Really Effective? 173
V. Does Natural Family Planning Make for Happy Marriages? 174

A. Artificial Contraception and Divorce 174
B. NFP and Enduring Marriages 175
VI. Conclusion: "The Word Is Very Near You" 177

EIGHT
CONTRACEPTION'S IDEOLOGICAL ROOTS: A COMPELLING RESPONSE 179

I. Why Is Contraception Flourishing? 180
A. Economic Factors 180
B. Ideological Roots 180
II. Origins of the Contraceptive Mentality:
Nineteenth Century Malthusianism 181
III. "What is Man?" — Eighteenth Century Rationalist Materialism 181
A. Sapere Aude: The Enlightenment 182
B. From Exaltation to Abasement:
A Reductive View of the Human Person 183
1. The Elimination of Mystery 183
2. The Opposition Between Faith and Reason 183
3. The Divorce of Faith and Culture 184
4. The Darkening of Reason: Radical Skepticism 185
IV. The Twentieth Century:
Reaping the Bitter Fruits of Enlightened Rationalism 186
A. Secular Humanism and Other Destructive "-isms" 186
B. "The Pulverization of the Person" 188
V. A Reply to Rationalist Materialism 190
A. Critique 190
1. Materialism Refuted 190
2. Skepticism Refuted 192
a) The Horizons of Reason:
Philosophy and the Empirical Sciences 192
b) The "Intelligent Design" Movement:
Opening the Empirical Sciences to Reason's Horizons 194
(1) Specified Complexity:
Detecting Intelligent Design Empirically 194
(2) Irreducible Complexity:
Intelligent Design in Biology — Darwinism Refuted 198
c) Skepticism: Self-destruction by Self-contradiction 200
3. Relativism Refuted 201
B. John Paul II's Compelling Response:
Fides et Ratio (Faith and Reason) 203
1. Humanity Today: A "Crisis of Meaning" 203
2. Why a Crisis? Man is a Being Who Seeks the Truth 205
3. To Resolve the Crisis:
Restoring Reason's Confidence in Itself 206
4. How to Restore Reason's Confidence—
Healing the Rupture Between Faith and Reason 206
a) Allies, Not Antagonists 206

b) Two Wings to Rise Toward Truth 208
5. To Seek the Truth in Love 208
6. The Truth is a Person: Christ! 210

NINE
CONTRACEPTION'S VIEW OF MEN AND WOMEN:
OBJECTS TO BE MANIPULATED 213

I. The Historical Drama of Contraception Unfolds 214
  A. The "Great Mystery" Is Threatened 214
  B. Planned Parenthood and a "New Sexual Order" 215
  C. Contraception: From Secular Ideology to Christian Heresy 215
II. The Catholic Church Defends the Inviolable
    Mystery of Married Love 216
  A. *Casti Connubii*: A Response to the Lambeth Conference 216
  B. Pius XII: Defending Married Love in the Decade of the Pill 218
  C. John XXIII: The Beginning of Dissent 218
  D. *Gaudium et Spes*: Married Love in the Mystery of God's Plan 220
III. *Humanae Vitae*: The Truth That Sets Married Love Free 221
  A. A Sign of Contradiction 221
  B. A New Phenomenon: Widespread Dissent 222
  C. Resisting Erroneous Theology:
    A Firm Defense of the Human Person 225
  D. Seeking to Win Over Theologians:
    "The Bruised Reed He Shall Not Break" 227
    1. 1989: The *Profession of Faith and Oath of Fidelity* 227
    2. 1990: The Instruction on the Ecclesial
      Vocation of the Theologian *Donum Veritatis* 228
    3. 1998: *Ad Tuendam Fidem* (To Defend the Faith) 230
  E. *Humanae Vitae's* Prophecies 231
    1. Conjugal Infidelity and a Lowering of Morality
      — Especially Among Young People 232
    Sex Education, Contraception, and Abortion 232
    2. Loss of Respect for Women 233
    3. A Dangerous Weapon in the Hands of Public Authorities 236
IV. Behind the Tragic Effects of Contraception:
    A Flawed Idea of the Human Person 238
  A. Persons in the Rationalist View:
    Individual Members of the Human Species 239
    1. A Fallacious Reduction 239
    2. Can Persons Be Treated as Numerical Individuals? 239
  B. Persons and Nature:
    From Legitimate Dominion to Absolute Autonomy 240
  C. Persons and Their Bodies:
    What Lies Hidden Behind Contraception 242
    1. The Essential Problem in the
      Responsible Transmission of Life 242

a) Persons: Self-Mastery Through Virtue 242
b) Self-Mastery and the Human Body 243
c) The Inner Meaning of the Conjugal Act. 244
2. The Essential Evil of the Contraceptive Act 245
3. Inevitable Effects of Contraception 246
a) Sexuality Becomes "Commonplace" 246
b) The Person Becomes an Object 247
D. Conclusion: The Contraceptive "Order of Things" 248

TEN
WHAT LIES HIDDEN BEHIND CONTRACEPTION 251

I. Cartesian Body-Soul Dualism 252
A. *"Cogito"*: A Quest for Certainty 253
B. Critique: A "Not-So-Methodical" Doubt 254
C. Man: An Embodied Spirit — A Response to Dualism 255
II. Implicit Biologism. 256
A. Is *Humanae Vitae* Just for Catholics? 256
1. Natural Law: Human Reason
Participates in God's Own Understanding 256
2. Characteristics of the Natural Moral Law 258
3. The Magisterium's Authority Regarding the Natural Law 259
B. *"Cogito ergo sum"* and the Alleged
Biologism of *Humanae Vitae* 262
1. The Accusation:
Enslaving Reason and Free Will to Biology. 262
2. Paul VI: Facing the Charge Squarely. 262
3. Underlying Errors in the Attack Against *Humanae Vitae* 263
a) Body-Soul Dualism and a False Abstraction
of the Biological Order. 263
b) Misinterpretation of the Natural Law 264
c) A Profound Irony:
The Biologism of *Humanae Vitae's* Critics 266
III. Selfish Utilitarianism. 267
A. Pleasure as the Object of Our Free Acts:
Utilitarianism's Critical Error. 268
B. The Utilitarian Principle:
Maximize Pleasure and Minimize Pain 269
C. Utilitarian Love: "The Harmonizing of Egoisms" 270
D. Instrumentalizing the Human Person 271
E. Contraception's Manifest Utilitarianism. 272
IV. Conclusion: The Resounding Words of *Familiaris Consortio* 272

ELEVEN
NATURAL FAMILY PLANNING VIEWS MEN AND WOMEN:
FREE PERSONAL SUBJECTS IN THEIR INVIOLABLE MYSTERY 275

I. A Transcendent Vision of the Person. 276

A. Personal Subjects in the Unity of Body and Soul 276
B. Freedom and Truth: The Inviolable Mystery of the Person 277
C. Man's Capacity for Truth: The Condition of Freedom 279
D. Duty: The Highest Manifestation of Freedom 280
II. True Human Love: Attraction, Affection, or Union of Persons? 283
  A. Love as Attraction: The Sexual Urge 284
    1. Sexual Attraction *vs.* Love: Acts of Man and Human Acts 285
    2. The Sexual Urge and Contraception: Can They Be Reconciled? . . 286
  B. Love as Affection: The Emotions 288
    1. The Vital Role of Emotions in Life and Love 288
    2. The Ambivalence of Sentimental Love 290
    3. The Need to Integrate Love 291
  C. Love as Goodwill: The Unification of Persons 293
  D. Betrothed Love: The Gift of Self 293
    1. The Divine Aspect of Love: To Desire God for the Beloved 295
    2. Love Put to the Test 295
III. Chastity: The Indispensable Condition of Love 298
  A. Continence:
    Obstacle to Tenderness, Spontaneity, and Affection? 299
    1. The Accusation 299
    2. Temperance, Chastity, and Continence:
      Are They the Same? 300
  B. Continence: Condition for Authentic
    Tenderness, Spontaneity and Affection 302
    1. An Eminently Positive Virtue 302
    2. A Virtue that Fosters Tenderness and Affection 303
    3. Spontaneity of the Passions or of the Person? 306
      a) Eros and *Ethos*: Called to Meet in the Human Heart 306
      b) Redemption: The Gift and Task
        of Conquering Spontaneity 308
    4. Living a True Communion of Persons 310
IV. Contraception *vs.* Natural Family Planning:
  The Essential Moral Difference 312
  A. Essential Difference in the Act 313
    1. The Three Factors of Morality 313
      a) The Object 314
      b) The Intention 315
      c) The Circumstances 316
    2. Good and Evil Acts 317
      a) Three to One: It Is Harder to Do
        Good than to Commit Evil 317
      b) Intrinsically Evil Acts 318
    3. Why a Contraceptive Act Is Essentially Different from
      Intercourse Only During the Infertile Periods 319
  B. Essential Difference in Attitudes 321
    1. Attitude Toward Procreation: Openness to Life 321

     a) Chastity Must Be a Moral Virtue, Not Just a Technique 322
     b) How to Practice Periodic Continence as a Virtue 323
  2. Attitude Toward One's Spouse: Love and Responsibility 324
  3. Attitude Toward God: "Respect for the Creator" 325
V. Conclusion: The Future of Humanity 326

TWELVE
"THROUGH HIM, WITH HIM, IN HIM":
    RESPONSIBLE PARENTHOOD AND THE SPIRITUALITY OF MARRIAGE . . . 329

I. Responsible Parenthood: Inseparably
  Linked to Marriage Spirituality 330
  A. Responsible Parenthood: General Attitudes 330
  B. Responsible Parenthood: Specific Questions 332
    1. Is There an Obligation for Married
      Persons to Have Children? 332
    2. Is the Obligation Absolute? 333
    3. What Are Just Reasons for Limiting Family Size? 334
    4. Should Parents Have Few Children? 335
II. The Strength to Live Responsible Parenthood:
  Marriage Spirituality 338
  A. Fundamental Element: The Gifts of the Holy Spirit 338
    1. Love Poured Out 338
    2. The Gift of Piety 339
    3. Contraception: The Antithesis of Conjugal Spirituality 340
  B. Prayer and the Sacraments 341
    1. "Lord, Teach Us to Pray" 341
    2. The Eucharist and the Sacrament of Reconciliation:
      Love that Knows No Bounds 342
  C. Marriage Spirituality: A Summary 343

CONCLUSION:
EVANGELIZING THE FAMILY IN THE THIRD CHRISTIAN MILLENNIUM 345

I. At a Crossroads 345
  A. Rome and Europe During the Jubilee Year 345
  B. Across the Atlantic: The Battle for America's Soul 346
II. Families: Evangelizers Impelled by Love 347
  A. Pope Paul VI: The Family's Evangelizing Mission 347
  B. Pope John Paul II: Encountering Christ the Evangelizer 348
    1. Who Is the Christ of John Paul II? 348
    2. Have We Encountered the Christ of John Paul II? 350
    3. God's Only Plan 350
III. To Set the World Ablaze 352
Select Bibliography 355
Index of Names 369
Index of Topics 373

Acknowledgments

Many people helped to make this book possible. I am sincerely grateful to all of them.

First and foremost, I would like to thank Father Marcial Maciel, LC, founder of the Legionaries of Christ, for his heroic witness of love for our Holy Father and selfless dedication to God's people. His example has been a guiding inspiration in the joyful task of writing about John Paul II's teachings.

Next my thanks go out to my superiors: Fathers Anthony Bannon, Antonio Bailleres, Emilio Díaz-Torre, Julio Martí, and Paul Moreau — and to all the priests, religious, and novices of the novitiate and humanities college of the Legionaries of Christ in Cheshire, Connecticut, where I teach. Without their constant prayers and encouragement, this book would not have become a reality. I am grateful to Andreas Kramarz, LC, and to Christopher O'Connor, LC, who generously assumed some of my classes, giving me the time necessary to complete the work.

Dave Pearson, features editor of the *National Catholic Register*, magnanimously dedicated himself to proofreading the manuscript. James Geerling also contributed to this task. Richard Tardiff, LC, and John Choi, LC, provided valuable help with technical aspects of the text. Fathers Antonio Rodríguez, LC, and Tarsicio Samaniego, LC, teamed with Kevin Donovan to achieve an exacting Spanish translation. They were granted the tireless help of Graciela Madero, who provided the official Vatican texts in Spanish of John Paul II's teachings that are cited in the book.

The following persons have generously supported this project: Katherine Blessington, Richard Pfundstein and his son, Greg, Jane and Marty Kiousis, Michael Toomey, Pete and Katy Fisher, and Anthony Sposato. Many thanks to each one, with the assurance of my prayers.

I cannot fail to express my sincere gratitude to Cardinal Angelo Sodano for his interest in this undertaking and his encouragement. I am deeply grateful to George Weigel for writing the Introduction.

Along with all these persons, I would like to thank John F. Kippley, founder of the Couple to Couple League, for his help.

Finally, I would certainly be remiss if I did not express my heartfelt gratitude to Dad, Mom, and my brothers and sisters: Carl, Carol, Heidi,

Greg, Ed, and Charlotte. Growing up with them on the first farm north of Currie, Minnesota, is what gave life to John Paul II's words on the beauty of Christian marriage and the family as an image of the self-giving love of the Blessed Trinity.

Father Walter Schu, LC
March 10, 2002

Abbreviations

Documents of Vatican II

DH   *Dignitatis Humanae.* Declaration on Religious Freedom.

DV   *Dei Verbum.* Dogmatic Constitution on Divine Revelation.

GS   *Gaudium et Spes.* Pastoral Constitution on the Church in the Modern World.

LG   *Lumen Gentium.* Dogmatic Constitution on the Church.

SC   *Sacrosanctum Concilium.* Constitution on the Sacred Liturgy.

Encyclicals of John Paul II

CA   *Centesimus Annus.* On the Hundredth Anniversary of *Rerum Novarum.* 1991.

DM   *Dives in Misericordia.* On the Mercy of God. 1980.

DetV   *Dominum et Vivificantem.* On the Holy Spirit in the Life of the Church and the World. 1986.

EV   *Evangelium Vitae.* The Gospel of Life. 1995.

FR   *Fides et Ratio.* Faith and Reason. 1998.

RH   *Redemptor Hominis.* The Redeemer of Man. 1979.

RM   *Redemptoris Missio.* The Mission of the Redeemer. 1990.

UUS   *Ut Unum Sint.* On Commitment to Ecumenism. 1995.

VS   *Veritatis Splendor.* The Splendor of Truth. 1993.

Post-Synodal Apostolic Exhortations of John Paul II

CL   *Christifideles Laici.* Lay Members of Christ's Faithful People. 1988.

CT   *Catechesi Tradendae.* Catechesis in Our Time. 1979.

FC   *Familiaris Consortio.* The Role of the Christian Family in the Modern World. 1981.

PDV   *Pastores Dabo Vobis.* I Will Give You Shepherds. 1992.

RP   *Reconciliatio et Poenitentia.* Reconciliation and Penance. 1984.

VC   *Vita Consecrata.* Consecrated Life. 1996.

Apostolic Constitutions of John Paul II

ECE   *Ex Corde Ecclesiae.* From the Heart of the Church. 1990.

FD   *Fidei Depositum.* The Deposit of Faith. 1992.

Apostolic Letters of John Paul II

LF   *Letter to Families.* 1994.

MD   *Mulieris Dignitatem.* The Dignity and Vocation of Women. 1988.

OS   *Ordinatio Sacerdotalis.* On Reserving Priestly Ordination to Men Alone. 1994.

SD   *Salvifici Doloris.* On the Christian Meaning of Human Suffering. 1984.

TMA   *Tertio Millennio Adveniente.* On Preparation for the Jubilee of the Year 2000. 1994.

Other Abbreviations

AAS   *Acta Apostolicae Sedis.* Rome, 1909—.

CCC   *Catechism of the Catholic Church.*

CIC   *Codex Iuris Canonici.* Code of Canon Law.

DS   Denzinger-Schönmetzer. Henry Denzinger and Adolf Schönmetzer, eds. *Enchiridion Symbolorum, Definitionum et Declarationum de Rebus Fidei et Morum,* 36th ed. (Freiburg : Herder, 1976).

NFP   Natural Family Planning.

ST   Thomas Aquinas, *Summa Theologiae.*

INTRODUCTION

In 1968, a bad year in a century replete with bad years, the arch-bishop of Kraków, Cardinal Karol Wojtyła, wrote a letter to his friend Henri de Lubac, the eminent French Jesuit theologian who was one of the intellectual architects of the Second Vatican Council. De Lubac and Wojtyła had gotten to know each other during the preparation of the Council's *Pastoral Constitution on the Church in the Modern World,* and the Frenchman was curious to learn something about his Polish colleague's current intellectual work. Cardinal Wojtyła's response — and his capitalization of one key word in it — was very suggestive:

> I devote my free moments to a work that is close to my heart and devoted to the metaphysical sense and mystery of the PERSON. It seems to me that the debate today is being played out on that level. The evil of our times consists in the first place in a kind of degrada-tion, indeed in a pulverization, of the fundamental uniqueness of each human person. This evil is even more of the metaphysical or-der than of the moral order. To this disintegration, planned at times by atheistic ideologies, we must oppose, rather than sterile polem-ics, a kind of "recapitulation" of the inviolable mystery of the person. . .

The language was technical and philosophical, but the message was clear: underwriting all the sorrows of the twentieth century — two world wars, three totalitarian systems, oceans of blood, mountains of corpses — were desperately deficient and defective ideas of the human person. Married to modern technology, those defective ideas of human nature, human origins, human community, and human destiny had proven to have lethal consequences. Faced with these challenges to the dignity of human life, the Church's task was to rescue the idea of the human person by boldly proclaiming Christian humanism as the anti-dote to the many defective humanisms that had made the twentieth century a valley of tears. Or so Wojtyła had suggested in a 1959 memo-randum to the commission preparing the agenda of Vatican II.

Karol Wojtyła brought these convictions with him to the papacy when he was elected the 263rd successor to St. Peter on October 16, 1978.

His challenge to Communist totalitarianism should be understood in this context: rather than acting primarily as a statesman or diplomat, John Paul II's role in the collapse of Communism was that of an evangelist, a pastor, and a witness to the inalienable dignity and value of every human person. John Paul II's challenge to the free societies of the twenty-first century is similar to the challenge he posed to twentieth-century tyrannies: unless the house of freedom is built on the solid foundation of respect for the dignity of every human life from conception until natural death, freedom will be insecure and freedom may even self-destruct.

John Paul II's Christian humanism is also the context in which to grapple with his extensive and profound teaching on marriage and the family, which Father Walter Schu explores in this book. For, in a long view of the cultural history of our times, the sexual revolution has been yet another episode in what Cardinal Wojtyła once described to Henri de Lubac as the "pulverization" of the human person. In this case, the meaning of human life is reduced to the pleasure principle, and freedom is understood as the capacity to pursue personal sexual satisfaction so long as "no one else" gets hurt — or no one in whom the state has declared an "interest." That familiar advertising slogan — "Just do it" — aptly summarizes the ersatz morality — and the demeaning idea of the human person that goes with it — that the sexual revolution carried into Western societies.

World Christianity's early response to the sexual revolution was not impressive. Much of liberal Protestantism simply surrendered to it. Pope Paul VI's 1968 encyclical *Humanae Vitae*, the first major papal attempt to address the implications of the sexual revolution after it had broken out into mainstream Western culture, courageously defended classic Catholic understandings of human sexuality, marriage, and procreation. At the same time, however, the encyclical caused a tremendous pastoral and theological controversy. When John Paul II was elected, ten years after *Humanae Vitae*, those ongoing controversies had contributed to a serious credibility problem for the Church on the entire range of issues involving marriage and family life. And just at the moment when the human wreckage caused by the sexual revolution had begun to cause some second thoughts among its former enthusiasts (especially among women), the Catholic Church, it seemed, had little to contribute to restructuring the argument.

John Paul II, committed to defending the dignity of the human person against the "pulverization" of the times, decided to do something about this at the very beginning of his pontificate. In 129 general audience addresses between 1979 and 1984, the Pope laid out a "theology of the body" that is, arguably, the most creative Christian response to the sexual revolution and its "pulverization" of the human person ever articulated. This revolutionary theology is at the philosophical and theological heart of John Paul II's teaching on marriage and the family, and so a brief summary of its main points may serve as a convenient entry-point for Father Schu's more extensive exploration of the Pope's thought on these issues.

The philosophical core of the "theology of the body" is a claim that Karol Wojtyła had worked out over many years of intense intellectual work: that there is what we might call a "Law of the Gift," a law of self-giving, built into the very structure of our humanity. None of us is the cause of our own existence; that is not simply a biological fact of life, according to Karol Wojtyła — it is a profoundly moral fact of life. Reflecting on that fact teaches us that we are to make of ourselves the gift to others that life itself is to us. According to the "Law of the Gift" written into the human heart, self-giving, not self-assertion, is the royal road to human flourishing.

These deep truths of the human condition, which Wojtyła believed could be demonstrated by a careful analysis of the way human beings think and choose morally, have enormous implications for meeting the challenge of the sexual revolution. Sex, as often experienced in today's sexual free-fire zone, is instinctive and impersonal. But that kind of sex, Wojtyła argued in his first book, *Love and Responsibility*, does not rise above the level of animal sexuality, which is also instinctive and impersonal. Sex that is an expression of self-giving love, not a use of the other for temporary gratification, is the only sex worthy of human beings.

This rich concept of sexual love also helps us understand the true meaning of chastity. Chastity, according to Wojtyła's analysis, is the "integrity of love." Chastity is the virtue that makes it possible for me to love another as a person. We are made free, Wojtyła argues, so that we can make a free gift of ourselves to others. We are free so that we can love freely, and thus love truly. Genuine freedom — the freedom that disposes of itself in self-giving — is the context of a genuinely humanistic sexual ethic. Marriage and the family are the schools in which we first learn these truths about loving as self-giving.

The theological core of John Paul's "theology of the body" is his profoundly sacramental sense of all of reality. Our embodiedness as male and female, the Pope teaches, is not an accident of evolutionary biology or a "cultural construct" (as certain feminist theories have it). Rather, that embodiedness and the mutuality built into it express some of the deepest truths of the world. They also teach us something about the world's Creator. John Paul even goes so far as to propose that sexual love within the bond of marital fidelity is an icon of the interior life of God the Holy Trinity, a community of mutual self-donation and mutual receptivity. Thus sexual love, within the bond of Christian marriage, is an act of worship.

It will be well into the twenty-first century before the Catholic Church, much less the wider culture, even begins to assimilate the contents of John Paul II's theology of the body. A secondary literature capable of unpacking these dense, compact audience addresses, and other key teachings of John Paul on marriage and the family, is badly needed — and Father Schu has done the Church and the world a genuine service by providing a good example of the right kind of "translation" of John Paul II's thought. May his work inspire others to take up this vital task in the future.

For the moment, though, it is worth noting that the Bishop of Rome, often assumed to be the custodian of a tradition deeply scarred by a Manichaean deprecation of human sexuality, has articulated a deeply humanistic response to the sexual revolution that says to the readers of *Playboy* and *Cosmopolitan* alike, "Human sexuality is far greater than you imagine."

And that, we may hope, can be the beginning of a revitalization of marriage and the family in the twenty-first century and beyond. For in a world where the temptation to remanufacture the human condition by manufacturing human beings will be omnipresent, nothing less than the future of humanity is at stake.

George Weigel
Senior Fellow: John M. Olin Chair in Religion and American Democracy
Ethics and Public Policy Center
Washington, D.C.

PROLOGUE:
A Gift to the Church and the World

"John Paul the Great"?

In the stillness of the evening on October 16, 1978, Pericle Cardinal Fellici stepped onto the central balcony of St. Peter's Basilica above a hushed and expectant crowd. His words rang out and echoed among the columns that embraced the square, *"Annuntio vobis gaudium magnum: Habemus Papam."* (I announce to you a great joy: We have a Pope.) At that moment the Church and the world could only begin to suspect the joy which would soon be theirs. For more than two decades these words have continued to echo, far beyond the confines of St. Peter's Square, to the ends of the earth.[1]

Now they resound in the silent dawn of the third Christian millennium, as it breaks upon us. The moment seems propitious to undertake the daunting task of a series of works dedicated to the thought and mission of the man who has led the Church and the world across the "threshold of hope" of the new millennium.

On January 25, 1999, the Holy Father was greeted in Aztec Stadium in Mexico City as "Juan Pablo Magno, John Paul the Great." Only two other popes in the history of the Church have received the title "great." They were St. Leo the Great in the fifth century, and St. Gregory the Great at the close of the sixth century.[2] Already in 1997 *Crisis* magazine dedicated the cover of its fifteenth anniversary issue to "John Paul the Great."[3] Father Richard John Neuhaus has made a similar claim in his recent book *Appointment in Rome.* He states, "If one considers the encyclicals alone — and, of course, they are only part of the many teaching documents of the pontificate — it is arguable that this is the most assertive teaching pontificate in the two thousand years of the Church's his-

---

[1] John Paul II, Encyclical Letter *Redemptoris Missio*, 1, "From the beginning of my pontificate I have chosen to travel to the ends of the earth in order to show this missionary concern."

[2] St. Leo I the Great, elected August 440; died November 10, 461. St. Gregory I the Great, consecrated September 3, 590; died March 12, 604.

[3] *Crisis*, November 1997.

tory, which reinforces the expectation that future generations will refer to John Paul the Great in the way that we have for centuries spoken of Leo the Great and Gregory the Great."[4]

Are these claims well founded? Will history bear them out?

As George Weigel observes in his definitive papal biography, *Witness to Hope*, a striking parallel exists between Popes Leo, Gregory, and John Paul II. Leo saved Rome from Attila and the Huns. Gregory preserved the civilized world from another barbarian people — the Lombards. And John Paul II? Surely there are no barbarians threatening humanity today.

As the third millennium dawned, a superficial glance at our world, from the perspective of globalization, Internet wonders, and unparalleled economic prosperity in many developed nations, seemed to indicate that all was well with mankind. Then September 11, 2001 changed that view of things forever. Thousands of innocent people died as the Twin Towers collapsed and the Pentagon burned in the worst acts of terrorism the world has ever known.

Untold misery and hatred are realities that engulf the lives of countless people in our world today. In the aftermath of September 11, many persons have begun to question the route humanity's future will take. We need pose but one simple question to send crashing to the ground the perilous construction which claims that ease and contentment have been secured. "Upon what fundamental reality does humanity's future depend?"

All civilizations throughout history have recognized one institution as the most vital cell of society itself: *the family*. At the same time, parents and children also form a "domestic church," where the Gospel is first transmitted from one generation to the next. John Paul II does not hesitate to proclaim, *"The future of humanity passes by way of the family."*[5]

In the United States and most Western nations, one out of every two marriages presently ends in divorce. There is not a single country in Europe where enough children are being born to replace the existing population. The same is true of the U.S., Canada, Japan, and the overwhelming majority of countries in the world today. Clearly, humanity's future is threatened.

Behind this threat lie forces "backed by very powerful resources . . . [which] seem to aim at the breakdown of the family."[6] These forces draw

---

[4] Richard John Neuhaus, *Appointment in Rome, The Church in America Awakening* (New York: Herder and Herder, Crossroad, 1999), p. 21.
[5] John Paul II, Apostolic Exhortation On the Role of the Christian Family in the Modern World *Familiaris Consortio*, 86.
[6] John Paul II, *Letter to Families*, 4.

their ideological might from false humanisms — reductive visions of men and women that deny their transcendent dimension and lead to a "pulverization of the fundamental uniqueness of each human person."[7]

From his very first days as Pope, John Paul II has shown himself to be an unswerving advocate of families. He unveiled a transforming vision of married love in the light of Christ's redemption — his "theology of the body" — during the Wednesday audiences from 1979 to 1984. The Holy Father's teachings truly open a new horizon for all married persons and families who have the courage to make them their own.

John Paul II has also defended the foundations of the family and humanity's future by tirelessly proposing an authentic Christian humanism, one that recognizes the transcendent greatness of human persons in their capacity to enter into communion with persons *par excellence* — the three Divine Persons of the Blessed Trinity.

The main goal of these pages is to enable each one of us who go through them to discover the treasure that is John Paul II's teaching on marriage and the family. The Holy Father's vision is capable of enriching our lives in a way we might barely suspect. It can bring us a joy and fullness we may never have imagined up to now. May that joy impel us to love, live, and spread faithfully our Holy Father's teachings. May we too defend the family and humanity's future at his side.

Throughout this book John Paul II will speak in his own words — words to be pondered, reflected upon and, above all, prayed over. The Holy Father's words must be prayed over, since the present work is not simply an intellectual study. If it were, it would not be faithful to the Pope's thinking. For the thought of John Paul II is directed without fail toward his mission. These pages strive to be an echo of the Holy Father's ardent appeal: "Open wide the doors to Christ!"

The book is designed in the form of a personal study guide. It can be read on one's own or serve as a basis for study circles and discussion groups. Passages from the Holy Father's encyclicals, apostolic exhortations and letters provide rich material for meditation. Quotes from experts on his thought and a select bibliography enable the reader to penetrate more deeply into John Paul II's compelling vision. A comprehensive outline format offers quick access to key quotations from the Holy Father's teachings — a resource for personal reflection, as well as for giving spiritual talks or retreats.

Three features are designed to make the guide "reader friendly":
1) *Preview* boxes reveal in a glance what lies just ahead and how it all fits together.

---

[7] 1968 Letter of Cardinal Karol Wojtyła to Jesuit theologian Henri de Lubac; as cited in George Weigel, "John Paul II and the Crisis of Humanism," *First Things*, December 1999, pp. 31-36, at 32.

2) *Points to look for* provide questions that help the reader discern the key aspects of each new topic as it unfolds.

3) *An outline format* aids in following and discovering the richness of the Holy Father's thought.

As this personal study guide enables us to experience some of the joy that drives and sustains John Paul II, may it help us bring many others to know the truth that will set them free[8] and reveal to them who they are — the One who is "the way, and the truth, and the life"[9] — Jesus Christ.

What Lies in Our Hands

With just a brief glance at how John Paul II has advanced the cause of the family, a vast panorama begins to open. If we lift our gaze to contemplate the other achievements of his more than two decades as Pope, we cannot but ask ourselves, "What has John Paul II done for the Church and the world?" In spite of all that has been accomplished, the answer is not yet clear, since the greatest part of his legacy is still to be determined. Why is this so? Precisely because the fullness of his legacy depends on each one of us.

It depends in a unique way upon mothers and fathers of families, as they strive to make a reality in their lives the truth that "love is . . . the fundamental and innate vocation of every human being."[10] They in turn will enable their children to experience the Father's merciful love.[11]

It depends on young people, as they walk along the path of life, to not be afraid,[12] to respond to the great things Christ expects from them. Will they answer the Holy Father's challenge that "the time for action is now?" Will they truly be "light to the world, as only young people can be light?"[13] Will they realize in the depths of their being that the future of the world and the Church in the third millennium rests in their hands?[14]

It depends on priests to respond to the Holy Father's call to deepen their love for Christ, the Good Shepherd, and to pattern their hearts on his. Then they will "be ready to go out as his image into the highways of the world to proclaim to all mankind Christ the way, the truth and the life."[15]

The Holy Father's legacy also depends on writers, artists and musicians to use their creative intuition "to enter into the heart of the mys-

---

[8] Cf. *Jn* 8:32.
[9] *Jn* 14:6.
[10] Familiaris Consortio, 11.
[11] Cf. Encyclical Letter *Dives in Misericordia*.
[12] First Papal Homily, October 22, 1978.
[13] John Paul II's address to young people at the Kiel Center, St. Louis, Missouri, January 26, 1999.
[14] Apostolic Letter *Tertio Millennio Adveniente*, 58.
[15] Apostolic Exhortation *Pastores Dabo Vobis*, 82.

tery of the Incarnate God and at the same time into the mystery of man,"[16] to make their many different paths lead to that "infinite Ocean of beauty where wonder becomes awe, exhilaration, unspeakable joy."[17] The need to do so is clear, since "humanity in every age, and even today, looks to works of art to shed light upon its path and its destiny."[18]

No less central is the role of teachers, who strive to be for their students, and for the rest of the faithful, "witnesses of the living truth of the Gospel and examples of fidelity to the Church."[19] University presidents and high-school principals are entrusted in a special way with the task of making universities and schools true centers where faith meets culture.[20]

All Christians bear the gentle yoke of striving for Christian unity, "without being discouraged at the difficulties that can appear or accumulate along that road; otherwise we would be unfaithful to the word of Christ, we would fail to accomplish His testament. Have we the right to run this risk?"[21] "Ecumenism is not only an internal question of the Christian communities. It is a matter of the love which God has in Jesus Christ for all humanity; to stand in the way of this love is an offense against him and against his plan to gather all people in Christ."[22]

All men and women of good will share a duty to safeguard the dignity of each human person. Will we live up to our task "of loving and serving, of defending and promoting human life?"[23]

Above all, the legacy of John Paul II depends on each one of us, as committed Christians, to respond to the Holy Father's ardent cry for a new springtime of evangelization in the Church.[24] Will his heartfelt appeal resound within our own hearts? "We cannot be content when we consider the millions of our brothers and sisters, who like us have been redeemed by the blood of Christ, but who live in ignorance of the love of God."[25] Will we carry out "a new evangelization — new in its ardor, new in its methods, new in its expressions?"[26]

Will each one of us respond to God's call in the inner sanctuary of our conscience, with a joy which no one except Christ can give? If we

---

[16] "Letter of John Paul II to Artists," April 4, 1999. Easter Sunday, 14.
[17] Ibid., 16.
[18] Ibid., 14.
[19] Apostolic Constitution *Sapientia Christiana*, Ch. 4.
[20] Cf. Apostolic Constitution *Ex Corde Ecclesiae*.
[21] Encyclical Letter *Redemptor Hominis*, 6.
[22] Encyclical Letter *Ut Unum Sint*, 99.
[23] Encyclical Letter *Evangelium Vitae*, 29.
[24] *Redemptoris Missio*, 2, 3. "I sense that the moment has come to commit all of the Church's energies to a new evangelization and to the mission *ad gentes*. No believer in Christ, no institution of the Church, can avoid this supreme duty: to proclaim Christ to all peoples" (*RM*, 3).
[25] *Redemptoris Missio*, 86.
[26] John Paul II, "The Task of the Latin American Bishop," Address to CELAM, March 9, 1983; English trans. in *Origins* 12 (March 24, 1983): 659-62, at 661.

do, then, when that distant future day arrives and the sun slowly sets on the third millennium, the mission of the Redeemer will no longer be just beginning.[27] No longer will it be true that two-thirds of the people in the world still do not know Christ. Many more will have discovered that he is the truth who fully reveals to them who they are, and gives them the strength to fulfill their destiny.[28] Many more will have come to the fullness of truth in the Holy Spirit,[29] a truth that sets them free[30] and transforms their lives forever.

Then, and only then, will the legacy of John Paul II be fulfilled. Then, and only then, will it become clear how much his pontificate has been and continues to be a gift to the Church and the world.

---

[27] *Redemptoris Missio,* 1.
[28] *Redemptor Hominis,* 10; cf. Second Vatican Council, Pastoral Constitution on the Church in the Modern World *Gaudium et Spes,* 22.
[29] Cf. Encyclical Letter *Dominum et Vivificantem.*
[30] Cf. *Jn* 8:32.

PART I

Mankind and the Family

ONE

The Future of Humanity

Preview

I. Society's First and Vital Cell

    A. A Crucial Relationship

    B. The "First Society"

        1. A Communion of Persons

        2. Communion and Community

        3. The Community of the Family and Society

II. A Domestic Church: Humanity's Transcendent Destiny

    A. The Family's Prophetic Role: "A Believing and Evangelizing Community"

        1. A Gift that Lasts Forever

        2. "In the Image of God"

Points to look for

1. Why does the future of humanity pass by way of the family?

2. When did John Paul II outline his theology of the body?

3. Why is the family the first and vital cell of society?

4. What facts can be cited to confirm that the decline of the family leads to society's deterioration?

5. What is meant by "a communion of persons"?

6. What is the difference between communion and community?

7. Based on the notions of communion, community, and the nature of the person, why can't the family be replaced by other forms of social organization?

8. Why must the moral values children need to acquire be transmitted in families, rather than simply being taught in schools?

9. What are the three aspects of Christ's saving mission in which the family participates within the life of the Church?

10. Why is the gift of faith that parents give to their children with God's grace such a transcendent one?

11. What facts can be cited to confirm the vital importance of a parent's role in the development of faith in a child?

Father Richard John Neuhaus has remarked that a sure way to discover the driving concerns of John Paul II is to look at the topics of the synods of bishops he has called. The very first world synod John Paul II convoked as Pope in 1980 dealt with the family. His Wednesday audiences also reveal what is close to the Holy Father's heart. On September 5, 1979, the Pope began a five-year series of general audiences focused precisely on marriage and the family. During these audiences he outlined his theology of the body.[31]

What gives rise to such concern? Why does John Paul II exclaim, "The Church perceives in a more urgent and compelling way her mission of proclaiming to all people the plan of God for marriage and the family"?[32] The reason is that mankind's very future is at stake. The Holy Father confirms what all people of good will must recognize: "*The future of humanity passes by way of the family.*"[33]

As Vatican II's Pastoral Constitution on the Church in the Modern World *Gaudium et Spes* points out, healthy families are vital for the well-being of all new persons who are born into the world.[34] Only by receiving the love of their mother and father within families can children begin to discover who they are as persons. Each child is welcomed as a gift from God. In their mutual family relationships, brothers and sisters growing up together start to realize that they are called to give themselves to others. They also perceive that the members of their family are valued for who they are, not for what they are able to do or produce.

Through Mom and Dad, discreetly present, always ready to stoop down toward them in their need, children discover who God is — they learn to pray. Under their parents' gentle, guiding hand they slowly begin to grasp the difference between right and wrong. In the daily give-and-take of family life, children learn how to be sincere, responsible, generous — how to forget about themselves and bring joy to those around them.

Even a quick glance at family life reveals how humanity's future depends on the family in two fundamental ways. First, the family is where new members are born into society and where they acquire basic social virtues. On the destiny of the family hangs the fate of society itself. Second, the future of the Church depends on the family, a "Church in min-

---

[31] John Paul II developed the theology of the body in a series of six cycles during 129 general audiences from September 5, 1979, through November 28, 1984. The cycles were interrupted briefly by the assassination attempt in May 1981. They were also postponed during the Holy Year of Redemption from February 1983 to May 1984. These audiences have been collected in the volume: John Paul II, *The Theology of the Body* (Boston: Pauline Books and Media, 1997).

[32] Post-Synodal Apostolic Exhortation On the Role of the Christian Family in the Modern World *Familiaris Consortio*, November 22, 1981, 3.

[33] *Familiaris Consortio*, 86.

[34] *GS*, 47.

iature (*Ecclesia domestica*),"[35] where the faith is passed on from one generation to the next. So mankind's ultimate and transcendent destiny is also at stake.

I. Society's First and Vital Cell
A. A Crucial Relationship

One year after the 1980 Synod of Bishops on the Family, John Paul II outlined its conclusions in the Apostolic Exhortation On the Role of the Christian Family in the Modern World, *Familiaris Consortio*. The Holy Father begins number 42 of *Familiaris Consortio* by reaffirming Vatican II's declaration: "The family is 'the first and vital cell of society.'"[36] Obviously society depends on the family for its physical prolongation. But the family is equally vital in forming the moral strength without which society would disintegrate. In light of events such as the Columbine High School killings, many people view with apprehension, if not alarm, the course society seems to be taking in America. Is there a direct relation to the state of the family?

Paul Johnson addresses this question in his book *A History of the American People*. He affirms what many analysts of American society considered to be "the decisive single development in America during the second half of the twentieth century: the decline of the family and of family life, and the growth in illegitimacy."[37] What have been the consequences of this decline?

> The enormous number of children born outside the family structure altogether, or raised in one-parent families, appeared to be statistically linked to most of the modern evils of American life: poor educational performance and illiteracy or semi-literacy, children out on the streets from an early age, juvenile delinquency, unemployment, adult crime, and, above all, poverty.[38]

It is not an empty claim that links the deterioration of the family with most of the ills afflicting society today. Statistics reveal a direct correlation between the two. Once again Paul Johnson cites a few decisive facts.

> In what was called 'the demoralization of American society,' a number of statistical indicators came together. In the thirty years 1960-90, while the US population rose by 41 percent, there was a 560 percent increase in violent crime, 200 percent in teenage suicide, 200 percent rise in divorce, over 400 percent rise in illegitimate births, 300 percent rise in children living in single-parent homes —

---

[35] *Familiaris Consortio*, 49. Cf. also Second Vatican Ecumenical Council, Dogmatic Constitution on the Church *Lumen Gentium*, 11; Decree on the Apostolate of the Laity *Apostolicam Actuositatem*, 11.

[36] *Apostolicam Actuositatem*, 11.

[37] Paul Johnson, *A History of the American People* (New York: HarperCollins, 1997), p. 971.

[38] Ibid.

producing *in toto* the significant fact that children formed the fastest-growing segment of the criminal population.[39]

Up to 1920, the proportion of children born to single women in the United States was less than 3 percent, roughly where it had been throughout the history of the country. . . . By the end of 1994 it [the illegitimacy rate] was 33 percent for the nation as a whole, 25 percent for whites, and 70 percent for blacks. In parts of Washington, capital of the richest nation in the world, it was as high as 90 percent.[40]

B. The "First Society"
1. A Communion of Persons

Why is the family the first and most vital cell of society? In 1994 the Holy Father responded to this question in his "Letter to Families," *Gratissimam Sane,* which he wrote on the occasion of the United Nations' International Year of the Family. First of all, the family is the most basic expression of man's social nature. Human beings can fulfill themselves as persons only through relationships with other persons. The unique bond between husband and wife leads to an intimate communion of persons: a sharing of their lives and their very selves with each other. Out of this personal communion, the community of the family arises. Thus, the family is the most basic community within society. All larger communities depend upon the family and so are called to uphold the rights and dignity of each family.

> The family has always been considered as the first and basic expression of man's social nature. Even today this way of looking at things remains unchanged. Nowadays, however, emphasis tends to be laid on how much the family, as the smallest and most basic human community, owes to the personal contribution of a man and a woman. The family is in fact a community of persons whose proper way of existing and living together is communion: *communio personarum.* Here too, while always acknowledging the absolute transcendence of the Creator with regard to his creatures, we can see the family's ultimate relationship to the divine "We." *Only persons are capable of living "in communion."* The family originates in a marital communion described by the Second Vatican Council as a "covenant," *in which man and woman "give themselves to each other and accept each other."*[41]

---

[39] Ibid., pp. 965-966. The source of these figures is William J. Bennett, *Index of Leading Cultural Indicators* (New York, 1993).

[40] Ibid., pp. 971-972. The source of these figures is Charles Murray, "Bad News About Illegitimacy," in *Washington Weekly Standard,* August 5, 1996.

[41] John Paul II, Letter to Families *Gratissimam Sane,* 1994, 7; citing the Pastoral Constitution on the Church in the Modern World *Gaudium et Spes,* 48.

2. Communion and Community

The Holy Father next explains the difference between communion and community. He describes how the intimate communion of two persons, husband and wife, gives rise to a first society: the community of the family. Since persons are made for communion, and the most intimate communion possible on a human level is that between family members, the family can never be replaced by any other form of social organization or sacrificed for the sake of "society itself."

> I have spoken of two closely related yet not identical concepts: the concept of "communion" and that of community. "*Communion*" has to do with the personal relationship between the "I" and the "thou." "*Community*" on the other hand transcends this framework and moves toward a "society," a "we." The family, as a community of persons, is thus the first human "society." It arises whenever there comes into being the conjugal covenant of marriage, which opens the spouses to a lasting communion of love and of life, and it is brought to completion in a full and specific way with the procreation of children: the "communion" of the spouses gives rise to the "community" of the family. The "community" of the family is completely pervaded by the very essence of "communion." On the human level, can there be any other "*communion*" comparable to that *between a mother and a child* whom she has carried in her womb and then brought to birth?[42]

3. The Community of the Family and Society

Since the family is where children first enter into relationships of intimate communion and so begin to realize themselves as persons, it is clear that the future of society rests upon the family. What will decide the type of persons who one day will be charting the course of nations in government, affecting the lives of millions as CEOs of multinational corporations, and forming future generations of young people in educational institutions? Families will determine the quality of these men and women — society's future leaders.

How do we assess the type of person someone is? We measure him primarily by his moral convictions and his consistency in living them. Adolf Hitler possessed many human qualities. He was brave, astute, intelligent, and had tremendous willpower. Yet, morally speaking, he was bankrupt. In evaluating Hitler as a person, everything depends on this last point.

The family is the irreplaceable community where a young person's moral character is forged. John Paul II reiterates this truth in his Letter to Families *Gratissimam Sane*. "And experience shows what an important role is played by a family living in accordance with the moral norm,

---

[42] John Paul II, *Letter to Families*, 7.

so that the individual born and raised in it will be able to set out without hesitation on the road of the good, which is *always written in his heart.*"[43]

No other institution can assume the family's role in helping children acquire the moral values they will need to become responsible members of society. This task cannot be left simply to schools. Father Marcial Maciel explains why not in a letter titled "The Home: School of Evangelization," written during the 1994 Year of the Family.

> [V]alues, unlike purely intellectual ideas, cannot be transmitted by academic instruction alone. They are transmitted through human relationships. A college professor can perhaps "teach" us that charity is a value; a mother at home who speaks words of forgiveness when she has been offended transmits the value of charity, irradiates charity, because she herself lives it.[44]

II. A Domestic Church: Humanity's Transcendent Destiny

Not only does society depend upon the family for its future well-being, so does the Church. As an *ecclesia domestica* the family is a "Church in miniature." It assumes an original and irreplaceable role in the Church's life and mission.[45] The family's unique role derives from its very nature. "Love and life constitute the nucleus of the saving mission of the Christian family in the Church and for the Church."[46] In fulfilling its unique responsibility, the family shares Christ's mission as prophet, priest, and king.

A. The Family's Prophetic Role: "A Believing and Evangelizing Community"

By sharing in Christ's prophetic mission, the family is called to become "a believing and evangelizing community."[47] Christian families are witnesses within society to God's love for his people and his enduring fidelity. Within themselves families also evangelize, as parents pass on the faith to their children through their words and the compelling witness of their lives. In his 1994 letter Father Maciel reflects on the transcendence of the gift of faith that parents give to their children with God's help.

1. A Gift that Lasts Forever

> There are some gifts that last a day, other gifts are forever. The gift of Christian faith will stay with your children during childhood and youth, throughout their years of maturity, in their old age, and into eternity. In heaven, when love and truth will shine forever,

---

[43] Ibid., 5.
[44] Father Marcial Maciel, LC, a letter to all members of the Regnum Christi Movement, "The Home: School of Evangelization," May 22, 1994, Feast of Pentecost (Hamden, CT: CIF, 1995), pp. 9-10.
[45] *Familiaris Consortio,* 49-50.
[46] Ibid., 50.
[47] Ibid., 51-54.

your children will be profoundly grateful to you for all you have done for them; but they will especially thank you for helping them to know and love God, the source of their happiness.[48]

2. "In the Image of God"

Not only do parents teach their children how to pray, enabling them to develop a personal relationship with God; parents actually represent God for their children. Father Maciel meditates on the profound truth that parents reflect the "image of God" for their sons and daughters.

A child's experience of his parents' love enables him to understand the infinitely good Father whom Christ sought to tell us about with his preaching. How beautiful and what a responsibility it is to know that the motherly and fatherly love you show your children is where they learn their relationship with God! What a privilege it is to be for your children a reflection of God, the Creator himself. By your word and example, by your love, you can help your children turn to God and to love him better.[49]

Just how crucial for children's faith in God is a close, loving relationship with their parents? Dr. Paul Vitz, noted psychologist of New York University, takes up this question with regard to fathers in his new book, *Faith of the Fatherless: The Psychology of Religion.* "On studying the lives of more than a dozen prominent atheists, Vitz discovered an alarming trend. In case after case he found that those who rejected God had suffered from a defective relationship with their earthly fathers. The fact that their fathers had died or abused or abandoned them seemed directly linked to their denial of God. Rejection of God followed on rejection of their fathers as inadequate and unworthy of trust."[50]

Friedrich Nietzsche, the German philosopher who proclaimed: "God is dead," and Sigmund Freud both disdained their weak and sickly fathers. Joseph Stalin was beaten unmercifully by his own father, as was Adolf Hitler. America's most outspoken atheist, Madalyn Murray O'Hair, despised her father so much that she once tried to kill him with a butcher knife.

As a control group, Vitz examined the lives of prominent religious believers from the same historical periods. What did he find? Every one of them enjoyed a strong, loving bond with his father, or with a male mentor who served as a father substitute. "The renowned French philosopher and mathematician Blaise Pascal was educated at home by his Catholic father, and the two had a close, affectionate relationship. John Henry Newman, Alexis de Tocqueville, Samuel Wilberforce, G.K. Ches-

---

[48] Father Marcial Maciel, LC, "The Home: School of Evangelization," pp. 4-5.
[49] Ibid., p. 11.
[50] Father Thomas Williams, LC, "The Power of a Father's Strong Faith," *National Catholic Register,* January 30, 2000, Vol. 76, No. 5, p. 9.

terton, and Dietrich Bonhoffer also enjoyed close, loving relationships with their earthly fathers, and went on to become great defenders of Christianity."[51]

Obviously the complex phenomenon of modern atheism stems from many factors and cannot be reduced to a single cause. Still, Vitz's work offers compelling evidence on how vitally important a good father is for the development of children's religious faith. Who can doubt that similar studies will reach the same conclusion regarding the crucial role of a loving mother in the faith of her children?

Even when a father is lost or absent in the most trying circumstances, a mother's caring presence can open a child to experience God's love. Father Werenfried van Straaten, O. Praem., founder of Aid to the Church in Need, tells the story of "Poor Little Rosemarie" in his book *Where God Weeps*. Father van Straaten begins the story by relating a somewhat perilous ferry-boat ride he undertook in India, during which he promised a young German nun named Sister Rosemarie that he would visit her orphanage. After describing the crossing, Father van Straaten flashes back to an incident that had occurred in the months following World War II.

> Shortly after the war one of my friends had in the course of a journey through Germany photographed a little refugee girl in a transit camp. He had also spoken to the mother, a war-widow driven away from Breslau. The little girl was the only one of her five children to survive their expulsion from Silesia. He sent me the photo with the mother's address and asked me to do something for her. That was the time when I was collecting bacon in Flanders for starving Germans. I was so struck by the expression on the child's face that I wrote an article on it called "Poor Little Rosemarie." I sent the mother a parcel of food and clothing with some chocolate and a doll for the little girl. I also added the photo and the translation of my article. I received a letter of thanks but never heard anything more of the mother and her daughter until I visited the young German nun and her orphanage in India.
>
> The orphanage proved to be a muddle of hovels and emergency sheds round a ramshackle stone house. There is also a school where, besides cooking and sewing, the children learn at least to write their names and the date of their birth. Unless they can do this they will never be allowed to vote and will remain for the rest of their lives without civil rights. The hospital that the nuns have built beside their orphanage — "God paid for it," said Sister Rosemarie — is not only for the children but for everyone. In the course of the last year 17,000 patients had been given free treatment. As

---

[51] Ibid.

there is hardly any nursing staff, the sick people's families do the nursing while their children play underneath the beds. . . .

Sister Rosemarie seems to know each child personally: "That blind girl with flowers in her black hair is a Mohammedan. Today the Moslems observe a feast day and the other children have decorated her with flowers. She was nothing but a lump of flesh when she was carried in here. Now she is the focal point of the others' love. That is why she will live. . . . That baby was found on the beach just before the tide came in. . . . That dear little boy has two little sisters here; the mother died of starvation and the father is unknown. . . . That little curly-head is a child of leper parents. The family left him behind in a hospital where he lived for three years with the other children under the beds without being noticed. . . . This baby weighed only two pounds when she was found in a dust-bin a month ago. Now she weighs five pounds. She will stay alive. . . . That very tiny one is six years old and was found playing with the corpse of her mother who had died of starvation. . . ."

And so it went on. Each child plays the chief part in its own terrible tragedy. Five hundred tragedies. And in each of them ten, thirty even fifty others are involved. Thousands of suffering people, creatures of God, the beloved of Jesus, whose misery was revealed to me in lurid colors by the sober commentary of this young nun. Her superior told me she had only been two years in India but for miles in the surrounding country she is known as "the angel of love." Deeply moved I went away. On my departure Sister Rosemarie asked me for my blessing and handed me an envelope. In this I found the long-forgotten photo of the little refugee girl from Breslau and the article I had sent to her mother nineteen years ago. On a card she had written that the doll and the chocolate had been for her the first proofs of God's goodness and that she owed her vocation to my article. That is why she took the name of Rosemarie when she entered the convent."[52]

---

[52] Werenfried van Straaten, O. Praem., *Where God Weeps*, (Netherlands: Oostpriesterhulp, 1970), pp. 16-19.

Preview

ONE: THE FUTURE OF HUMANITY *(continued)*

II. A Domestic Church: Humanity's Transcendent Destiny *(continued)*

    B. The Family's Priestly Role: "A Community in Dialogue with God"

    C. The Family's Kingly Role: "A Community at the Service of Man"

    D. *Ecclesia Domestica*: Society's Best Ally

Points to look for

1. What are the three principal ways in which the family participates in Christ's priestly mission?

2. Why does the Sacrament of Marriage find its source in the Eucharist?

3. Why should families never hesitate to approach the Sacrament of Reconciliation in their struggles to live up to Christ's teachings?

4. Why is it so vital that parents pray with their children?

5. Why does the Christian family's mission as a domestic Church fortify and not contradict its role as society's most vital cell?

6. How does the family's participation in Christ's kingly mission make it one of society's best allies?

7. What dramatic change has occurred in the United States during the past five decades regarding the relationship between religion and society?

B. The Family's Priestly Role: "A Community in Dialogue with God"

There are three principal ways in which the family shares Christ's priestly mission as "a community in dialogue with God."[53] "The Christian family is continuously vivified by the Lord Jesus and called and engaged by him in a dialogue with God through the sacraments, through the offering of one's life, and through prayer."[54]

In the family's daily life, the Eucharist and the sacrament of Reconciliation help bring to fulfillment the sanctifying power of the sacrament of Matrimony. Since Christian marriage is a reflection of Christ's love for his bride,[55] the Church, marriage finds its very source in the Eucharist. For it is in the Eucharist that Christ renews his self-giving sacrifice, even to the point of shedding his blood for his people. So the Eucharist is a fountain of charity for families. Sharing in Christ's body and blood should be a continual source of apostolic dynamism.

The Eucharist is the very source of Christian marriage. The Eucharistic Sacrifice, in fact, represents Christ's covenant of love with the

---

[53] Cf. *Familiaris Consortio,* 55-62.
[54] Ibid., 55.
[55] Cf. Eph 5.
[56] Cf. Jn 19:34.

Church, sealed with his blood on the Cross.[56] In this sacrifice of the New and Eternal Covenant, Christian spouses encounter the source from which their own marriage covenant flows, is interiorly structured and continuously renewed. As a representation of Christ's sacrifice of love for the Church, the Eucharist is a fountain of charity. In the Eucharistic gift of charity the Christian family finds the foundation and soul of its "communion" and its "mission": by partaking in the Eucharistic bread, the different members of the Christian family become one body, which reveals and shares in the wider unity of the Church. Their sharing in the Body of Christ that is "given up" and in his Blood that is "shed" becomes a never-ending source of missionary and apostolic dynamism for the Christian family.[57]

In addition to participating in the Eucharist, family members should frequently receive the sacrament of Reconciliation to grow in holiness and live Gospel truths in the midst of society. Through confession both parents and children "are led to an encounter with God, who is 'rich in mercy,'[58] who bestows on them his love which is more powerful than sin,[59] and who reconstructs and brings to perfection the marriage covenant and the family communion."[60]

Christ died in unspeakable agony upon the cross so that he could forgive our sins in the sacrament of Reconciliation. We make an act of gratitude to him each time we approach this sacrament in humble repentance and with a firm resolution to be faithful to his grace in the future. The sacrament of Reconciliation has the power to transform our weakness into strength and our misery into love. After Peter denied Christ three times, one look of forgiveness from Jesus gave the first Pope the courage to be crucified for his Lord.

Along with the sacraments of the Eucharist and Reconciliation, prayer gives Christian families the strength to offer their lives to God each day, amidst the joys and sorrows of striving to follow Christ's will in everything. Just how important is family prayer? John Paul II, a man whose prayerful depth strikes all who encounter him, responds clearly. The Holy Father quotes his predecessor, Pope Paul VI, also a man of deep prayer.

> Only by praying together with their children can a father and mother — exercising their royal priesthood — penetrate the innermost depths of their children's hearts and leave an impression that the future events in their lives will not be able to efface. Let us listen again to the appeal made by Paul VI to parents: "Mothers, do you

---

[57] *Familiaris Consortio*, 57.
[58] Eph 2:4.
[59] Cf. John Paul II, Encyclical *Dives in Misericordia*, 13: *AAS* 72 (1980), 1218-1219.
[60] *Familiaris Consortio*, 58.

teach your children the Christian prayers? Do you prepare them, in conjunction with the priests, for the sacraments that they receive when they are young: Confession, Communion and Confirmation? Do you encourage them when they are sick to think of Christ suffering, to invoke the aid of the Blessed Virgin and the saints? And you, fathers, do you pray with your children, with the whole domestic community, at least sometimes? Your example of honesty in thought and action, joined to some common prayer, is a lesson for life, an act of worship of singular value. In this way you bring peace to your homes: *Pax huic domui*. Remember, it is thus that you build up the Church."[61]

These moving passages on how prayer affects lives show that there is no opposition between the family as a domestic Church and the family as society's most vital cell. On the contrary, the strength that Christian families acquire from prayer and the sacraments, enabling them to live the transforming message of the Gospel in the heart of society, makes them one of society's best allies. John Paul II comments on this fact with regard to prayer. "Far from being a form of escapism from everyday commitments, prayer constitutes the strongest incentive for the Christian family to assume and comply fully with all its responsibilities as the primary and fundamental cell of human society."[62]

C. The Family's Kingly Role: "A Community at the Service of Man"

What does it mean that the family shares Christ's role not only as prophet and priest, but also as king?[63] "Just as Christ exercises his royal power by serving us,[64] so also the Christian finds the authentic meaning of his participation in the kingship of his Lord in sharing his spirit and practice of service to man."[65] A true Christian is able to discover Christ in each fellow human being. "In each individual, especially in the poor, the weak, and those who suffer or are unjustly treated, love knows how to discover a fellow human being to be loved and served."[66]

D. *Ecclesia Domestica*: Society's Best Ally

The true meaning of the Christian family's role as prophet, priest, and king reveals that the family, as a domestic Church, is really society's best ally. Throughout most of the history of the United States, the faith passed on and lived by families has been regarded as a vital element of the social fabric. In his farewell address, George Washington went so far

---

[61] Ibid., 60, citing Paul VI, General Audience Address, August 11, 1976: *Insegnamenti di Paolo VI*, XIV (1976), 640.
[62] Ibid., 62.
[63] Ibid., 63-64.
[64] Cf. Mk 10:45.
[65] *Familiaris Consortio*, 63.
[66] Ibid., 64.

as to say that the republic was based on two pillars — religion and the Constitution. This view of religion has perdured until recent times. Paul Johnson presents a startling portrait of how much has changed within our country during the last five decades.

> Until the second half of the twentieth century, religion was held by virtually all Americans, irrespective of their beliefs or non-belief, to be not only desirable but an essential part of the national fabric. It is worth recalling De Tocqueville's observation that Americans held religion "to be indispensable to the maintenance of free institutions." Religion was identified first with republicanism, then with democracy, so as to constitute the American way of life, the set of values, and the notions of private and civil behavior which Americans agreed to be self-evidently true and right. In consequence, those who preached such values from the pulpit or who most clearly, even ostentatiously, upheld them from the pews, were acknowledged to be among the most valuable citizens of the country. Whereas in Europe, religious practice and fervor were often, even habitually, seen as a threat to freedom, in America they were seen as its underpinning. In Europe religion was presented, at any rate by the majority of its intellectuals, as an obstacle to "progress," in America, as one of its dynamics.

> From the 1960s, this huge and important difference between Europe and America was becoming blurred, perhaps in the process of disappearing altogether. It was one way in which America was losing its uniqueness and ceasing to be the City on the Hill. For the first time in American history there was a widespread tendency, especially among intellectuals, to present religious people as enemies of freedom and democratic choice. There was a further tendency among the same people to present religious practice of any kind which was conducted with zeal as "fundamentalist," a term of universal abuse.[67]

---

[67] Paul Johnson, *A History of the American People*, pp. 967-968.

TWO

Mankind's Future at Risk: Assaults on the Family

Preview

I. Beyond Tears: The Rise of Planned Parenthood

II. "Male and Female He Created Them": The Threat of Same-Sex Partnerships
  A. A Question of "Tolerance" and Civil Rights?
  B. The Homosexual Agenda: To Destroy Marriage
    1. The Eradication of Marriage: an Overt Goal
    2. Why Same-Sex Partnerships Undermine Marriage
      a) Socially
      b) Legally
    3. Refuting "Same-Sex Partnership Status" as a Civil Right
    4. The Ultimate Goal of Homosexual Activists: Redefine Creation and Redemption
      a) "In the Beginning"
      b) Redeemed by Christ's Blood
      c) A Society that Would Oppose Christ's Redemption?
      d) True Compassion: "Go, and Sin No More"
  C. "Clear and Present Danger": Homosexual Advances Already Secured
    1. The Corporate Scene, Universities, and Municipalities
    2. The Courts
    3. The American Psychological Association
      a) Immoral Behavior as a Civil Right
      b) Just the Facts: A Quest for Young People
        (1) "Facts" or an Agenda?
        (2) Legal Threats and Academic Censorship
  D. The Church's Liberating Teaching on Homosexuality
  E. Our Duty as Christians and Citizens

Points to look for

1. What facts can be cited to show that the family is truly being threatened in society today?

2. What are some of the concrete forces working to undermine marriage and the family?

3. What are the goals and purpose of Planned Parenthood, as described by its founder, Margaret Sanger?

4. What facts can be cited to show the pervasive influence of Planned Parenthood during this past century?

5. What sophisms does the homosexual movement employ to give a semblance of credibility to the case for same-sex partnerships?

6. Why do homosexual activists seek not merely tolerance, but the eradication of marriage itself?

7. How does the recognition of same-sex partnerships undermine marriage as a social institution?

8. How would the legal recognition of "homosexual marriage" or same-sex "domestic partnerships" undermine marriage?

9. How can the claim be refuted that same-sex partnership status is a civil right, and to deny this fact is to discriminate against homosexual persons?

10. How do homosexual activists seek to redefine the order of creation and redemption?

11. What have been the historical consequences for civilizations that have socially condoned homosexual behavior, weakening marriage and the family? Why?

12. Why is the refusal to sanction same-sex partnerships not at variance with true compassion for homosexual persons?

13. How is the position of the American Psychological Association as to whether homosexuality is a disorder in direct contradiction with Church teaching?

14. What is the APA's position on whether same-sex couples should be allowed to adopt children? Why is this position so destructive?

15. How does the Church offer true liberation for persons with homosexual tendencies?

16. What critiques could be made of the document *Just the Facts About Sexual Orientation and Youth?*

The growth of an antagonistic view toward religion, especially toward public expressions of religious belief, certainly strikes a blow against the family. But this is only one of many attacks being waged against the family today. Every Christian, every concerned citizen, has a duty to love and defend society's most vital cell. What does it mean to love the family? In the conclusion of *Familiaris Consortio,* the Holy Father reviews the different ways we can do so. One of them is surprising at first glance, but crucial. *"Loving the family means identifying the dangers and evils that menace it, in order to overcome them."*[68]

A 200 percent rise in divorce, a 400 percent rise in illegitimate births, and a 300 percent rise in children living in single-parent homes from 1960 to 1990 certainly reveal that the family is being threatened. Are these menacing evils simply the product of inexorable social and technological

[68] *Familiaris Consortio,* 86. Italics mine.

change? Or are there concrete forces working to undermine the family? John Paul II affirms that the latter is true.

> Unfortunately various programs backed by very powerful resources nowadays seem to aim at the breakdown of the family. At times it appears that concerted efforts are being made to present as "normal" and attractive, even to glamorize, situations which are in fact "irregular." Indeed, they contradict "the truth and love" which should inspire and guide relationships between men and women, thus causing tensions and divisions in families, with grave consequences particularly for children. The moral conscience becomes darkened; what is true, good and beautiful is deformed; and freedom is replaced by what is actually enslavement.[69]

What are some of these "programs backed by very powerful resources" that are pursuing the breakdown of the family? Foremost among them ranks the organization founded in the 1920's as the "American Birth Control League" — now known by the more innocuous-sounding title of "Planned Parenthood." In more recent decades, Planned Parenthood has not infrequently discovered powerful allies in international organizations such as the United Nations, the International Monetary Fund, and the World Bank. The courts have often taken sides against the family, as the 1973 *Roe v. Wade* decision attests — striking out against life itself within the mother's womb. Educational experiments such as values clarification and biologically oriented sex education have done much to undermine fundamental family values. Not to be overlooked are media forays such as *The Simpsons* and *Honey I Burnt the Kids,* ridiculing fatherhood.

I. Beyond Tears: The Rise of Planned Parenthood

How aptly John Paul II has described the twentieth century as "a century of tears." From Auschwitz to the gulags, from the "killing fields" of Cambodia to the unnamed dwellings of China's Cultural Revolution, human tears have flowed without ceasing. Tears of fathers and mothers, and of children. Tears of all races and religions.

Could anything be more terrible than the cruelty and human misery which have given rise to so many tears? Yes. For only a heart that loves is able to weep. The twentieth century has witnessed another, more silent, assault upon humanity. Unlike the gulags, this attack has not passed into history, but continues unabated into the third millennium. It strikes at "the fundamental and innate vocation of every human being"[70] — the call to love. And it does so precisely by undermining an institution whose very essence is to foster love: the family.

---

[69] Letter to Families, 4.
[70] *Familiaris Consortio,* 11

Who has launched this most thriving crusade against humankind? One of the forgotten figures of the past century: Margaret Sanger — the founder of Planned Parenthood.

Margaret Sanger? Was she not a liberal woman of immense compassion who was so moved by the plight of poor mothers and families in the early decades of the twentieth century that she dedicated her entire life to their cause? Was their misery not the reason she edited the *Birth Control Review* from 1917 to 1938 and founded the American Birth Control League, whose name was later changed to Planned Parenthood of America in 1942? Did not the suffering poor beyond American borders motivate her to launch the International Planned Parenthood Federation in 1948? Sanger's defenders would have us believe so.

Margaret Sanger herself (1879-1966) knew what it meant to be poor. One of eleven children of poverty-stricken Irish immigrant parents, Sanger soon rose to affluence when she dropped out of nursing school after only three months to marry a wealthy architect and eventually settle in New York's Greenwich Village. There Sanger became closely associated with leading figures in the eugenics movement, many of whom played a prominent role in the foundation of Planned Parenthood.

The eugenics circle held that some races and individual members of the human species were genetically superior to others. These superior members should be encouraged to reproduce, while the births of inferior members such as the poor or minorities were to be regulated. The ultimate solution to the problem of poverty when viewed in these terms was remarkably simple: Eliminate the poor!

Did Margaret Sanger truly adopt such a view of the human person and espouse such goals? Her own words speak for themselves. In the May 1919 edition of *Birth Control Review*, she wrote, "More children from the fit, less from the unfit — that is the chief aim of birth control." The November 1921 edition declared, "Birth control: to create a race of thoroughbreds."

Sanger outlined her new philosophy in her 1922 book *Pivot of Civilization*. In it she sharply criticized philanthropists who provided free maternity care to poor mothers. According to Sanger these acts of generosity "encourage the healthier and more normal sections of the world to shoulder the burden of unthinking and indiscriminate fecundity of others; which brings with it, as I think the reader must agree, a dead weight of human waste. Instead of decreasing and aiming to eliminate the stocks that are most detrimental to the future of the race and the world, it tends to render them to a menacing degree dominant." [71]

---

[71] Margaret Sanger, *Pivot of Civilization* (New York: Brentano's, 1922), p. 177.

The founder of Planned Parenthood saw contraception, sterilization, and eventually abortion as the panacea for eliminating all human suffering. Elasah Drogin notes the following in her book *Margaret Sanger: Father of Modern Society.* "Through the 284 pages of *Pivot of Civilization,* there is not one word written about fair labor laws, fair housing requirements, a more equitable distribution of wealth, or even the simple responsibility of caring for one's neighbor."[72]

Sanger's disdain was not confined to the poor, whom she often referred to as "human weeds." It extended to minorities such as blacks. In a private letter to Clarence Gamble dated October 19, 1939, she revealed her ultimate goal towards blacks and how it could best be attained. "The most successful educational approach to the Negro is through a religious appeal. We do not want word to go out that we want to exterminate the Negro population, and the minister is the man who can straighten out that idea if it ever occurs to any of their more rebellious members."[73]

The following lines from *Pivot of Civilization* allow a particularly telling glimpse of Sanger's "compassion" and her motives. "Remember our motto: if we must have welfare, give it to the rich, not to the poor. . . . We are paying for and even submitting to the dictates of an ever increasing, unceasingly spawning class of human beings who never should have been born at all."[74]

Sanger's views naturally led her to strike out against the institution of marriage and the family. She wrote, "The marriage bed is the most degenerating influence in the social order."[75] Sanger advocated instead a "voluntary association" between sexual partners. She thus sought to supplant the family as the most fundamental unit of society with relationships directed toward individual sexual gratification.

How successful has been the campaign to reconstruct society launched by Margaret Sanger and Planned Parenthood, her life's cause? A few facts reveal the pervasive influence of Sanger's movement on humanity's course in the twentieth century. As a United Nations study has indicated, in the year 2000 the United States, Canada, China, Japan and every country in Europe have fallen below zero population growth. (Immigration helps boost the numbers in America.) Worldwide, at least 61 countries are failing to replace their populations.

Since the 1973 *Roe v. Wade* abortion decision, an average of 1.5 million unborn babies have been aborted each year in the United States.

---

[72] Elasah Drogin, *Margaret Sanger: Father of Modern Society,* (New Hope: CUL, 1989), p. 43.
[73] As cited in Drogin, p. 33.
[74] As cited in Drogin, pp. 45 and 52.
[75] David Kennedy, *Birth Control in America, The Career of Margaret Sanger* (New Haven: Yale University Press, 1970), p. 23. As cited in Drogin, p. 15.

Twenty-five percent of white women's pregnancies have ended in abortion, while 40 percent of minority pregnancies have been aborted. In 1990 more than 70 percent of the married women in the United States were using contraceptives.[76]

Without exception, all the sad consequences of contraception that Pope Paul VI foresaw in his 1968 encyclical *Humanae Vitae* have come to pass.

Can the twenty-first truly become a century of healing and wiping away tears? Tens of thousands of Americans who march for life in Washington, D.C. each year think that it can. So do countless mothers and fathers who still believe that a child is God's most precious gift. And since human history has become the history of salvation with Christ's birth, death, and resurrection, there are certainly grounds for hope.

II. "Male and Female He Created Them": The Threat of Same-Sex Partnerships
A. A Question of "Tolerance" and Civil Rights?

Homosexual activists claim that same-sex "domestic partnerships" and even the oxymoron of "gay marriage" represent a simple issue of tolerance. To deny the equivalent of marital status to homosexual couples is to violate their basic civil rights — besides manifesting blatant "homophobia."

In a pluralistic society like America's, should not homosexual behavior be regarded as an "alternative lifestyle"? After all, it is claimed, the only goal of the homosexual movement is for same-sex couples to form "non-traditional" families that co-exist peacefully beside traditional families — father, mother, children, and relatives.

B. The Homosexual Agenda: To Destroy Marriage

Two issues must be clearly faced. First, do homosexuals merely seek to be tolerated within society? The facts belie this claim. Second, would it ever be possible to achieve the goal of "innocuous" same-sex partnerships flourishing side-by-side with traditional families as an ideal in a pluralistic society? No. The moment society accords equal recognition to homosexual couples, it undermines marriage and the family. Society begins to sow the seeds of its own self-destruction.

1. The Eradication of Marriage: An Overt Goal

Michaelangelo Signorile, a leading homosexual activist, speaks quite candidly. He urges fellow activists

---

[76] Figures are based on information supplied by the Population Research Institute of Washington, D.C.

... to fight for same-sex marriage and its benefits and then, once granted, redefine the institution of marriage completely, to demand the right to marry not as a way of adhering to society's moral codes but rather to debunk a myth and radically alter an archaic institution that as it now stands keeps us down. The most subversive action lesbians and gay men can undertake — and one that would perhaps benefit all of society — is to transform the notion of "family" entirely.[77]

Is Signorile perhaps a lone voice, not representative of the homosexual movement as such? Thomas Stoddard, leader of the campaign for homosexuals in the military and former president of the Lambda Legal Defense Fund, now known as the Lambda Legal Defense and Education Fund, a homosexual legal foundation, has this to say about the need to alter marriage.

I must confess at the outset that I am no fan of the "institution" of marriage as currently constructed and practiced.... Why give it such prominence? Why devote resources to such a distant goal? Because marriage is, I believe, the political issue that most fully tests the dedication of people who are not gay to full equality for gay people, and also the issue most likely to lead ultimately to a world free from discrimination against lesbians and gay men. Marriage is much more than a relationship sanctioned by law. It is the centerpiece of our entire social structure, the core of the traditional notion of "family."[78]

Lesbian activist Paula Ettelbrick, policy director for the National Center for Lesbian Rights, opposes the very notion of marriage itself as oppressive to homosexual persons. Her objectives are far-reaching. "We must keep our eyes on the goals of providing true alternatives to marriage and of radically reordering society's views of reality."[79]

2. Why Same-Sex Partnerships Undermine Marriage
a) Socially

Social recognition of same-sex partnerships as the equivalent of marriage by corporations in granting benefits, and by universities and municipalities in formulating their policies, weakens marriage. Robert H. Knight, Director of Cultural Studies at the Family Research Council, tells why. First of all, such recognition sends a clear signal that marriage is no longer considered "a priority worth encouraging above other kinds of relationships."[80] Second, same-sex activity is legitimized, fos-

---

[77] Michaelangelo Signorile, "Bridal Wave," *Out*, December/January 1994, p. 161.
[78] Thomas Stoddard, "Why Gay People Should Seek the Right to Marry," essay in *Lesbians, Gay Men and the Law*, William B. Rubenstein, ed. (New York: The New Press, 1993), pp. 398, 400.
[79] Paula Ettelbrick, "Since When Is Marriage a Path to Liberation?" in Rubenstein, *op. cit.*, p. 405.
[80] Robert H. Knight, "How Domestic Partnerships and 'Gay Marriage' Threaten the Family," www.frc.org / issues in depth / homosexual culture, report of June 1994, p. 1.

tering homosexuals' claims that they should be able to adopt children. The healthy sexual identity of these children would be put in grave peril, as would their ability to one day raise sound families of their own. Third, recognition of same-sex partnerships undermines the need for procreation as the basis of marriage, along with the kinship structure essential to the stability of communities and societies. Fourth, it mocks the idea of commitment, since domestic partners can generally be changed several times within a single year. Finally, such recognition breeds cynicism by defying the common understanding of marriage as a permanent commitment between husband and wife, the authentic foundation for any family worthy of the name.[81]

b) Legally

Granting protection and benefits under the law to same-sex partnerships goes even further than social recognition toward destroying marriage. Fortunately, at present not a single state recognizes "gay marriage." In 1996 Congress enacted a federal defense of marriage bill that defined marriage as being between one man and one woman. Were a single state to grant homosexual couples marital status in the future, an immediate constitutional crisis would ensue. Couples from any other state could travel to the state in question, become recognized as married, then return to their own home state and sue for equal recognition there under the "full faith and credit clause" of the United States Constitution. The Supreme Court would eventually have to decide the issue and could, in a single stroke, redefine marriage for all fifty states.

Even if the oxymoron "homosexual marriage" is not specifically employed, granting equal "benefits, protection, and security" under the law to same-sex "domestic partnerships" or "civil unions," as the Vermont state legislature has done, delivers a devastating blow to marriage.[82] The claim that such a law is not the equivalent to recognizing "homosexual marriage" rests on semantic sophistry. In plain terms: it is a lie. When such behavior is granted legal benefits and protection, the law establishes it as a social reality, as an equivalent to marriage, even if the term is never used. Still further, the law then begins to shape the moral conscience of society itself, which tends to regard any legally-sanctioned behavior as morally acceptable.

3. Refuting "Same-Sex Partnership Status" as a Civil Right

We have already discovered how false is the claim that the homosexual movement merely seeks "tolerance" within society. Homosexual activists overtly strive to eradicate marriage, either by redefining it into

---

[81] Ibid., pp. 1-2.
[82] It is a terrible irony that the Vermont state senate followed the lead of the House and approved the bill on Tuesday of Holy Week during the Jubilee Year 2000. Vermont's governor implicitly acknowledged the widespread public opposition to the bill within Vermont by signing it in a private ceremony.

non-existence or by eliminating it entirely. Even if this were not their explicit goal, social and legal recognition of same-sex partnerships inevitably undermines marriage.

What about the charge made by homosexual activists that they are being discriminated against if their same-sex partnerships are not granted equal legal status with heterosexual marriage? They often invoke the violation of black persons' civil rights that occurred when the law forbade interracial marriages. No analogy, they contend, could better describe their present situation.

First of all, the analogy being appealed to does not hold up under scrutiny. Skin color is a benign, non-behavioral characteristic. It cannot be equated with an orientation based precisely on freely chosen behavior to affirm a violation of civil rights. No moral behavior that violates the natural law and the very foundations of society, such as homosexuality, can ever be the object of civil rights. Second, present marriage laws in no way discriminate against homosexual persons. They have just as much right under the law to marry someone of the opposite sex as do heterosexual persons. While homosexual couples do not have the right to receive legal marital status, neither can heterosexual persons attempt to form same sex-partnerships and claim marriage benefits.

The law adheres to the definition of marriage found in *Webster's Dictionary*. It is as follows: "a: the state of being united to a person of the opposite sex as husband or wife; b: the mutual relation of husband and wife: wedlock; c: the institution whereby men and women are joined in a special kind of social and legal dependence for the purpose of founding and maintaining a family."[83] When homosexual activists claim they are being discriminated against and their civil rights violated by present marriage laws, they are making an accusation that is completely false in an effort to achieve their true purpose of eradicating marriage itself.

4. The Ultimate Goal of Homosexual Activists: Redefine Creation and Redemption
a) "In the Beginning"

From a social and legal perspective, homosexual activism is an attempt to change the very essence of marriage and the family. It is an effort to reconstruct fundamental public moral convictions, "radically reordering society's views of reality." What dimension does the homosexual campaign assume when judged from a Christian viewpoint? It becomes nothing less than the attempt to redefine creation and redemption.

---

[83] *Webster's Third New International Dictionary of the English Language Unabridged* (Springfield: Merriam-Webster Inc., 1981), p. 1284.

God's Word in Sacred Scripture reveals to us the Creator's plan for each human person. "So God created man in his own image, in the image of God he created him; male and female he created them" (Gn 1:27). The Book of Genesis goes on to add, "Therefore a man leaves his father and his mother and cleaves to his wife, and they become one flesh" (Gn 2:24).

Divine revelation assures us that being created male and female is a reflection of God's very image. The communion to which husband and wife are called in marriage reflects the self-giving communion of Father, Son, and Holy Spirit. Can any group, any law, any society, ever take it upon itself to alter God's creative plan for humanity? The future does not bode well for those who would try.

But man has indeed tried. His first attempt to alter God's plan took place in the Garden of Eden. It is called the Fall — original sin. Who can ever begin to fathom the terrible consequences of this attempt in the bitter fruit of man's inhumanity to man throughout the centuries? Only God himself could ever restore the agonizing wound wrought by sin. And God did so when he sent his only begotten Son to enter human history as the Redeemer of man.

b) Redeemed by Christ's Blood

Christ restored man and woman to the Father's original plan "in the beginning," before sin. Jesus clearly reveals that he has redeemed marriage when the Pharisees ask him whether divorce is allowed. Christ answers that Moses permitted divorce due to the hardness of their hearts. He then pronounces the following decisive words: "But from the beginning of creation, 'God made them male and female.' 'For this reason a man shall leave his father and mother and be joined to his wife, and the two shall become one.' So they are no longer two but one. What therefore God has joined together, let not man put asunder."[84] Christ plainly manifests that, thanks to him, marriage has become once again what God originally meant it to be.

What was the price that Christ had to pay in order to transform marriage and restore it to God's original plan? He sweat drops of his own blood in the Garden of Gethsemane. Blood poured steadily from the flesh that was torn open on his back as he was scourged at the pillar. Rivulets of blood trickled down his face when he allowed himself to be crowned with thorns. Streams of blood flowed from his hands and feet, nailed to the cross, before he was able to pronounce the words, "Father, forgive them," and, finally, "It is accomplished."

How sobering to ponder what God's only Son endured in order to redeem our fallen human nature and restore God's original plan for

---

[84] Mk 10:6-9.

marriage and the family. As St. Paul exclaims, "You were bought with a price."[85]

c) A Society that Would Oppose Christ's Redemption?

What will be the fate of a society that comes to sanction behavior which is objectively opposed to God's creative plan, restored by Christ at the price of his redeeming blood? History imparts a clear lesson. Robert Knight of the Family Research Council cites research done by the late Harvard sociologist Pitirim Sorokin.

> Analyzing studies of cultures spanning several thousand years on several continents, Sorokin found that virtually all political revolutions that brought about societal collapse were preceded by sexual revolutions in which marriage and family were no longer accorded premiere status. . . .[86]

> Self-governing people require a robust culture founded on marriage and family, which nurture the qualities that permit self-rule: deferred gratification, self-sacrifice, respect for kinship and law, and property rights. These qualities are founded upon sexual restraint, which permits people to pursue long-term interests, such as procreating and raising the next generation, and securing benefits for one's children.

> According sex outside marriage the same protections and status as the marital bond would destroy traditional sexual morality, not merely expand it. One can no more "expand" a definition or moral principle than one can continually expand a yardstick and still use it as a reliable measure.[87]

d) True Compassion: "Go, and Sin No More"

Not only do Christians and all people of good will safeguard the very future of society by refusing to sanction homosexual behavior, but they also serve the best interests of homosexual persons themselves. The accusation is often made that those who would defend God's plan lack compassion toward homosexual persons. "He lacks compassion" — no charge more serious than this one could be leveled against someone today. But G.K. Chesterton once said that compassion is the only thing which remains after society has lost all of its moral principles.

Compassion is certainly not bad. It is a Christian virtue. No one could possibly be found more compassionate than Christ himself. There is not a single time in any of the Gospels when he did not come to the aid of someone who cried out, "Have pity on me." Even under the ex-

---

[85] 1 Cor 7:23.

[86] Pitirim Sorokin, *The American Sex Revolution* (Boston: Porter Sargent Publishers, 1956), pp. 77-105.

[87] Robert Knight, "How Domestic Partnerships and 'Gay Marriages' Threaten the Family," pp. 8-9.

cruciating torment of the cross, when the condemned thief asked him for mercy, Christ replied, "Today you will be with me in Paradise."[88]

But just what is true compassion? Does it mean telling someone, "I understand, I feel your pain, continue doing exactly what you are doing"? Homosexual behavior is destructive. It wounds people physically, psychologically, and spiritually. How could it not do so, when it violates the natural law, when it goes against the way God created us as persons? Homosexual behavior contravenes the human dignity of persons who surrender to it, just as any sin diminishes the sinner.

Christ was compassionate. He forgave the woman caught in the act of adultery when everyone else was ready to stone her. But the depths of Christ's compassion were also expressed in the very next words he spoke to her: "Go, and do not sin again."[89] Christ's command called upon the woman to rise to her true dignity as a person by overcoming sin in her life. It opened before her "the glorious freedom of the children of God."[90] Still, Christ did much more for the woman caught in adultery than give her a command that would ennoble her. He also imparted to her the grace and the strength she needed to fulfill his command. And the price Christ paid in order to do so was his death upon the cross.

St. Paul exclaims in his letter to the Galatians, "For freedom Christ has set us free." Then he hastens to add, "Stand fast, therefore, and do not submit again to a yoke of slavery."[91] Each person is called to conquer sin and attain true freedom, "lest the cross of Christ be emptied of its power."[92]

Christ's cross can give homosexual persons the strength to conquer the freedom Christ has won for them. It can also give Christians the courage to publicly defend marriage and the family, even at the risk of being politically incorrect, "fundamentalist," or even "uncompassionate." When the day arrives in which each of us must render an account to Christ for our lives, he will ask us whether we have done so. His message in the Gospel is clear. "Whoever is ashamed of me and of my words, the Son of Man will be ashamed of when he comes in his glory and in the glory of the Father and of the holy angels."[93]

C. "Clear and Present Danger": Homosexual Advances Already Secured

As the third millennium dawns, what is the panorama that unfolds before us regarding marriage, the family, and the future of our society?

---

[88] Lk 23:43.
[89] Jn 8:11.
[90] Rm 8:21.
[91] Gal 5:1.
[92] 1 Cor 1:17.
[93] Lk 9:26.

The signs of the times are less than reassuring. While California became the thirty-first state to pass a defense of marriage act through a popular referendum in March 2000, a single court case would be enough for the Supreme Court to redefine the institution of marriage. The 1973 *Roe v. Wade* decision undermining life, the very reason for being of the family, is not a heartening precedent.

1. The Corporate Scene, Universities, and Municipalities

For the present, most corporations resist extending family benefits to same-sex partners. As of 1994, only six of the Fortune 1000 companies had instituted domestic partnership plans.[94] Still, some very big names have already done so. Among them are Time Warner, Levi-Strauss, Apple, Lotus, Microsoft, and Ben and Jerry's. Institutions such as Minnesota Public Radio and the Federal National Mortgage Association have also joined their numbers.[95] Among the institutions that promote homosexuality through diversity training and officially sanctioned homosexual employees' groups are AT&T, U.S. West, Xerox, and federal agencies such as the departments of Transportation, Agriculture, Health and Human Services, and Housing and Urban Development.[96]

Not surprisingly, California tops the list of states in which cities have extended employee benefits to same-sex partners. These include San Francisco, Los Angeles, Berkeley, Laguna Beach, Santa Cruz and West Hollywood. Other cities that have followed the lead of their progressive compatriots are Seattle and Madison (Wisconsin).

Many universities have extended benefits such as campus housing to same-sex couples. These include Stanford, the University of Chicago, Harvard, Columbia, Dartmouth, Iowa, Iowa State, the University of Wisconsin, Minnesota, Northwestern, Indiana, and MIT.[97] Even more numerous are the universities which sanction "diversity training" and official homosexual organizations. It is certainly not a pleasant scene for parents to contemplate as their sons and daughters graduate from high school and prepare to leave home.

2. The Courts

In a more glorious epoch, the courts could have been counted upon as a bulwark of defense for the family. The U.S. Supreme Court described marriage in an 1888 decision as "creating the most important relation in life, as having more to do with the morals and civilization of a people than any other institution."[98]

---

[94] David J. Jefferson, "Gay Employees Win Benefits for Partners at More Corporations," The *Wall Street Journal*, March 18, 1994, p. A-1.

[95] Jefferson, *Wall Street Journal*, op. cit., and Thomas A. Stewart, "Gay in Corporate America," *Fortune*, December 16, 1991, p. 50.

[96] Knight, "How Domestic Partnerships and 'Gay Marriages' Threaten the Family," p. 2.

[97] "Report of the 14.06 Task Force," University of Michigan, March 29, 1994, pp. 3-5.

[98] *Maynard v. Hill*, 125 U.S. 190, 205 (1888).

Today, through judicial activism, the courts are often on the leading edge of the movement to redefine marriage and the family. In Hawaii the state supreme court attempted to rewrite marriage so that same-sex couples would attain equal legal recognition. Only an amendment to the state constitution, approved by an overwhelming seventy percent of the people, enabled the state legislature to pass a law defining marriage as a union between one man and one woman. A similar drama took place in Alaska. History has repeated itself most recently in Vermont, where, on December 20, 1999, the state supreme court ordered the legislature to pass a "domestic partnership" bill, granting equal "protection, benefits, and security" under the law to homosexual couples as to husband and wife. In a scant four months, Vermont's legislature and governor tragically complied. Matt Daniels, executive director of Alliance for Marriage in Washington, D.C., accurately describes the present situation.

> Public opinion polls reveal that most Americans continue to regard the term "homosexual marriage" as an oxymoron. This is because most Americans — as well as most people around the world — acknowledge the important link between marriage as a legal institution and the procreative potential of the union of a man and a woman.

> In effect, without acknowledging it in so many words, most Americans still recognize the natural law basis for the social institution of marriage. If the day ever comes when American law refuses to acknowledge the natural law foundation of marriage and the family, the law of the nation will have become substantially untethered from the fabric of social reality itself.[99]

3. The American Psychological Association
a) Immoral Behavior as a Civil Right

With over 159,000 members, the American Psychological Association is the largest organization of professional psychologists not only in the United States, but also in the entire world. How is this association wielding its extensive influence in the struggle for the future of marriage and the family?

In 1975 the American Psychological Association made a momentous decision. Its council of representatives voted to support the action taken two years earlier by the American Psychiatric Association. It removed homosexuality from the Association's official list of mental disorders. The council of representatives went on to adopt the following resolution:

---

[99] Matthew Daniels, "Vermont Legislature Threatens Marriage," *National Catholic Register*, March 12-18, 2000, Vol. 76, No. 11, pp. 1, 15, at 15.

Homosexuality per se implies no impairment in judgment, stability, reliability, or general social and vocational capabilities; further, the American Psychological Association urges all mental health professionals to take the lead in removing the stigma of mental illness that has long been associated with homosexual orientations.[100]

In a single blow the APA declared that homosexuality is not a disorder, but rather a completely normal sexual orientation, and exhorted all of its 159,000 members to promote this "sea change." The APA then took another incredible step. "Further, the American Psychological Association supports and urges the enactment of civil rights legislation at the local, state and federal levels that would offer citizens who engage in acts of homosexuality the same protections now guaranteed to others on the basis of race, creed, color, etc."[101]

Can we truly believe the words our eyes have just read? The largest professional association of psychologists in the world is now campaigning to grant the status of a civil right to behavior that openly contradicts the understanding of marriage and the nature of man and woman which has guided every civilization since the beginning of recorded history. The APA actively seeks to give legal protection to behavior that the Judeo-Christian tradition condemns as immoral. What will be the fate of our country if such measures are adopted? What is already the fate of suffering homosexual persons who come seeking help to psychologists who follow the APA line?

A final question that must be asked is how deeply the APA's position will affect families. The first ones to suffer will be young, innocent children. Here is the policy statement of the APA on allowing same-sex couples to adopt children: "The sex, gender identity, or sexual orientation of natural, or prospective adoptive or foster parents should not be the sole or primary variable considered in custody or placement cases."[102] In other words, a same-sex couple should enjoy the same privilege as a husband and wife in being allowed to adopt children. The most elementary knowledge of a child's need for both father and mother decries the untenable position of the APA.

b) *Just the Facts:* **A Quest for Young People**
(1) "Facts" or an Agenda?

The APA is fully conscious of its impact on young people through the field of education. Awareness of their influence led the APA to join a

---

[100] Policy Statements on Lesbian, Gay, and Bisexual Concerns, *"Discrimination Against Homosexuals," adopted by the American Psychological Association Council of Representatives on January 24-26, 1975, at www.apa.org.*

[101] Ibid.

[102] *Policy Statements on Lesbian, Gay, and Bisexual Concerns,* "Child Custody or Placement," adopted by the American Psychological Association Council of Representatives on September 2 & 5, 1976, at ibid.

coalition of nine other professional organizations in publishing a twelve-page pamphlet entitled *Just the Facts About Sexual Orientation and Youth*. In the fall of 1999, this pamphlet was sent out to the heads of all 14,700 public school districts in the U.S. Other members of the coalition included the National Education Association, the American Federation of Teachers, the American Association of School Administrators, and the American Academy of Pediatrics.

Why was the factsheet distributed? Its authors are quite direct: due to alarm over efforts to help young people with homosexual tendencies overcome this disorder.

> The reason for publishing this factsheet now is the recent upsurge in aggressive promotion of "reparative therapy" and "transformational ministry." "Reparative therapy" refers to psychotherapy to eliminate individuals' sexual desires for members of their own gender. "Transformational ministry" refers to the use of religion to eliminate those desires. Since mid-1998, a number of organizations have invested significant resources in the promotion of "reparative therapy" and "transformational ministry" in the press, in conferences targeting educators, and in television and newspaper ads. This factsheet provides information from physicians, counselors, social workers, psychologists, legal experts, and educators who are knowledgeable about the development of sexual orientation in youth and the issues raised by "reparative therapy" and "transformational ministry."[103]

Just what "issues are raised" by these efforts to enable young people to live according to the truth of their identity as human persons? According to *Just the Facts*, "The promotion of 'reparative therapy' and 'transformational ministry' is likely to exacerbate the risk of harassment, harm, and fear."[104] The central position of the pamphlet is outlined in the following paragraphs.

> The term "reparative therapy" refers to psychotherapy aimed at eliminating homosexual desires and is used by people who do not think homosexuality is one variation within human sexual orientation, but rather still believe homosexuality is a mental disorder. The most important fact about "reparative therapy," also sometimes known as "conversion" therapy, is that it is based on an understanding of homosexuality that has been rejected by all the major health and mental health professions. The American Academy of Pediatrics, the American Counseling Association, the American Psychiatric Association, the American Psychological Association, the National Association of School Psychologists, and the National

---

[103] *Just the Facts About Sexual Orientation and Youth: A Primer for Principals, Educators & School Personnel*, at www.apa.org / public interest, p. 2.
[104] *Just the Facts About Sexual Orientation and Youth*, p. 3.

Association of Social Workers, together representing more than 477,000 health and mental health professionals, have all taken the position that homosexuality is not a mental disorder and thus there is no need for a "cure."

The Diagnostic and Statistical Manual of Mental Disorders, published by the American Psychiatric Association and defining the standard of the field, does not include homosexuality as a mental disorder. All other major health professional organizations have supported the American Psychiatric Association in its declassification of homosexuality as a mental disorder in 1973. Thus, the idea that homosexuality is a mental disorder or that the emergence of same-gender sexual desires among some adolescents is in any way abnormal or mentally unhealthy has no support among health and mental health professional organizations.[105]

In asserting that there is no support among health and mental health professionals for the idea that homosexuality is a disorder or that same-gender sexual desires are abnormal, *Just the Facts* chooses to omit a few salient facts to the contrary. "A 1977 survey conducted by the journal *Medical Aspects of Human Sexuality* reported that 69 percent of the 10,000 psychiatrists polled considered homosexuality a pathological adaptation."[106]

Why does *Just the Facts* not mention that Masters and Johnson reported a 71.6 percent success rate for patients leaving homosexuality after a follow-up of six years?[107] The "factsheet" also fails to acknowledge the following statement from the president of the National Association for Research and Therapy of Homosexuality (N.A.R.T.H.): "There is at present sufficient evidence that in a majority of cases homosexuality can be successfully treated by psychoanalysis."[108] Here is yet another statement from a leading expert on homosexuality relegated into nonexistence by the "factsheet": "There is, nevertheless, continuing conviction among most, although not all, dynamically oriented psychiatrists in

---

[105] Ibid., p. 5.

[106] Yvette Cantu, "Recovery Change and Homosexuality: What the Experts Have to Say," at www.frc.org/issues in depth/homosexual culture.

[107] William H. Masters and Virginia E. Johnson, *Homosexuality in Perspective* (Boston: Little, Brown and Company, 1979), pp. 402 and 408. (William H. Masters obtained his M.D. from the University of Rochester. Positions held: professor of clinical obstetrics and gynecology for the School of Medicine of Washington University; director of the Reproductive Biological Research Foundation; and co-director and chairman of the board of the Masters and Johnson Institute. Virginia E. Johnson obtained her M.D. from the University of Missouri. Positions held: research director of the Reproductive Biological Research Foundation and co-director of the Masters and Johnson Institute.)

[108] Charles W. Socarides, M.D., *Homosexuality* (New York: Jason Aronson, 1978), p. 3. (Positions held include clinical professor of psychiatry at Albert Einstein College of Medicine. In 1995, he received the Distinguished Professor Award from the Association of Psychoanalytic Psychologists, British Health Service.)

general, and psychoanalysts in particular, that homosexuality can and should be changed to heterosexuality."[109]

What conclusion suggests itself after considering what *Just the Facts* asserts and the facts it pretends do not exist? Rather than a "scientific factsheet," the pamphlet takes on the appearance of an agenda that is being promoted.

(2) Legal Threats and Academic Censorship

The "factsheet" concludes with threatening legal tones and an appeal for academic censorship among the nations' schools. Through a clever sleight-of-hand tactic, *Just the Facts* manipulates the issue, attempting to identify any view of the human person — that is, any legitimate scientific anthropology which regards homosexuality as a disorder — with a religious stance. The "factsheet" then proceeds to warn against introducing such a view in a public educational context, invoking no less an authority than the U.S. Constitution and the separation of church and state.

> Like all students, those who are or are perceived to be lesbian, gay, or bisexual are protected by the Establishment Clause of the First Amendment, which, among other things, requires the separation of church and state. For example, public schools may not promote religion, endorse particular religious beliefs or seek to impose such beliefs on students. Also, a guidance counselor in a public school context may not attempt to persuade a gay, lesbian or bisexual student of the religious belief of some that homosexuality is a sin, or otherwise seek to impose a negative religious view of being gay, lesbian or bisexual on the student.[110]

Next the "factsheet" cites a 1996 Wisconsin legal case in which a student received a settlement of nearly one million dollars from a school that failed to stop anti-gay harassment directed against him. From protection against harassment, the document then crafts the amazing extrapolation that any difference in treatment constitutes inequality. "The legal mandate of equality for gay and non-gay students alike is not limited to circumstances of harassment; it applies to all decisions a public school official might make that would treat lesbian, gay, and bisexual students differently."[111] Does this mean that third graders could sue for discrimination if not allowed to enter fourth-grade classes? They are certainly being treated differently than fourth graders. Would not ramps for handicapped students also constitute discrimination under this criterion?

---

[109] Dr. Richard A. Isay, "Homosexuality and Psychiatry," *Psychiatric News* (February 7, 1992), p. 3. (Positions held: clinical professor of psychiatry at Cornell Medical College and chair of the American Psychiatric Association Committee on Gay, Lesbian, and Bisexual Issues.)
[110] *Just the Facts About Sexual Orientation and Youth*, p. 8.
[111] Ibid., p. 9.

Just the Facts completes its *tour de force* with a subtle appeal for academic censorship. It notes the prerogative public schools enjoy of deciding not to disseminate certain information to their students. The "factsheet" displays no qualms in pointing out to educators what sort of materials should never reach students' eyes: ". . .School officials should be deeply concerned about the validity and bias of materials or presentations that promote a change to a person's sexual orientation as a 'cure' or suggest that being gay, lesbian, or bisexual is unhealthy."[112] Must it be said that a professional body such as the American Psychological Association, united with the National Education Association and other influential organizations, feels called upon to urge public schools to violate such a cherished American value as academic freedom — all for the cause of advancing the homosexual agenda? As the Latin orator Cicero once exclaimed, "*O tempora, o mores!*"[113]

D. The Church's Liberating Teaching on Homosexuality

The APA's position that homosexuality is not a disorder stands in open contradiction to the teachings of the Church. But the APA does echo the Catholic teaching that all unjust discrimination against homosexual persons is wrong. As sons and daughters of God, redeemed by Christ's blood, homosexual persons should be treated with understanding and compassion. The Catechism clearly states this truth.

> The number of men and women who have deep-seated homosexual tendencies is not negligible. This inclination, which is objectively disordered, constitutes for most of them a trial. They must be accepted with respect, compassion, and sensitivity. Every sign of unjust discrimination in their regard should be avoided. These persons are called to fulfill God's will in their lives and, if they are Christians, to unite to the sacrifice of the Lord's Cross the difficulties they may encounter from their condition.[114]

Does avoiding unjust discrimination imply granting civil rights to homosexual behavior? The answer here is a resounding "no." While the homosexual tendency itself constitutes an objective disorder and is not a sin, surrendering to that tendency and committing homosexual acts is a sin. These acts violate God's law as revealed both in divine revelation and by the natural law. All men and women are responsible in conscience for following the dictates of the natural law. No government or society can ever legitimately condone behavior that directly violates the natural law.

---

[112] Ibid.

[113] "Oh times, oh customs!" (Cicero's First Speech Against Cataline, Chapter One)

[114] *Catechism of the Catholic Church*, 2358. The quotation is taken from the second English edition, published in 2000, which incorporates the modifications from the *Editio Typica*, (Rome-Washington, D.C.: Libreria Editrice Vaticana-U.S.C.C., 1997).

Basing itself on Sacred Scripture, which presents homosexual acts as acts of grave depravity,[115] tradition has always declared that "homosexual acts are intrinsically disordered."[116] They are contrary to the natural law. They close the sexual act to the gift of life. They do not proceed from a genuine affective and sexual complementarity. Under no circumstances can they be approved.[117]

By being faithful to the truth of the human person, created male and female in the image of God, the Church lives out authentic compassion toward homosexual persons. Her message is a liberating call. Those who would encourage persons with homosexual tendencies to surrender to their passions actually confine and restrain them. In the end, they make them slaves of a disorder that can often be overcome and can always be transformed, with the help of God's grace — not without suffering — into a path toward holiness. Christ exclaims in the Gospel, "You will know the truth, and the truth will make you free."[118]

Homosexual persons are called to chastity. By the virtues of self-mastery that teach them inner freedom, at times by the support of disinterested friendship, by prayer and sacramental grace, they can and should gradually and resolutely approach Christian perfection.[119]

E. Our Duty as Christians and Citizens

In the face of the numerous assaults being launched against the family today, each of us must rise to its defense. We are called to defend the family not just as Christians, but also as citizens of our beloved country. The family is not only a domestic Church, it is also the most fundamental and vital cell of society. It is the first community of persons, upon which all other communities depend.

The nature of marriage and the family is not simply a Catholic question. It cannot even be categorized as a religious issue. It is a question of natural law that must be respected by every man and woman of good will. America was founded on the natural law. In the Declaration of Independence, the founding fathers appealed to the rights to which *the law of Nature and of Nature's God*" entitled them.

It would be wishful thinking to believe that parents can assure the future of their children simply by loving them, teaching them the faith, and transmitting correct moral values. To be a responsible parent today, it is not enough to raise a good family. The future of all children and grandchildren will be determined in large part by the society in which

---

[115] Cf. Gen 19:1-29; Rom 1:24-27; 1 Cor 6:10; 1 Tim 1:10.
[116] Congregation for the Doctrine of the Faith, *Persona humana*, 8.
[117] *CCC*, 2357.
[118] Jn 8:32.
[119] *CCC*, 2359.

they come to live. Are Christian parents prepared to meet the challenge entailed in helping shape the path of that society? The fate of their children depends on their resolve.

Preview

Two MANKIND'S FUTURE AT RISK: ASSAULTS ON THE FAMILY *(continued)*
III. Radical Feminism at the U. N.: "A Gender Perspective"
    A. Dramas on the World Stage
    B. The Overt Goal of Radical Feminism: Redefine Equality
    C. A More Pernicious Goal: Redefine Gender Itself
    D. Consequences of a Gender Perspective: The Manipulation of Human Rights
    E. How Did Radical Feminism Come About?
        1. The Early 1960s: Liberal Feminism

        2. The Late 1960s: Radical Feminists and Neo-Marxism

        3. Are Radical Feminists Really Marxists?

    F. Really Radical Feminism: From Marxism to Deconstruction
    G. Cardinal Ratzinger Assesses U.N. Ideologies
    H. Our Response to the U.N. As Christians

Points to look for

1. What are NGOs and PrepComs? How have they become a source of ideological pressure at the United Nations?

2. In what way do radical feminists seek to redefine equality between men and women?

3. What is the "gender perspective"? How does it involve a differentiation between the word "gender" and the word "sex"?

4. How does the "gender perspective" imply a manipulation of fundamental human rights?

5. What is liberal feminism?

6. How did liberal feminism give way to radical feminism?

7. How does Neo-Marxism constitute the foundation of radical feminism?

8. Why is Neo-Marxist radical feminism so destructive to the human person?

9. What is "deconstructionism"? How does it influence radical feminism?

10. What critique does Cardinal Joseph Ratzinger level against the U.N.'s ideology of "women's empowerment" and "women's fulfillment"?

11. How does the U.N. radical feminist ideology lead to an eclipse of the "philosophy of love"?

12. What should be our response as Christians to the United Nations?

III. Radical Feminism at the U.N.: "A Gender Perspective"
A. Dramas on the World Stage

In 1994 the United Nations held an international conference on population and development in Cairo. The following year a similar conference on women took place at Beijing. Apparently they represented two worthwhile U.N. endeavors, seeking to confront issues of deep concern in the world today. Yet in these two conferences a world-scale drama unfolded in which not only the future of the family was at stake, but the very definition of what it means to be human, created "male and female" in God's image.

Had it not been for the diligent efforts of John Paul II and the coalition of countries that the Vatican delegations to these two conferences were able to muster, abortion would probably be an internationally recognized human right today. Instead of checking either the box marked "Male" or the one labeled "Female" when filling out any sort of questionnaire, we might well be selecting from among five different genders. How is it possible that such a state of affairs has come to hold sway at the U.N.?

Cairo and Beijing reveal the profound evolution that has taken place within the United Nations since the Universal Declaration of Human Rights was proclaimed in 1948. Many new ideological forces are at play behind the scenes. Often the most powerful of them come not from delegations which represent individual states, but from non-governmental organizations, or NGOs. Among the NGOs, two are especially noted for their clout: The International Planned Parenthood Federation (IPPF) and the Women's Environment and Development Organization (WEDO). Both of these organizations share a common ideology: radical feminism.

Precisely at international U.N. conferences, these NGOs are able to wield their influence most effectively. Often they are able to dominate the preparatory committee meetings, or "PrepComs," prior to the conferences. These PrepComs, in which discussion takes place of draft documents drawn up previously, are of crucial importance. Only those phrases from the drafts that delegates specifically request to be put into brackets can be debated at the international conferences themselves. Unsuspected forms of manipulation occur at the PrepComs in the attempt to muscle through ideologically "loaded" documents. Delegates from poorer countries are often intimidated and at times not even recognized by the chair. Persistent efforts are made to deny passes to Vatican delegates or even to occupy their seats in the committee rooms.

International conferences and the PrepComs leading up to them have become a preferred way for radical feminists and similar ideological groups to impose their agenda upon the world community. They are thus able to circumvent the legislative process of the U.N. member nations, making use of a new class of appointed United Nations' bureaucrats who are not responsible before any public election. Although the final documents resulting from the conferences do not possess the binding force of law, they are viewed as holding moral authority once approved by the international community, and are utilized as a means of pressure by agencies such as the International Monetary Fund and the World Bank. Nafis Sadik, who served as secretary general at the Cairo conference on population, claims that these international conferences now occupy seventy percent of the U.N.'s work.[120]

B. The Overt Goal of Radical Feminism: Redefine Equality

What exactly constitutes radical feminism, and why are the goals it seeks to achieve, in large part through the U.N., so destructive to the family? The noted journalist Dale O'Leary thoroughly investigated the origins and scope of radical feminism for her book *The Gender Agenda: Redefining Equality*.[121] The analysis which follows is based in large part upon her work.[122]

Radical feminists seek to redefine equality between men and women, so that it no longer consists of equal dignity as persons, but instead entails identity of functions and roles. A paper distributed at the PrepCom for Beijing illustrates the point. Co-authored by Frances Kissling, president of Catholics for a Free Choice, and Mary Hunt, the paper was entitled, "Equal is as Equal Does." The document called for a "feminist anthropology" based "on the radical equality of women and men," where "community, rather than family, is the 'programmatic focus.'"[123]

It is worth noting that Mary Hunt is a member of WATER (Women's Alliance for Theology, Ethics, and Ritual) for Women-Church Convergence. At a radical feminist "Re-Imaging" conference in Minneapolis in 1993, she proposed substituting friendship as a metaphor for family. "Imagine sex among friends as the norm. . . . Pleasure is our birthright of which we have been robbed in religious patriarchy. . . . I picture friends, not families, basking in the pleasure we deserve because our bodies are holy."[124]

---

[120] Cf. Dale O'Leary, *The Gender Agenda: Redefining Equality* (Lafayette, LA: Vital Issues Press, 1997), p. 41.
[121] Cf. previous footnote for publishing information.
[122] Most of the primary sources referred to are also cited by O'Leary in her book.
[123] As cited in O'Leary, *The Gender Agenda*, p. 79.
[124] Re-Imaging Conference, quoted in *HLI Reports* (January 1995), p. 6.

C. A More Pernicious Goal: Redefine Gender Itself

The strategy for redefining equality between men and women is to promote a "gender perspective," as evidenced by the statement which was issued by the Vienna regional preparatory meeting for Beijing. "A new gender contract involves an active and visible policy of mainstreaming a gender perspective into all relevant political economic and social policy fields at central, regional, and local levels."[125]

What precisely is a gender perspective? It is an ideological stance in which the word "gender" is no longer a synonym for the biological sex of male or female. A speech made by Bella Abzug to the Beijing PrepCom reveals the motive for enlarging the parameters of gender. "The meaning of the word *gender* has evolved as differentiated from the word *sex* to express the reality that women's and men's roles and status are socially constructed and subject to change."[126]

The word "gender" appeared over 200 times in the draft of the Platform for Action for the Beijing women's conference. One article states: "In many countries, the differences between women's and men's achievements and activities are still not recognized as the consequences of socially constructed gender roles rather than immutable biological differences."[127] The word "mother," on the other hand, could scarcely be encountered. Little wonder, since radical feminists wage a veritable war on motherhood as a socially constructed role foisted upon women.

In the redefinition of gender we are confronted with the most pernicious aspect of the feminist agenda, one that is utterly destructive of the human person, both men and women alike, created "male and female" by God "in the beginning." Incredible as it may seem, the claim is made that there are not merely two human genders, but *five*. And what might these be? Male, female, homosexual, lesbian, and bisexual or transsexual.

Surely it is impossible to "progress" any further than this? An even more radical goal is sought by some: *gender fluidity.* Kate Bornestein, a man who underwent a sex change, defines this ominous-sounding concept. "Gender fluidity is the ability to freely and knowingly become one or many of a limitless number of genders, for any length of time, at any rate of change. Gender fluidity recognizes no borders or rules of gender."[128]

---

[125] As cited in O'Leary, *The Gender Agenda,* p. 68.
[126] As cited in Ibid., pp 86-87.
[127] As cited in Ibid., p. 30.
[128] Kate Bornestein, *Gender Outlaw: On Men, Women and the Rest of Us* (New York: Rutledge, 1994), p. 115.

D. Consequences of a Gender Perspective: The Manipulation of Human Rights

It is not surprising that the sudden appearance of three new genders should be accompanied by the emergence of never-before-seen fundamental and inalienable human rights. Two all-encompassing ones are "sexual and reproductive rights." The former implies "respect for women's bodily integrity and decision-making as well as their right to express their sexuality with pleasure and without fear of abuse, disease, or discrimination. It requires access to voluntary, quality, reproductive and sexual health information, education and services."[129] Reproductive rights entail access to abortion on demand and contraception of all kinds.

The extension of inalienable rights to embrace the killing of innocent, unborn babies, as well as the most perverse and immoral sexual behavior, inexorably leads feminists to identify new enemies of human rights: religious fundamentalists and the Catholic Church. Naturally, among religious fundamentalists are included all who possess firm moral convictions that certain forms of behavior are simply wrong. In a Cairo human rights series, Copeland and Hernández declare, "This demand for elemental human rights is being met with opposition by religious fundamentalists of all kinds, with the Vatican playing a leading role in organizing religious opposition to reproductive rights and health, including even family-planning services."[130]

The blind ideological commitment of radical feminists leads to tragic results, as everything is reduced to gender, sexual freedom, contraception and abortion, while the real needs of women are ignored. To the delegates representing the international community gathered at Beijing, a group of lawyers issued a stark press release, based on eyewitness testimony that called attention to the plight of Tibetan women under the Chinese Communist regime:

> The villagers were informed that all women had to report to the tent for abortions and sterilizations or there would be grave consequences. For the women who went peacefully to the tents and did not resist, medical care was given. The women who refused to go were taken by force, operated on, and given no medical care. Women nine months pregnant had their babies taken out. . . . We saw many girls crying, heard their screams as they waited for their turn to go into the tent, and saw the growing pile of fetuses build outside the tent, which smelled horrible. During the two weeks of

---

[129] Rhonda Copeland and Berta Esperanza Hernández, "Sexual and Reproductive Rights and Health as Human Rights: Concepts and Strategies; An Introduction for Activists" (Cairo: *Human Rights Series*, 1994), p. 2.

[130] Ibid., p. 3.

this mobilization, all pregnant women were given abortions, followed by sterilization, and every woman of childbearing age was sterilized.[131]

What was the U.N. response to this agonizing plea? Tibetan women were manipulated by their feminist "supporters" into unknowingly promoting "reproductive rights." Added to the press release being circulated was the following: "That Tibetan women be provided with access to health care facilities to ensure availability of safe and effective birth control methods, safe abortions and sterilizations, should Tibetan women choose such options."[132] Tibet's call for international intervention went unheeded.

E. How Did Radical Feminism Come About?
1. The Early 1960s: Liberal Feminism

When the feminist movement emerged upon the scene in the early 1960s, it took the form of "liberal" or "equity" feminism. It quite justly held that women should have as much liberty in society as men. At the same time, liberal feminism insisted that the individual should be considered separately from the group.

The movement's strong points consisted of advocating a woman's right to vote in all countries, to hold public office, to have access to equal education, and to receive equal employment opportunities. The limitations of liberal feminism stemmed first of all from a failure to recognize the real and obvious differences between men and women. Many laws which feminists regarded as "discriminating" didn't attempt to oppress women, but sought to compensate for these differences and protect women. An exaggerated stress on the individual tended to ignore the importance of the family as a social unit. Finally, big government was overemphasized as a solution to all problems, including women's.

In the late 1960s, the shift took place from liberal to radical feminism. Liberal feminists had sought to work within the existing order of society, striving to achieve greater equality for women. Radical feminists repudiated them precisely because liberal feminists didn't recognize that it was "necessary to change the whole existing social structure in order to achieve women's liberation."[133]

---

[131] International Committee of Lawyers for Tibet, "Denial of Tibetan Women's Right to Reproductive Freedom" (San Francisco, CA, March 1, 1995), p. 10. The press release was based on the eyewitness account of Chinese mobile birth control teams in Tibetan villages in 1987. Cited in O'Leary, *The Gender Agenda*, p. 82.

[132] Cited in Ibid., p. 83.

[133] Alison Jagger, "Political Philosophies of Women's Liberation," *Feminism and Philosophy*, eds. Vetterling-Braggin, Elliston and English (Totowa, NJ: Littlefield, Adams & Co., 1977), p. 9.

2. The Late 1960s: Radical Feminists and Neo-Marxism

How did such a drastic shift in viewpoint come about — one that would lead to efforts not only to alter society itself, but to change the very definition of man and woman? What ideology underlies the radical feminist stance? The answer is surprising, almost hard to believe: *Neo-Marxism!*

The Neo-Marxist underpinnings of radical feminism begin to seem more plausible if we put ourselves back into the context of the late 1960s. It is the height of the Cold War and the arms race. The Vietnam War is raging, with fears that if Ho Chi Minh were to triumph, country after country would fall in a Southeast Asia "domino effect." Within the Church, liberation theology is at its apogee in Latin America, applying Marxist interpretation to Sacred Scripture. Christ is portrayed as a political liberator of the oppressed poor classes. John Paul II will not be elected for twenty more years. The year 1989 and the fall of the Berlin Wall are still on the distant horizon.

Today nearly everyone is familiar with Marxist economic theory, which views history as a continuous class struggle, culminating in the oppression of the working proletariat by capitalists. Violent revolution is the only way out. The proletariat must forcibly take back the means of production, abolishing private property and establishing a classless, socialist state.

Fewer people are acquainted with the teachings of Karl Marx and his companion, Frederick Engels, on women and the family. The following significant quote is taken from Engels' 1884 work, *The Origin of the Family, Private Property and the State*. "In an old unpublished manuscript written by Karl Marx and myself in 1846, I find the words: 'The first division of labor is that between man and woman for the propagation of children.' And today I can add: The first class opposition that appears in history coincides with the development of the antagonism between man and woman in monogamous marriage, and the first class oppression coincides with that of the female sex by the male."[134]

Engels goes on to outline the Marxist equivalent of the Book of Genesis, with its primordial paradise. In the early ages of human existence, mankind lived in classless societies composed of matrilineal family units, where private property was unknown and oppression non-existent. Then Marxist original sin occurred. Men insisted on recognition of their fatherhood, enslaved women in marriage, created the patriarchal family, and established private property. Class struggle and oppression followed.

---

[134] Frederick Engels, *The Origin of the Family, Private Property and the State* (New York: International Publishers, 1942), p. 58.

According to Engels, "The overthrow of the mother-right was the *world historical defeat of the female sex*. The man took command of the home also; the woman was degraded and reduced to servitude; she became the slave of his lust and a mere instrument for the production of children."[135] What is needed to liberate women? "The first condition for the liberation of the wife is to bring the whole female sex back into public industry, and that this in turn demands the abolition of the monogamous family as the economic unit of society."[136]

3. Are Radical Feminists Really Marxists?

Things are beginning to sound hauntingly familiar. But could it in fact be true? Are radical feminists really neo-Marxists? The very title of a programmatic book by an extreme feminist ideologue, Shulamith Firestone, is more than revealing: *The Dialectic of Sex*. In its pages Firestone affirms the following:

> So that just as to assure elimination of economic classes requires the revolt of the underclass (the proletariat) and, in a temporary dictatorship, their seizure of the means of *production*, so to assure the elimination of sexual classes requires the revolt of the underclass (women) and the seizure of control of *reproduction*: the restoration to women of ownership of their own bodies, as well as feminine control of human fertility, including both the new technology and all the social institutions of child-bearing and childrearing. And just as the end goal of socialist revolution was not only the elimination of the economic class privilege but of the economic class *distinction* itself, so the end goal of feminist revolution must be, unlike that of the first feminist movement, not just the elimination of male *privilege* but of the sex *distinction* itself; genital differences between human beings would no longer matter culturally. [137]

A Marxist philosophy absurdly applied to human sexuality leads to a destructive attempt to redefine the human person, and an open quest for the most perverse behavior. Firestone indicates the ultimate goals her revolution seeks. "A reversion to an unobstructed *pansexuality* — Freud's 'polymorphous perversity' — would probably supersede hetero/homo/bi-sexuality."[138]

F. Really Radical Feminism:
From Marxism to Deconstructionism

It would not seem possible to go beyond radical neo-Marxist feminism. But another step has indeed been taken. Many radical feminists have adopted the post-modernist philosophy of deconstructionism. Ac-

---

[135] Ibid., p. 50.
[136] Ibid., p. 66.
[137] Shulamith Firestone, *The Dialectic of Sex* (New York: Bantam Books, 1972), pp. 10-11; as cited in O'Leary, *The Gender Agenda*, p. 104.
[138] Ibid., p. 12.

cording to this view of things, words do not actually describe reality. They simply impose an arbitrary structure on objects. "Words are deconstructed by proving that a word serves a political purpose, giving one group power over another. According to deconstructionist theory, once the word is stripped of its power, people will be liberated. . . . In the end, everything can be deconstructed."[139]

Judith Butler, another analyst of feminist thought, describes the absurdity of what happens when gender itself is deconstructed. "When the constructed status of gender is theorized as radically independent of sex, gender itself becomes a free-floating artifice, with the consequence that *man* and *masculine* might just as easily signify a female body as a male one, and *woman* and *feminine* a male body as a female one."[140]

Absolutely no dialogue whatever is possible with those who assume a deconstructionist position. Dale O'Leary points out why. "Truth, reality, logic, scientific evidence, verifiable research — these are just words to the feminists."[141] History, science, and religion were made up by men to oppress women. Women must remake them to be liberated.

David Horowitz, a former 1960s radical himself, imparts a biting critique of left-wing ideologies such as radical feminism, so destructive toward everything that it means to be human.

> Compassion is not what motivates the Left, which is oblivious to the human suffering its generations have caused. What motivates the Left is the totalitarian Idea: the Idea that is more important than reality itself. . . . What motivates the Left is an Idea whose true consciousness is this: *Everything human is alien.* Because everything that is flesh-and-blood humanity is only the disposable past. This is the consciousness that makes mass murderers of well-intentioned humanists and earnest progressives.[142]

G. Cardinal Ratzinger Assesses U.N. Ideologies

Five years after the Beijing conference, from September 6-8, 2000, the U.N. held its "Millennium Summit" in New York, which marked the largest gathering of heads of state and government in history. Cardinal Joseph Ratzinger, Prefect of the Congregation for the Doctrine of the Faith, in an interview with the Italian journal *Avvenire,* used the occasion to severely criticize the United Nations' ideological proposal for a new world order based on the degradation of sexuality through "gender equality" and the elimination of women's very femininity. Ratzinger

---

[139] O'Leary, *The Gender Agenda*, p. 111.

[140] Judith Butler, *Gender Trouble: Feminism and the Subversion of Identity* (New York: Routledge, 1990), p. 6.

[141] O'Leary, *The Gender Agenda*, p. 110.

[142] David Horowitz and Peter Collier, *Destructive Generation: Second Thoughts about the '60s* (New York: Summit Books, 1989), p. 288.

noted that the Cairo and Beijing conferences manifested "a real and proper philosophy of the new man and new world. The peculiarity of this new anthropology, which should be at the base of the New World Order, is evident especially in the image of woman, in the ideology of 'Women's Empowerment,' born from the Beijing Conference. The objective of this ideology is woman's fulfillment. However, the principal obstacles to her fulfillment are the family and maternity."[143]

What are the sad consequences of this ideology, which dominates U.N. agencies? "Woman must be liberated especially of what characterizes her, namely, her feminine specificity. This must be annulled before a 'gender equity' and 'equality,' before an indistinct and uniform human being, in whose life sexuality has no other meaning than a voluptuous drug, that can be used without any criteria."[144]

When sexuality is reduced to hedonism, the result is an eclipse of the "philosophy of love." The eclipse of love can be seen above all in a fear of motherhood, where the supreme gift of a child becomes instead a threat to the quest for selfish fulfillment. "In the fear of maternity that has taken hold of a great part of our contemporaries, there is at stake something that is even more profound: In the end, the other is always an antagonist who deprives us of a part of life, a threat to our self and our free development."[145]

Cardinal Ratzinger's final assessment is pronounced in no uncertain terms. His words are completely frank, and so they offer the best hope of reclaiming our very humanity from false ideologies that would destroy us. "Today there is no longer a 'philosophy of love,' but only a 'philosophy of selfishness.' It is precisely here that people are deceived. In fact, at the moment they are advised not to love, they are advised, in the final analysis, not to be human."

H. Our Response to the U.N. as Christians

In light of the forces at play in the United Nations, what should be our attitude toward this institution as Christians? Should we perhaps desire its dissolution? Cardinal Ratzinger offers an initial response. "For this reason, at this stage of the development of the new image of the new world, Christians — and not just them but in any case even more than others — have the duty to protest."[146]

John Paul II provides a further, sure guideline based on his own example. Almost in the wake of the Beijing women's conference, the Pope addressed the U.N. on October 5, 1995, the 50th anniversary of its foun-

---

[143] As reported by the Zenit News Service, September 15, 2000.
[144] Ibid.
[145] Ibid.
[146] Ibid.

dation. The Holy Father appealed to the U.N.'s own founding principles, especially to the Universal Declaration of Human Rights of 1948. He spoke of the quest for freedom, for true freedom based on the truth of who we are.

Finally he offered the members of the U.N., often sorely led astray by false and reductive views of humanity, a new vision of the human person — a vision capable of inspiring hope and of stirring noble souls to respond to its challenge.

> We must learn not to be afraid; we must rediscover a spirit of hope and a spirit of trust. . . . As a Christian, my hope and trust are centered on Jesus Christ. . . . I come before you as a witness: a witness to human dignity, a witness to hope, a witness to the conviction that the destiny of all nations lies in the hands of a merciful providence.
>
> We must not be afraid of the future. We must not be afraid of man. It is no accident that we are here. Each and every human person has been created in the "image and likeness" of the one who is the origin of all that is. We have within us the capacities for wisdom and virtue. With these gifts, and with the help of God's grace, we can build in the next century and the next millennium a civilization worthy of the human person, a true culture of freedom. We can and must do so! And in doing so, we shall see that the tears of this century have prepared the ground for a new springtime of the human spirit.[147]

---

[147] John Paul II, "Address to the United Nations," October 5, 1995, 16-17.

PART II

Defending Marriage and Family: John Paul II's Theology of the Body

THREE

The Exalted Dignity of Marriage: A Vision of the Human Person Born of Faith

Preview

I. The Only Creature God Willed for Itself
    A. Why Are Persons So Unique?
        1. Only Persons Can *Love*
        2. Only Persons Are *Responsible*
    B. Why Are Persons So Fragile?
        Transcendent Greatness and Inescapable Dependence
    C. Loving and Using: The Personalistic Norm
        1. Using
        2. The Personalistic Norm
        3. A Dilemma
        4. A Response: Christ's New Commandment
        5. Love and Marriage
II. Man Can Only Find Himself in the Sincere Gift of Self
III. Only Christ Fully Reveals Man to Himself

Points to look for

1. How does John Paul II defend marriage in a compelling way?
2. How has the Holy Father arrived at his exalted vision of the nature of marriage?
3. What are three fundamental aspects of our identity as persons found in *Gaudium et Spes* 22 and 24?
4. Why are persons the only corporeal beings who are able to love?
5. What does it mean that we have an "inner" or "spiritual" life?
6. What is Karol Wojtyła's definition of a "person"?
7. What does it mean that man is both an object in the world and a conscious, free subject?
8. Why are we responsible as persons for loving or failing to love?
9. What does it mean "to use" an object?

10. What is the personalistic norm?

11. What apparent dilemma arises from our dependence on others on the one hand and the personalistic norm on the other?

12. How does Christ's new commandment resolve this apparent dilemma in our relationships with other persons?

13. What is the only proper and adequate attitude towards a person?

14. What is the common end of husband and wife in married love?

15. What is the *law of the gift*?

16. Why can we fully come to discover who we are as persons only by giving ourselves in love?

17. Why does Christ alone fully reveal man to himself?

If everything the Church has taught through the ages about marriage and the family were to be collected into one volume, it would total an impressive six thousand pages. But the most remarkable fact is that four thousand of those pages have been written by John Paul II.[148] Who can doubt that our present Pope has been one of the greatest defenders of marriage and the family against the forces seeking to undermine them?

John Paul II has upheld marriage most powerfully by expressing in a compelling way its supreme dignity according to God's original plan, restored by Christ at the price of his own blood. As he outlined his theology of the body in a five-year series of Wednesday audiences beginning in 1979, the Holy Father went so far as to proclaim that the conjugal union of husband and wife, their marital embrace, is an icon of the self-giving love of the Blessed Trinity.[149] The fruits of love and holiness that the marital embrace engenders in husband and wife, the children they bring into this world through their mutual self-giving, reflect the fruitfulness of God's creative love. Even further, the communion of persons (*communio personarum*) between the spouses and then among other members of the family images the divine communion of the Father, Son and Holy Spirit.

How has John Paul II arrived at such an exalted vision of marriage and the family? He has done so through intense meditation, penetrated by faith, on God's revelation about man and woman in Sacred Scripture, beginning with the Book of Genesis. Then he has reflected philosophically on the consequences entailed in these divinely revealed truths regarding human persons in order to construct an "adequate anthropology," a "total vision of man," as Pope Paul VI called for in his encyclical

---

[148] Christopher West, "John Paul II's Theology of the Body," audiocassette (Cincinnati: Couple to Couple League, 1998).

[149] Cf. John Paul II, General Audience of November 14, 1979, in *Theology of the Body* (Boston: Pauline Books and Media, 1997), pp. 45-48.

Humanae Vitae.[150] In the light of who we are as persons, created man and woman in the image of God and redeemed by Christ, the transcendent beauty of marriage shines forth in all its splendor.

Let us journey with gratitude and wonder along the path John Paul II has forged, to catch at least a glimmer of his vision of marriage and the family. The beauty of what God has done in creating man and woman, and restoring them to his original plan in Christ, is more than the human heart can grasp.[151]

An Adequate Anthropology
I. The Only Creature God Willed for Itself

If we seek to discover the nature of the human person and penetrate into the mystery of who we are, where is the surest point to begin? The firmest foundation upon which to build a total vision of man, an adequate anthropology, is God's own revelation about our identity. After all, we are his creatures, the work of his hands. John Paul II turns to the Conciliar document *Gaudium et Spes*, which draws directly upon divine revelation in Sacred Scripture, to formulate a comprehensive view of the human person.

Numbers 22 and 24 of *Gaudium et Spes* present three fundamental aspects of what it means to be human. First of all, man is the only creature whom God has willed not as a means for anything else, but simply for himself. Secondly, even though it may seem paradoxical, each person can discover his own identity and come to realize himself only by giving himself away — by freely giving himself in love. "This likeness reveals that man, who is the only creature on earth which God willed for itself, cannot fully find himself except through a sincere gift of himself" (*GS*, 24). Christ proclaims in the Gospel, "Whoever would save his life will lose it, and whoever loses his life for my sake will find it."[152] The third key mark of our identity is that only Christ fully reveals to us who we are. "Christ, the final Adam, by the revelation of the mystery of the Father and his love, fully reveals man to man himself and makes his supreme calling clear" (*GS*, 22).

Bishop Karol Wojtyła pondered the implications of the truth that each person is willed by God for himself in his book on married love between husband and wife, *Love and Responsibility*.[153] Published in 1960,

---

[150] Pope Paul VI calls for a "total vision of man" in number 7 of his 1968 encyclical *Humanae Vitae*.

[151] I am indebted to Christopher West for the conception of this presentation of John Paul II's theology of the body. I have drawn upon his audiocassette series and his study guide *Naked Without Shame: Sex and the Christian Mystery* (Carpentersville, IL: GIFT Foundation, 2000).

[152] Mt 16:25.

[153] *Love and Responsibility* is available in an English translation by H.T. Willetts (New York: Farrar, Straus and Giroux, 1981). For an excellent analysis of the book see Rocco Buttiglione, *Karol Wojtyła, The Thought of the Man Who Became Pope John Paul II*, foreword by Michael Novak, translated by Paolo Guietti and Francesca Murphy (Grand Rapids, Michigan: Eerdmans, 1997), Chapter 4, Love and Responsibility, pp. 83-116.

the book offered a coherent response to the sexual revolution of the 1960s even as it exploded upon the Western world. This new revolution has swept away the happiness of countless lives, with a violence to the human person in some ways no less severe than the Bolshevik in Russia.

Being willed for ourselves as persons by God makes us unique. Karol Wojtyła asks himself what is the essential characteristic of that uniqueness.

A. Why Are Persons So Unique?
1. Only Persons Can *Love*

One truth stands out above all others. *"Love is exclusively the portion of human persons."*[154] Animals, trees, and stones simply do not love. Neither do majestic, snow-peaked mountains, nor does the boundless expanse of the sea. Only persons can love.

What is it that makes a person to be a person, someone capable of love? We are persons because of our intelligence and freedom. By our reason we can know the truth, and we tend toward it. By the freedom of our will we tend toward the good. Because of our intelligence and freedom, we are beings who possess an *inner life*, a *spiritual life*.[155] Human beings are at the crossroads between two worlds: the physical universe and the spiritual. We are the only physical beings who are aware of our own existence, of who we are, the only ones who can ask ourselves, "Why am I here? What is the cause of everything? What is the purpose of my life?" Thanks to our intelligence and freedom, we are *moral* beings. We are the only ones who can experience within ourselves the obligation, the duty, to do good and avoid evil.[156]

Karol Wojtyła defines a person as a being with the capacity for this inner life. *"A person is an objective entity, which as a definite subject has the closest contacts with the whole (external) world and is most intimately involved with it precisely because of its inwardness, its interior life.* It must be added that it communicates thus not only with the visible world, but also with the invisible, and, most importantly, with God. This is a further indication of the person's uniqueness in the visible world."[157]

A great deal is contained within this definition of person. First of all, Wojtyła notes that a person is an objective entity. That is, persons are beings with a definite nature, who exist as objects in the world, just like eagles or trees or towering skyscrapers. We come into contact with other persons; they are objects of our knowledge and experience in the same way that we are objects of others' experience.

---

[154] Karol Wojtyła, *Love and Responsibility*, p. 29.
[155] Ibid., pp. 22-23.
[156] We experience this obligation as an absolute one: moral evil must never be committed. This experience is a call from the One who is absolute, speaking within our conscience — that inner sanctuary where we are alone with God (cf. *Gaudium et Spes*, 16).
[157] Karol Wojtyła, *Love and Responsibility*, p. 23.

What distinguishes persons from all other objects in the world is the fact that, as part of our nature, we are endowed with intellect and will. Thanks to these two faculties, we are not only objects, but also conscious subjects. We are aware of ourselves in all of our relations with the external world and can freely choose the way we will relate not only to objects, but also to other conscious subjects like ourselves. Ultimately, we freely decide how we will respond to God himself.

So, on the one hand, persons are existing objects in the world, with a specifically determined nature. On the other hand, we are conscious subjects, able to transcend the entire visible world and enter into a personal relationship with God. Here we catch a glimpse of the synthesis Karol Wojtyła, the philosopher, has achieved between traditional Thomism, which emphasizes the objective nature of man, and modern personalist philosophy. Personalism seeks to discover man as an intelligent, free subject, penetrating into the drama of his lived experience.

2. Only Persons Are *Responsible*

Because of our freedom, we are *responsible* as persons for whether or not we truly love. We are responsible for our own destiny and, at least in part, for the destiny of others. We shape who we are, we create ourselves as persons by our free moral choices. In the degree that our choices influence the free moral decisions of others, we also are responsible for helping shape their destiny. Love and responsibility are inseparable. They are both the consequence of freedom. We are responsible for loving or failing to love.

B. Why Are Persons So Fragile?
Transcendent Greatness and Inescapable Dependence

What is revealed by the fact that we are free and capable of loving, even loving God himself? What can we discover from the truth that we are also responsible for loving, for shaping our destiny? These aspects of being a person show our *transcendence*. They are the mark of our greatness, the "image of God" stamped upon our being, the source of our inalienable rights and dignity.

But there is another equally fundamental characteristic of persons. We are *dependent*. We are incomplete. We are not sufficient for ourselves. We depend on others for our existence, our very being. We depend on our relationships with other persons in order to even become aware of ourselves as persons. We rely on others to help us discover our path in life and follow it, to fulfill ourselves as persons, to be happy. We also depend on many *things*, on many objects, merely to survive.

If we are so dependent, if our life is a continuous succession of relationships with other persons and even with other objects, a question must be raised. How are we to act toward other persons and toward things? How are we to treat them? Here the fact that persons alone are willed for themselves by God comes to the fore. A fundamental distinction arises between loving and using.

C. Loving and Using: The Personalistic Norm
1. Using

"To use means to employ some object of action as a means to an end — the specific end which the subject has in view. . . . In the nature of things the means is subordinated to the end, and at the same time *subordinated to some extent to the agent."*[158] When an artist uses oil paints of varied hues, as well as brushes of diverse texture and size, in an attempt to convey upon a canvass the glory of Christ's resurrection, all of these materials he employs are subordinate to his final end: the completed work of art. Some of the oil paints may be entirely consumed in the process of painting, and the brushes worn out, never to be utilized again. The materials are subordinated not only to the final end of the completed painting, but also to the artist who makes use of them. As persons we use the objects of the whole created universe to achieve our ends.

What is the norm that governs our use of things? "Intelligent human beings are only required not to destroy or squander these natural resources, but to use them with restraint, so as not to impede the development of man himself, and so as to ensure the coexistence of human societies in justice and harmony."[159] In other words, our duty in the use of things is not to the objects themselves, but to our fellow men, who also have a right to utilize them for their own well-being and development as persons.

But what happens when other persons and not things become the objects of our acts? What norm governs our relationship with them? Can other persons be a means to our own fulfillment and happiness? We can neither realize ourselves nor be happy without them, but can we "use" persons like we "use" things?

The answer is a resounding *no.* "Nobody can use a person as a means towards an end, no human being, nor yet God the Creator."[160] How can we emerge from this apparent dilemma of being dependent on

---

[158] Ibid., p. 25.

[159] Ibid.

[160] Ibid., p. 27. Wojtyła continues, "On the part of God, indeed, it is totally out of the question, since, by giving man an intelligent and free nature, he has thereby ordained that each man alone will decide for himself the ends of his activity, and not be a blind tool of someone else's ends. Therefore, if God intends to direct man towards certain goals, he allows him to begin to know those goals, so that he may make them his own and strive towards them independently. In this amongst other things resides the most profound logic of revelation: God allows man to learn His supernatural ends, but the decision to strive towards an end, the choice of course, is left to man's free will. God does not redeem man against his will."

other persons, yet at the same time not being able to use them? The response lies in the personalistic norm.

2. The Personalistic Norm

Wojtyła formulates this absolute prohibition against using the person as a means in the *personalistic norm*,[161] which is the fundamental axis of his ethical thinking. In formulating the norm, he reworks the categorical imperative of the eighteenth-century German philosopher Immanuel Kant.[162] The personalistic norm states, "Whenever a person is the object of your activity, remember that you may not treat that person as only the means to an end, as an instrument, but must allow for the fact that he or she, too, has, or at least should have, distinct personal ends."[163]

How fundamental is this norm? "This principle, thus formulated, lies at the basis of all the human freedoms, properly understood, and especially freedom of conscience."[164] Why is the personalistic norm true? Why can a person never be only a means to an end? As the norm itself indicates, a person can never be treated as a means because of what it signifies to be a person. "A person must not be *merely* the means to an end for another person. This is precluded by the very nature of personhood, by what any person is. For a person is a thinking subject, and capable of taking decisions: these, most notably, are the attributes we find in the inner self of a person. This being so, every person is by nature capable of determining his or her aims. Anyone who treats a person as the means to an end does violence to the very essence of the other, to what constitutes its natural right."[165]

A young man may come to fall deeply in love with a young woman and reach the conclusion that he can never be happy in life without her. But if he truly loves her, he realizes that he must respect who she is as a person, what she desires in life. He cannot treat her simply as a means to his own happiness. He cannot compel her to love him or to marry him.

3. A Dilemma

But now the dilemma with which we have been confronted emerges in all its force. On the one hand, we can never use persons as a means. On the other hand, we are dependent on other persons. We cannot realize ourselves or be happy without them. We cannot

---

[161] A norm is a rule and measure of human acts, *"regula et mensura humanorum actuum,"* (*Summa Theologiae*, I-II, q. 90, a.1).

[162] The categorical imperative of Kant states, "Act always in such a way that the other person is the end and not merely the instrument of your action." (As cited in *Love and Responsibility*, pp. 27-28.)

[163] Wojtyła, *Love and Responsibility*, p. 28.

[164] Ibid.

[165] Ibid., pp. 26-27.

achieve the end of fulfilling our destiny by simply relying on ourselves and our use of things in the natural world. How is it possible to resolve this quandary?

4. A Response: Christ's New Commandment

The response to the dilemma is found in Christ's new commandment: "Love one another as I have loved you" (Jn 15:12). For loving is the opposite of using. In its negative formulation the personalistic norm testifies that we can never treat a person as an object of use, as a means to an end. What form does the norm acquire when stated positively? "In its positive form the personalistic norm confirms this: *the person is a good towards which the only proper and adequate attitude is love.*"[166] Wojtyła affirms that in a broad sense Christ's new commandment can be identified with the personalistic norm. "Strictly speaking the commandment says: 'Love persons,' and the personalistic norm says: 'A person is an entity of a sort to which the only proper and adequate way to relate is love.'"[167]

What is there in the nature of love that makes it preclude the use of one person by another? In love two or more persons are joined together seeking a common good. Though they are dependent upon each other, they are not using one another, since both desire the same good and have made it their own goal internally, within their inner depths as persons.

> If we go on to seek a positive solution to this problem we begin to discern love, to catch a preliminary glimpse of it, so to speak, as the only clear alternative to using a person as the means to an end, or the instrument of one's own action. Obviously, I may want another person to desire the same good which I myself desire. Obviously, the other must know this end of mine, recognize it as a good, and adopt it. If this happens, a special bond is established between me and this other person: the bond of a *common good* and of a common aim. This special bond does not mean merely that we both seek a common good; it also unites the persons involved internally, and so constitutes the essential core round which any love must grow. In any case, love between two people is quite unthinkable without some common good to bind them together. This good is the end which both these persons choose. *When two different people consciously choose a common aim* this puts them on a footing of equality, and precludes the possibility that one of them might be subordinated to the other. . . . Man's capacity for love depends on his willingness consciously to seek a good together with others, and to subordinate himself to that good for the sake of others, or to others for the sake of that good.[168]

---

[166] Ibid., p. 41. Italics are mine.
[167] Ibid.
[168] Ibid., pp. 28-29.

The young man who falls in love with a young woman can certainly hope that she will come to love him as well. He might spend time with her, bring her flowers, and even boast of his past exploits as a high school football star. Eventually he may dare to speak of how happy they would be spending their lives together. The two of them may begin to ponder the beauty of having children and raising a family. Over time, a bond has been formed between the young couple. They have both come to freely desire a common good: giving their lives to one another and bringing up a family. A basis has been established for love. They will become a source of happiness for one another — but not by using each other as means. Instead, they will each freely seek the good of the other and of their children from within their depths as persons.

5. Love and Marriage

The example of the young couple reveals how this vision of love as the common attitude of people toward the same good applies to married love between husband and wife. *"Marriage is one of the most important areas where this principle is put into practice. . . .* Such an end [the common end of husband and wife], where marriage is concerned, is procreation, the future generation, a family, and, at the same time, the continual ripening of the relationship between two people, in all the areas of activity which conjugal life includes. . . . *Love is the unification of persons."*[169]

A husband and wife celebrating their golden jubilee, who have watched their children grow up together, who have been by each other's side "in joy and in sorrow, in sickness and in health,"[170] have become united as persons in a way few others can ever be in life. Often a slight glance or a brief silence is enough to communicate their inner self to each other. How noble human love can become when it is touched by the grace of God!

II. Man Can Only Find Himself in the Sincere Gift of Self

We have discovered a fundamental consequence that springs from the first truth of our nature as persons. Since persons are willed by God for their own sake, the only adequate response toward a person is love. The second truth of our nature arises from the first. As persons created for communion with other persons, we can only come to fully realize ourselves and discover our own identity by giving ourselves to others in love. John Paul II spoke of this *law of the gift* inscribed in our very being during his Wednesday audiences outlining his theology of the body.

---

[169] Ibid., pp. 28 and 38.
[170] From the formula of the marriage vows.

The gift reveals, so to speak, a particular characteristic of personal existence, or rather, of the essence of the person. When God-Yahweh said, "It is not good that man should be alone," (Gn 2:18) he affirmed that "alone," man does not completely realize this essence. He realizes it only by existing "with someone" — and even more deeply and completely — by existing "for someone."[171]

III. Only Christ Fully Reveals Man to Himself

The third fundamental aspect about our identity as persons is expressed by John Paul II in his first encyclical, *Redemptor Hominis.* "Man cannot live without love. He remains a being that is incomprehensible for himself, his life is senseless, if love is not revealed to him, if he does not encounter love, if he does not experience it and make it his own, if he does not participate intimately in it. This, as has already been said, is why Christ the Redeemer 'fully reveals man to himself'" (*RH*, 10). Called in the very nature of our being as persons to love and be loved, we can only discover who we are by experiencing love.

In the seasons of the Church's liturgical year, we enter anew into the experience of a love that surpasses the most ardent longings of our human heart. At Christmas we gaze in silent wonder upon the eternal Son of the Father, shivering as a helpless baby under the night sky to redeem us. "For God so loved the world that he gave his only Son, that whoever believes in him should not perish but have eternal life."[172] During Lent and Holy Week, we discover that Christ's love goes even further. "Greater love has no man than this, that a man lay down his life for his friends."[173]

The Easter Season allows us to experience the transforming effects of Christ's sacrificial love. St. Paul's intimate, personal experience moves him to go one step beyond Christ's own words in describing our Redeemer's love for us. "Why, one will hardly die for a righteous man — though perhaps for a good man one will even dare to die. But God proves his love for us in that while we were yet sinners Christ died for us."[174] Christ did more than lay down his life for his friends — he made us his friends by redeeming us from sin in agony upon the cross.

The joy expressed on John Paul II's countenance each time he encounters people also radiates through his written words, as he contemplates the transforming power of Christ's death and resurrection on our human lives.

---

[171] John Paul II, General Audience of January 9, 1980, in *Theology of the Body*, p. 60.
[172] Jn 3:16.
[173] Jn 15:13.
[174] Rm 5:7-8.

In the mystery of the redemption man becomes newly "expressed" and, in a way, is newly created. He is newly created! "There is neither Jew nor Greek, there is neither slave nor free, there is neither male nor female; for you are all one in Christ Jesus."[175] The man who wishes to understand himself thoroughly — and not just in accordance with immediate, partial, often superficial, and even illusory standards and measures of his being — he must with his unrest, uncertainty and even his weakness and sinfulness, with his life and death, draw near to Christ. He must, so to speak, enter into Him with all his own self, he must "appropriate" and assimilate the whole of the reality of the Incarnation and Redemption in order to find himself. If this profound process takes place within him, he then bears fruit not only of adoration of God but also of deep wonder at himself. How precious must man be in the eyes of the Creator, if he "gained so great a Redeemer,"[176] and if God "gave his only Son" in order that man "should not perish but have eternal life."[177]

The great mystery of our redemption, in which Christ not only reveals to us who we are, but also transforms us into a new creation, begins within the heart of a family. "If in fact Christ 'fully discloses man to himself,'[178] he does so beginning with the family in which he chose to be born and grow up. . . . The *only-begotten Son,* of one substance with the Father, '*God from God* and Light from Light,' *entered into human history through the family.*"[179]

---

[175] Gal 3:28.
[176] *Exsultet* at the Easter Vigil.
[177] Cf. *Jn* 3:16. The entire text of John Paul II cited is from *Redemptor Hominis*, 10.
[178] *Gaudium et Spes*, 22.
[179] *Letter to Families*, 2.

FOUR

The Whole Human Person at a Glance

Preview

I. Between Two Worlds: The Rational Faculties

II. Where It All Begins: Sense Knowledge

III. Born To Obey Reason: The Emotions
  A. Seeking Good and Avoiding Evil: The Concupiscible Passions
  B. When Good is Difficult and Evil Threatens: The Irascible Passions
  C. The Emotions Among Themselves: How Should They Relate?
  D. The Emotions Meet Reason and Will: What Should Happen?

IV. Fully Human Love: Will or Emotion?

Points to look for

1. How do the rational faculties of intellect and will put human persons on the horizon between two worlds?

2. How can it be proven that the human intellect is not material, but is rather a spiritual faculty?

3. How can it be proven that the human will is spiritual?

4. What are the two functions of the intellect? What does each function entail?

5. What is the relationship between the intellect and the will?

6. What is prudence? Where does it reside?

7. What is justice? Where does it reside?

8. What relationship exists between the truths we know with our rational intellect and those we know through our sense knowledge?

9. How do memory and imagination differ in animals and in human beings?

10. What is sense appetite?

11. What are passions or emotions?

12. What are the two different groups of emotions? Which emotions pertain to each group?

13. What relationship should exist between these two groups of emotions?

14. What do love, desire, and joy consist of? How are they related?

15. What relationship should exist between the emotions on the one hand, and the will and reason on the other?

16. What are temperance and fortitude? Where does each of them reside?

17. What is the nature of fully human love? How does it relate to the emotion of love?

18. Why does the emotional experience of love alone not justify physical or sexual intimacy between a man and woman?

19. What is the relationship between the emotions and Christian moral perfection?

Now that we have outlined the three basic truths about the human person revealed by faith, it is necessary to consider briefly St. Thomas Aquinas' structural vision of man. The anthropology of Aquinas underlies John Paul II's theology of the body. The Holy Father's teachings on human love cannot be understood in all of their depth and beauty without first pausing to sketch a brief philosophical portrait of human nature.

I. Between Two Worlds: The Rational Faculties

The chart to the right reveals that the drama of the human person is played out at the crossroads between two worlds. By our rational faculties of intellect and will, we are spiritual beings, open to the infinite. At the same time, we are bodily creatures. As such, we exercise the powers of sensory knowledge and are influenced by sense appetites. These appetites are more commonly known as emotions or passions. Finally, we possess the vegetative powers of reproduction, growth, and nutrition that are common to all living, material beings.

Is it possible to prove that our intellect and will are spiritual? Perhaps man is nothing more than a rather skillful chimpanzee. What can be said in response to those who would claim that humans are simply glorified animals — and not so glorified at that, given the harm we often inflict on our fellow human beings and on the environment in which we live?

Material things are by nature individual, singular, and limited. They are made up of parts outside of parts. All acts of an entity that is exclusively material must necessarily be material as well, since a thing's way of acting follows from the nature of its being. *Agere sequitur esse*.[180] This basic truth is expressed in the popular adage, "You can't get blood from a turnip." Material acts in turn are always directed toward material objects. With my bodily act of sight I perceive individual, material things:

---

[180] "Acting follows being." Cf. Thomas Aquinas, *In Libros Sententiarum, in III Sententiarum, Distinctio 3, Quaestio 2, Articulus 1, corpus; Summa Contra Gentiles, Liber 3, Capitulus 69, n. 20.*

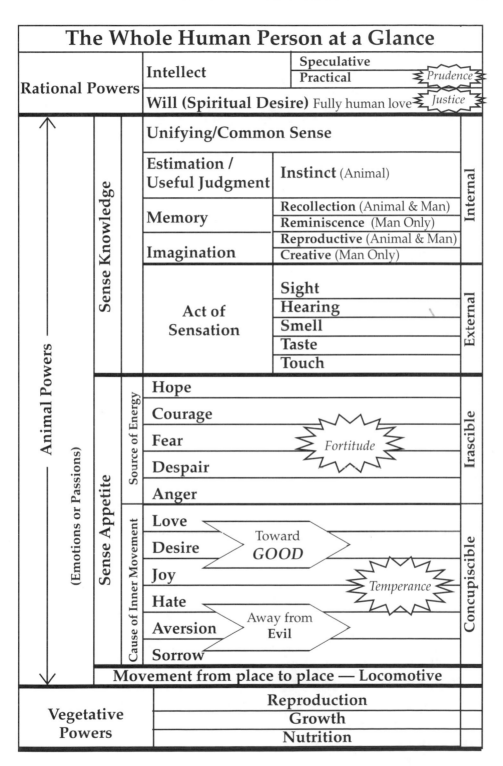

The Whole Human Person at a Glance

Rational Powers	**Intellect**	Speculative	
		Practical	*Prudence*
	Will (Spiritual Desire) Fully human love		*Justice*

Sense Knowledge (Internal)

Unifying/Common Sense	
Estimation / Useful Judgment	**Instinct** (Animal)
Memory	**Recollection** (Animal & Man)
	Reminiscence (Man Only)
Imagination	**Reproductive** (Animal & Man)
	Creative (Man Only)

Act of Sensation (External)

- **Sight**
- **Hearing**
- **Smell**
- **Taste**
- **Touch**

Sense Appetite

Source of Energy — Irascible:
- **Hope**
- **Courage**
- **Fear** — *Fortitude*
- **Despair**
- **Anger**

Cause of Inner Movement — Concupiscible:
- **Love** — Toward *GOOD*
- **Desire**
- **Joy** — *Temperance*
- **Hate** — Away from Evil
- **Aversion**
- **Sorrow**

Movement from place to place — Locomotive

Animal Powers (Emotions or Passions)

Vegetative Powers	**Reproduction**
	Growth
	Nutrition

the familiar tree outside my office window, the computer screen in front of me that has inexplicably gone blank. My sense of taste allows me to savor specific delicacies: a hot slice of pepperoni pizza or a sweet wedge of Italian pastry such as *mille foglie*.

A first proof that our rational faculties of intellect and will are not material, but spiritual, leaps out at us. The intellect transcends singular, material objects to grasp what is universal. From the experience of my own individual father, my intellect is able to form the abstract, universal concept "father," which can be applied to any father anywhere — even to God in an analogical way. This is clearly a spiritual act, since my material eye is capable of seeing no such universal "father." The most it can do is perceive many individual fathers at once, if they all stand close together. A faculty capable of a spiritual act must itself be spiritual. So my intellect has to be spiritual, since it performs spiritual acts in order to grasp its spiritual and universal object — truth itself. Finally, I myself must have a spiritual as well as a bodily nature, if I possess a spiritual faculty: the intellect.

Yet a second fact of experience irrefutably proves that the intellect is spiritual. No material act is able to reflect back upon itself. My hand may grasp a book and pick it up to begin reading, but my hand cannot grasp itself. My eye can see the book and perceive each printed page, but it is utterly incapable of seeing its own act of seeing. When I actually begin the intellectual act of reading the book, however, everything changes. Not only do I come to know the content of the book, I am also aware of my act of reading. I can reflect on my own act of knowing the content of the book, and know that I know it. Otherwise, I could never be sure of being ready for an upcoming exam, if the book in question happens to be a text for a class that I'm taking. So, once again, it is necessary to conclude that my intellect is a spiritual faculty.

Two different functions of my rational intellect can be distinguished: speculative and practical. The speculative function enables me to know and contemplate theoretical truths or concepts. The mystery of the Trinity, the theory of relativity, the relationship between slavery and the Civil War are all objects of speculative knowledge. The intellect's practical function enables me to discern what concrete actions I should undertake in order to foster my own good and the good of others. For this reason the cardinal virtue of *prudence* resides in the practical intellect. Prudence "disposes the practical reason to discern, in every circumstance, our true good and to choose the right means for achieving it."[181]

Having examined the intellect, we now turn our attention to the second rational faculty: the will. Is the will really spiritual? Does it not tend

---

[181] *CCC*, 1835; cf. 1806.

toward individual, material objects that are good? Almost everyone enjoys a good movie, or an exciting game of basketball or tennis. On a higher plane, we all value good friends and desire to follow a worthwhile path in life. Does not each of these examples involve concrete, particular choices that we make because our will feels attracted to them as good?

It is true that in this life we can choose the good only in limited, particular situations. But this very experience within ourselves of the freedom to choose can only be explained by the fact that our will tends toward universal good — toward the infinite horizon of Goodness itself. Here the paradoxical limits of our earthly life continuously reassert themselves. Whenever I make a choice, I exclude all other possible choices. If I decide to undertake a pilgrimage to Rome for Holy Week of the Jubilee Year, then I cannot spend Good Friday or Easter Sunday in Jerusalem. Both options attract my will, since both are good. But I am free to choose between them, since neither is Absolute Goodness, which would draw my will irresistibly. For that same reason, there is also a sense of loss after I decide to go to Rome, for another good has been sacrificed.

Only when we are face to face with God in heaven will this paradox be overcome. Then, when our will is wholly caught up in God's infinite goodness, we shall be supremely free — beyond the limits of freedom of choice. This great reality is expressed by St. Augustine's timeless words in Book I of the *Confessions*. "You have made us for yourself, and our heart is restless until it rests in you."[182]

Thus the will, like the intellect, must be spiritual, since it freely chooses concrete, individual goods only within the spiritual horizon of the universal good. The fact that we experience a sense of loss at the individual choices we make, since they exclude all other choices, is proof that our will is open to universal goodness. It is for that goodness that we have been made.

There is an intimate relationship between our rational powers of intellect and will. As the faculty of spiritual desire, our will naturally seeks what reason reveals to be a good for our whole person. Our true good entails recognizing what we owe to God and to others. Thus, the cardinal virtue of *justice* resides primarily in the will. Justice is "the moral virtue that consists in the constant and firm will to give their due to God and neighbor."[183]

Countless examples can be discovered of the will following reason's guide. Once my reason discerns that it would be a supreme good for me

---

[182] St. Augustine, *Confessions*, translated by John K. Ryan, (New York: Doubleday Image Books, 1960), p. 43.
[183] CCC, 1807.

in life to respond to God's call and become a missionary in China, then my will impels me to study the Chinese language, to learn Chinese culture, and to penetrate more deeply into the truths of the faith. My will moves me to attain the long-awaited day, of proclaiming Christ for the first time to people who have never heard the Gospel.

II. Where It All Begins: Sense Knowledge

Our spiritual faculties of intellect and will, which open us to universal truth and absolute goodness, are inextricably linked with our bodily nature. All of our intellectual knowledge originates in the senses. It is due to our sense knowledge (our ability to see, hear, smell, taste, and touch individual objects) that we are able to abstract from them, rising to the level of universal concepts and truths. Thomas Aquinas expresses this fact about human knowing numerous times throughout his works.[184]

Besides acquiring sense knowledge through the five external senses, we also make use of four internal sensory powers: unifying or common sense, estimation or useful judgment, memory, and imagination. Although animals possess these sensory powers as well, they differ in man, since our rational intellect penetrates them. Thanks to the unifying sense, we perceive objects as a whole and do not merely receive a continuous, unrelated flow of sounds, smells, and visual images. Estimation is an immediate judgment, at the level of our senses, prior to reason, as to whether an object is harmful or useful to us. The corresponding power in animals is instinct. A young lamb does not have to be taught by its mother to flee from an approaching wolf. It does so instinctively.

Memory also differs in man and animals. In the latter this power is limited to simple recollection, a recalling of something past. In addition to recollection, man is capable of reminiscence. Through laws of association, such as calling to mind related persons or occurrences, he can bring himself to remember a once-forgotten event. In imagination, too, man's reason enables him to transcend the mere reproductive imagination of animals, which makes it possible for them to imagine an object no longer present. Man's imagination is not only reproductive, but also creative. He can invent a new reality that has never even existed, by

---

[184] "*Intellectus humanus a potentiis sensitivis accipit suae cognitionis originem.*" (The human intellect takes the origin of its knowledge from the sensitive powers), (*Compendium Theologiae, Liber 1, c. 128*). "*Humana cognitio a sensu initium sumit,*" (Human knowledge takes its beginning from the senses), (*In Librum de Causis, Lectio 7*). "*Cognitio nostra incipit a sensu et terminatur ad intellectum*" (Our knowledge begins from the senses and ends in the intellect), (*In Libros Sententiarum, in III Sententiarum, Distinctio 26, Quaestio 1, Articulus 5, corpus*). "*Cognitio intellectus nostri tota derivatur a sensu*" (All the knowledge of our intellect is derived from the senses), (*In Boethii de Trinitate, Pars 1, Questio 1, Articulus 3, corpus 3*). The classical Scholastic formulation of this truth is the following, "*Nihil in intellectu quod prius non fuerit in sensu,*" (Nothing is in the intellect that was not first in the senses).

combining various known images with his intellect. Tolkien's characters in the *Lord of the Rings* trilogy are a stirring example of creative imagination.[185]

III. Born To Obey Reason: The Emotions

Just as the will is the faculty of spiritual desire that responds to the universal good discerned by reason, so the sense appetite is attracted to particular goods perceived through sense knowledge. "Feelings or passions are emotions or movements of the sensitive appetite that incline us to act or not to act in regard to something felt or imagined to be good or evil."[186] We are presented with two types of objects by our sensory cognitive powers: those which themselves are good or evil for us, and those which are useful for attaining a difficult good or for avoiding an impending evil. Thus, we possess two corresponding groups of emotions: the concupiscible passions, directed toward good or evil objects themselves, and the irascible passions, aimed at means for attaining difficult goods or avoiding evils.

A. Seeking Good and Avoiding Evil: The Concupiscible Passions

Of the six concupiscible passions, the most fundamental is *love*, aroused by the attraction of the good.[187] The essence of love is complacence in the person or object loved.[188] Love creates *desire* for the absent good, which is the second emotion. When desire attains its object, we experience the emotion of *joy*: delight in the good possessed. Joy brings to fulfillment the movement begun by love and desire. It is the point of arrival, the emotion in which the human heart and the entire person come to rest.[189]

When we are confronted with evil, three opposite emotions arise. We feel *hatred* or displeasure toward the evil object, which generates *aversion*. If the evil cannot be avoided, we feel *sorrow* or sadness at its possession. These six emotions of the concupiscible or pleasure appetite are restrained by *temperance*. The cardinal virtue of temperance "moderates the attraction of pleasures and provides balance in the use of created goods."[190]

---

[185] For a more complete explanation of the human person's sensory powers of knowing, see Anna A. Terruwe, M.D. and Dr. Conrad W. Baars, M.D., *Psychic Wholeness and Healing* (New York: Alba House, 1981), pp. 7-10.

[186] CCC, 1763.

[187] Cf. CCC, 1765.

[188] *Summa Theologiae* I-II, q 26, a 2, c.

[189] "*Prima ergo immutatio appetitus ab appetibili vocatur amor, qui nihil est aliud quam complacentia appetibilis; et ex hac complacentia sequitur motus in appetibile, qui est desiderium; et ultimo quies, quae est gaudium.*" (Accordingly, the first change wrought in the appetite by the appetible object is called *love*, and is nothing else than complacency in that object; and from this complacency results a movement towards that same object, and this movement is *desire*; and lastly, there is rest which is *joy*.) *Summa Theologiae* I-II, q 26, a 2, c.

[190] CCC, 1809.

That Christ experienced all of these emotions in the Gospels reveals how completely he "humbled himself to share in our humanity."[191] At the Garden of Gethsemane he cried out, "My soul is very sorrowful; even to death; remain here and watch with me" (Mt 26:38).

B. When Good is Difficult and Evil Threatens: The Irascible Passions

Amidst the trials and vicissitudes of our journey through life, harsh evils often menace the good we desire. Formidable obstacles arise — both within and outside of ourselves — that would prevent us from attaining it. A second group of emotions responds to these challenges: the irascible passions. *Hope* inspires confidence that we will be able to reach the goal, in spite of the narrow road ahead. Its opposite is *despair*. *Courage* impels us to overcome evils, while *fear* shrinks before them when they seem overpowering. *Despair* fills us if the good seems lost forever. *Anger* arises when an evil persists in the face of our resistance or when a good remains beyond our grasp, despite all efforts.

Hope and courage are strengthened, fear is mitigated, despair resisted, and anger channeled by the fourth cardinal virtue: *fortitude.* This virtue "ensures firmness in difficulties and constancy in the pursuit of the good."[192] Christ reveals to us in Gethsemane the intimate relationship between the emotions, the virtue of fortitude, and our personal union with God. Jesus' insistent prayer, even to the point of sweating blood, gained him the necessary fortitude to overcome the sadness and fear that threatened to prevent him from drinking the chalice of his Father's will for our redemption.

C. The Emotions Among Themselves: How Should They Relate?

Now that the panorama of our six concupiscible emotions and five irascible passions has unfolded before us, a natural question arises. How do these two groups of emotions relate to one another? Should one group have priority in a person with a mature, balanced emotional life? The response is clear. Since the concupiscible appetite seeks objects that are good in themselves, it takes precedence. In fact, the irascible emotions exist only so that the concupiscible appetite may reach its goal. Thus, irascible passions should always be subordinate to concupiscible emotions and directed toward them.[193]

Let us consider the relationship between these two groups of emotions in a concrete case. The concupiscible appetite enters first upon the

---

[191] From the priest's prayer *sotto voce* during the offertory at Mass.

[192] *CCC*, 1808.

[193] "*Passiones irascibilis et principium habent a passionibus concupiscibilis, et in passiones concupiscibilis terminantur.*" (The irascible passions both arise from and terminate in the passions of the concupiscible faculty.) *Summa Theologiae* I-II, q 25, a 1, c.

stage. Love of Christ in the Eucharist engenders the desire to be with him at least a few minutes each day. But this good presents itself as difficult to attain. On my first attempt to make a visit to the Eucharist during lunch hour, I discover that all of the churches in the area where I work are locked outside of the times for Mass. The irascible passion of hope arises from my desire and impels me to continue searching. Finally, I discover a parish with perpetual adoration one half hour away from my workplace. Courage moves me to get up a half hour earlier each morning and arrive to the adoration chapel before work. These two irascible passions lead once more to the concupiscible appetite, as I experience the joy of being with Christ.

We have seen the relationship between the two groups of emotions. Is there also a hierarchy among the concupiscible passions themselves? Yes. "The most fundamental passion is love.... All other affections have their source in this first movement of the human heart toward the good."[194] Without exception, the other emotions arise because of love. We desire what we love and experience joy when we possess the good object that is loved. We experience hatred and aversion toward those things that threaten our possession of what we love. We feel sorrow when the evil cannot be avoided. Our irascible passions arise out of the usefulness judgment that certain objects may help us attain a difficult good that we love, while others may hinder us.

D. The Emotions Meet Reason and Will: What Should Happen?

We have sketched the proper relationship that should exist among emotions of the sense appetite. But a further question remains. How should emotions relate to our rational faculties of intellect and will? St. Thomas Aquinas responds to this query by affirming that the emotions naturally obey reason. "*Appetitus sensitivus in nobis ... natus est obedire rationi.*" (The sensitive appetite in us is born to obey reason.)[195] To say that our emotions are meant to follow the dictates of reason is equivalent to saying that they should be directed by our will, which follows reason's guidance. "*Appetitus sensitivus natus est moveri ab appetitu rationali.*" (The sensitive appetite is born to be moved by the rational appetite.)[196]

When the rational faculties consistently succeed in guiding the emotions, an individual is stable and mature. His reason judges whether a given emotion that arises within him toward a sense object is in accordance with his true, universal good as a person. If it is, reason directs the will to foster the emotion. If it is not, reason instructs the will to ab-

---

[194] *CCC*, 1765, 1766.
[195] *Summa Theologiae* I-II, q 74, a 3, ad 1.
[196] *Summa Theologiae* I-II, q 50, a 3, ad 3. (Note: The rational appetite is the will.)

negate the passion. A happily-married businessman may begin to feel an emotional attraction toward one of his female colleagues. His reason warns him immediately that this sentiment contradicts both his true good and hers. It then directs his will to restrain the emotion, avoiding situations which would stimulate it.

Submitting the emotions to the guidance of reason and will in this way does not lead to a repressed or stunted personality. Harmony results in the person as a whole, even on those occasions when the natural appetite is momentarily checked. That is because the appetite is repressed in its particular object, but realized in its general object: the true good of the person. By guiding our sentiments with reason, we grow in emotional maturity and develop strength of character. We acquire an authentic, consistent personality.

What happens when our passions do not obey reason, and instead follow their own, particular inclinations? There may be a momentary feeling of satisfaction, but it soon gives way to a deeper, more all-encompassing existential experience: that of *guilt*. The experience of guilt testifies both to the emotions' proper subordination to reason and to the unity of the entire person.

Let us suppose that I have been exerting myself for several hours on an afternoon hike along one of the scenic routes skirting Italy's Sorrentine Peninsula. While taking in the majestic sweep of blue Mediterranean waters, I gradually become aware that the autumn sun has begun to drain me. Then, just around a sharp bend in the road, a vineyard of succulent Italian grapes, ripe for the harvest, presents itself. A sudden craving for one of the gleaming clusters invades me. I clamber over the low stone wall separating me from the object of my desire, and soon find myself delighting in the tender fare. What could be compared with this moment of bliss?

But then, as my craving is gradually satiated, a new sensation begins to make itself felt. A hoe leaning up against the stone wall catches my eye. The careful manner in which each bunch of vines has been pruned attracts my attention. I begin to wonder to whom this vineyard might belong, and how its owner would feel about my having devoured one of his diligently cultivated clusters of grapes. A hand-carved wooden sign on the metal gate into the vineyard, hitherto unnoticed, now stares at me in silent accusation: *Proprietà privata. Vietato l'ingresso.* (Private property. No trespassing.) With a rueful frown, I somberly make my way back over the stone wall, realizing that I have paid a high price for an instant of blissful delight.

This example reveals how reason penetrates the sense appetite, elevating passions to the plane of the person as a whole and judging them in that light. Thus, guilt does not consist of simply knowing with my intellect that I have done something wrong. Guilt touches the emotions. In its psychological aspect, it is an experience of discomfort, of incompleteness. In its moral character, it penetrates to the most intimate core of my person: the conscience, that inner sanctuary where I am alone with God.[197]

While guilt is primarily a negative experience, arising from the judgment of my conscience that I have done evil, it carries with it a pledge of hope in God's mercy.[198] It also reveals how reason ennobles the passions, enabling us to see the relation of a particular satisfaction to the universal good. We are capable of pursuing the good not in a strictly egocentric way, but for the sake of the good itself. Reason also allows us to see ourselves in relation to the universal good. In this light, our passions can help us seek the good of others unselfishly. Through the transforming power of grace, under reason's guide, our passions can impel us to fulfill Christ's new commandment of love.

IV. Fully Human Love: Will or Emotion?

No reality of human life has been more pondered in prose, song, and verse than love. We have seen that love is the most fundamental emotion, giving rise to all the others. But is human love simply an emotional experience, a sentiment? What is the essence of this mysterious phenomenon, strong enough to consume the whole person, as the Song of Songs hauntingly conveys?

> Set me as a seal upon your heart,
>   as a seal upon your arm;
> For love is strong as death,
>   jealousy is cruel as the grave.
> Its flashes are flashes of fire, a most vehement flame.
> Many waters cannot quench love,
>   neither can floods drown it.
> If a man offered for love all the wealth of his house,
>   it would be utterly scorned.
>
> (Song of Songs 8:6-7)

Naturally, true human love profoundly resonates within the emotional sphere. It reaches the *heart*, "in the biblical sense of the depths of one's being, where the person decides for or against God."[199] But a person's inner depths rest on a more stable foundation than emotions. The spiritual faculties of intellect and will confer upon the person his transcendent dignity. They form part of his inmost core. So human love in its fullness is first and foremost an act of the will. "To love is to will

---

[197] Cf. *Gaudium et Spes*, 16.
[198] Cf. *CCC*, 1781.
[199] *CCC*, 368, cf. Jer 31:33; Deut 6:5, 29:3; Isa 29:13; Ezek 36:26; Mt 6:21; Lk 8:15; Rm 5:5.

the good of another."[200] Karol Wojtyła avows this truth in a compelling way in *Love and Responsibility.* "What is most essential to love is affirmation of the value of the person: this is the basis on which the will of the loving subject strives for the true good of the beloved person, the entire and perfect good, the absolute good, which is identical with happiness."[201]

Wojtyła then goes on to distinguish between authentic love as an act of the will, as a commitment of one's whole self to the good of the other person, and love as an emotion. He argues against the view that the emotion of love gives men and women the right to physical intimacy and to sexual intercourse.

> This is a mistaken view, for love as an emotional experience, even if it is reciprocated, is very far from being the same as love completed by commitment of the will. This last requires that each of two persons chooses the other, on the basis of an unqualified affirmation of the value of the other person, with a view to a lasting union in matrimony, and with a clearly defined attitude to parenthood. Love between persons possesses — and must possess — a clear-cut objective purpose. Love as an emotional-affective experience often has a purely subjective character, and is from the ethical point of view immature. We have said several times . . . that transient erotic experiences must not be confused with love.[202]

To conclude, how should we judge love as an emotion, and the emotions as a whole, in relation to fully human love? Our call to love is identical with our responsibility to seek what is morally good. So another way to phrase the same question would be the following: "What is the relationship between the passions or emotions and the moral life?" The *Catechism* responds directly to this query. "In themselves passions are neither good nor evil. They are morally qualified only to the extent that they effectively engage reason and will. . . . Passions are morally good when they contribute to a good action, evil in the opposite case." [203] In the words of St. Augustine, passions "are evil if love is evil and good if it is good."[204]

As the Song of Songs expresses, authentic human love of the will penetrates the emotions and is enriched by them, so that the whole person is caught up in love. Karol Wojtyła succinctly formulates this relationship. "Affirmation of the person influences the emotions in such a way that the value of the person is not just abstractly understood, but

---

[200] *CCC*, 1766, citing St. Thomas Aquinas, *Summa Theologiae*, I-II, 26, 4, corp. art.
[201] Wojtyła, *Love and Responsibility*, p. 183.
[202] Ibid., p. 185.
[203] *CCC*, 1767, 1768.
[204] *CCC*, 1766, citing *De civ. Dei* 14, 7, 2: PL 41, 410.

deeply felt."[205] The light that radiates from John Paul II's countenance each time he encounters one of God's people reveals how profoundly he himself lives the words he has written. The *Catechism* sums it all up. "Moral perfection consists in man's being moved to the good not by his will alone, but also by his sensitive appetite, as in the words of the psalm: 'My heart and flesh sing for joy to the living God.'"[206]

FIVE

The Three States of Man

Preview

I. Original Man
   A. Original Solitude
   B. Original Unity
   C. Original Nakedness
   D. "Naked without Shame": The Nuptial Meaning of the Body
      1. The Body Reveals Divine Mysteries
      2. The Body Reveals Man
      3. The Body Reveals Man and Woman as a Gift for Each Other
      4. Creation Itself: A First and Fundamental Gift
      5. Freedom: Condition for the Gift of Self
      6. The Nuptial Meaning of the Body and Procreation
      7. The Nuptial Meaning of the Body: A Final View

Points to look for

1. Into what two parts are the Holy Father's Wednesday audiences on the theology of the body divided? What are the three cycles of each part?

2. To what does John Paul II's theology of the body refer in its essential nucleus?

3. What does John Paul II mean by "original human experiences"?

4. What is original solitude?

5. How does the union of Adam and Eve both relieve and at the same time confirm original solitude?

6. What is original nakedness?

7. Why did Adam and Eve experience no shame, even though they were naked?

8. How does the body reveal divine mysteries?

9. How does the body reveal man?

10. What is the nuptial meaning of the body?

11. How does the nuptial meaning of the body reflect the structure of creation itself and the nature of God's creative act?

12. How is freedom an essential condition for the gift of self?

13. What does the nuptial meaning of the body reveal about procreation and who we are as persons?

The foundations for an adequate anthropology, for a total vision of man, have been laid with the three fundamental truths about who we are as persons. We alone among all creatures have been willed by God for ourselves. Further, we are beings able to discover ourselves fully only by giving ourselves in love. In the end, only Christ reveals to us the fullness of who we are through his self-giving love that transforms our very nature.

This theological sketch of the human person, a vision born of faith, has been complemented by a philosophical view of man, attained through reason. We have seen how our spiritual faculties of intellect and will enable us to transcend the material world and reach the horizon of universal truth and goodness. Our passions, when guided by reason and will, make it possible for us to rise to the fullness of humanity. We do so by striving toward the good, even in the face of obstacles, and loving it with all our heart.

To understand even more deeply the drama of our present condition, it is necessary to gaze upon the origins of mankind, weigh the nature of our historical journey through time, and contemplate the destiny to which we are called. John Paul II does precisely that in his Wednesday audiences when he considers the three states of man: original man, historical man, and eschatological man. Original man designates the state in which God created us before that terrible and mysterious reality appeared upon the stage — sin. Historical man signifies, first of all, human persons in our present condition, tainted by sin. But historical man has now become redeemed man, transformed from within by the saving grace of Christ's death upon the cross and his resurrection. Eschatological man evokes the fulfillment of our destiny at the end of time, when Christ will establish new heavens and a new earth, and God will be all in all.

The Holy Father considers these three states of man in three cycles of Wednesday audiences. Then, once the whole panorama has been unfolded, he applies this all-encompassing vision of who we are in another three series of audiences — first, to the celibate vocation, second, to the married vocation, and, finally, to the nature of conjugal love and fruitfulness. Only in light of the complete vision of man that the Holy Father develops is it possible to understand in all of its truth and beauty the Church's teaching on married love and responsible parenthood. In today's world it is very easy to be misled by fragmented sketches of who we are as persons. "We are children of an age in which, owing to the development of various disciplines, this total vision of man may easily be rejected and replaced by multiple partial conceptions."[207]

---

[207] John Paul II, General Audience of April 2, 1980, in *Theology of the Body*, pp. 87-88.

It is from the truth of the total vision of man that John Paul II's theology of the body springs. What is the essential nucleus of this theology? In a single sentence, it could be defined as follows: "This truth concerns the meaning of the human body in the structure of the personal subject."[208] In other words, our body is not simply a physical object. It is part of who we are as persons, as conscious subjects. Nor are the human acts we freely perform with our body mere physical, biological actions. They possess an intrinsic meaning that derives from the personal meaning of our body. Let us embark upon the journey into the mystery of our human condition, revealed through our bodies, and the vocation to which we are called.

I. Original Man

What does John Paul II mean when he refers to "original man" and his "original human experiences"? Is he inclining perhaps toward a literalist interpretation of the Book of Genesis? Does he look upon the creation story as a scientific, empirical account of man's emergence upon the world stage? The answer here is a definite "no." The Holy Father explains the precise meaning of these terms. "Speaking of original human experiences, we have in mind not so much their distance in time, as rather their basic significance. The important thing is not that these experiences belong to man's prehistory (to his 'theological prehistory'), but that they are always at the root of every human experience."[209] In other words, the divinely inspired account of Genesis describes the foundational elements that underlie our experience — essential for understanding who we are as persons.

A. Original Solitude

Adam's most profound experience in the Garden of Eden was that of original solitude. He named each of the animals God had created as they passed before him, but, even in their midst, he remained utterly alone. Adam felt intense solitude because he alone among God's creatures was a person. Only he possessed self-awareness and self-determination. Only he was called to love. God recognizes Adam's solitude. He declares, "It is not good that the man should be alone."[210]

B. Original Unity

God relieves Adam's solitude by creating Eve. Adam recognizes in Eve the one he has been searching for, but has been unable to find among any of God's other creatures. He exclaims, "This at last is bone of my bones and flesh of my flesh."[211] Original solitude is transformed into *original unity* between man and woman when the two "become one

---

[208] General Audience of April 2, 1980, in Ibid., p. 88.
[209] General Audience of December 12, 1979, in Ibid., p. 51.
[210] Gn 2:18.
[211] Gn 2:23.

flesh."[212] At the same time, the unity of man and woman confirms their solitude in the midst of all other creatures. For they alone are called to reflect the image of God by giving themselves to each other in love.

It is precisely the experience of solitude that leads man and woman to recognize their uniqueness as persons and to reach out to one another to form a communion of persons (*communio personarum*) that is an image of God's own communion in the three persons of the Blessed Trinity. Here we arrive at one of John Paul II's most unique contributions to theology. In the past, man's individual humanity, residing primarily in his intellect and free will, has been viewed as the principal way we reflect God's image. John Paul II transcends this vision. He affirms that the call to communion is what is deepest within us as persons, created "in the image of God."

> Man became "the image and likeness" of God not only through his own humanity, but also through the communion of persons which man and woman form right from the beginning. . . . Man becomes the image of God not so much in the moment of solitude as in the moment of communion. Right "from the beginning," he is not only an image in which the solitude of a person who rules the world is reflected, but also, and essentially, an image of an inscrutable divine communion of persons. . . . Obviously, that is not without significance for the theology of the body. *Perhaps it even constitutes the deepest theological aspect of all that can be said about man.*[213]

What does this communion of persons entail? What is that deepest aspect within ourselves as persons, of which the Holy Father speaks? It is that we are made "for" others, to give ourselves away to them. Only by living in loving communion with others, and above all with God, can we be fulfilled. "The communion of persons means existing in a mutual 'for,' in a relationship of mutual gift. This relationship is precisely the fulfillment of man's original solitude."[214]

C. Original Nakedness

After the account of Eve's creation and her reception by Adam, there follows one of the most beautiful lines in the Book of Genesis. "And the man and his wife were both naked, and were not ashamed" (Gn 2:25). This verse reveals another essential aspect of humanity's primordial state: *original nakedness*. How important is this notion for grasping the nature of man as revealed by God himself in Sacred Scripture? The Holy Father responds, "In the first biblical draft of anthropology, it is not something accidental. On the contrary, it is precisely the key for its full and complete understanding."[215]

---

[212] Gn 2:24.
[213] John Paul II, General Audience of November 14, 1979, in *Theology of the Body*, pp. 46-47.
[214] General Audience of January 9, 1980, in Ibid., p. 61.
[215] General Audience of December 12, 1979, in Ibid., p. 52.

The fact that Adam and Eve were not ashamed of being naked does not mean they were shameless. Rather, it indicates that they saw each other as persons, in the fullness of their bodily reality — male and female — with the vision of God, the Creator. "And God saw everything that he had made, and behold, it was very good" (Gn 1:31). "They see and know each other with all the peace of the interior gaze, which creates precisely the fullness of the intimacy of persons."[216]

D. "Naked Without Shame": The Nuptial Meaning of the Body

What intrinsic meaning does the human body possess? It is a meaning Adam and Eve were able to perceive in all its fullness, with the purity of heart that marked their *original innocence* before the fall. Actually, several different levels of meaning are conveyed by the human body.

1. The Body Reveals Divine Mysteries

At its deepest level, the human body reveals divine mysteries. What is the hidden, invisible mystery that the human body reveals above all? Nothing less than man and woman's call to participate in the Trinitarian life of God himself. John Paul II affirms this truth in no uncertain terms. "The body, and it alone, is capable of making visible what is invisible: the spiritual and the divine. It was created to transfer into the visible reality of the world the mystery hidden since time immemorial in God, and thus be a sign of it."[217]

Adam and Eve reveal to each other the mystery of God's love as a call to live in a communion of persons, to participate in the divine life. The pinnacle of the body revealing God, making him visible, is reached in the Incarnation, when the Word takes on flesh. John proclaims in the first chapter of his Gospel, "No one has ever seen God; the only Son, who is in the bosom of the Father, he has made him known" (Jn 1:18). The Holy Father comments on the fundamental importance of the Incarnation for the theology of the body. "Through the fact that the Word of God became flesh, the body entered theology through the main door."[218]

2. The Body Reveals Man

While the human body makes visible God's invisible reality, it also reveals man. And it does so by manifesting what is unique to man among all other creatures — he is a personal subject. When Adam names each of the animals, their bodies manifest their objective form of existence as individuals of a species. Only when God presents Eve to him does he exclaim, "This one is bone of my bone and flesh of my flesh" (Gn 2:23). Eve's body reveals her to Adam as a conscious subject just like him, a person to be loved.

---

[216] General Audience of January 2, 1980, in Ibid., p. 57.
[217] General Audience of February 20, 1980, in Ibid., p. 76.
[218] General Audience of April 2, 1980, in Ibid., p. 88-89.

In the light of the preceding analysis of all the "bodies" which man has come into contact with and has defined, conceptually giving them their name (*animalia*), the expression "flesh of my flesh" takes on precisely this meaning: the body reveals man. . . . Exclaiming in this way, he [Adam] seems to say that here is a body that expresses the person. . . . The whole biblical narrative, and in particular the Yahwist text, shows that the body through its own visibility manifests man. In manifesting him, it acts as intermediary, that is, it enables man and woman, right from the beginning, to communicate with each other according to that *communio personarum* willed by the Creator precisely for them.[219]

3. The Body Reveals Man and Woman as a Gift for Each Other

The body reveals human persons as man or woman. In doing so, it manifests the essential core of being a person: the call to give oneself in love to another person, and to receive in turn his or her gift of self. This law of the gift, inscribed in our very nature, expresses the *nuptial meaning of the body*. "The human body, with its sex, and its masculinity and femininity . . . includes right from the beginning the nuptial attribute, that is, the capacity of expressing love, that love in which the person becomes a gift and — by means of this gift — fulfills the meaning of his being and existence."[220]

Adam and Eve were naked yet experienced no shame because they saw with the purity of original innocence the nuptial meaning of the body. They perceived in the nakedness of each other's body not an object to be used for their own selfish gratification, but a person to be loved. Just how essential to human life is this perception that Adam and Eve enjoyed in complete fullness before they sinned? John Paul II responds, "The awareness of the meaning of the body . . . — in particular its nuptial meaning — is the fundamental element of human existence in the world."[221]

4. Creation Itself: A First and Fundamental Gift

Why is the nuptial meaning of the body so essential? Because it personifies in us, as conscious subjects, the very structure of creation itself and the meaning of God's creative act. All of creation is a gift from God to man. As a gift, creation reveals to us that God is love — for selfless giving flows only from one who loves.

This is the body — a witness to creation as a fundamental gift, and so a witness to Love as the source from which this same giving

---

[219] General Audiences of November 14, 1979; January 9, 1980; and December 19, 1979; in Ibid., pp. 47, 61, 56.
[220] General Audience of January 16, 1980, in Ibid., p. 63.
[221] General Audience of January 16, 1980, in Ibid., p. 66.

springs. Masculinity and femininity — namely, sex — is the original sign of a creative donation and an awareness on the part of man, male-female, of a gift lived in an original way. Such is the meaning with which sex enters the theology of the body.[222]

Man receives creation as a gift from God, who is pure self-giving love. Thanks to the nuptial meaning of the body, created male and female, man reflects the structure of creation as a gift within his depths as a person. Husband and wife are able to give themselves in love to one another with their entire being. They are capable of entering into a loving communion of persons. Their mutual gift of self is an echo of the gift that is all of creation.

5. Freedom: Condition for the Gift of Self

The most fundamental condition in order to be able to give ourselves in love is freedom. The fact that we are free elevates us to the dignity of being subjects. No human person is simply an object of nature, an individual of a species, as every plant or animal is. Only a free, conscious subject can be aware of himself and possess his "self" in order to be able to give himself away. The deeper our inner freedom, the greater is our capacity to give ourselves to another simply for his own sake as another subject like us — another person. The more our freedom is tainted by our passions, the more we tend to treat others as objects for our own gratification. Before sin, Adam and Eve possessed perfect freedom. The Holy Father describes their situation, their ability to live the nuptial meaning of the body in its fullness.

> In the narrative of creation (especially in Genesis 2:23-25) the woman is certainly not merely an object for the man. They both remain in front of each other in all the fullness of their objectivity as creatures, as "bone of my bones and flesh of my flesh," as male and female, both naked. Only the nakedness that makes woman an object for man, or vice versa, is a source of shame. The fact that they were not ashamed means that the woman was not an "object" for the man nor he for her.

> Interior innocence as purity of heart made it impossible somehow for one to be reduced by the other to the level of a mere object. The fact that they were not ashamed means they were united by awareness of the gift. They were mutually conscious of the nuptial meaning of their bodies, in which the freedom of the gift is expressed and all the interior riches of the person as subject are manifested.[223]

6. The Nuptial Meaning of the Body and Procreation

Adam and Eve discover in their bodies the capacity to give themselves as a gift to each other — not simply as objects, but as personal

---

[222] General Audience of January 9, 1980, in Ibid., p. 62.
[223] General Audience of February 20, 1980, in Ibid., p. 75.

subjects. This self-giving love is fulfilled in the act of conjugal union, when they become one flesh. The marital act, by its very nature, points to another dimension of the nuptial meaning of the body: the husband and wife's gift of self is inseparably linked to procreation. John Paul II reflects on these two aspects of marital union.

> In this way, the reality of the conjugal union, in which the man and the woman become one flesh, contains a new and, in a way, definitive discovery of the meaning of the human body in its masculinity and femininity. But in connection with this discovery, is it right to speak only of "sexual life together"? We must consider that each of them, man and woman, is not just a passive object, defined by his or her own body and sex, and in this way determined "by nature." On the contrary, because they are a man and a woman, each of them is "given" to the other as a unique and unrepeatable subject, as "self," as a person.[224]

> However, in the knowledge which Genesis 4:1 speaks of, the mystery of femininity is manifested and revealed completely by means of motherhood, as the text says: "She conceived and bore. . . ." The woman stands before the man as a mother, the subject of the new human life that is conceived and develops in her, and from her is born into the world. Likewise, the mystery of man's masculinity, that is, the generative and fatherly meaning of his body, is also thoroughly revealed.[225]

Thus, the fullness of the nuptial meaning of the body is revealed in fatherhood and motherhood. Both parents recognize each other and themselves in the new offspring born into the world from their act of self-giving love. "Procreation brings it about that the man and the woman (his wife) know each other reciprocally in the 'third,' sprung from them both. Therefore, this knowledge becomes a discovery. In a way it is a revelation of the new man, in whom both of them, man and woman, again recognize themselves, their humanity, their living image."[226]

The procreative meaning of the body, revealed in the conjugal act, brings man and woman to a further discovery. They come to realize that God himself plays a role in their fatherhood and motherhood. It is he who enables them to bring a son or daughter, a new human life, into the world. "In giving birth, the first woman is fully aware of the mystery of creation, which is renewed in human generation. She is also fully aware of the creative participation that God has in human generation, his work and that of her husband, since she says: 'I have begotten a man with the help of the Lord.'"[227]

---

[224] General Audience of March 5, 1980, in Ibid., p. 79.
[225] General Audience of March 12, 1980, in Ibid., p. 81.
[226] Ibid.
[227] Ibid., p. 82.

7. The Nuptial Meaning of the Body: A Final View

We have seen that the human body is much more than an object of nature possessed by us. It expresses who we are as persons; it reveals our capacity to transcend the physical world around us and reflect the image of God himself. At the same time, the body reveals that what lies deepest within our being is the call to give ourselves to others in love. The gift of self is always fruitful. Within married love this fecundity attains a direct cooperation with God's own creative act, when a child, a new human being, is born into the world. "In the beginning," before sin, the nuptial meaning of the body was revealed in all of its fullness. The Holy Father sums up the different levels of meaning expressed by the body in God's original plan.

> As we pointed out previously, in the state of original innocence nakedness did not express a lack. Rather, it represented full acceptance of the body in all its human and therefore personal truth.
>
> As the expression of the person, the body was the first sign of man's presence in the visible world. In that world, right from the beginning, man was able to distinguish himself, almost to be individualized — that is, confirm himself as a person — through his own body. It had been marked as a visible factor of the transcendence in virtue of which man, as a person, surpasses the visible world of living beings (*animalia*). In this sense, the human body was from the beginning a faithful witness and a tangible verification of man's original solitude in the world. At the same time, by means of his masculinity and femininity, it became a limpid element of mutual donation in the communion of persons.
>
> In this way, the human body bore in itself, in the mystery of creation, an unquestionable sign of the image of God.[228]

---

[228] General Audience of May 14, 1980, in Ibid., p. 113.

Preview

FIVE THE THREE STATES OF MAN *(continued)*

II. Historical Man
    A. Tainted by Sin
        1. The Appearance of Shame
        2. Lust: The Source of Shame
        3. The Nuptial Meaning of the Body in Peril
            a) From a Person to an Object
            b) From Free Self-Giving to Appropriation
        4. "The Heart — A Battlefield Between Love and Lust"
            a) "More Devious than Any Other Thing"
            b) A Quest for Love: The Twofold Meaning of Shame
            c) Shame and the Nature of the Human Person

Points to look for

1. According to John Paul II, what is the essence or central meaning of Adam and Eve's sin?

2. Why do Adam and Eve feel ashamed of their nakedness after their sin?

3. What emotion always accompanies shame?

4. How does lust threaten the nuptial meaning of the body?

5. What does the Holy Father mean when he says that lust transforms a relationship of mutual self-giving into one of appropriation?

6. What is meant by the "heart"?

7. What positive aspect of shame offers a pledge of hope for man's redemption?

8. What does the Holy Father mean by the opposition in the human heart between the spirit and the body?

9. What is the somewhat defensive aspect of shame's positive dimension?

10. What is the deepest, inner meaning of shame's positive dimension?

11. How does the experience of shame confirm the metaphysical nature of the human person as a being who possesses an inner life?

12. How does shame confirm the truth that the human person is the only creature willed by God for itself?

II. Historical Man
A. Tainted by Sin

Before the dawn of recorded history, a mysterious event occurred. This one incident continues to leave its mark upon every person born into the world — Adam and Eve sinned. Tempted by the devil, they disobeyed God. They turned from the one who had breathed life into them, created the entire universe as their home, and given each one to the other as a surpassing gift.

How could this ever have happened? The human spirit cannot penetrate the *mysterium iniquitatis,* the mystery of evil. What was the essence of Adam and Eve's sin? In what did it consist? John Paul II responds that the moment of sin is the moment in which *"the gift is questioned in man's heart."*[229] When Adam and Eve question God's gift, they also doubt "the love from which creation has its origin as donation."[230]

> Questioning in his heart the deepest meaning of the donation, that is, love as the specific motive of the creation and of the original covenant (cf. Gn 3:5), man turns his back on God-love, on the Father. In a way he casts God out of his heart. At the same time, he detaches his heart and almost cuts it off from what "is of the Father." Thus, there remains in him what "is of the world."[231]

Historical man emerges upon the scene as someone tainted by sin. He is the one who, "at the beginning of his earthly vicissitudes, found himself 'inside' the knowledge of good and evil, breaking the covenant with his Creator."[232] In the morning of his existence, man lost original innocence. Throughout history, humanity has continued to feel the effects of this loss in an unbroken saga of wars, cruelties, and sufferings.

The Holy Father penetrates into sin's effects on human life through an illuminating meditation on two passages from Sacred Scripture. The first is the story of man's fall in Genesis, Chapter 3. The second is a single verse from Christ's Sermon on the Mount. "You have heard that it was said, 'You shall not commit adultery.' But I say to you that every one who looks at a woman lustfully has already committed adultery with her in his heart" (Mt 5:27-28).

1. The Appearance of Shame

After Adam and Eve sin by disobeying God, they experience something never felt before: shame. They are suddenly ashamed in front of one another. One verse from Genesis resonates with the tragedy that has just occurred in their mutual relationship. "Then the eyes of both were opened, and they knew that they were naked; and they sewed fig leaves together and made themselves aprons" (Gn 3:7).

A still greater desolation is immediately revealed. Man and woman are ashamed not only in front of one another, but also before God. Shame brings with it a second emotion never before experienced: fear. "A certain fear always belongs to the essence of shame."[233] Adam and Eve feel compelled to hide themselves from the One who created them out of love.

---

[229] General Audience of April 30, 1980, in Ibid., p. 110. Italics are mine.
[230] Ibid.
[231] Ibid., p. 111.
[232] General Audience of April 23, 1980, in Ibid., p. 106.
[233] General Audience of May 14, 1980, in Ibid., p. 112.

And they heard the sound of the Lord God walking in the garden in the cool of the day, and the man and his wife hid themselves from the presence of the Lord God among the trees of the garden. But the Lord God called to the man, and said to him, "Where are you?" And he said, "I heard the sound of you in the garden, and I was afraid, because I was naked; and I hid myself" (Gn 3:8-10).

2. Lust: The Source of Shame

Why do Adam and Eve suddenly feel ashamed in front of each other and in the presence of God? They were naked before their sin, yet felt no shame. Is it their own bodies they have now become ashamed of? Adam and Eve are not so much ashamed of their bodies as they are of a new phenomenon that has arisen within them — lust. The triple concupiscence St. John describes has made itself a reality in their lives: "the lust of the flesh and the lust of the eyes and the pride of life."[234] Genesis reveals the appearance of these three forms of lust in a single verse: "So when the woman saw that the tree was good for food, and that it was a delight to the eyes, and that the tree was to be desired to make one wise, she took of its fruit and ate; and she also gave some to her husband, and he ate."[235]

Lust causes Adam and Eve to be ashamed of their own nakedness. It does so because of the way they now have come to view each other's body: no longer as a person to be loved, but as an object to be used for selfish gratification. Eve covers herself as if to say, "Adam — stop looking at me like that." Although lust has come to taint historical man, the fact that our first parents experience shame reveals that their nature has not been totally corrupted by sin. For only someone who continues to realize that a person must be valued precisely as a person can feel ashamed of his reaction to treat that person as an object for his own sensual pleasure. Hope remains for the redemption of the human person, even after sin.

3. The Nuptial Meaning of the Body in Peril
a) From a Person to an Object

Adam and Eve's experience of shame leads them to modesty: They sew aprons to cover themselves. This shame and consequent modesty reveal that lust has not completely destroyed the nuptial meaning of the human body. But sin's concupiscence does constantly threaten the nuptial meaning. It does so, first of all, by reducing the other person's body to an object for enjoyment. As a result, lust questions whether the other is really a person willed by God for his or her own sake. The Holy Father describes these two consequences of lust.

---

[234] 1 Jn 2:16.
[235] Gn 3:6.

The nuptial meaning of the body has not been completely suffo-
cated by concupiscence, but only habitually threatened. . . . It deprives man of the dignity of giving, which is expressed by his body
through masculinity and femininity. In a way it depersonalizes
man, making him an object "for the other." Instead of being "together with the other" — a subject in unity, in the sacramental unity
of the body — man becomes an object for man, the female for the
male and vice versa. . . .

Violating the dimension of the mutual giving of the man and the
woman, concupiscence also calls into question the fact that each of
them was willed by the Creator "for his own sake." In a certain
sense, the subjectivity of the person gives way to the objectivity of
the body. Owing to the body, man becomes an object for man — the
female for the male and vice versa. Concupiscence means that the
personal relations of man and woman are unilaterally and reduc-
tively linked with the body and sex, in the sense that these relations
become almost incapable of accepting the mutual gift of the person.
They do not contain or deal with femininity/masculinity according
to the full dimension of personal subjectivity. They do not express
communion, but they remain unilaterally determined by sex.[236]

b) From Free Self-Giving to Appropriation

In the state of original innocence, man's will, guided by his intellect,
exercised complete dominion over his passions. Adam and Eve loved
each other as persons, with a love of the will that moved them to give
their entire life, their whole self, to one another. Emotional love and
sense desire always followed from the spiritual desire of the will and co-
incided with it. So our first parents were supremely free.

Sin changes all that. The fall destroys the original harmony of the
human person. Concupiscence unleashes the passions to pursue their
own course, often in open defiance of the will and against the true good
of the person that the intellect discerns. As a result, the interior freedom
of giving oneself is lost. Instead, lust seeks to grasp the body of the other
as an object for the passions to enjoy. A relationship of mutual self-giving is changed to one of appropriation — of possessing and using the
other. The Holy Father penetrates this reality of our fallen nature.

Concupiscence entails the loss of the interior freedom of the gift.
The nuptial meaning of the human body is connected precisely
with this freedom. Man can become a gift — that is, the man and
the woman can exist in the relationship of mutual self-giving — if
each of them controls himself. Manifested as a "coercion *sui generis*
of the body,"[237] concupiscence limits interiorly and reduces self-

---

[236] General Audience of July 23, 1980, in Ibid., pp. 126-127.
[237] *Sui generis* could be rendered "of a kind."

control. For that reason, in a certain sense it makes impossible the interior freedom of giving. Together with that, the beauty that the human body possesses in its male and female aspect, as an expression of the spirit, is obscured. The body remains as an object of lust and, therefore, as a "field of appropriation" of the other human being. In itself, concupiscence is not capable of promoting union as the communion of persons. By itself, it does not unite, but appropriates. The relationship of the gift is changed into the relationship of appropriation.[238]

4. "The Heart — A Battlefield between Love and Lust"
a) "More Devious than Any Other Thing"

The new situation of historical man after the fall is eloquently summed up by John Paul II in a single phrase. "The heart has become a battlefield between love and lust."[239] Jeremiah, a prophet who endured the treachery of his own people, pondered in his writings the power of evil that seeks to take possession of men. In the grip of the *mysterium iniquitatis,* our hearts often become a mystery to ourselves.

> The heart is deceitful above all things
> and desperately corrupt;
> who can understand it?
> I the Lord search the mind and try the heart,
> to give every man according to his ways,
> according to the fruit of his doings. (Jer 17:9-10).

What takes place within our heart reveals the fundamental truth about who we are. We know instinctively that if someone has a good heart, he is a good person. The prophets continually implore the people of Israel, "Harden not your hearts." But what precisely do we mean by the "heart"? Is it a separate faculty, like reason or will? Is the heart the same thing as the sensitive appetite, the seat of our emotions? More than a precise anthropological term, the "heart" is a biblical concept that refers to the inner depths of the person. So the heart entails not only our emotions, but also our reason and will, our conscience, where we decide either for or against God. Because of sin, the motives of our heart at times remain a mystery to us. The *Catechism* vibrantly describes the meaning of the human heart.

> The heart is the dwelling-place where I am, where I live; according to the Semitic or Biblical expression, the heart is the place "to which I withdraw." The heart is our hidden center, beyond the grasp of our reason and of others; only the Spirit of God can fathom the human heart and know it fully. The heart is the place of decision, deeper than our psychic drives. It is the place of truth, where we

---

[238] Ibid., p. 127.
[239] General Audience of July 23, 1980, in Ibid., p. 126.

choose life or death. It is the place of encounter, because as image of God we live in relation: it is the place of covenant.[240]

John Paul II expresses in succinct form the Catechism's description of the human heart. In a sense, our heart is what makes us to be individual, personal subjects. "Man is unique and unrepeatable above all because of his heart, which decides his being from within. The category of the heart is, in a way, the equivalent of personal subjectivity."[241]

The internal division wrought by sin that we constantly experience within us is described by John Paul II as an "opposition in the human heart between spirit and body."[242] The emotions of our sensitive appetite are no longer subject in a harmonious way to our spiritual faculties of reason and will. Instead, they often seek to pursue their own path to self-gratification. Nor do reason and will themselves always tend toward our true good, but are often tainted by motives such as spiritual pride or vanity. So our life on earth presents itself as a constant battle to conquer our own heart. In the words of Job, "*Militia est vita hominis super terram*" (The life of man on earth is a warfare).[243]

b) A Quest for Love: The Twofold Meaning of Shame

The ambiguity of the human heart after sin is reflected in the twofold nature of shame. Before considering shame's double aspect, we must ask ourselves, "What is shame? When does it occur?" Karol Wojtyła offers a response. "*The phenomenon of shame arises when something which of its very nature or in view of its purpose ought to be private passes the bounds of a person's privacy and somehow becomes public.*"[244] This answer provides an initial, general definition of shame.

In its twofold nature in the sexual sphere, shame is, first of all, a negative emotional experience, since it arises from one's own lust or from being looked upon by another with lust — as a sensual object to be used. But the experience of shame also encompasses a positive dimension. It springs from an intimate desire to respect the value of the other person precisely as a person, as a conscious subject and not an object of sensual gratification. "The feeling of shame goes with the realization that a person of the other sex must not be regarded (even in one's private thoughts) as an object of use. . . . Only the person can feel shame, because only it of its very nature cannot be the object of use."[245]

Shame leads to sexual modesty. The desire to safeguard the personal value of another and one's own value by modesty is a somewhat defen-

---

[240] *CCC*, 2563.
[241] General Audience of December 3, 1980, in *The Theology of the Body*, p. 177.
[242] General Audience of July 30, 1980, in Ibid., p. 128; cf. p 130.
[243] Job 7:1.
[244] Wojtyła, *Love and Responsibility*, p. 174.
[245] Ibid., p. 178.

sive aspect of shame's positive dimension. But behind this defensive reflex lies hidden a much deeper aspiration: the longing to inspire love. While modest persons tend to conceal sexual values, they do so because they seek to inspire in persons of the opposite sex, not a reaction of sensuality, but a deeper response of love toward their whole person. A woman desires that a man come to love her for who she is, and the same is true for him. Wojtyła describes this profound, inner meaning of shame.

> This spontaneous urge to conceal sexual values, and the sexual character of certain feelings, which we encounter in men and women has, however, another and deeper meaning. It is not just a matter of hiding anything that might produce a sexual reaction in another person, nor yet of internally hiding from one's own reaction to a person of the other sex. For this shrinking from reactions to mere sexual values goes together with the longing to inspire love, to inspire a 'reaction' to the value of the person, and with the longing to experience love in the same sense — the first perhaps stronger in women, the second in men, but one should not suppose that either is exclusive to either of the sexes. A woman wants to be loved so that she can show love. A man wants to love so that he can be loved. In either case, sexual modesty is not a flight from love, but on the contrary the opening of a way towards it. *The spontaneous need to conceal mere sexual values bound up with the person is the natural way to the discovery of the value of the person as such.*[246]

Wojtyła succinctly recaps the two meanings hidden within shame's positive dimension. "Shame has, however, a dual significance: It means flight, the endeavor to conceal sexual values so that they do not obscure the values of the person as such, but it also means the longing to inspire or experience love."[247]

c) Shame and the Nature of the Human Person

Our experience of shame is an existential proof of the metaphysical nature of the person.[248] Since a person possesses the rational or spiritual faculties of intellect and will, he is a being marked by an interior life. Shame, as the need to conceal certain experiences, cannot be explained without this sphere of inner life. That is why it is impossible for animals to experience shame. They can feel fear, and shrink away from an evil that threatens. But shame is impossible for them, since they possess no

---

[246] Ibid., p. 179.

[247] Ibid., p. 182.

[248] The metaphysical nature of the person refers to the type of being a person is. Metaphysically, human persons differ from other beings, such as animals, plants, or inanimate objects. A person's moral nature, which reveals how he should act, derives from his metaphysical nature, from the type of being that he is. When we perform actions that are morally good, we are acting consistently with regard to our nature as persons. When we commit morally evil acts, we contradict our very being as persons.

conscious self-awareness, no capacity for reflection, and hence no interior realm, where shame arises. Wojtyła comments on this fact.

> It [shame] can only be understood if we heavily emphasize the truth that the existence of the person is an interior one, i.e., that the person possesses an interior peculiarly its own, and that from this arises the need to conceal (that is, to retain internally) certain experiences or values, or else to withdraw with them into itself. Fear does not exhibit this inwardness, it is a simple reaction to an evil perceived, imagined, or experienced. No interior is necessary to this reaction, whereas shame cannot be conceived of without it.[249]

Besides confirming that persons are beings with an interior life, the experience of shame also bears out the Church's teaching that man is the only creature willed by God for its own sake.[250] Another classical definition of the person as *alteri incommunicabilis* (not communicable to another) expresses this truth about who we are. Wojtyła reflects on this essential aspect of the person. Because of our very nature, we must freely choose to reveal ourselves, to give ourselves as a gift to others, if we are to be truly known and, in a certain way, possessed by them.

> The person is its own master (*sui juris*);[251] no one else except God the Creator has or can have any proprietary right in relation to it. It is its own property, it has the power of self-determination, and no one can encroach upon its independence. No one can take possession of the person unless the person permits this, makes a gift of itself from love. This objective inalienability (*alteri incommunicabilitas*) and inviolability of the person finds expression precisely in the experience of sexual shame. *The experience of shame is a natural reflection of the essential nature of the person.*[252]

These reflections on shame, both its negative and positive dimensions, and how it reflects the nature of the human person, lead to a more specific definition of shame itself. "*Shame is a tendency, uniquely characteristic of the human person, to conceal sexual values sufficiently to prevent them from obscuring the value of the person as such.* The purpose of this tendency is self-defense of the person, which does not wish to be an object to be used by another, whether in practice or merely in intention, but does wish to be an object of love."[253]

---

[249] Wojtyła, *Love and Responsibility,* p. 175.
[250] Cf. *Gaudium et Spes,* 24.
[251] (of its own right)
[252] Wojtyła, *Love and Responsibility,* p. 178.
[253] Ibid., p. 187.

Preview

FIVE THE THREE STATES OF MAN (continued)

II. Historical Man (continued)
  A. Tainted by Sin
  B. Redeemed by Christ's Blood
    1. An Appeal to the Heart: The Sermon on the Mount
    2. The Redemption of the Body
    3. Life According to the Spirit
      a) A New Power at Work Within Us
      b) A New Freedom
      c) Purity: The Fruit of Life According to the Spirit
        (1) Twofold Dimension of Purity: Moral Virtue
            and Gift of the Holy Spirit
        (2) Twofold Dignity of the Body: Personal Spirit and Indwelling of the
            Holy Spirit
      d) Life According to the Spirit: Ethical Norm and Anthropological Truth
      e) The Fruit of Purity in the Holy Spirit: Joy

Points to look for

1. How are Christ's words in Matthew 5:27-28 both an accusation of the human heart and an appeal to man's heart?

2. Why should we not regard the human heart with continual distrust, despite sin and our fallen human nature?

3. What should be our attitude toward the human heart and toward our own heart?

4. Who are the three "masters of suspicion" and how has each of them viewed the human heart with complete distrust?

5. How can we be sure that lust does not represent what is deepest in man's heart?

6. How is it possible for a husband to commit adultery in his heart with his own wife?

7. Why should we not fear the severity of Christ's words regarding adultery in the heart?

8. Why is the truth of our redemption in Christ the truth that will make us free?

9. What are the two alternatives that lie open before us in the drama of our earthly life?

10. What is the new freedom Christ has won for us by the power of his redemption?

11. What is the generic and the specific meanings of purity?

12. Why does self-control enhance our dignity as persons?

13. Why is purity necessary in order to fulfill the "law of the gift" inscribed in us?

14. What is the meaning of the statement that purity is both a moral virtue and a gift of the Holy Spirit?

15. What is the reward of purity?

16. What is the twofold dimension of the dignity of the human body?

17. How does Christ's call to live purity of heart express both a normative, ethical truth and an anthropological truth about the human person?

18. How do the fruits of life according to the Spirit more than compensate the struggle needed to overcome life according to the flesh?

B. Redeemed by Christ's Blood
1. An Appeal to the Heart: The Sermon on the Mount

The experience of shame reveals to us the ambiguity hidden within man's heart after sin. So what should be our attitude toward the human heart, and even toward our own heart? Should the heart be regarded with suspicion or trust? In the Gospel of John, the people acclaim Christ because of his miracles on his first entry into Jerusalem. Yet John tells us, "But Jesus did not trust himself to them, because he knew all men and needed no one to bear witness of man; for he himself knew what was in man" (Jn 2:25).

Christ, our Creator and Redeemer, more than anyone, knows who man is, what lies hidden within the recesses of the human heart. So Christ's attitude toward the heart should guide our own. The Holy Father penetrates the depths of Christ's attitude, revealed in one of his phrases from the Sermon on the Mount. "You have heard that it was said, 'You shall not commit adultery.' But I say to you that everyone who looks at a woman lustfully has already committed adultery with her in his heart" (Mt 5:27-28).

At first glance these words appear to be an accusation directed against the heart. While this may be true on the surface, at a much deeper level they represent an appeal. Christ appeals to the human heart, to the inner man. He calls us to be pure, not only in our outward actions, but even in our inmost thoughts. Ultimately, he invites each person in the secret of his inner self to scale the heights of God's original plan for man and woman before sin.

So what should the presence of sin in our own hearts and the hearts of others imply for us? John Paul II responds in light of Christ's words. "Does this mean that it is our duty to distrust the human heart? No! It only means that we must keep it under control."[254]

The temptation can be strong to accuse the heart and distrust it suspiciously. Three modern figures who have profoundly influenced mankind's course are described by the French philosopher Paul Ricoeur as "masters of suspicion": Freud, Marx, and Nietzsche.[255] Their three systems are based upon the threefold lust hidden within the human heart. One common tie unites their diverse accounts of who man is: They each present a *reductive* vision of the human person. The three systems all contain an element of truth about man. That is what makes them so appealing — and seductive. But all three accounts attempt to reduce the entire person to that single aspect of truth they have discov-

---

[254] General Audience of July 23, 1980, in *The Theology of the Body*, p. 126.
[255] General Audience of October 29, 1980, in Ibid., p. 165. Cf. Paul Ricoeur, *Le conflit des interpretations* (Paris: Seuil, 1969), pp. 149-150.

ered. When faced with the transcendent reality that is the human person, any system which is *reductive* is also *destructive.*

Each school submits a partial, distorted response to the psalmist's perennial question, "What is man?"[256] Nietzsche reduces man to his "will to power," his desire for dominion over others. Nietzsche's quest for the "superman," who affirms his own will as supreme, reflects the "pride of life." What have been the consequences of this reductive view of man? Fascism and Naziism. Is it possible even to begin to describe the sufferings these ideologies have wrought upon mankind?

Marx asserts that man is simply what he produces. Only through the production of material goods can persons overcome a profound sense of alienation. Man is nothing more than the "lust of the eyes." The fruits of this second reductive vision of man have been the untold horrors of the Communist empire.

Freud affirms that man is no more than his libido, his drive for sexual pleasure. In the end, all human motivations can be reduced to the sexual urge. The human person is completely dominated by the "lust of the flesh." What bitter fruits have matured from this third reductive vision of man? The incalculable emotional and psychological suffering produced by the sexual revolution — countless broken lives, many of them wasted away in the very springtime of youth.

Though Christ seems to accuse man's heart, his words in Matthew 5:27-28 do not allow us to stop where these men did, regarding the human heart with continual suspicion. Christ's words reveal that there is something deeper than lust within man. Lust cannot be viewed as the definitive key for interpreting who man is. These words of Christ are such that, "while manifesting the whole reality of desire and lust, they do not permit us to make this lust the absolute criterion of anthropology and ethics, that is, the very core of the hermeneutics of man."[257]

2. The Redemption of the Body

Sin does not constitute the definitive word regarding man's nature or his destiny. Christ has redeemed us from sin at the price of his blood, shed in agony upon the cross. Christ gave us the strength to answer his own appeal to our hearts by his Incarnation, the bitter suffering of his passion, and his victorious resurrection. St. Paul refers to this marvelous new reality that penetrates the life of every person who responds to God's grace as "the redemption of our bodies."[258]

---

[256] Psalm 8.
[257] General Audience of October 29, 1980, in Ibid., p. 166. (Hermeneutics is the study of the methodological principles of interpretation. It is most often spoken of with regard to the interpretation of the Bible, as in, "a correct Biblical hermeneutics." But the Holy Father uses the term here to refer to the proper principles for interpreting the nature of the human person.)
[258] Rm 8:23.

Christ's words, appealing to a new way of life, are certainly demanding. By identifying adultery not simply with a bodily action, but with the intentions of the heart, Christ reveals that his grace is meant to penetrate into the inner core of our person. For the intentions of our heart ultimately define who we are. Carrying Christ's words to their logical conclusion, John Paul II made an observation during his Wednesday audience of October 8, 1980, that became a subject of immediate controversy. It is possible for a husband to look lustfully at his own wife, and so commit adultery with her in his heart. "Adultery in the heart is committed not only *because* a man looks in this way at a woman who is not his wife, but *precisely* because he looks at a woman in this way. Even if he looked in this way at the woman who is his wife, he could likewise commit adultery in his heart."[259]

How is it possible for a husband to commit adultery with his own wife? He may allow lust to move him, so that he sees his wife no longer as a person, with whom he enters into loving communion through the conjugal act. Rather, she becomes reduced by him to an object to satisfy his sexual urge. If a husband, or a wife, for that matter, allows this to occur within him, he has committed adultery with his spouse in his heart. The Holy Father develops this point.

> The lust which, as an interior act, springs from this basis . . . changes the very intentionality of the woman's existence "for" man. It reduces the riches of the perennial call to the communion of persons, the riches of the deep attractiveness of masculinity and femininity, to mere satisfaction of the sexual need of the body (the concept of "instinct" seems to be more closely linked with this). As a result of this reduction, the person (in this case, the woman) becomes for the other person (the man) mainly an object of the potential satisfaction of his own sexual need. In this way the mutual "for" is distorted, losing its character of communion of persons in favor of the utilitarian function. A man who looks in this way, as Matthew 5:27-28 indicates, uses the woman, her femininity, to satisfy his own instinct. Although he does not do so with an exterior act, he has already assumed this attitude deep down, inwardly deciding in this way with regard to a given woman. This is what adultery committed in the heart consists of. Man can commit this adultery in the heart also with regard to his own wife, if he treats her only as an object to satisfy instinct.[260]

In the face of this reality, we may be tempted to cry out, as the apostles did, "If such is the case of a man with his wife, it is expedient not to marry."[261] Left to our own strength, our dismay would be well-

---

[259] General Audience of October 8, 1980, in *The Theology of the Body*, p. 157.
[260] Ibid.
[261] Mt 19:10.

founded. But Christ does not command us to rise to a new way of life in full keeping with our dignity as persons, and then leave us on our own. He gives us the grace we need to answer his appeal through prayer, the sacraments, and the sufferings of our daily life united with his own passion. He has won for us the "redemption of our bodies" — and at what a price! The Holy Father asks how we should respond to Christ's appeal. "Are we to fear the severity of these words, or rather have confidence in their salvific content, in their power?"[262]

John Paul II reviews in a profoundly moving way the new horizons opened for our lives by the "redemption of the body." The truth of our redemption in Christ, a truth that we are called to strive for and live out each day of our lives, is without question the truth that will make us free.[263]

> Summing up, it can be said briefly that Christ's words according to Matthew 5:27-28 do not allow us to stop at the accusation of the human heart and to regard it continually with suspicion. But they must be understood and interpreted above all as an appeal to the heart. This derives from the nature of the ethos of redemption. On the basis of this mystery, which St. Paul defines as "the redemption of the body" (Rm 8:23), on the basis of the reality called "redemption" . . . we cannot stop only at the accusation of the human heart on the basis of desire and lust of the flesh. Man cannot stop at putting the heart in a state of continual and irreversible suspicion due to the manifestations of the lust of the flesh and libido. . . . Redemption is a truth, a reality, in the name of which man must feel called, and "called with efficacy." He must realize this call also through Christ's words according to Matthew 5:27-28, reread in the full context of the revelation of the body. Man must feel called to rediscover, nay more, to realize the nuptial meaning of the body. He must feel called to express in this way the interior freedom of the gift, that is, of that spiritual state and that spiritual power which are derived from mastery of the lust of the flesh.
>
> Man is called to this by the word of the Gospel, therefore from "outside," but at the same time he is also called from "inside." The words of Christ, who in the Sermon on the Mount appealed to the heart, induce the listener, in a way, to this interior call. If he lets them act in him, he will be able to hear within him at the same time almost the echo of that "beginning." . . . Christ's words bear witness that the original power (therefore also the grace) of the mystery of creation becomes for each of them power (that is, grace) of the mystery of redemption. That concerns the very nature, the very substratum of the humanity of the person, the deepest impulses of

---

[262] Ibid., p. 159.
[263] Cf. Jn 3:16.

the heart. Does not man feel, at the same time as lust, a deep need to preserve the dignity of the mutual relations, which find their expression in the body, thanks to his masculinity and femininity? Does he not feel the need to impregnate them with everything that is noble and beautiful? Does he not feel the need to confer on them the supreme value which is love?

Rereading it, this appeal contained in Christ's words in the Sermon on the Mount cannot be an act detached from the context of concrete existence. It always means — though only in the dimension of the act to which it is referred — the rediscovery of the meaning of the whole of existence, the meaning of life, which also contains that meaning of the body which here we call "nuptial." The meaning of the body is, in a sense, the antithesis of Freudian libido. The meaning of life is the antithesis of the interpretation "of suspicion." This interpretation is radically different from what we rediscover in Christ's words in the Sermon on the Mount. These words reveal not only another ethos, but also another vision of man's possibilities. It is important that he, precisely in his heart, should not feel irrevocably accused and given as a prey to the lust of the flesh, but that he should feel forcefully called in this same heart. He is called precisely to that supreme value that is love. He is called as a person in the truth of his humanity, therefore also in the truth of his masculinity or femininity, in the truth of his body. He is called in that truth which has been his heritage from the beginning, the heritage of his heart, which is deeper than the sinfulness inherited, deeper than lust in its three forms. The words of Christ, set in the whole reality of creation and redemption, reactivate that deeper heritage and give it real power in human life.[264]

3. Life According to the Spirit
a) A New Power at Work Within Us

On the cross Christ won for us a new life through the transforming power of his redemption. This new life is Christ's very own spirit, the Holy Spirit, dwelling within us. It is "a real power that operates in man and is revealed and asserts itself in his actions."[265]

Though Christ has won for us new life according to the Spirit, at the same time, this life must be conquered by us. For we experience within ourselves an intimate opposition to this new life, a resistance that St. Paul describes as "life according to the flesh." The battle between these two conflicting forces plays out the drama of human existence. "The desires of the flesh are against the Spirit, and the desires of the Spirit are against the flesh" (Gal 5:17).

---

[264] General Audience of October 29, 1980, in *The Theology of the Body*, pp. 167-168.
[265] General Audience of December 17, 1980, in *Ibid.*, p. 193.

All protagonists in the history of salvation have had to choose between these two alternatives. Moses presented this inexorable decision to the Israelites in the desert. "I call heaven and earth to witness against you this day, that I have set before you life and death, blessing and curse; therefore choose life."[266] These are the two ways open to man in Psalm 1. He who follows the way of life according to the Spirit will be "like a tree planted near running water." But those who follow the desires of the flesh are "like chaff which the wind drives away."

St. Paul describes the works produced by each of these two ways of life — these two irreconcilable forces struggling to gain the victory in every person's earthly existence. "Now the works of the flesh are plain: fornication, impurity, licentiousness, idolatry, sorcery, enmity, strife, jealousy, anger, selfishness, dissension, party spirit, envy, drunkenness, carousing, and the like. I warn you, as I warned you before, that those who do such things shall not inherit the kingdom of God. But the fruit of the Spirit is love, joy, peace, patience, kindness, goodness, faithfulness, gentleness, self-control . . ." (Gal 5:19-23). The outcome of this unfolding confrontation could not possibly be more crucial. For, as St. Paul warns, nothing less than our eternal destiny is at stake.

b) A New Freedom

In the drama of redemption, we see played out within each person the battle over freedom that is being waged on a global scale. What does freedom really mean? For those who live according to the flesh, it implies freedom *from* any restriction on concupiscence, on the desires of the passions. Freedom *from* is equivalent to license. St. Paul warns against this false view of freedom. "Only do not use your freedom as an opportunity for the flesh. . . ."[267] What are the fruits of freedom as license? Once again, St. Paul speaks clearly. "Be sure of this, that no fornicator or impure man, or one who is covetous (that is, an idolater), has any inheritance in the kingdom of God."[268]

Christ reveals to us the truth about freedom. Freedom is not an end in itself. Freedom is *for* love. Only in Christ's supreme commandment, "Love one another as I have loved you,"[269] is freedom fulfilled. But Christ not only reveals to us the inner meaning of freedom, he also bestows this new freedom upon us through his redemption. Christ sends his Holy Spirit, whose transforming power at work within us makes it possible to fulfill Christ's new command, to become truly free with the freedom of love. St. Paul exclaims, "For freedom Christ has set us free."[270] He then proclaims both the need to conquer this freedom and

---

[266] Dt 30:19.
[267] Gal 5:13.
[268] Eph 5:5.
[269] Jn 15:12.
[270] Gal 5:1.

its profound, inner meaning. "For you were called to freedom, brethren; only do not use your freedom as an opportunity for the flesh, but through love be servants of one another. For the whole law is fulfilled in one word, 'You shall love your neighbor as yourself.'"[271]

The Holy Father succinctly describes the freedom to which we are called. "Christ realized and manifested the freedom that finds its fullness in charity, the freedom thanks to which we are servants of one another. In other words, that freedom becomes a source of new works and life according to the Spirit."[272]

c) Purity: The Fruit of Life According to the Spirit

The freedom of love, given to us through life in the Holy Spirit, is vitally expressed in purity. Authentic love and purity are inseparable. "Purity is a requirement of love. It is the dimension of its interior truth in man's heart."[273]

But just what is meant by purity? The Holy Father refers to purity in both a generic and a specific sense. "In the first case, everything that is morally good is pure, and on the contrary, everything that is morally bad is impure."[274] In the specific sense, purity can be equated with the virtue of chastity. St. Paul lists fornication, impurity, and licentiousness as the first three sins against the flesh, against chastity, in the letter to the Galatians.

A key passage in which St. Paul describes the role of purity is found in his first letter to the Thessalonians. "For this is the will of God, your sanctification: that you abstain from immorality; that each one of you know how to control his own body in holiness and honor, not in the passion of lust like heathen who do not know God."[275] The first section of these verses reveals what could be viewed as a somewhat negative aspect of purity: resisting the passion of lust. We see that the virtue of temperance, the capacity for controlling the desires of the sensitive appetite, belongs necessarily to purity.[276] But the eminently positive function of purity can be seen in St. Paul's exhortation to control our own body "in holiness and honor."

Abstention and self-control are closely connected and dependent on each other. Self-mastery enables us to attain our dignity as persons. For a person is essentially someone who is aware of himself and possesses himself. Only when a person has achieved self-mastery can he fulfill the law of the gift inscribed in his nature and give himself away out of love.

---

[271] Gal 5:13-14.
[272] General Audience of January 14, 1981, in Ibid., p. 198.
[273] General Audience of December 3, 1980, in Ibid., p. 177.
[274] General Audience of January 14, 1981, in Ibid., p. 198.
[275] 1 Th 4:3-5.
[276] Cf. General Audience of January 28, 1981, in Ibid., p. 200.

The reward Christ promises in the sixth beatitude to those who are pure compensates beyond measure our daily struggle to live this virtue. "Blessed are the pure in heart, for they shall see God."[277] But the recompense of purity is not reserved for the life to come. "Even now it enables us to see *according to* God, to accept others as 'neighbors'; it lets us perceive the human body — our own and our neighbor's — as a temple of the Holy Spirit, a manifestation of divine beauty."[278]

(1) Twofold Dimension of Purity: Moral Virtue and Gift of the Holy Spirit

Purity itself possesses a twofold dimension. It is, first of all, a moral virtue, a subjective capacity we are able to acquire through constant human effort. But purity is also a gift of the Holy Spirit, a sublime manifestation of "life according to the Spirit."[279] Another gift, that of piety, is closely linked with purity, as the Holy Father explains.

> If purity prepares man to "control his own body in holiness and honor" (1 Th 4:3-5), piety, which is a gift of the Holy Spirit, seems to serve purity in a particular way. It makes the human subject sensitive to that dignity which is characteristic of the human body by virtue of the mystery of creation and redemption. "Do you not know that your body is a temple of the Holy Spirit within you? . . . You are not your own" (1 Cor 6:19). Thanks to the gift of piety, Paul's words acquire the eloquence of an experience of the nuptial meaning of the body and of the freedom of the gift connected with it, in which the profound aspect of purity and its organic link with love is revealed.[280]

The Holy Father affirms that the gift of piety enables us to penetrate in a new way into the beauty of purity and its vital role in true love. Our motives for living purity are not simply out of respect for the other and for ourselves as human persons, but above all because the Holy Spirit dwells within each one of us. God himself is truly present in the hidden depths of each person living in the state of grace. Only someone whose heart is pure is able to perceive how the nuptial meaning of the body enables us to give ourselves freely, not simply to other human persons, but to God himself dwelling within them.

John Paul II speaks in moving terms of the dignity we acquire as persons through the virtue and gift of purity. God is glorified in our bodies, and we are able to catch a glimpse of his own eternal beauty reflected within us.

> Purity as the virtue is the capacity of controlling one's body in holiness and honor. Together with the gift of piety, as the fruit of the in-

---

[277] Mt 5:8.
[278] CCC, 2519.
[279] Cf. General Audience of February 11, 1981, in *The Theology of the Body*, p. 206.
[280] General Audience of March 18, 1981, in Ibid., p. 209.

dwelling of the Holy Spirit in the temple of the body, purity brings about in the body such a fullness of dignity in interpersonal relations that God himself is thereby glorified. Purity is the glory of the human body before God. It is God's glory in the human body, through which masculinity and femininity are manifested. From purity springs that extraordinary beauty which permeates every sphere of men's common life and makes it possible to express in it simplicity and depth, cordiality and the unrepeatable authenticity of personal trust.[281]

(2) Twofold Dignity of the Body: Personal Spirit and Indwelling of the Holy Spirit

The call to purity arises from the twofold dignity of the human body. First of all, our body possesses an innate dignity because of our personal, human spirit that constitutes us as personal subjects. Our body is an essential aspect of our personal identity. It is not simply an object that we possess. The Holy Father goes so far as to affirm that in a certain sense we *are* our body.

> Certainly, it is possible to describe the human body, to express its truth with the objectivity characteristic of the natural species. But such a description — with all its precision — cannot be adequate (that is, commensurable with its object). It is not just a question of the body (intended as an organism, in the somatic sense) but of man, who expresses himself through that body and in this sense *is*, I would say, that body.[282]

Christ has conferred a new and much higher dignity upon the human body. By his Incarnation, Christ takes on a human body, making it the body of the God-man. As a result, Christ elevates in a supernatural way the body of every man. Through the transforming power of his redemption, Christ enables each person's body to become a temple of the Holy Spirit, who dwells within us by grace.

> In Paul's eyes, it is not only the human spirit, thanks to which man is constituted as a personal subject, that decides the dignity of the human body. But even more so it is the supernatural reality constituted by the indwelling and the continual presence of the Holy Spirit in man — in his soul and in his body — as the fruit of the redemption carried out by Christ.[283]

St. Paul explains why purity acquires a new force and must be pursued with greater vigor thanks to Christ's redemption. "Shun immorality. Every other sin which a man commits is outside the body; but the immoral man sins against his own body. Do you not know that your

---

[281] General Audience of March 18, 1981, in Ibid., p. 209.
[282] General Audience of February 4, 1981, in Ibid., pp. 202-203.
[283] General Audience of February 11, 1981, in Ibid., p. 206.

body is a temple of the Holy Spirit within you, which you have from God? You are not your own; you were bought with a price. So glorify God in your body."[284]

John Paul II ponders what Christ has done for us by redeeming our bodies. In *Redemptor Hominis* the Pope marveled that we have been newly created. In his Wednesday audiences he reflects that Christ has given each one of us back to ourselves in a new way, with a transcendent dignity and a greater freedom — the freedom of the Holy Spirit, who dwells within us.

> Through redemption, every man has received from God again, as it were, himself and his own body. Christ has imprinted new dignity on the human body — on the body of every man and every woman, since in Christ the human body has been admitted, together with the soul, to union with the Person of the Son-Word. With this new dignity, through the redemption of the body, a new obligation arose at the same time. Paul writes of this concisely, but in an extremely moving way: "You were bought with a price" (1 Cor 6:20). The fruit of redemption is the Holy Spirit, who dwells in man and in his body as in a temple. In this Gift, which sanctifies every man, the Christian receives himself again as a gift from God. This new, double gift is binding. The Apostle refers to this binding dimension when he writes to believers, aware of the Gift, to convince them that one must not commit unchastity. One must not sin "against one's own body" (1 Cor 6:18). He writes: "The body is not meant for immorality, but for the Lord, and the Lord for the body" (1 Cor 6:13).[285]

d) Life According to the Spirit:
Ethical Norm and Anthropological Truth

Christ's call to purity of heart in the Sermon on the Mount expresses a normative, ethical truth about the human person. His words are the norm for our conduct. We must strive to live up to them and be pure, not merely in our actions, but also within the depths of our person — in our heart. At the same time, Christ's words contain an essential, anthropological truth about man. They reveal that, through redemption, we have become new persons. Through the power of the Holy Spirit, we are able to overcome the threefold lust within us and fulfill Christ's command to be pure of heart.

Do Christ's words imply that we can now return to original innocence? No. They are quite realistic in what they call man to. They at once acknowledge the tendency to sin at work within us, while offering the hope of being able to rise above that concupiscence of the flesh that

---

[284] 1 Cor 6:18-20.
[285] General Audience of February 11, 1981, in Ibid., pp. 206-207.

made St. Paul exclaim, "Who will deliver me from this body of death?" (Rm 7:24). The Holy Father gives an overview of the twofold truth revealed by Christ's words, which offer man a new freedom. Still, it is a freedom that must always be conquered anew amidst the tensions of this earthly life.

> But Christ's words are realistic. They do not try to make the human heart return to the state of original innocence, which man left behind him at the moment when he committed original sin. On the contrary, they indicate to him the way to a purity of heart which is possible and accessible to him even in the state of hereditary sinfulness. This is the purity of the man of lust. However, he is inspired by the word of the Gospel and open to life according to the Spirit (in conformity with St. Paul's words), that is, the purity of the man of lust who is entirely enveloped by the redemption of the body Christ carried out. For this reason we find in the words of the Sermon on the Mount the reference to the heart, that is, to the interior man. The interior man must open himself to life according to the Spirit, in order to participate in evangelical purity of heart, to rediscover and realize the value of the body, freed through redemption from the bonds of lust. The normative meaning of Christ's words is deeply rooted in their anthropological meaning, in the dimension of human interiority.[286]

e) **The Fruit of Purity in the Holy Spirit: Joy**

Reflecting upon the struggles of our own life, which on more than one occasion have surely elicited from us a cry similar to St. Paul's, we may feel tempted to ask ourselves, "Is it really worth it?" We might even implore God to show us the fruits of life according to the Spirit in a manner we can grasp hold of, so that we can be convinced, once and for all, that the conquest is worth the fight.

Since the Lord knows what we need even before we ask, he has already answered our plea. To discover the fruits of life in the Holy Spirit, one has to do no more than gaze upon the countenance of John Paul II. His face radiates what each one of us seeks to experience in life: joy. It is a joy that fills his whole being and overflows to each person he encounters, often moving them to tears with a single glance or gesture, and, at times, simply with his presence.

Who could doubt that a joy such as this is worth fighting for? Indeed, it is this very joy that often invades us when we least expect it to sustain us in the fight. It is a joy that seems to delight in catching us unaware. Often a single glimpse suffices to make us yearn for its fulfillment in the life to come. How convincing are the Holy Father's words in light of the witness of his life!

---

[286] General Audience of April 1, 1981, in Ibid., pp. 212-213.

The satisfaction of the passions is one thing, and the joy that man finds in mastering himself more fully is another thing. In this way he can also become more fully a real gift for another person.

The words Christ spoke in the Sermon on the Mount direct the human heart toward this joy. We must entrust ourselves, our thoughts and our actions to them, in order to find joy and give it to others.[287]

Would it not be wonderful if simple, clear directions could be given that would enable us to set off confidently along the path towards that joy? What is the secret for experiencing a joy like the Holy Father's? Father Marcial Maciel, who has lived a life filled with difficulties and every type of suffering imaginable, does not hesitate to affirm that his most profound experience throughout his days has been joy. In one of his letters, he reveals the path to that joy. "The extension of Christ's Kingdom! . . . How I would like to instill in you this powerful longing of my life, full of worries and troubles, but overflowing with meaning and an inexpressible joy: *the joy that our Lord and God grants to those who have made him the sole, driving passion of their poor, fleeting existence.*"[288]

When we have come to make Christ the sole, driving passion of our lives, when we have allowed him to strip us of our egotism, of our secret desires to be esteemed and highly regarded, of our fears about what others will think of us, then we will begin to experience a taste of that freedom he has come to give. When the only thing that matters to us in life is the extension of Christ's Kingdom, that he be known and loved in the lives of men and women, in the hearts of young people and children, then the joy that drives and sustains John Paul II will start to become a deep reality in our lives.

---

[287] General Audience of April 1, 1981, in Ibid., pp. 213-214.
[288] Letter of Father Marcial Maciel, LC, May 22, 1983, To Consecrated Regnum Christi Members, in *Lecturas Sacerdotales*, p. 1321. My translation. (Italics are mine.)

Preview

FIVE THE THREE STATES OF MAN *(continued)*
I. Original Man
II. Historical Man
III. Eschatological Man
  A. "He truly has risen! Alleluia!"
  B. What Will Heaven Be Like?
    Similarities and Differences
  C. A Completely New State of Human Life
    1. Spiritualization of the Body
    2. Divinization of the Body
    3. Face-to-Face Vision of God
    4. Communion of Saints
    5. Perfection of the Human Subject
    6. Fulfillment of the Nuptial Meaning of the Body

Points to look for

1. What are the three states of man that must be understood in order to arrive at a "total vision" of the human person? Why?
2. What is the twofold meaning of Christ's resurrection?
3. What are some of the similarities between heaven and our present earthly life?
4. What is one profound difference that will characterize our life in heaven?
5. What does the spiritualization of the body in heaven entail?
6. What is meant by the divinization of the human body?
7. What are two fundamental aspects of seeing God "face to face" in heaven?
8. What is the unity of all human persons in heaven referred to as?
9. Why is it worth all our prayers, struggles and sacrifices to arrive to heaven?
10. Will we be completely absorbed by God in heaven?
11. How can the nuptial meaning of the body be completely fulfilled in heaven if there is no marriage?
12. Why can there be no marriage in heaven?
13. How is virginity the definitive realization of the nuptial meaning of the body?
14. How does the beauty of marriage enable us to see more clearly the beauty of the consecrated life?

III. Eschatological Man

Under the guiding hand of John Paul II, the panorama of a total vision of the human person has been unfolding before our eyes. By insightful, theological penetration into a few verses from the Book of Genesis, simultaneously applying to these verses what we know of our present human condition, the Holy Father has traced God's original plan for man and woman at the dawn of creation, before sin. In doing so, he has brought to light fundamental truths about our nature and our destiny. Our very bodies reveal that we have been called to live a *communio personarum* (communion of persons) by giving ourselves in love. This "law of the gift" inscribed in us, the nuptial meaning of the body, is a revelation of God himself. It reflects the eternal communion of self-giving love among the three persons of the Blessed Trinity.

Through sin, historical man has lost his original innocence. That intimate, personal communion between husband and wife expressed by the words "and they become one flesh"[289] is endangered, and at times destroyed, by the threefold lust which threatens to reduce the other person to an object of sensual pleasure. A relationship of mutual self-giving can be degraded to one of appropriation. But historical man has been redeemed by Christ at the price of his own blood upon the cross. Christ's redemption recreates us. The horizons of a new life according to the Holy Spirit offer the hope of conquering the way of the flesh.

---

[289] Gn 2:24.

We have contemplated the origins of mankind and our present human condition. To reach a total vision of man, a third aspect about who we are as persons must be pondered: our future destiny. "The world is not man's eternal destiny, but the kingdom of God."[290] Christ's redemption has opened for us the gates of heaven. There we will experience complete happiness and fulfillment, in union with the three Persons of the Blessed Trinity. At the same time, the opposition between the spirit and the flesh within us will be definitively overcome. We will possess ourselves to the full, newly created in Christ. John Paul II dedicates the third cycle of his Wednesday audiences on the theology of the body to contemplating eschatological man:[291] the fulfillment of our eternal destiny with God, after the resurrection of our bodies.[292]

A. "He truly has risen! Alleluia!"

The Holy Father's reflections on our ultimate fulfillment as persons, once this earthly life has ended, are centered on a single verse from the Gospel of Matthew. "In the resurrection they neither marry nor are given in marriage, but are like angels in heaven."[293] The resurrection of each one of us, after our death, is founded entirely upon Christ's resurrection. Chapter 15 of the First Letter to the Corinthians penetrates into the meaning of the resurrection, as St. Paul, filled with emotion, ponders what Christ has done for us.

Christ's resurrection has a twofold meaning. First of all, it definitively reveals who God is. He is a God of life, a God who is faithful to his promises. At the same time, the resurrection confirms that everything Christ has taught, all that he has said he would do for mankind, is true. "The resurrection of Christ is the last and the fullest word of the self-revelation of the living God as 'not the God of the dead, but of the living' (Mk 12:27). It is the last and fullest confirmation of the truth about God. . . ."[294]

The second fundamental meaning of Christ's resurrection is that it achieves our victory over sin and death. All persons can look forward in hope to their own resurrection by participating in Christ's death and rising. "Furthermore, the resurrection is the reply of the God of life to the historical inevitability of death, to which man was subjected from the moment of breaking the first covenant and which, together with sin, entered his history."[295]

---

[290] General Audience of July 14, 1982, in Ibid., p. 296.
[291] The word *eschatology* is derived from the Greek (ἔσχατος, last) and means the science of the last things. In Catholic theology, individual eschatology considers death, particular judgment, purgatory, heaven, and hell. Collective eschatology deals with the end of the world, the second coming of Christ, the resurrection of the dead, and the general judgment.
[292] This third cycle of nine audiences extends from November 11, 1981, through February 10, 1982.
[293] Mt 22:30.
[294] General Audience of January 27, 1982, in *The Theology of the Body*, p. 250.
[295] Ibid.

B. What Will Heaven Be Like? Similarities and Differences

John Paul II proclaims, "The resurrection constitutes the definitive accomplishment of the redemption of the body."[296] By redeeming our body, the resurrection opens to us the gates of heaven. But what exactly does the final redemption of our body entail? What will heaven be like? St. Paul once was granted an experience of heaven. He could only describe it as "what no eye has seen, nor ear heard, nor the heart of man conceived, what God has prepared for those who love him."[297]

In popular imagery, heaven is often depicted as a place where people recline upon clouds, endlessly stroking the harp. This representation has done much to give heaven a bad name, especially among vigorous young people or those who have retained their youthful spirit at the twilight of a life etched by deep human joys and sorrows. One thing is certain: Christ never speaks this way about heaven in the Gospels. He describes heaven as a banquet — a wedding feast. Those moments of deepest joy and intimate fulfillment in this life are but a fleeting glimpse of the happiness that awaits us when we shall be immersed forever in God's love.

Some things will not change in heaven. Most fundamentally, after the resurrection of the body, each one of us will retain our own personal, human identity in the psychosomatic unity of body and soul.[298] Even Christ continues to possess his human body, with his five wounds still visible, now glorified.[299] The Holy Father explains the teaching of the union of our body and soul in heaven.

> The truth about the resurrection clearly affirmed, in fact, that the eschatological perfection and happiness of man cannot be understood as a state of the soul alone, separated (according to Plato: liberated) from the body. But it must be understood as the state of man definitively and perfectly "integrated" through such a union of the soul and the body, which qualifies and definitively ensures this perfect integrity.[300]

As the years pass in our earthly life, our present material body becomes less and less capable of performing the feats it was once able to accomplish. Twenty-mile hikes, an inviting challenge a few summers back, somehow become transformed into an ominous prospect. Our speed and endurance on the soccer field diminishes, until we eventually find ourselves watching from the sidelines while others play.

---

[296] General Audience of January 27, 1982, in Ibid., p. 252.

[297] 1 Cor 2:9.

[298] The term "psychosomatic" is derived from the Greek ψυχή, meaning "soul," and the Greek σῶμα, meaning "body." It refers to the body-soul unity of our human nature.

[299] Father Richard John Neuhaus ponders this mystery in one chapter from his book *Death on a Friday Afternoon*, titled "The Scars of God."

[300] General Audience of December 2, 1981, in Ibid., p. 240.

Still, as our material body weakens, hastening us towards death, it enables our spirit to grow in beauty and virtue through ever deeper, more purified acts of self-giving love. The physical spending of our present body, like a candle that consumes itself, enriches the life of our soul. Our bodily death can be viewed as a birth to a radically new way of life in eternity, just like an unborn baby must go beyond its embryonic existence within the womb in order to be born into the fullness of earthly life.[301]

Does our body simply prepare our soul for eternal life and then disintegrate into the earth from which we were formed? This cannot be the case, due to our identity as human persons in the unity of body and soul. "The spiritual and immortal soul is the principle of unity of the human being, whereby it exists as a whole — *corpore et anima unus*[302] — as a person."[303] Since our soul is of its very nature ordered to a body and is the form of the body,[304] our body too has been promised the resurrection and will share in the glory of eternal life in heaven.[305] "In fact, *body and soul are inseparable*: in the person, in the willing agent and in the deliberate act *they stand or fall together.*"[306]

Since our soul will be united to our risen, glorified body in heaven, we will remain male or female, just as we have been created by God. What a compelling sign that each person is unique and unrepeatable! We remain so not only in this life, but for all eternity. At the same time, this eschatological reality is a powerful confirmation that being a man and being a woman are each inimitable ways of reflecting the image of God. "The words, 'They neither marry nor are given in marriage' seem to affirm at the same time that human bodies, recovered and at the same time renewed in the resurrection, will keep their masculine or feminine peculiarity."[307]

On the other hand, profound differences will also characterize our life in heaven. Foremost among them is the fact that marriage will no longer exist. "In the resurrection they neither marry nor are given in marriage."[308] It may seem paradoxical that we remain male or female if there is no marriage. This apparent paradox must lead us to conclude that the meaning of being a man or a woman goes beyond marriage and

---

[301] Cf. Mieczysław A. Krąpiec, O.P., *I-Man: An Outline of Philosophical Anthropology* (New Britain, CT: Mariel Publications, 1983), pp. 335-362, especially pp. 360-361.
[302] "One in the unity of body and soul." Second Vatican Ecumenical Council, Pastoral Constitution on the Church in the Modern World *Gaudium et Spes*, 14.
[303] *Veritatis Splendor*, 48.
[304] Cf. Ecumenical Council of Vienne, Constitution *Fidei Catholicae*: DS, 902; Fifth Lateran Ecumenical Council, Bull *Apostolici Regiminis*: DS, 1440.
[305] Cf. *Veritatis Splendor*, 48.
[306] Ibid., 49.
[307] General Audience of December 2, 1981, in *The Theology of the Body*, p. 239.
[308] Mt. 22:30.

procreation. "The sense of being a male or a female in the body will be constituted and understood in that age in a different way from what it had been from the beginning, and then in the whole dimension of earthly existence."[309]

C. A Completely New State of Human Life

Christ's words reveal how profound will be the transformation wrought by our own resurrection to life eternal in heaven. He confirms this great reality in the Book of Revelation. "Behold, I make all things new."[310] John Paul II declares, "The resurrection means not only . . . the re-establishment of human life in its integrity by means of the union of the body and the soul, but also a completely new state of human life itself."[311] Just what does this new state of life entail?

1. Spiritualization of the Body

In the first place, Christ's words, "They are like angels in heaven,"[312] make it possible to deduce "a spiritualization of man according to a different dimension from that of earthly life (and even from that of the beginning itself)."[313] But this spiritualization of the body does not mean we will become pure spirits, identical to angels — otherwise the resurrection of the body would be meaningless. The Gospel context indicates clearly that in heaven we will keep our human nature in the unity of body and soul.

Spiritualization of the body refers rather to the definitive triumph of "life according to the Spirit" over "life according to the flesh" in man. It signifies the restoration of harmony between the spiritual and the physical in us. No more will we experience St. Paul's anguished cry, "I see in my members another law at war with the law of my mind."[314]

> In the resurrection the body will return to perfect unity and harmony with the spirit. Man will no longer experience the opposition between what is spiritual and what is physical in him. Spiritualization means not only that the spirit will dominate the body, but, I would say, that it will fully permeate the body, and that the forces of the spirit will permeate the energies of the body. . . . The resurrection will consist in the participation of all that is physical in man in what is spiritual in him. At the same time it will consist in the perfect realization of what is personal in man.[315]

---

[309] Ibid.
[310] Rv 21:5.
[311] Ibid., p. 238.
[312] Mt 22:30.
[313] Ibid., p. 239.
[314] Rm 7:23.
[315] General Audience of December 9, 1981, in Ibid., p. 241.

2. Divinization of the Body

Not only will our body be spiritualized in heaven, but our entire humanity will also be divinized through direct participation in the inner life of God himself. Christ reveals this aspect about the new state of heavenly life in Luke 20:36, when he proclaims that those judged worthy to attain the resurrection are not only equal to angels, but also "sons of God." In heaven "penetration and permeation of what is essentially human by what is essentially divine will then reach its peak, so that the life of the human spirit will arrive at such fullness which previously had been absolutely inaccessible to it."[316]

3. Face-to-Face Vision of God

The divinization of our body that results from participating directly in God's own life is described by St. Paul as seeing God "face to face." In heaven, we will experience the joy of living in a personal, loving communion with God. But that joy will become even greater, because we will be able to contemplate the communion of love between the three Persons of the Blessed Trinity. "The eschatological communion (*communio*) of man with God, constituted thanks to the love of perfect union, will be nourished by the vision, face to face, of contemplation of that more perfect communion — because it is purely divine — which is the Trinitarian communion of the divine Persons in the unity of the same divinity."[317]

In heaven we will be able to give ourselves completely to God with no hindrance of sin, no passions, egotism, fears, attachments, or lack of generosity to tarnish the fullness of our gift. Yet that complete and absolute "freedom of the gift" does not constitute the most sublime wonder of eternal life. By clinging to the mysteries of the Incarnation and the Eucharist, our hearts gain the courage to ponder what surpasses all we could dare hope for. In heaven God, our Creator and Redeemer, will give himself to us! Christ promises in the Gospel, "Blessed are those servants whom the master finds awake when he comes; truly, I say to you, he will gird himself and have them sit at table, and he will come and serve them."[318] The Holy Father describes God's self-communication to us. "This is the most personal self-giving by God, in his very divinity, to man, to that being who, from the beginning, bears within himself the image and likeness of God."[319]

The experience of God's self-giving to us is beatitude: perfect happiness. "This will constitute the beatifying experience of the gift of himself

---

[316] General Audience of December 9, 1981, in Ibid., p. 242.
[317] General Audience of December 16, 1981, in Ibid., p. 243.
[318] Lk 12:37.
[319] General Audience of December 9, 1981, in Ibid., p. 243.

on God's part, which is absolutely superior to any experience proper to earthly life."[320] Even now, on earth, we experience each day God's constant self-giving to us. The quiet splendor of a sunrise, an act of kindness from someone near us, an insight during prayer are all moments of God's gift of himself. On occasion God may even concede to us an experience of his goodness that is almost overwhelming. Yet these are all mere glimpses of how God will love us in heaven — in utter fullness at each moment, and forever. It is worth any struggle or sacrifice to arrive there! It is worth every silent tear we may shed, every prayer and supplication to ensure that each person whose life has in some way been entrusted to us by God will make it there as well!

4. Communion of Saints

In heaven we will not only live in perfect, beatifying communion with the Trinity, but also in complete unity with all redeemed men and women: the communion of saints. We will all be united through our communion with God. Man will rediscover himself "not only in the depths of his own person, but also in that union which is proper to the world of persons in their psychosomatic constitution. This is certainly a union of communion. . . . For this reason we profess faith in the 'communion of saints' (*communio sanctorum*), and we profess it in organic connection with faith in the resurrection of the dead."[321]

What will it be like to be reunited with our loved ones who have preceded us on our journey back to God? What joy and gratitude will fill us when we encounter all those persons whose hidden prayers and sacrifices have enabled us to discover our vocation in life and remain faithful to it until the end of our earthly pilgrimage? What will be our first words to Mary, our mother? What will we say to St. Ignatius of Loyola or St. Francis of Assisi? We could ask St. Thomas Aquinas how much he loved Christ in the Eucharist in order to be able to write the *Adoro Te Devote*. And since it is heaven, we won't have to wait for his response. We will be able to feel his love for Christ burning within our own hearts.

Heaven! A brief contemplation is motive enough for each of us to repeat with renewed fervor those words the priest pronounces *sotto voce* before receiving Christ in the Eucharist during Mass: "Keep me faithful to your teachings, and never let me be parted from you."

5. Perfection of the Human Subject

Our intimate communion with God and with all of the saints in heaven will bring about our complete fulfillment, our perfection as human subjects. The immediate, overwhelming experience of God's love

---

[320] General Audience of December 16, 1981, in Ibid., p. 244.
[321] Ibid.

will not absorb us until we lose our personal identity, a goal some forms of Eastern mysticism would strive for as an ideal. Rather, that experience of love will lead us to discover our own identity to the full. It is precisely for that love that we have been created and redeemed. The Holy Father ponders this reality.

> This intimacy — with all its subjective intensity — will not absorb man's personal subjectivity, but rather will make it stand out to an incomparably greater and fuller extent.[322] . . . Those who participate in the future world, that is, in perfect communion with the living God, will enjoy a perfectly mature subjectivity.[323]

6. Fulfillment of the Nuptial Meaning of the Body

In heaven the nuptial meaning of the body will be completely fulfilled. Yet at the same time, there will be no marriage. How can we resolve this paradox? The answer lies in the fact that the nuptial significance of the body in its most fundamental aspect reveals our call to live in a communion of persons. The supreme and definitive communion we are called to is with the three Persons of the Blessed Trinity, intimately sharing their very life in heaven. Marriage between a man and a woman is a temporal expression, within history, of the definitive nuptial union of heaven. Then, each of us will be a bride of Christ, the bridegroom, enjoying the eternal happiness of giving ourselves to him in response to God's own gift of himself. John Paul II reflects on the temporal and eternal dimensions of the nuptial meaning of the body.

> The original and fundamental significance of being a body, as well as being, by reason of the body, male and female — that is precisely the nuptial significance — is united with the fact that man is created as a person and called to a life in *communione personarum*.[324] Marriage and procreation in itself do not determine definitively the original and fundamental meaning of being, as a body, male and female. Marriage and procreation merely give a concrete reality to that meaning in the dimensions of history.[325]

So, paradoxically, the definitive realization of the nuptial meaning of the body lies not in earthly marriage, but in virginity. The body's virginity will be fully expressed in heaven because the only adequate response to God's outpouring of love will be to give ourselves entirely to him in all that we are as personal subjects. That is why the exclusive self-giving between husband and wife in marriage, even though it is done for love of God, can no longer exist in heaven. As we give ourselves entirely to God, we will also be giving ourselves to all others in

---

[322] General Audience of December 9, 1981, in Ibid., p. 242.
[323] General Audience of December 16, 1981, in Ibid., p. 244.
[324] The communion of persons.
[325] General Audience of January 13, 1982, in Ibid., p. 247.

him. Thus, John Paul II affirms, "That nuptial meaning of being a body will be realized, therefore, as a meaning that is perfectly personal and communitarian at the same time."[326] So the communion of saints will be the definitive marriage between Christ and his bride, the Church.

In the light of marriage and the nuptial meaning of the body, we can also see the beauty of the call to celibacy, to the virginity of consecrated life. Those consecrated to Christ through poverty, chastity, and obedience make present on earth, in anticipation, that virginal, yet spousal, union with God that each person will live for all eternity in heaven. The Holy Father enables us to catch a glimpse of heaven's glorious reality.

> The reciprocal gift of oneself to God — a gift in which man will concentrate and express all the energies of his own personal and at the same time psychosomatic subjectivity — will be the response to God's gift of himself to man. In this mutual gift of himself by man, a gift which will become completely and definitively beatifying, as a response worthy of a personal subject to God's gift of himself, virginity, or rather the virginal state of the body, will be totally manifested as the eschatological fulfillment of the nuptial meaning of the body, as the specific sign and the authentic expression of all personal subjectivity. In this way, therefore, that eschatological situation in which "They neither marry nor are given in marriage" has its solid foundation in the future state of the personal subject. This will happen when, as a result of the vision of God face to face, there will be born in him a love of such depth and power of concentration on God himself, as to completely absorb his whole psychosomatic subjectivity.[327]

---

[326] Ibid., pp. 247-248.
[327] General Audience of December 16, 1981, in Ibid., p. 244.

SIX

A Total Vision of Man: Three Applications

Preview

I. "Virginity for the Kingdom of Heaven": The Celibate Vocation
   A. The Nature of the Call to Celibacy
   B. The Inner Meaning of Celibacy for the Kingdom
      1. A Charismatic Sign of Our Eternal Destiny
      2. A Decisive Turning Point in Revealing the Meaning of the Body
   C. What Moves Someone To Choose Celibacy?
   D. Celibacy and Marriage
      1. Two Complementary Vocations
         a) How Marriage Sheds Light on Celibacy
         b) How Celibacy for the Kingdom Affirms Marriage
      2. Is the Celibate Vocation Superior?
      3. Only Charity is Supreme
      4. Celibacy and Marriage: Living the Redemption of the Body

Points to look for

1. What are the three states of man John Paul II has reflected upon in order to attain a total vision of who we are as persons?

2. What are the three applications the Holy Father makes of this total vision of man?

3. How do Christ's words in Matthew 19:10-12 show that celibacy is a counsel and not a command?

4. Why is virginity for the sake of the kingdom both voluntary and supernatural?

5. How is celibacy a charismatic sign of our eternal destiny?

6. Why does Christ's call to virginity for the kingdom mark a decisive turning point in revealing the meaning of the body?

7. What moves a person to freely live his entire life in celibacy?

8. Why are celibacy and marriage two complementary vocations and not two opposing ways of life?

9. How does marriage shed light on the inner meaning of celibacy?

10. How does celibacy affirm the vocation of marriage?

11. Is the celibate vocation superior to marriage? In what sense?

12. What is the sole criterion of Christian perfection? How can this be proven?

13. Why does living in an objective state of perfection within a religious institute not necessarily guarantee a higher degree of personal Christian perfection?

14. How do both celibacy and marriage give witness to the redemption of the body?

We have accompanied John Paul II in three cycles of Wednesday audiences from September 1979 to February 1982. The Holy Father has reflected upon the three states of man in order to develop an adequate anthropology, a total vision of who we are as persons. He has contemplated the very origins of man at the dawn of creation, before sin. Next he has pondered our present reality as historical man — tainted by sin, yet redeemed by Christ. Finally, he has considered the destiny to which we are called: to live as eschatological man in intimate, loving communion with the Blessed Trinity forever in heaven.

Now the Holy Father proceeds to make three vital applications of this total vision of the human person. First he contemplates the celibate vocation in light of who man is. Next he considers the vocation to married life. Finally, he reflects upon the nature of married love and fruitfulness. With what magnanimity has John Paul II responded to Paul VI's request in his encyclical *Humanae Vitae* for a total vision of man, so that the Church's teaching on conjugal love and regulating childbirth could be clearly understood!

> In considering the problem of birth regulation, as in the case of every other problem regarding human life, one must look beyond partial perspectives — whether biological or psychological, demographic or sociological — and make one's consideration in light of an integral vision of man and his vocation, not only his natural and earthly vocation, but also his supernatural and eternal one.[328]

I. "Virginity for the Kingdom of Heaven": The Celibate Vocation

John Paul II ponders the nature and inner meaning of the vocation to celibacy by reflecting upon two verses from Chapter 19 of Matthew's Gospel.[329] Christ has just reaffirmed the indissolubility of marriage, proclaiming that to divorce and remarry is to commit adultery. The disciples, aghast, respond in a utilitarian way: "If such is the case of a man with his wife, it is not expedient to marry."[330]

---

[328] Pope Paul VI, Encyclical *Humanae Vitae*, 1968, no. 7.

[329] John Paul II reflected upon the celibate vocation in a series of fourteen general audiences delivered between March 10, 1982, and July 21, 1982.

[330] Mt 19:10.

Christ does not retreat from his position. He knows that the graces of redemption he is about to win through the bitter sufferings of his passion will give men and women the strength to fulfill God's original plan for marriage. Christ replies to the disciples by revealing a completely new and challenging vocation: virginity for the kingdom of heaven. "Not all men can receive this saying, but only those to whom it is given. For there are eunuchs who have been so from birth, and there are eunuchs who have been made eunuchs by men, and there are eunuchs who have made themselves eunuchs for the sake of the kingdom of heaven. He who is able to receive this, let him receive it."[331]

A. The Nature of the Call to Celibacy

Christ's concise words reveal much about the nature of the call to celibacy. It is, first of all, a counsel, not a command. "In the Church's doctrine the conviction exists that these words do not express a command by which all are bound, but a counsel which concerns only some persons — precisely those who are able 'to receive it.'"[332] Since Christ's invitation is a counsel only for some, God has not destined most people to celibacy. It is ". . . a choice that is proper to a rather exceptional vocation, and not one that is universal and ordinary."[333]

A second key aspect of Christ's call to celibacy is that it is both voluntary and supernatural in character. "It is voluntary, because those pertaining to this category 'have made themselves eunuchs,' and it is supernatural, because they have done so 'for the kingdom of heaven.'"[334] The decision to live celibacy must be a mature and free choice. This choice is motivated by love for Christ and a desire to consecrate one's entire life, poor though it may be, to establishing his kingdom.

Finally, Christ's words make no attempt to hide the self-sacrifice implied by virginity for the sake of the kingdom. "Continence means a conscious and voluntary renouncement of that union [between husband and wife] and all that is connected to it in the full meaning of life and human society. The man who renounces matrimony also gives up procreation as the foundation of the family."[335]

B. The Inner Meaning of Celibacy for the Kingdom
1. A Charismatic Sign of Our Eternal Destiny

We have considered three aspects of the nature of celibacy, but what is celibacy's inner meaning? Why did Christ invite some persons to live in perpetual virginity for the sake of the kingdom? Celibacy is, in its es-

---

[331] Mt 19:11-12.
[332] General Audience of March 10, 1982, in Ibid., p. 263.
[333] General Audience of March 31, 1982, in Ibid., p. 271.
[334] General Audience of March 17, 1982, in Ibid., p. 265.
[335] General Audience of April 7, 1982, in Ibid., p. 274.

sence, a charismatic sign of our future life in heaven after the resurrection. There people will no longer marry[336] because God will be "everything to everyone."[337]

In heaven the fullness of the nuptial meaning of our bodies will be revealed in our intimate communion with God, receiving the gift of God himself and giving all that we are to him. Through our communion with God, we will also be united with all persons. John Paul II reflects on how consecrated persons make this future reality, in a certain way, present in our historical, earthly life.

> Such a human being, man and woman, indicates the eschatological virginity of the risen man. In him there will be revealed, I would say, the absolute and eternal nuptial meaning of the glorified body in union with God himself through the "face to face" vision of him, and glorified also through the union of perfect intersubjectivity. This will unite all who participate in the other world, men and women, in the mystery of the communion of saints.

> Earthly continence for the kingdom of heaven is undoubtedly a sign that indicates this truth and this reality. It is a sign that the body, whose end is not the grave, is directed to glorification.[338]

2. A Decisive Turning Point in Revealing the Meaning of the Body

If Christ's proclamation that marriage was indissoluble startled the Apostles, his call to virginity for the kingdom must have shocked them even more. The Apostles' Jewish faith could in no way have prepared them for this new teaching. The Holy Father remarks, "In this environment Christ's words determine a decisive turning point."[339]

Why do Christ's words open a completely new dimension regarding the meaning of the body? "In the tradition of the old covenant, marriage and procreative fruitfulness in the body were a religiously privileged condition."[340] God promised Abraham descendents as numerous as the stars in the sky in reward for his faith. Ever since that time, the Jewish people had looked upon parents' fecundity as a sign of God's favor.

Now Christ reveals a new type of fruitfulness: "the supernatural fruitfulness of the human spirit which comes from the Holy Spirit."[341] Those who sacrifice physical paternity or maternity, by consecrating their lives to Christ, discover that they become spiritual fathers or mothers to countless persons. They share more directly in the work of redemption by following the way of life Christ himself chose to live.

[336] Cf. Mk 12:25.
[337] 1 Cor 15:28.
[338] General Audience of March 24, 1982, in Ibid., p. 267.
[339] General Audience of March 17, 1982, in Ibid., p. 266.
[340] General Audience of March 24, 1982, in Ibid., p. 269.
[341] General Audience of March 24, 1982, in Ibid., p. 270.

"Whoever consciously chooses such continence, chooses, in a certain sense, a special participation in the mystery of the redemption (of the body). He wishes in a particular way to complete it, so to say, in his own flesh (cf. Col 1:24), finding thereby also the imprint of a likeness to Christ."[342]

When the likeness of Christ is born in someone, abundant fruit cannot but result. Virginity for the kingdom yields the most copious of fruits: It wins for countless persons that gift more precious than life itself — the gift of faith — a gift that endures to life eternal. Mary of Nazareth, who is both virgin and mother, is the supreme example of spiritual fruitfulness. "Mary's divine maternity is . . . a superabundant revelation of that fruitfulness in the Holy Spirit to which man submits his spirit when he freely chooses continence in the body, namely, continence for the kingdom of heaven."[343]

C. What Moves Someone to Choose Celibacy?

Persons who freely choose to live their entire life in celibacy feel the attraction of Christ's Kingdom and long to see that kingdom established in all hearts. The Holy Father expresses the force of this kingdom. "The kingdom of heaven is certainly the definitive fulfillment of the aspirations of all men, to whom Christ addressed his message. It is the fullness of the good that the human heart desires beyond the limits of all that can be his lot in this earthly life."[344]

But there is another equally profound motive that impels someone to choose celibacy: the intimate experience of Christ's love. The Psalmist cries out:

I waited patiently for the Lord;
he inclined to me
and heard my cry.[345]

When a person becomes aware that the Lord of the universe, in his infinite majesty, has stooped down to a poor, insignificant creature and given himself with the love of a spouse, that person feels overwhelmed. Father Marcial Maciel converses with God about this experience on his seventy-eighth birthday. "I do not know how much of my life still lies ahead of me, but I do know that You have loved me incomprehensibly, and that Your heart, the heart of a benevolent God, has been an ocean of love for this little created being, imperfect, miserable, and great before Your eyes only because of the love with which You look at him."[346]

---

[342] General Audience of March 31, 1982, in Ibid., p. 271.
[343] General Audience of March 24, 1982, in Ibid., p. 269.
[344] General Audience of April 21, 1982, in Ibid., p. 280.
[345] Psalm 40:1-2.
[346] *Eighty Years in Step with the Church* (Selected Writings and Talks of Father Marcial Maciel, L.C.), (Cheshire, CT: Novitiate and Juniorate of the Legionaries of Christ, 2000), p. 90.

A single response lies open: to give one's entire life to a God who became man so that he could suffer immeasurably in his passion and continue to pour himself out, day after day, in the silent oblation of the Eucharist. John Paul II speaks of the power Christ's self-giving love possesses to transform the human heart.

> It is natural for the human heart to accept demands, even difficult ones, in the name of love for an ideal, and above all in the name of love for a person. (By its very nature, love is directed toward a person.) Therefore in that call to continence for the sake of the kingdom of heaven, first the disciples themselves, and then the whole living Tradition of the Church, will soon discover the love that is referred to Christ himself as the Spouse of the Church, the Spouse of souls. He has given himself to them to the very limit, in the paschal and Eucharistic mystery.

> In this way, continence for the sake of the kingdom of heaven, the choice of virginity or celibacy for one's whole life, has become in the experience of Christ's disciples and followers the act of a particular response of love for the divine Spouse. Therefore it has acquired the significance of an act of nuptial love, that is, a nuptial giving of oneself for the purpose of reciprocating in a particular way that nuptial love of the Redeemer. It is a giving of oneself understood as renunciation, but made above all out of love."[347]

D. Celibacy and Marriage
1. Two Complementary Vocations

We have begun to catch a glimpse of some startling similarities between marriage and virginity for the kingdom. In fact, these two apparently disparate vocations are closely intertwined. Each one complements and illuminates the other. "On the strength of Christ's words it can be asserted that marriage helps us to understand continence for the kingdom of heaven. Not only that, but also continence itself sheds a particular light on marriage viewed in the mystery of creation and redemption."[348]

> Marriage and continence are neither opposed to each other, nor do they divide the human (and Christian) community into two camps (let us say, those who are "perfect" because of continence and those who are "imperfect" or "less perfect" because of the reality of married life). But as it is often said, these two basic situations, these two "states," in a certain sense explain and complete each other as regards the existence and Christian life of this community.[349]

---

[347] General Audience of April 28, 1982, in *The Theology of the Body*, pp. 281-282.
[348] General Audience of March 31, 1982, in Ibid., p. 272.
[349] General Audience of April 14, 1982, in Ibid., p. 276.

a) How Marriage Sheds Light on Celibacy

Just how does marriage help reveal more clearly the nature of the call to celibacy? The nuptial meaning of the human body, created by God as male and female, enables husband and wife to make a mutual gift of themselves in conjugal love. In their masculinity and femininity, they exist "for" one another. This same nuptial meaning of the body allows celibate persons to renounce the exclusive gift of themselves to a spouse and give themselves entirely to Christ. The "for" each other of husband and wife becomes virginity "for" the kingdom. Just as true conjugal love must be total, faithful, and fruitful by its very nature, so must consecration to Christ in virginity. The physical parenthood of married love points to the spiritual paternity or maternity that results from an authentic living of consecrated celibacy.

> Conjugal love which finds its expression in continence for the kingdom of heaven must lead in its normal development to paternity or maternity in a spiritual sense (in other words, precisely to that fruitfulness of the Holy Spirit we have already spoken about), in a way analogous to conjugal love, which matures in physical paternity and maternity, and in this way confirms itself as conjugal love.[350]

b) How Celibacy for the Kingdom Affirms Marriage

While married love helps reveal the inner nature of virginity for the kingdom, celibacy in turn affirms and sheds light on the vocation of marriage. Those who renounce married life through celibacy do so in full and conscious awareness of the value of conjugal love, to which human persons are ordered by being created male and female. "In order for man to be fully aware of what he is choosing (continence for the sake of the kingdom), he must also be fully aware of what he is renouncing."[351] Even though it may seem a paradox, those who freely choose consecrated virginity enable men and women to perceive more clearly the resplendent beauty of marriage. John Paul II hastens to add, "It is known that many statements in the Gospel are paradoxical, and those are often the most eloquent and profound."[352]

The enduring, spiritual fruitfulness of celibacy also points to the culmination that the physical parenthood of marriage is meant to attain. Being a parent implies above all the education and care of each new child brought into the world. Children's spiritual formation, a task that will shape their eternal destiny, rests first and foremost in their parents' hands. The Holy Father comments on this aspect of marriage, one that is brought more clearly to light by the celibate vocation. "For its part,

---

[350] General Audience of April 14, 1982, in Ibid., p. 278.
[351] General Audience of May 5, 1982, in Ibid., p. 285.
[352] Ibid.

physical procreation also fully responds to its meaning only if it is completed by paternity and maternity in the spirit, whose expression and fruit is all the educative work of the parents in regard to the children born of their conjugal corporeal union."[353]

2. Is the Celibate Vocation Superior?

We have seen that celibacy for the kingdom and marriage are two complementary vocations which mutually affirm one another. Still, the question has often been raised, "Is the celibate vocation superior to marriage?" Clearly, the first answer to be given is that for each person the specific vocation God has called him or her to is absolutely superior — the only one to be chosen, the path to holiness, joy, and complete fulfillment in life. Every vocation is a gift from God, a call of love. Since the Lord is faithful to his promises, he always gives the graces needed to follow that call. The Holy Father reflects on St. Paul's beautiful words about the gift from God.

> "I wish that all were as I myself am. But each has his own special gift from God, one of one kind and one of another" (1 Cor 7:7). . . . The gift received by persons who live in marriage is different from the one received by persons who live in virginity and choose continence for the sake of the kingdom of God. All the same, it is a true gift from God, one's own gift, intended for concrete persons. It is specific, that is, suited to their vocation in life.[354]

For each person the only thing that matters is to discover and pursue the vocation God has prepared with love from all eternity. Yet, it can still be asked whether one type of vocation is superior on the objective plane. Here the reply must be that celibacy for the kingdom is objectively superior to marriage. But this does not mean continence is in itself more perfect than conjugal love, or that there is anything impure in the one flesh union of husband and wife. No shades of Manichaeism can be found either in the words of St. Paul or the Church's Magisterium developed by John Paul II.[355]

Celibacy is objectively superior, not due to continence itself, but precisely because it is lived *for the kingdom.* Celibacy must be valued within the context of the three evangelical counsels: poverty, chastity, and obedience. Christ reveals in the Gospels that the counsels are a way to perfection when he invites the rich young man to sell everything and fol-

---

[353] General Audience of April 14, 1982, in Ibid., p. 278.

[354] General Audience of July 7, 1982, in Ibid., p. 295.

[355] Manichaeism was a complex, dualistic Eastern religion, essentially Gnostic in character. Its founder, Mani, was born in 214 A.D. A central tenet of Manichaeism was the dualistic opposition between the uncreated principles of Good-Evil, Light-Darkness. The material world was considered by Manichaeism to be evil, in opposition to the spiritual. Thus, the human body and acts of human sexuality were looked upon as evil. St. Augustine was influenced by Manichaeism in the period leading up to his conversion. As bishop, the saint became a firm adversary of the Gnostic sect, strongly condemning its errors.

low him, "If you would be perfect. . . ."[356] The Holy Father notes that this is why a certain theological tradition speaks of consecrated life through the counsels as a state of perfection (*status perfectionis*).[357]

Indeed, Christ himself, who is both God and man, chose to live the evangelical counsels during his earthly life. John Paul II reflects on the implications of this reality in his apostolic exhortation *Vita Consecrata* (*Consecrated Life*).

> His [Christ's] way of living in chastity, poverty and obedience appears as the most radical way of living the Gospel on this earth, a way which may be called *divine*, for it was embraced by him, God and man, as the expression of his relationship as the Only-Begotten Son with the Father and with the Holy Spirit. This is why Christian tradition has always spoken of the *objective superiority of the consecrated life*.[358]

3. Only Charity is Supreme

Reflecting upon consecrated celibacy as a state of perfection leads us to the one criterion that is the measure of every Christian life — the only one that finally may be called supreme. For what is the sole measure of all Christian perfection? *Charity.* St. Paul exclaims: "If I speak in the tongues of men and of angels, but have not love, I am a noisy gong or a clanging cymbal. And if I have prophetic powers, and understand all mysteries and all knowledge, and if I have all faith, so as to remove mountains, but have not love, I am nothing. If I give away all I have, and if I deliver my body to be burned, but have not love, I gain nothing."[359]

Father Marcial Maciel observes that charity is the very core of Christianity. "To speak about charity means to speak about the center, essence, and supreme perfection of all Christian life. Because all of Christ's teaching on how we must lead our life in this world is distilled in the practice of charity. . . . Furthermore, I do not believe that there can be true holiness, true piety, true union with God, or genuine apostolic zeal in someone who doesn't practice charity."[360]

After affirming the objective superiority of consecrated celibacy as a state of perfection, John Paul II is quick to add that those persons truly attain Christian perfection who excel in the practice of charity. While the counsels naturally help one to grow in Christian love, it is not infrequently the case that Christians who live in the "world" practice a more heroic charity than consecrated men and women. Wherever love

---

[356] Mt 19:21.
[357] General Audience of April 14, 1982, in *The Theology of the Body*, p. 277.
[358] John Paul II, Post-Synodal Apostolic Exhortation *Vita Consecrata* (March 25, 1996), 18.
[359] 1 Cor 13:1-3.
[360] Father Marcial Maciel, LC, "Gospel Charity" (Hamden, CT: CIF, 1994), pp. 5-7.

abounds, the spirit of the counsels is being lived, and Christian perfection is being conquered.

> Perfection of the Christian life . . . is measured with the rule of charity. It follows that a person who does not live in the state of perfection (that is, in an institute that bases its life plan on vows of poverty, chastity, and obedience), or in other words, who does not live in a religious institute but in the "world," can *de facto* reach a superior degree of perfection — whose measure is charity — in comparison to the person who lives in the state of perfection with a lesser degree of charity. In any case, the evangelical counsels undoubtedly help us to achieve a fuller charity. Therefore, whoever achieves it, even if he does not live in an institutionalized state of perfection, reaches that perfection which flows from charity, through fidelity to the spirit of those counsels. Such perfection is possible and accessible to every person, both in a religious institute and in the "world."[361]

4. Celibacy and Marriage:
Living the Redemption of the Body

Both the faithful living of consecrated virginity for the sake of the kingdom and the daily living for one another of husband and wife are eloquent testimony of that great victory Christ has won for us: the redemption of our bodies. Only through grace's transforming power is it possible to achieve this continuous triumph of self-giving love over sin, over selfishness and egotism. To conquer anew each day, in the midst of struggles and opposition, the freedom of the gift offers renewed hope of the final victory humanity longs for: victory over death to be with God forever. John Paul II speaks of this reality. "The hope of every day manifests its power in human works and even in the very movements of the human heart, clearing a path, in a certain sense, for the great eschatological hope bound with the redemption of the body."[362]

---

[361] General Audience of April 14, 1982, in *The Theology of the Body*, p. 277.
[362] General Audience of July 21, 1982, in Ibid., p. 301.

Preview

Six A Total Vision of Man: Three Applications *(continued)*

I. "Virginity for the Kingdom of Heaven": The Celibate Vocation

II. "As Christ Loves the Church": The Vocation to Married Life
    A. Analogy and Mystery: To Glimpse the Transcendent
    B. Sacrament: the Hidden Mystery Made Visible
        1. From the Mystery of Creation and Redemption to the Seven Sacraments:
           A Fundamental Analogy
        2. The Keystone of Ephesians 5

Points to look for

1. What is an analogy?

2. What is a mystery?

3. Why are both analogy and mystery vitally important in coming to grips with the meaning of human existence?

4. What is the most striking characteristic of God's love for his people?

5. What is a sacrament in the restricted, theologically technical sense of the term?

6. What is the broader, Biblical and patristic notion of sacrament?

7. Why does John Paul II call marriage the "primordial sacrament"?

8. In what sense is the Church itself a sacrament?

9. What is the "hidden mystery" of God's plan that St. Paul speaks of in Ephesians 1?

10. How does the analogy of marriage help us to understand more deeply the mystery of Christ's redemptive love?

11. What does John Paul II declare to be the keystone of Ephesians 5? Why?

II. "As Christ Loves the Church": The Vocation to Married Life

Patiently and firmly, in a series of Wednesday general audiences spanning more than two and a half years, John Paul II advanced toward his goal. He sketched a total vision of the human person created in the image of God and redeemed by Christ from the power of sin and death. The Holy Father unfolded the nuptial meaning of the human body: the call to love as God loves, written in our very being. Upon this foundation, in a fifth cycle of audiences on the sacramentality of marriage, the Pope revealed how the sacrament of matrimony penetrates into the very heart of the mystery of creation and redemption.[363] St. Paul describes with reverent awe this great mystery of our being created and redeemed — God's eternal plan for us — in Chapter One of his Letter to the Ephesians.

---

[363] The series of twenty-two general audiences on the sacramentality of marriage extends from July 28, 1982 through February 9, 1983.

> Blessed be the God and Father of our Lord Jesus Christ, who has blessed us in Christ with every spiritual blessing in the heavenly places, even as he chose us in him before the foundation of the world, that we should be holy and blameless before him. He destined us in love to be his sons through Jesus Christ, according to the purpose of his will, to the praise of his glorious grace which he freely bestowed on us in the Beloved. In him we have redemption through his blood, the forgiveness of our trespasses, according to the riches of his grace which he lavished upon us. For he has made known to us in all wisdom and insight the mystery of his will, according to his purpose which he set forth in Christ as a plan for the fullness of time, to unite all things in him, things in heaven and things on earth (Eph 1:3-10).

In a profound meditation on Chapter Five of this same Letter to the Ephesians, John Paul II affirms that marriage, at its deepest level, is an embodiment of this very mystery of creation and redemption. It signifies nothing less than God's eternal plan of salvation for mankind. "That mystery, as God's salvific plan in regard to humanity, is in a certain sense the theme of all revelation, its central reality."[364] Let us ponder St. Paul's text along with the Holy Father.

> Be subject to one another out of reverence for Christ. Wives, be subject to your husbands, as to the Lord. For the husband is the head of the wife as Christ is the head of the Church, his body, and is himself its Savior. As the Church is subject to Christ, so let wives also be subject in everything to their husbands. Husbands, love your wives, as Christ loved the Church and gave himself up for her, that he might sanctify her, having cleansed her by the washing of water with the word, that he might present the Church to himself in splendor, without spot or wrinkle or any such thing, that she might be holy and without blemish. Even so husbands should love their wives as their own bodies. He who loves his wife loves himself. For no man ever hates his own flesh, but nourishes and cherishes it, as Christ does the Church, because we are members of his body. "For this reason a man shall leave his father and mother and be joined to his wife, and the two shall become one flesh." This mystery is a great one, and I am saying that it refers to Christ and the Church; however, let each one of you love his wife as himself, and let the wife see that she respects her husband (Eph 5:21-33).

A. Analogy and Mystery: To Glimpse the Transcendent

John Paul II deftly unfolds the fundamental analogy expressed within these verses: The union between husband and wife embodies God's salvific love for mankind, a love that reaches its supreme fulfillment in Christ's spousal union with his body, the Church. In order to ac-

---

[364] General Audience of September 8, 1982, in *The Theology of the Body*, p. 322.

company the Holy Father to the summit of his reflections, we must pause for a moment and look more closely at two crucial concepts: analogy and mystery. Both are vitally important in coming to grips with the meaning of our earthly existence.

Just what is an analogy and what is it good for? Fundamentally, it is a comparison between realities that are in some way similar and in other ways diverse. A term that contains several different levels of meaning, all of which share something in common, is analogous. The Greek word *analogía* (ἀναλογία) means "proportion." In an analogy a certain quality or perfection is applied to two or more subjects in a way that is proportional: "partly the same, partly different."[365]

One of the most important analogies in philosophy is the analogy of being (*analogia entis*). Stones, lions, humans, and angels are all beings — they all exist. So all of them have *being* in common. Yet at the same time, their *manner* of being is different. They exist in different ways. Lions, humans, and angels are all living beings, while stones are not. Humans are both physical and spiritual, while angels are strictly spiritual beings.

Analogies are vital in striving to grasp the meaning of our existence, since human life in many aspects remains a mystery to us. Life is often a mystery because it comes from the One whose existence infinitely surpasses us: God himself. A mystery is a hidden reality or secret. It is a truth that exceeds human comprehension. Mysteries are not irrational, that is, dark and obscure. On the contrary, they transcend our limited human reason. They are so resplendent with light that they blind our eyes, preventing us from gazing directly upon them.

Analogies enable us to catch at least a glimpse of the mysteries that enfold our life. By offering a comparison between what we do understand and the transcendent, analogies allow us to grasp at least a portion of what remains a mystery. They make it possible to understand the mystery in a real, though limited way. Pope Leo XIII has described the dogma of the Trinity as "the greatest of all mysteries, since it is the foundation and origin of all."[366]

Every human person is, in a true sense, a mystery. When we reveal clearly to someone we trust what we think and feel, we are opening to them a hint of the mystery of our being. In the same way, if God wishes to reveal himself to mankind and draw us into his friendship, he must share with us his own inner mystery. John Paul II affirms that the fundamental analogy through which God reveals the hidden secrets of his mystery is found in Chapter Five of the Letter to the Ephesians.

---

[365] *Summa Theologiae*, I, q 13, a 5, c.
[366] Leo XIII, *Divinum illud munus*, ActSSed 29 (1897), 645.

"God is love."[367] The pure, self-giving love with which the three Persons of the Blessed Trinity love one another is also poured upon humanity. Christ tells his apostles at the Last Supper, "As the Father has loved me, so have I loved you, abide in my love."[368] How can the mystery of this love be described? God's love for his people is *spousal*. It is the love of a bridegroom who gives himself up for his bride. The hidden mystery of God's love was first made visible at the dawn of creation, in the primordial marriage of Adam and Eve.

If a single word had to be used to characterize God's spousal love, that word would be *fidelity*. God remains a faithful spouse, even when his bride turns away from him through sin. The prophets never tire of proclaiming Yahweh's *hesed*, his steadfast love, in spite of the infidelity of his chosen people, Israel. Though Israel makes herself a harlot by worshipping false gods, Yahweh is prepared to take her back. The Fourth Eucharistic Prayer of the *Roman Missal* exalts God's steadfast love, "Again and again you offered a covenant to man, and through the prophets taught him to hope for salvation."

In the face of mankind's sin, God's faithful love becomes *mercy*. God the Father is so "rich in mercy"[369] that he sent his only begotten Son. Christ restored us to life when we were dead through our sins by giving himself up as a bridegroom for his bride, the Church. Christ's spousal union with his Church, his redemptive sacrifice for her on Calvary, is the source of the Church's very sacramentality. All of the graces that flow from the seven sacraments pour out of the pierced side of Christ.

Now it becomes clear why John Paul II declares, "[T]he visible sign of marriage 'in the beginning,' inasmuch as it is linked to the visible sign of Christ and the Church . . . transfers the eternal plan of love into the 'historical' dimension and makes it the foundation of the whole sacramental order."[370] The marriage between Adam and Eve marks the first time that God's invisible love is visibly manifested as a loving communion of persons. This invisible love of God is now made visible each time the sacraments are celebrated. But the spousal union of Christ with the Church that marriage embodies, his redemptive sacrifice for her, is the source of all the sacraments. So marriage can be looked upon, in a way, as a first or foundational sacrament. The Holy Father goes on to add, "In a certain sense all the sacraments of the new covenant find their prototype in marriage as the primordial sacrament."[371]

---

[367] 1 Jn 4:8.
[368] Jn 15:9.
[369] Eph 2:4.
[370] General Audience of September 29, 1982, in *Theology of the Body*, pp. 332-333.
[371] General Audience of October 20, 1982, in Ibid., p. 339.

B. Sacrament: The Hidden Mystery Made Visible

To grasp more fully the depth and beauty of John Paul II's teaching, we must pause for a moment and ask ourselves what is meant by "sacrament." This term is profoundly analogous. The Holy Father employs several different levels of meaning contained within the word "sacrament." First, there is the restricted, theologically technical use of "sacrament" as referring to the seven sacraments of the Church. The *Catechism* provides a strict definition: "The sacraments are efficacious signs of grace, instituted by Christ and entrusted to the Church, by which divine life is dispensed to us."[372] This definition reveals the common meaning that underlies the various analogous uses of "sacrament." A sacrament is always a visible sign of an invisible mystery. But it is not just an ordinary sign, one that simply points to the hidden reality. It is an *efficacious* sign: It not only reveals, but also makes present the mystery it signifies.[373]

The seven sacraments confer grace through the liturgical rite by which they are celebrated.[374] The liturgical action consists of two elements: the *form*, or words spoken, and the specific *matter* of the sacrament. The Holy Father states, "In this sense each of the seven sacraments of the Church is characterized by a determinate liturgical action, made up of words (the form) and the specific sacramental 'matter.' This is according to the widespread hylomorphic theory deriving from Thomas Aquinas and the whole scholastic tradition."[375] In the concrete case of the Eucharist, the form consists of the words of consecration, spoken by the priest. The bread and wine are the matter of the sacrament.

1. From the Mystery of Creation and Redemption to the Seven Sacraments: A Fundamental Analogy

The Holy Father begins to focus upon the specific meaning of "sacrament" as one of the seven efficacious signs of grace only in the second

---

[372] *CCC*, 1131.

[373] John Paul II teaches, "The sacrament consists in the 'manifesting' of that mystery in a sign which serves not only to proclaim the mystery, but also to accomplish it in man. The sacrament is a visible and efficacious sign of grace. Through it, that mystery hidden from eternity in God is accomplished in man, that mystery which Ephesians speaks of at the very beginning" (cf. Eph 1:9). (General Audience of September 8, 1982, in *Theology of the Body*, p. 323.)

[374] "The visible rites by which the sacraments are celebrated signify and make present the graces proper to each sacrament" (*CCC*, 1131).

[375] General Audience of October 20, 1982, in *Theology of the Body*, p. 341. The term "hylomorphic" comes from the Greek words ὕλη (matter) and μορφή (form). The Aristotelian-Thomistic hylomorphic theory asserts that all physical bodies are composed of two essential principles: matter and form. Since matter and form are principles of being within objects, and not concrete, existing beings, such as a tree or a person, they can never be seen or experienced in any way. Still, they must necessarily be real, because certain facts of experience cannot be explained without them. An example is the fact of different individuals within a species. Lassie and Old Yeller are both dogs because they possess the same form. Yet they are distinct, individual dogs since they have different matter.

part of his audiences on the sacramentality of marriage. First he lays the foundations of the whole sacramental order by developing the broader Biblical and patristic meaning of "sacrament." Here the Latin *sacramentum* (sacrament) is identical with the Greek *mystérion* (mystery). It refers to the invisible mystery of God himself, hidden from all eternity, but made visible through creation. Since creation makes visible the hidden mystery of God pondered by St. Paul in Chapter One of the Letter to the Ephesians, John Paul II declares that we can speak of the "sacrament of creation" in an analogous sense.

> In relationship to this rather restricted meaning, we have used in our considerations a wider and perhaps also more ancient and fundamental meaning of the term "sacrament." Ephesians, especially 5:21-33, seems in a particular way to authorize us to do so. Here sacrament signifies the very mystery of God, which is hidden from eternity; however, not in an eternal concealment, but above all, in its very revelation and actuation (furthermore, in its revelation through its actuation).[376]

Within the sacrament of creation, marriage between Adam and Eve emerges as the *primordial sacrament*. It is instituted by God in the very beginning. The one-flesh union of our first parents is an image of the self-giving love of the three persons of the Blessed Trinity. It was meant by God to pass on original grace, supernatural life, to future generations of mankind — until sin intervened.

The hidden mystery of God's plan is restored and brought to fulfillment in the "sacrament of redemption," mankind's salvation won by Christ. "Redemption signifies, as it were, a 'new creation.'"[377] Just what is the great hidden mystery that is brought to completion? John Paul II responds, "It is the mystery of God's call of man in Christ to holiness, and the mystery of his predestination to become his adopted son."[378] St. Paul expresses this mystery of creation and redemption in tones of awed wonder:

> Blessed be the God and Father of our Lord Jesus Christ, who has blessed us in Christ with every spiritual blessing in the heavenly places, even as he chose us in him before the foundation of the world, that we should be holy and blameless before him. He destined us in love to be his sons through Jesus Christ, according to the purpose of his will, to the praise of his glorious grace which he freely bestowed on us in the Beloved (Eph 1:3-6).

We have seen that creation and redemption are sacraments in the broadest, analogical meaning of the term: making visible God's hidden

---

[376] General Audience of October 20, 1982, in Ibid., p. 341.
[377] General Audience of October 27, 1982, in Ibid., p. 344.
[378] General Audience of September 8, 1982, in Ibid., p. 323.

mystery. Christ's redemptive act, which is at the same time his act of spousal union with the Church, is the source of the Church's sacramentality — that is, of the seven sacraments in the strict sense. So the Church herself can also be considered a sacrament in an intermediate, analogical way. The Second Vatican Council's Dogmatic Constitution on the Church *Lumen Gentium* confirms this teaching. "The Church is in Christ in the nature of a sacrament — a sign and instrument, that is, of communion with God and of unity among all men" (*LG*, 1).

John Paul II clarifies the meaning of this passage. "This text of Vatican II does not say: 'The Church is a sacrament,' but 'It is in the nature of a sacrament.' Thereby it indicates that one must speak of the sacramentality of the Church in a manner that is analogical and not identical in regard to what we mean when we speak of the seven sacraments administered by the Church by Christ's institution."[379]

In his general audience of October 20, 1982, the Holy Father presents a compact summary of his reflections on the "great mystery" of Christ's union with the Church. It is a spousal union that reflects God's eternal, steadfast love for mankind. Every Christian marriage is a living reflection of this love.

> In this sense we spoke also of the sacrament of creation and of the sacrament of redemption. On the basis of the sacrament of creation, one must understand the original sacramentality of marriage (the primordial sacrament). Following upon this, on the basis of the sacrament of redemption one can understand the sacramentality of the Church, or rather the sacramentality of the union of Christ with the Church. The author of Ephesians presents this under the simile of marriage, the conjugal union of husband and wife.[380]

2. The Keystone of Ephesians 5

In Chapter Five of Ephesians, St. Paul quotes Genesis 2:24. He does so in order to link the one flesh union of Adam and Eve to Christ's union with the Church. "'For this reason a man shall leave his father and mother and be joined to his wife, and the two shall become one.' This is a great mystery, and I mean it in reference to Christ and the Church."[381] John Paul II affirms, "This is the most important point of the whole text, in a certain sense, the keystone."[382]

By linking Adam and Eve's marital union to Christ, St. Paul reveals the unchanging fidelity of God's love for mankind. From the very be-

---

[379] General Audience of September 8, 1982, in Ibid., p. 323.
[380] General Audience of October 20, 1982, in Ibid., p. 342.
[381] Eph 5:31-32.
[382] General Audience of September 8, 1982, in Ibid., p. 321.

ginning God has loved humanity as a husband loves his wife. Christ has brought this love to a fulfillment surpassing all hopes, giving himself up to ransom his unfaithful bride and restore her to himself. St. Paul shows how God's salvific plan "unites marriage, as the most ancient revelation (manifestation) of the plan in the created world, with the definitive revelation and manifestation — the revelation that 'Christ loved the Church and gave himself up for her' (Eph 5:25), conferring on his redemptive love a spousal character and meaning."[383]

What does the revelation of God's love as spousal unveil to us about its inner depths? Essentially, it allows us to perceive that God's love is self-giving. He who created the earth and the heavens with all their array, he who is worshipped day and night by hosts of angels in his resplendent holiness, this same God gives himself in love to his poor creatures — to each one of us.

> The analogy of spousal love seems to emphasize especially the aspect of the gift of self on the part of God to man, "for ages" chosen in Christ. . . . It is a total (or rather radical) and irrevocable gift in its essential character, that is, as a gift. . . . In a certain sense, it is all that God could give of himself to man, considering the limited faculties of man, a creature.[384]

---

[383] General Audience of September 8, 1982, in Ibid., pp. 321-322.
[384] General Audience of September 29, 1982, in Ibid., p. 331.

Preview
SIX A TOTAL VISION OF MAN: THREE APPLICATIONS *(continued)*

I. "Virginity for the Kingdom of Heaven": The Celibate Vocation
II. "As Christ Loves the Church": The Vocation to Married Life *(continued)*
   C. A Twofold Analogy: Understanding Marriage Itself
      1. "Out of Reverence for Christ"
      2. A Sacrament of Hope
      3. Marriage as a Sacrament: The Conjugal Union of Husband and Wife
         a) "I take you as my wife. . . . I take you as my husband":
            The Matter and Form of Marriage
         b) "Living in the Truth": The Language of the Body
         c) Speaking the Language of the Body in Truth: To Create a Culture of Life

Points to look for
1. What is the true meaning of St. Paul's exhortation, "Wives, be subject to your husbands"?

2. What is the meaning of St. Paul's phrase, "out of reverence for Christ," in the mutual subjection of married love?

3. How is the analogy in Ephesians 5 twofold?

4. How does Ephesians 5 enable us to understand the depths of Christian marriage?

5. What does the Holy Father say is the test and the measure of true love?

6. What is the twofold hope offered by marriage?

7. Why does this hope extend not just to husband and wife, but to all mankind?

8. What are the form and the matter of the sacrament of Matrimony?

9. What is the language of the body?

10. Is the body itself the author of its own language?

11. In what sense is the human person the author of the language of the body?

12. In what sense is God, the Creator, the author of the language of the body?

13. What does it mean to "reread the language of the body in truth"?

14. What does it mean to tell a lie with the body?

15. Why is it essential for the sacrament of Matrimony that husband and wife speak the language of the body *in truth* in their conjugal union?

16. Why is contraception "telling a lie with the body"?

17. What is the effect of contraception on marriage?

18. By speaking the language of the body in truth in their conjugal union, how do husband and wife help create a culture of life?

C. A Twofold Analogy: Understanding Marriage Itself

Up to the present we have seen how the reality of marriage helps us grasp more deeply the mystery of Christ's redemptive love. But the analogy of Ephesians 5 is twofold. It works in opposite directions. Christ's spousal union with his Church also enables us to perceive under a new light the most profound meaning of marriage itself. John Paul II elaborates this point.

> As we can see, the analogy operates in two directions. On the one hand, it helps us to understand better the essence of the relationship between Christ and the Church. On the other, at the same time, it helps us to see more deeply into the essence of marriage to which Christians are called. In a certain sense, the analogy shows the way in which this marriage, in its deepest essence, emerges from the mystery of God's eternal love for man and for humanity. It emerges from that salvific mystery which is fulfilled in time through the spousal love of Christ for the Church.[385]

1. "Out of Reverence for Christ"

St. Paul begins his reflections on marriage with a tenet that is often considered controversial today. "Wives, be subject to your husbands, as to the Lord. For the husband is the head of the wife as Christ is the head

---

[385] General Audience of August 18, 1982, in *The Theology of the Body*, p. 313.

of the Church, his body, and is himself its Savior. As the Church is subject to Christ, so let wives also be subject in everything to their husbands."[386] Some would have us believe that this particular teaching of St. Paul is culturally conditioned, reflecting the prevailing domination of men over women in his society.

Such a reading of the Apostle's words would be quite superficial. It fails to perceive the profound beauty or grasp the depths of meaning in Christian marriage. Just what does St. Paul urge when he says a wife should be subject to her husband? His very next sentence clarifies what he intends. "Husbands, love your wives, as Christ loved the Church and gave himself up for her."[387]

For the Church, being subject to Christ means above all experiencing Christ's redeeming love. It is a love that transforms and makes holy her members, a love that washes their feet and sweats tears of blood for them, a love that seeks only their good without the slightest trace of self-interest. So when St. Paul exhorts wives to be subject to their husbands, he is actually encouraging them to experience their husbands' love for them. The Holy Father stresses this crucial interpretation of the Apostle's words.

> The husband is above all, *he who loves* and the wife, on the other hand, is *she who is loved.* One could even hazard the idea that the wife's submission to her husband, understood in the context of the entire passage of Ephesians (5:21-33), signifies above all the "experiencing of love." This is all the more so since this submission is related to the image of the submission of the Church to Christ, which certainly consists in experiencing his love.[388]

The words with which St. Paul begins his teaching on marriage further clarify the meaning of the above passage: "Be subject to one another out of reverence for Christ."[389] Husband and wife are to discover Christ in each other, loving and serving the Lord in the person of their spouse. So when St. Paul exhorts wives to be subject to their husbands, he "does not intend to say that the husband is the lord of the wife and that the interpersonal pact proper to marriage is a pact of domination of the husband over the wife."[390] Instead, both husband and wife are subject to one another in the mutual self-donation that is love.

> Love makes the husband simultaneously subject to the wife, and thereby subject to the Lord himself, just as the wife to the husband. The community or unity which they should establish through mar-

---

[386] Eph 5:22-24.
[387] Eph 5:25.
[388] General Audience of September 1, 1982, in Ibid., p. 320.
[389] Eph 5:21.
[390] General Audience of August 11, 1982, in Ibid., p. 310.

riage is constituted by the reciprocal donation of self, which is also a mutual subjection. Christ is the source and at the same time the model of that subjection, which, being reciprocal "out of reverence for Christ," confers on the conjugal union a profound and mature character.[391]

In fact, the Holy Father goes so far as to say that the husband's self-donation to his wife with a complete absence of self-interest is the test of his love for her. True, disinterested love seeks only the good of the person loved. It longs to discover all the good that is there, and even creates goodness in the one loved. How many young men was St. John Bosco able to rescue from the streets and a future life of crime, transforming them into heroic Christians, because of his selfless love for them? "That good which he who loves creates, through his love, in the one that is loved, is like a test of that same love and its measure."[392]

Now we can see more clearly the hidden depths that are concealed within the sacrament of marriage. Far transcending a mere human love between a man and a woman, sacramental marriage embodies and makes present the very love of Christ for his Church. Christian marriage lives up to its name only when the self-giving love of Christ is present and active between the spouses.

> Marriage corresponds to the vocation of Christians only when it reflects the love which Christ the Bridegroom gives to the Church his Bride, and which the Church (resembling the "subject" wife, that is, completely given) attempts to return to Christ. This is redeeming love, love as salvation, the love with which man from eternity has been loved by God in Christ: ". . . even as he chose us in him before the foundation of the world, that we should be holy and blameless before him. . . ." (Eph. 1:4).[393]

2. A Sacrament of Hope

Marriage, renewed and constituted as one of the seven sacraments of the Church by Christ, has become a luminous sacrament of hope. The hope that radiates from Christian marriage for all mankind emerges from the redemption of the body and its transforming power. "According to Christ's words (cf. Mt 19:4), marriage is a sacrament from the very beginning. At the same time, on the basis of man's historic sinfulness, it is a sacrament arising from the mystery of the redemption of the body."[394]

The hope offered by the sacrament of Matrimony is twofold. First of all, marriage holds out the possibility of overcoming sinfulness in this

---

[391] Ibid.
[392] General Audience of September 1, 1982, in Ibid., p. 319.
[393] General Audience of August 18, 1982, in Ibid., p. 312.
[394] General Audience of November 24, 1982, in Ibid., p. 347.

life. The gift of the Holy Spirit, won for us by Christ's redemption, enables husband and wife to triumph over selfishness and give themselves in freedom to one another. This temporal hope of defeating sin through self-giving love leads to a second hope — one for the life to come. Marriage opens the eschatological hope of experiencing Christ's own gift of himself forever in heaven.

> As much as concupiscence darkens the horizon of the inward vision and deprives the heart of the clarity of desires and aspirations, so much does "life according to the Spirit" (that is, the grace of the sacrament of marriage) permit man and woman to find again the true freedom of the gift, united to the awareness of the spousal meaning of the body in its masculinity and femininity.[395]

The hope offered by marriage, renewed and redeemed by Christ, is a free gift. But it is also a hope that must be conquered. Day by day husband and wife strive to mold their personalities to one another, anticipate each other's needs, strengthen and console one another in the wonderful task of being a parent. As they do so, they attain the holiness that the sacrament imparts. "Marriage as a sacrament derived from the mystery of redemption is given to historical man as a grace and at the same time as an ethos."[396] Christ's gift of the sacrament entails an ethical responsibility for man and woman to live up to its demands, the demands of holiness. It is "'assigned' to man as a duty through the reality of the redemption."[397]

How is this duty conferred on the human person? It is bestowed in the most intimate way possible, penetrating to the very depths of who he is and longs to become. "It is assigned to his heart, to his conscience, to his looks, and to his behavior."[398] Husband and wife are forged into a new creation; they become a new man and woman in Christ when they live up to the challenges of married life. Christ is not satisfied if their outward behavior conforms to the moral law. The sufferings and joys of their life together are the occasions which allow the Master to enter the inner sanctuary of their hearts and consciences.

---

[395] General Audience of December 1, 1982, in Ibid., p. 349.

[396] General Audience of December 1, 1982, in Ibid., p. 348. (In his General Audience of November 5, 1980 [in Ibid., p. 169], John Paul II speaks of the general meaning the term "ethos" has acquired in philosophy and theology. "It embraces in its content the complex spheres of good and evil, depending on human will and subject to the laws of conscience and the sensitivity of the human heart." In other words, *ethos* goes beyond *ethics*, which outlines a set of moral principles or values. Ethos includes these moral principles as embodied not only in the guiding beliefs of a people, but also within their character and sentiments, within their very moral nature as individuals or a group.)

[397] General Audience of November 24, 1982, in Ibid., p. 346.

[398] General Audience of November 24, 1982, in Ibid., p. 347. In this same audience the Holy Father refers to the heart as "that intimate place where good and evil struggle in man — sin and justice, concupiscence and holiness." Ibid.

Once inside, he slowly begins to open doors, allowing his light to shine into rooms that may have been sealed for years. At times this process is painful. It is much more comfortable to pull down the shades when the first rays of dawn burst through our window than to let the piercing sunlight rouse us from slumber. But if we force ourselves out of bed and are able to gaze upon the silent splendor of a new sunrise, joy and gratitude overwhelm us. In the same way, as the years slip past, filled with self-giving love in happiness and sorrow, husband and wife begin to experience the liberating presence of their Redeemer, claiming absolute dominion over their entire selves. Soon they long for him to open any door of their heart that may remain shut, to enter any secret chamber still reserved for themselves. Many times each day they raise a silent colloquy to their Lord: "With the light of your heart, dispel the darkness of my heart."

The hope offered by redeemed marriage is not just for husband and wife. In this great sacrament all men and women can discover more fully who they are and with what confidence they may lay claim to attaining their eternal destiny. Marriage reveals that Christ's love for his Church, for each one of his people, is at the same time spousal and redemptive.

> The Pauline image of marriage, inscribed in the "great mystery" of Christ and of the Church, brings together the redemptive dimension and the spousal dimension of love. In a certain sense it fuses these two dimensions into one. Christ has become the spouse of the Church. He has married the Church as a bride, because "He has given himself up for her" (Eph 5:25).[399]

The union between the spousal and the redemptive aspects of love, revealed by Christ, reflects the deepest meaning of the human body. As spousal, love is self-giving. The self-giving love that we are capable of achieving through our bodies helps redeem us and win the redemption of those we love. John Paul II affirms that the convergence between these two meanings of the body is fundamental for each person to understand his or her very reason for existing. "That linking of the spousal significance of the body with its redemptive significance is equally essential and valid for the understanding of man in general, for the fundamental problem of understanding him and for the self-comprehension of his being in the world."[400]

---

[399] General Audience of December 15, 1982, in Ibid., p. 352.
[400] General Audience of December 15, 1982, in Ibid., pp. 352-353.

3. Marriage as a Sacrament:
The Conjugal Union of Husband and Wife
a) "I take you as my wife. . . . I take you as my husband":
The Matter and Form of Marriage

Christian marriage offers hope both to the spouses and to all of mankind that it is possible to conquer once more the freedom of the gift. Men and women are capable of freely giving themselves to one another with selfless love, thanks to Christ. The hope held out by marriage arises from the saving reality of grace, which the sacrament of matrimony effects — grace won for us by Christ's redemption of our bodies. After contemplating the horizons of this new hope opened by grace, John Paul II goes on to consider matrimony as a sign: one that makes present the grace it signifies.

The Holy Father poses the fundamental question, "What precisely constitutes the sacramental sign of matrimony?" This apparently simple query is actually composed of two parts: "What is the form and what is the matter of the sacrament of Matrimony?" John Paul II affirms that Ephesians 5 provides a solid foundation for reflecting on this question, although it deals with marriage as a sacrament in the analogical sense and not as one of the seven sacraments. "Even though Ephesians does not speak directly and immediately of marriage as one of the sacraments of the Church, the sacramentality of marriage is especially confirmed and closely examined in it."[401]

Ephesians 5 examines the inner nature of marriage, clearly pronounced to be a sacrament in the Gospels. It is Christ himself who restores marriage as a primordial sacrament established by the Father "in the beginning." At the same time, Christ constitutes matrimony as one of the Church's seven sacraments, opening it to the salvific power of grace.

> In the presence of those with whom he was conversing, in the Gospels of Matthew and Mark (cf. Mt 19; Mk 10), Christ confirmed marriage as a sacrament instituted by the Creator at the beginning. If in conformity with this he insisted on its indissolubility, he thereby opened marriage to the salvific action of God, to the forces which flow from the redemption of the body."[402]

When is the great reality of this sacrament constituted? What are the essential elements of marriage — its matter and form? Unlike most of the seven sacraments, matrimony is not conferred by the priest. He is simply an official witness of the Church during the marriage ceremony. According to the Latin tradition, husband and wife are the ministers

---

[401] General Audience of October 27, 1982, in Ibid., p. 342.
[402] General Audience of November 24, 1982, in Ibid., p. 345.

who confer the sacrament of Matrimony upon one another.[403] Thus, it is their words of consent which are the *form* of the sacrament. Their words signify and bring into being the life-long covenant of mutual self-giving that is marriage.

> "I take you as my wife"; "I take you as my husband." These words are at the center of the liturgy of marriage as a sacrament of the Church. . . . With these words the engaged couple enter the marriage contract and at the same time receive the sacrament of which both are ministers.[404]

The words of consent alone, however, do not constitute marriage as a sacrament. They do not represent the fullness of the sacramental sign. The very persons of the husband and wife, their own bodies in their masculinity and femininity, enabling the spouses to give themselves in love by becoming "one flesh," are essential for the *matter* of the sacrament.

> Both of them, as man and woman, being the ministers of the sacrament in the moment of contracting marriage, constitute at the same time the full and real visible sign of the sacrament itself. The words spoken by them would not, *per se*, constitute the sacramental sign of marriage unless there corresponded to them the human subjectivity of the engaged couple and at the same time the awareness of the body, linked to the masculinity and femininity of the husband and wife.[405]

Even the words of consent, along with the persons of the spouses as male and female, do not constitute the fullness of the sacramental sign. The words express the couple's intent to enter into marriage. They establish marriage as a personal communion of life and love in the order of *intentionality*. The words of the formula reflect this personal communion: "I promise to be faithful to you always, in joy and in sorrow, in sickness and in health, and to love and honor you all the days of my life."[406] But marriage is fully constituted only when the intention of the spouses becomes a *reality* through the marital union of sexual intercourse. John Paul II ponders that the sacramental word of consent is, in itself, "merely the sign of the coming into being of marriage."[407] It is the conjugal union of husband and wife that makes a concrete reality their mutual gift of self to one another. The Holy Father states:

> The coming into being of marriage is distinguished from its consummation, to the extent that without this consummation the marriage is not yet constituted in its full reality. The fact that a marriage

---

[403] Cf. *CCC*, 1623.
[404] General Audience of January 5, 1983, in *The Theology of the Body*, p. 354.
[405] Ibid., p. 356.
[406] Ibid., p. 354.
[407] Ibid., p. 355.

is juridically contracted but not consummated (*ratum — non consummatum*) corresponds to the fact that it has not been fully constituted as a marriage. Indeed, the very words "I take you as my wife — husband" . . . can be fulfilled only by means of conjugal intercourse. This reality (conjugal intercourse) has moreover been determined from the very beginning by institution of the Creator: "Therefore a man leaves his father and his mother and cleaves to his wife, and they become one flesh" (cf. Gn 2:24).[408]

So every time husband and wife give themselves to each other in the marital embrace of conjugal union, *if they do so in truth*, they are renewing the sacramental reality of their marriage. They deepen their mutual love by opening it to the presence of the Holy Spirit, whom they received through the sacrament of Matrimony "as the communion of love of Christ and the Church.[409] The Holy Spirit is the seal of their covenant, the ever-available source of their love and the strength to renew their fidelity."[410]

b) "Living in the Truth": The Language of the Body

The need for husband and wife to give themselves to each other *in truth* during the act of conjugal union brings us to an essential aspect of John Paul II's theology: *the language of the body*. The Holy Father affirms that the human body, created male and female, "speaks" a language of its own.

The body itself "speaks." It speaks by means of its masculinity and femininity. It speaks in the mysterious language of the personal gift. It speaks ultimately — and this happens more frequently — both in the language of fidelity, that is, of love, and also in the language of conjugal infidelity, that is, of adultery.[411]

Is the body itself the author of its own language? It is not. The Old Testament prophets see the covenant of love between God and his people embodied in marriage. The language of faithfulness or infidelity that husband and wife express to each other through their bodies reflects the Chosen People's fidelity to God or their betrayal of him. Husband and wife are presented with the challenge of living up to the language of the body, just as the Chosen People are called to remain faithful to their God. The spousal language inscribed in the body is not invented by the body itself. John Paul II states: "In the texts of the prophets the human body speaks a 'language' which it is not the author of."[412]

---

[408] Ibid.
[409] Cf. Eph 5:32.
[410] CCC, 1624.
[411] General Audience of January 12, 1983, in *The Theology of the Body*, p. 359.
[412] Ibid.

Who, then, is the author of the language which the human body speaks? In a certain sense each one of us, as a human person, man or woman, is the author of the language of the body, just as Shakespeare is truly the author of *Macbeth*. We speak through our bodies the language of self-giving, of fidelity, of love. We allow our bodies to speak for us, on our behalf.

> It is obvious that the body as such does not "speak," but man speaks, rereading that which requires to be expressed precisely on the basis of the "body," of masculinity and femininity of the personal subject, indeed, on the basis of what can be expressed by man only by means of the body.
>
> In this sense man — male or female — does not merely speak with the language of the body. But in a certain sense he permits the body to speak "for him" and "on his behalf," I would say, in his name and with his personal authority. In this way even the concept "prophetism of the body" seems to be well founded. The prophet spoke "for" and "on behalf of" — in the name and with the authority of a person.[413]

The Holy Father adds that it is not simply a question of allowing the body to speak on our behalf. There are certain fundamental aspects of human life, of who we are as persons, which we are absolutely unable to express except through our bodies. Our most basic vocation is the call to live in a loving communion of persons. But we cannot do so except through our bodies. John Paul II elaborates this point.

> However, man cannot, in a certain sense, express this singular language of his personal existence and of his vocation without the body. He has already been constituted in such a way from the beginning, in such wise that the most profound words of the spirit — words of love, of giving, of fidelity — demand an adequate language of the body. Without that they cannot be fully expressed. We know from the Gospel that this refers both to marriage and also to celibacy for the sake of the kingdom.[414]

In one sense we are the authors of the language of the body as human persons. But we are not its ultimate author. Shakespeare made use of the English language in a profound and insightful way when he wrote *Macbeth*. Still, he did not invent English as such, and was obliged to utilize the language in accordance with the inner meaning it already possessed.

Who is the ultimate author of the language of the body? God himself is the author, the Creator of our body, the one who has inscribed a

---

[413] General Audience of January 26, 1983, in Ibid., pp. 363-364.
[414] General Audience of January 12, 1983, in Ibid., p. 359.

certain, intrinsic meaning in its structure and acts. "God himself origi-
nated this language by creating man as male and female — a language
which has been renewed by Christ. This enduring language of the body
carries within itself all the richness and depth of the mystery, first of creation and then of redemption."[415]

We are called to reread the language of the body in truth — the
truth of the intrinsic meaning it possesses in itself and its acts. In a similar way Shakespeare made use of the English language already constituted. If our intentions correspond to the inner meaning of the language
of the body, we are living in the truth. If, on the other hand, we attempt
to confer on our actions a meaning that contradicts the significance they
possess in themselves, we are falsifying the language of the body. We
are telling a lie with our bodies. In the Garden of Gethsemane, Judas
greeted Christ with a kiss of friendship. But he meant that kiss to betray
his Master. Everyone recognizes immediately the terrible nature of violating in this way the intimate language of the body.

John Paul II points out the vital importance of living the language of
the body in truth for the sacrament of Matrimony. The language of the
body, he affirms, constitutes the communion of persons formed by marriage. It expresses and makes a reality the mutual self-giving of husband
and wife.

> In this way the enduring and ever-new language of the body is not
> only the "substratum," but in a certain sense, it is the constitutive
> element of the communion of the persons. The persons — man and
> woman — become for each other a mutual gift. They become that
> gift in their masculinity and femininity, discovering the spousal sig-
> nificance of the body and referring it reciprocally to themselves in
> an irreversible manner — in a life-long dimension.[416]

When the Old Testament prophets discover in marriage an analogy
of God's faithful covenant with his people, they reveal that conjugal fidelity is the truth of the language of the body among spouses. Committing adultery means lying with the body. "In the writings of the prophets, who catch a fleeting glimpse of the analogy of the covenant of
Yahweh with Israel in marriage, the body speaks the truth through fidelity and conjugal love. When it commits adultery it speaks lies; it is
guilty of falsity."[417]

Just how necessary is speaking the language of the body *in truth* for
marriage? John Paul II declares that it is an essential element. In fact, the
language of the body, spoken in truth, is needed in order to *constitute* the
sacramental sign of marriage — to make the sacrament of Matrimony

---

[415] General Audience of January 19, 1983, in Ibid., p. 362.
[416] General Audience of January 5, 1983, in Ibid., p. 356.
[417] General Audience of January 12, 1983, in Ibid., p. 360.

come into being as a reality. "We can then say that the essential element for marriage as a sacrament is the language of the body in its aspects of truth. Precisely by means of that, the sacramental sign is constituted."[418]

What are the consequences of the need for husband and wife to speak the language of the body in truth in order to constitute the sacramental sign of matrimony? If husband or wife perform the conjugal act after their wedding due to moral or physical violence or coercion, the marriage has not been truly consummated.[419] The sacramental sign has not been fully realized. The act of self-giving love, establishing a bond that lasts a lifetime, which conjugal union is meant to be, has not really taken place.

To be true to the language of the body, the conjugal act must also be open to life.[420] This is so because, by its intimate structure, the conjugal act not only unites husband and wife intimately, but is also ordered to generating offspring.[421] As a result, married couples who practice contraception tell a lie with their bodies each time they engage in the act of conjugal union. They perform an act whose inner language, written by God himself, speaks of life. Yet they themselves are not open to life, and prevent their act of conjugal union from being so.

On an objective plane, they do not renew the sacramental power of their marriage, as conjugal union is meant to do. How could they, if their act remains closed to the presence of the Holy Spirit, "the Lord and Giver of Life"?[422] Christopher West sums up well the relationship between the conjugal love of husband and wife and openness to fertility: "Love leads to life, and life comes from love. The language of the body is the revelation of the life-giving love of God."[423]

c) Speaking the Language of the Body in Truth: To Create a Culture of Life

Who is not aware of the pervasive forces of the culture of death, which threaten the very foundations of society itself? The culture of death menaces human persons when they are most vulnerable. Abortion takes the lives of helpless babies within their mother's wombs. Euthanasia kills men and women in the weakness of old age or serious illness.

---

[418] Ibid.

[419] Cf. *CIC*, 1061. See also the commentary regarding this canon in *The Code of Canon Law: A Text and Commentary*, James S. Coriden, Thomas J. Green, Donald E. Heintschel, eds. (Mahwah, NJ: Paulist Press, 1985), p. 745.

[420] Cf. *Humanae Vitae*, 9; *Familiaris Consortio*, 13, 50; *CCC*, 1643.

[421] Cf. *HV*, 12; *FC*, 32.

[422] We proclaim the truth that the Holy Spirit is the "Lord and Giver of Life" each time we recite the Creed. John Paul II has made this truth the Latin title of his 1986 encyclical on the Holy Spirit: *Dominum et Vivificantem.*

[423] Christopher West, audiocassette series *Naked Without Shame: Sex and the Christian Mystery. Reflections on Pope John Paul II's Theology of the Body* (Carpentersville, IL: GIFT Foundation, 2000), Tape 6, "Sacramentality of Marriage."

All Christians, all people of good will, must respond to these perilous threats by creating a culture of life. Where must this culture of life begin? There can be no place of origin for an authentic and enduring culture of life other than that most intimate sanctuary where human life itself comes into being through God's creative plan: the marital union of husband and wife.

How vital it is for husband and wife to speak the language of the body in truth each time they lovingly give themselves to one another, in light of the struggle for the future of human life itself that is raging in the world today! What a transcendent responsibility is placed upon their shoulders, and what a glorious call they receive from the Lord to live heroically their Christian vocation! May all people who seek the good of mankind join in fervent prayer, that husbands and wives will have the courage to lay the lasting foundations of a culture of life within the hidden sanctuary of their self-giving love to one another.

Preview

Six A Total Vision of Man: Three Applications (continued)

III. "Love and Fruitfulness": Reflections on Humanae Vitae
    A. The Song of Songs: "Truth and Freedom — the Foundation of True Love"
        1. "My Sister, My Bride": Love Reveals the Person
        2. "A Garden Enclosed": The Freedom of the Gift and the Inviolable Mystery of the Person
    B. The Book of Tobit: Love as a "Test of Life and Death"
        1. A Struggle Between Good and Evil: The Objective Dimension of Human Love
        2. Conjugal Life as Liturgical: The Splendor of Redeemed Love

Points to look for

1. What is the most obvious meaning of the Song of Songs?

2. What further meaning have mystical writers such as St. John of the Cross discovered in the Song of Songs?

3. Why does St. John of the Cross exclaim that all the works of nature leave him wounded and unsatisfied?

4. What characteristic does one who is in love acquire, as revealed by the Spiritual Canticle?

5. What characteristic of love does the soaring lyric poetry of the Song disclose?

6. What aspect of love can be discovered in the groom calling his bride his "sister"?

7. What do the metaphors "a garden enclosed, a fountain sealed" reveal about the nature of authentic love?

8. How is married love in its objective dimension a struggle between good and evil?

9. Why are the sacraments necessary for husband and wife to remain faithful to one another all the days of their life?

10. Why does John Paul II affirm that the conjugal life of married couples is in a certain way liturgical?

III. "Love and Fruitfulness": Reflections on *Humanae Vitae*

John Paul II declared 1983 an extraordinary Holy Year to commemorate 1,950 years since Christ's redeeming death upon the cross. During the Holy Year he interrupted his series of audiences on human love in the divine plan. In May 1984, the Holy Father began the sixth and final cycle of the series, applying the total vision of man he had traced previously to Paul VI's teaching on married love and fruitfulness in his encyclical *Humanae Vitae*.[424] John Paul II views the final cycle of reflections on love and fruitfulness as the "crowning" of all he has previously illustrated.[425] Let us attempt to glimpse with the Holy Father the splendor of human love when touched by grace.

A. The Song of Songs: "Truth and Freedom — the Foundation of True Love"

The Song of Songs is one of the most intriguing books of the Old Testament. In its most obvious meaning, it is a love poem. The Song extols the beauty and attraction of human love between a young man and woman. Attitudes toward the Song of Songs have varied greatly. At times its reading has been discouraged due to its "profane" content. Yet great mystics have been inspired by it to write their most intense verses. The following lines from the Song moved St. John of the Cross to compose his timeless "Spiritual Canticle."

> On my bed at night I sought him
> whom my heart loves —
> I sought him but I did not find him.
> I will rise then and go about the city;
> in the streets and crossings I will seek
> Him whom my heart loves.

---

[424] The concluding cycle of John Paul II's theology of the body contains 21 general audiences, delivered between May 23, 1984, and November 28, 1984. Some commentators place the first five audiences on the Song of Songs and the Book of Tobit at the end of the previous cycle on the sacramentality of marriage. The Holy Father himself, however, indicates on May 23 that they belong as a preface to the final cycle. It is true that the content of these audiences deals in large part with the sacramental sign of marriage, but this serves to lay the foundations for the direct reflections on *Humanae Vitae*, which follow.

[425] Cf. General Audience of May 23, 1984, in *The Theology of the Body*, p. 368.

I sought him but I did not find him.
The watchmen came upon me
As they made their rounds of the City:
Have you seen him whom my
heart loves?   (Sg 3:1-3)

The "Spiritual Canticle" of St. John of the Cross discovers in the Song, hidden within the beloved's pursuit of her lover, the soul's ardent search for God — pierced to the heart by Christ's love. At every turn the soul finds traces of the divine Lover's footprints: on the morning dew, in a patch of wheat. Though so near, the Lover flees, and is always just beyond reach. The soul cannot rest until she encounters the one her heart seeks.[426]

CÁNTICO ESPIRITUAL
Esposa

1. ¿Adonde te escondiste,
Amado, y me dejaste con gemido?
Como el ciervo huiste
Habiéndome herido;
Salí tras ti clamando,
     y eras ido.

2. Pastores, los que fueredes
Allá, por las majadas al otero,
Si por ventura vieredes
Aquel que yo más quiero,
Decidle que adolezco, peno y muero.

3. Buscando mis amores,
Iré por esos montes y
riberas,
Ni cogeré las flores
Ni temeré las fieras,
Y pasaré los fuertes y
fronteras.

4. ¡Oh bosques y espesuras,
Plantadas por la mano del Amado;
Oh prado de verduras,
De flores esmaltado,
Decid si por vosotros ha pasado!

5. Mil gracias derramando,
Pasó por estos sotos con presura,

THE SPIRITUAL CANTICLE
Bride

1. Where have you hidden,
Beloved, and left me moaning?
You fled like the stag
After wounding me;
I went out calling You,
     and You were gone.

2. Shepherds, you that go
Up through the sheepfolds to the hill,
If by chance you see
Him I love most,
Tell Him that I sicken, suffer, and die.

3. Seeking my Love
I will head for the mountains and for
 watersides,
I will not gather flowers,
Nor fear wild beasts;
I will go beyond strong men and
frontiers.

4. O woods and thickets
Planted by the hand of my Beloved!
O green meadow,
Coated, bright, with flowers,
Tell me, has He passed by you?

5. Pouring out a thousand graces,
He passed these groves in haste;

---

[426] Stanzas 1-7 of *The Spiritual Canticle* which follow, both the original Spanish and the English translation, are taken from *The Collected Works of St. John of the Cross,* translated by Kieran Kavanaugh, OCD, and Otilio Rodriguez, OCD, (Washington, D.C.: ICS Publications, 1979), pp. 712-713.

Y yéndolos mirando,	And having looked at them,
Con sola su figura	With his image alone,
Vestidos los dejó de hermosura.	Clothed them in beauty.

6. Ay, ¿quién podrá sanarme?	6. Ah, who has the power to heal me?
Acaba de entregarte ya de vero,	Now wholly surrender yourself!
No quieras enviarme	Do not send me
De hoy ya más mensajero,	Any more messengers,
Que no saben decirme lo que quiero.	That cannot tell me what I must hear.

7. Y todos cuantos vagan,	7. All who are free
De ti me van mil gracias	Tell me a thousand graceful things
refiriendo,	of You;
Y todos más me llagan,	All wound me more
Y déjame muriendo	And leave me dying
Un no sé qué que quedan	Of, ah, I-don't-know-what behind
balbuciendo.	their stammering.

Even though the drama of each person's ardent quest for God lies hidden within the Song of Songs, John Paul II views its most obvious meaning as developing Adam's exclamation upon first seeing Eve: "This one, at last, is bone of my bones and flesh of my flesh."[427] Adam's words express wonder and admiration, and, even more, the sense of fascination before Eve. These sentiments are developed more fully in the Song of Songs through the dialogue between the young man and woman. "The point of departure as well as the point of arrival for this fascination — mutual wonder and admiration — are in fact the bride's femininity and the groom's masculinity, in the direct experience of their visibility."[428]

The expressions of love uttered by the bride and groom focus on the body, but that is only natural, since through the body an attraction arises for the other *person*. It is that attraction for the other "I" which "in the interior impulse of the heart generates love."[429] The soaring lyric poetry in the Song of Songs discloses a moving aspect of love. The Holy Father observes, "Love unleashes a special experience of the beautiful, which focuses on what is visible, but at the same time involves the entire person."[430] To love someone is to perceive a beauty within him or her that may well lie hidden from others who do not gaze with the eyes of love.

1. "My Sister, My Bride": Love Reveals the Person

John Paul II reserves a special commentary for one of the titles the groom uses to address his beloved. He calls her "my sister, my bride."[431]

---

[427] Gn 2:23.
[428] General Audience of May 23, 1984, in *The Theology of the Body*, p. 369.
[429] Ibid.
[430] Ibid.
[431] Sg 4:9.

In a way, these words are more poignant than many of the terms of endearment commonly addressed to a beloved. By calling his bride his "sister," the groom recognizes her complete humanity, the fullness of who she is as a person. She is much more to him than someone who can satisfy the natural human desire for love. "Through the name 'sister,' the groom's words tend to reproduce, I would say, the history of the femininity of the person loved. They see her still in the time of girlhood and they embrace her entire 'I,' soul and body, with a disinterested tenderness."[432]

A mark of authentic love is that it reveals the one loved in complete fullness as a person, inspiring a tender, selfless devotion toward him or her. What is the fruit of this disinterested recognition of the other as a person? Peace. "This is the peace of the body, which in appearance resembles sleep ('Do not arouse, do not stir up love before its own time'). . . . 'So am I in your eyes, like one who has found peace' (Sg 8:10)."[433] The peace engendered by authentic love is a compelling testimony of the image of God in the human person, created male and female. As St. Peter Chrysologus comments in one of his sermons, "Peace. . . . is God's will; it is the sweetness of Christ and the perfection of sanctity. . . . We should guard peace before all the virtues, for God is always present in peace."[434]

2. "A Garden Enclosed": The Freedom of the Gift and the Inviolable Mystery of the Person

The groom describes with perceptive metaphors his bride, already recognized as his sister:

> You are an enclosed garden, my sister, my bride,
>   an enclosed garden, a fountain sealed (Sg 4:12).

These evocative comparisons bring to light the far-reaching consequences of the personhood the groom has fully acknowledged in his beloved. As a person, the woman is "master of her own mystery."[435] She alone can freely decide to reveal the mystery of herself to her lover. She is the one who must choose in complete freedom to make a gift of herself in love. The bride responds to this invitation by entrusting herself to the groom. So the metaphors at the same time express the mutual and exclusive belonging to one another of the future spouses.

> The language of metaphors — poetic language — seems to be in this sphere especially appropriate and precise. The "sister bride" is for the man the master of her own mystery as a "garden enclosed" and a "fountain sealed." The language of the body reread in truth keeps pace with the discovery of the interior inviolability of the

---

[432] General Audience of May 30, 1984, in Ibid., p. 371.
[433] Ibid.
[434] From a sermon of St. Peter Chrysologus in *The Divine Office: The Liturgy of the Hours According to the Roman Rite, Volume III*, (London: Collins, 1974), pp. 99*-100*.
[435] General Audience of May 30, 1984, in *The Theology of the Body*, p. 372.

person. At the same time, this discovery expresses the authentic depth of the mutual belonging of the spouses who are aware of belonging to each other, of being destined for each other: "My lover belongs to me and I to him" (Sg 2:16; cf. 6:3).[436]

With a peace that arises from the groom's recognition of her freedom to make a gift of her very self, the bride entrusts her life to the one she loves. The Holy Father insists that only when planted in such soil can authentic love grow and mature. "The freedom of the gift is the response to the deep awareness of the gift expressed by the groom's words. Through this truth and freedom that love is built up, which we must affirm is authentic love."[437]

B. The Book of Tobit: Love as a "Test of Life and Death"
1. A Struggle Between Good and Evil:
The Objective Dimension of Human Love

The Song of Songs exalts the subjective dimension of human love. It conveys the language of the body in its emotive power. The Book of Tobit, on the other hand, emphasizes love's objective dimension. Married love is a struggle between good and evil. In its poetic transport, the Song of Songs proclaims love to be "strong as death."[438] The dramatic story of Tobit and Sarah, whose seven previous husbands all die on their wedding night before consummating the marriage, through the work of a demon, reveals that married love is a true "test of life and death."[439]

The Book of Tobit makes plain that the test of marriage is a lifelong vocation from God to union and self-giving love. Only through prayer, with the grace that comes from the author of marriage, can husband and wife emerge victorious in the struggle to conquer lust with love in the depths of the human heart.

John Paul II notes how the Song of Songs seems almost unaware of the objective struggle between good and evil. But even this fact reveals a deep truth about love: The fullness of love enables a person to experience peace even in the midst of the battle to overcome one's own passions and the mysterious forces of sin within the heart. "The spouses of the Song live and express themselves in an ideal or abstract world, in which it is as though the struggle of the objective forces between good and evil did not exist. Is it not precisely the power and the interior truth of love that subdues the struggle that goes on in man and around him?"[440]

---

[436] Ibid.
[437] Ibid.
[438] Sg 8:6.
[439] General Audience of June 27, 1984, in Ibid., p. 376.
[440] Ibid.

At the same time, the objective dimension of human love as a conquest through effort and prayer, revealed in the Book of Tobit, is even more deeply moving, according to the Holy Father. Here human love takes on all the drama of the free decisions and choices that shape human existence.

> The truth and the power of love are shown in the ability to place oneself between the forces of good and evil which are fighting in man and around him, because love is confident in the victory of good and is ready to do everything so that good may conquer. As a result, the love of the spouses in the book of Tobit is not confirmed by the words expressed by the language of loving transport as in the Song of Songs, but by the choices and the actions that take on all the weight of human existence in the union of the two. The language of the body here seems to use the words of the choices and the acts stemming from the love that is victorious because it prays.[441]

2. Conjugal Life as Liturgical: The Splendor of Redeemed Love

Sarah and Tobit were able to overcome the evil demon which had slain her previous husbands by the fervent prayer they raised to God on their wedding night. Their prayer makes clear that married love is a call to holiness. Only if husband and wife continuously grow in holiness through the joys and sorrows, the bliss and suffering, of giving themselves to one another and their children, will they be able to remain faithful all the days of their life.

Since married love has been touched from within by the power of Christ's redemption, one of the greatest sources of strength for husband and wife in their quest for holiness are the sacraments — the very sources of redemptive grace. John Paul II calls attention to their effect on the human person.

> The sacraments inject sanctity into the plan of man's humanity. They penetrate the soul and body, the femininity and the masculinity of the personal subject, with the power of sanctity. All of this is expressed in the language of the liturgy. It is expressed there and brought about there.[442]

In a special way the sacrament of matrimony confers upon husband and wife the graces they need to grow in love and holiness through each event of their married life. The action of grace enables the language of the liturgy to become incarnate as the language of their bodies in the joys and vicissitudes of each day. Husband and wife know the simple delight of greeting each other after the hectic day's work has been ac-

---

[441] Ibid.
[442] General Audience of July 4, 1984, in Ibid., p. 378.

complished. They also experience the deep and profound joy of discovering that a new child will be born to them. Together they face the challenges of transmitting the faith to their children. They strengthen and console one another in sadness, when loved ones die or doubts about their family's future may arise.

All of these experiences are elevated by the liturgy to the dimension of mystery. The Holy Father goes even further. That most intimate act of love between husband and wife, their conjugal union, becomes in a certain way a liturgical act. "Thus liturgical language, that is, the language of the sacrament and of the *mysterium*, becomes in their life and in their living together the language of the body in a depth, simplicity and beauty hitherto altogether unknown. . . . In this way, conjugal life becomes in a certain sense liturgical."[443]

Married love, redeemed by Christ, has been undergoing a challenge in the present and past century that has rocked it to its very foundations. For four years during his Wednesday audiences, John Paul II laid the groundwork to confront that challenge. In his sixth cycle, reflections on *Humanae Vitae*, he faced it directly. If we truly love marriage and the family, if we ardently long to foster them, we too must meet this test along with the Holy Father. The challenge can be voiced in a single word: *contraception*.

---

[443] Ibid., p. 380.

Natural Family Planning vs. Contraception: Two Irreconcilable Views of the Human Person

"Love and All That Is Opposed to Love": The Development of Natural Family Planning and Contraception

Preview

I. Contraception: Just What Is at Stake?

II. The Development of Modern Forms of Contraception

    A. "Contraception": An Authoritative Definition
    B. Barrier Methods of Contraception
    C. Sterilization
    D. A Revolutionary Development: The Pill
        1. Is It Effective?
        2. Is It Safe?
        3. Is It Moral?

III. Is There a Reliable Alternative? — Natural Family Planning

    A. The Fertility Cycle
    B. Calendar Rhythm: A First, Ineffective Form of NFP

Points to look for

1. Why does John Paul II affirm that even more is at stake than a fundamental moral teaching of the Church in the question of natural family planning *vs.* contraception?

2. What are the two irreconcilable views of the human person that lie behind choosing to practice natural family planning or contraception?

3. What is contraception?

4. What is the Church's teaching as to whether contraception is morally acceptable?

5. Are barrier methods of contraception effective or healthy?

6. What are some of the dangers sterilization poses to physical and psychological health?

7. What scientific discovery made possible both the development of the Pill and effective forms of natural family planning?

8. What are some of the health hazards to women who use the Pill?

9. Besides the fact that it is a form of contraception, why else is the use of the Pill in its various forms immoral?

10. What is the role of the hormone FSH in a woman's fertility cycle?

11. What are the roles of the hormones estrogen and progesterone in the cycle?

12. During how many days of her menstrual cycle is a woman fertile?

13. Why did calendar rhythm prove to be an inadequate method of natural family planning?

I. Contraception: Just What is at Stake?

The severe challenge of contraception was first launched against married love in the second half of the 1800s. Since then it has come to assume truly menacing dimensions. Catholic thinker Sean Inherst conveys the intense drama of the present attack on God's plan for man and woman, not hesitating to identify the contraceptive ideology as a modern heresy: "anti-conceptionism." Inherst affirms that John Paul II's theology of the body, by explaining how married love is at the heart of God's entire plan of salvation, will one day gain the victory over this new threat to the faith and to humanity.

> I'm sure we are living in that age which Catholics of the future will describe as the near-triumph of the heresy of anti-conceptionism. They will recount that this heresy had not only threatened millions of souls but millions of bodies as well. As has always been the case in the history of theological development, in the future they will recognize that this attack against the original plan of God, disclosed in the future as His "marital plan," will have been vanquished by a precise theological elaboration of the place of the marital covenant at the very heart and center of the economy of salvation.[444]

In his 1994 "Letter to Families," John Paul II affirmed that today "the family is placed at the center of the great struggle between good and evil, between life and death, between love and all that is opposed to love."[445] Many different forces enter into that struggle. But at its very core is the ideology of contraception.

For John Paul II a lot is at stake in the present drama of contraception. It is even more than a question of the Church's moral teaching, al-

---

[444] From Sean Inherst's private correspondence, cited by Christopher West in *Naked without Shame: Sex and the Christian Mystery — Study Guide*, p. 21.
[445] *Letter to Families*, 23.

ready pronounced in the first centuries of Christianity. The difference between contraception and natural family planning is so fundamental that it penetrates to the very heart of who we are as persons. The Holy Father affirms that the difference is *"both anthropological and moral."*[446] Behind the scenes in the disparity between contraception and recourse to the rhythm of the woman's cycle lie "two irreconcilable concepts of the human person and of human sexuality."[447]

When a husband and wife decide to practice natural family planning and not to contracept, they do more than make a moral decision regarding their act of conjugal union. They choose in favor of an authentic Christian vision of human persons as free, personal subjects. If a couple decides to practice contraception, they are opting, consciously or not, for a materialistic concept of the person as an object that can be manipulated.

Nothing less than the Christian heritage of our dignity as persons is on the line in the silent drama of contraception. Will we continue to view others and ourselves as utterly unique beings, open to the transcendent mystery of the divine, whose own personal mystery no one has a right to violate? Or will we begin to consider persons as nothing more than material individuals of the human species, members who possess their own bodies as mere objects which can be manipulated at will?

It would be hard to imagine higher stakes in the game. That is why John Paul II deemed it crucial to respond in a compelling way to Pope Paul VI's appeal for a "total vision of man."[448] Over the course of five years of Wednesday audiences, John Paul II elaborated this total vision or "theology of the body," in light of which the Church's teaching on the regulation of births could shine brightly before all men and women of good will.

Yet we may feel tempted to ask ourselves, "Is the alternative between contraception and natural family planning really as stark as John Paul II makes it out to be? How exactly does choosing whether or not to use the Pill imply two irreconcilable concepts of the person and sexuality?" The best way to answer these questions is by tracing the origins of the contraceptive mentality and the philosophy that lies behind it. These origins pass through nineteenth-century Malthusianism to the

---

[446] *Familiaris Consortio*, 32 (emphasis in the original).
[447] Ibid.
[448] *Humanae Vitae*, 7. Paul VI states in number 7: "The problem of birth, like every other problem regarding human life, is to be considered, beyond partial perspectives — whether of the biological or psychological, demographic or sociological orders — in the light of an integral vision of man and of his vocation, not only his natural and earthly, but also his supernatural and eternal vocation."

rationalist materialism of the Enlightenment. That journey will be undertaken in Chapter 8.

In Chapter 7 we will examine some fundamental questions which precede the philosophical and moral drama that is being played out. Just what is meant by artificial contraception and natural family planning? How did they develop? Is NFP a truly effective, scientific method for regulating birth, or is it simply a course of action undertaken by pious people in which "anything could happen"? On a purely medical and human plane, how do artificial forms of contraception compare with NFP regarding the health and well-being of the wife or husband?

II. The Development of Modern Forms of Contraception

Efforts to artificially limit births have been made since the earliest times. But the modern birth-control movement and methods of contraception trace their origins back to the neo-Malthusians of the 1860's. Responding to Thomas Malthus' 1798 theory of impending overpopulation, the neo-Malthusians advocated contraception as the solution. The earlier discovery of vulcanized rubber in 1839 facilitated the production of condoms, which they promoted as an effective means of birth control.

A. "Contraception": An Authoritative Definition

Artificial contraceptives have proliferated in the twentieth century. Their variety of forms leads to the question: "What precisely constitutes artificial contraception?" Pope Paul VI gives an authoritative definition in his 1968 encyclical *Humanae Vitae* (Of Human Life). Contraception is "every action which, either in anticipation of the conjugal act, or in its accomplishment, or in the development of its natural consequences, proposes, whether as an end or as a means, to render procreation impossible."[449] Just a few sentences later, Paul VI goes on to reaffirm the Church's constant teaching that all such actions are intrinsically evil (*intrinsece inhonestum*).[450] The *Catechism of the Catholic Church* reiterates Paul VI's condemnation of all forms of unnatural contraception as intrinsically evil in number 2370.

B. Barrier Methods of Contraception

The first part of the twentieth century was marked by a proliferation of barrier methods of contraception. Most are still widely marketed today. They attempt to prevent sperm penetration and fertilization of the ovum. Among them are condoms (male and female), diaphragms, cervical caps, the sponge, and spermicidal jelly or foam. Since they all have problems of effectiveness, at times more than one are used together.

These methods have obvious aesthetic objections. It is hard for the couple not to feel that they are defending themselves from one another,

---

[449] *Humanae Vitae*, 14.
[450] Ibid.

rather than offering themselves in an act of total self-giving love. Each of these forms of contraception is also notoriously ineffective. A fact sheet by Dr. Hanna Klaus, M.D. in Mary Shivanandan's book *Crossing the Threshold of Love* indicates a percentage of unplanned pregnancies ranging from 12 to 28 percent for adults, depending on the method utilized. Among adolescents the rate of unplanned pregnancies ranges from 18 to 28 percent.[451] A similar method, that of early withdrawal, has an unplanned pregnancy rate of between 15 and 40 percent.

Besides being ineffective and aesthetically offensive, on a human or medical plane, how do these methods affect the couples who use them? Withdrawal causes frustration of the partners. Jellies and foams can produce allergic reactions. Allegations have been made in medical literature that they can also cause birth defects. In one legal case a 5 million dollar judgment was rendered against a pharmaceutical firm when a child was born with birth defects to parents using the company's contraceptive jelly.[452]

A married woman and journalist, Ruth Lasseter, describes how she and her husband, Rollin, were beguiled into using one of these contraceptives after the birth of their first child, and the effects it had on them.

> One of the "help for new mothers" booklets that was given me at the hospital contained an advertisement for spermicidal foam. It featured a picture of a sweet young mother holding a tiny infant to her breast; the caption read: "You gave him life. Now, give him yourself." The serpent at his most eloquent! . . . Like Eve and her apple, I showed it to Adam and bade him eat.

> When we discovered that we were pregnant and would have another baby within a year of the first, we quarreled seriously and viciously for the first time in our marriage. I had hated using the foam; it made me feel cheap. Rollin, taken unprepared, was annoyed at the prospect of another baby; he felt tricked by me.

> The bitterness of this first quarrel *should* have alerted us to the effects of contraception on married love and trust.[453]

Another similar form of contraception is the Intra-Uterine Device (IUD). One extremely important difference is that, in addition to preventing the sperm from uniting with the ovum, at times the IUD also

---

[451] Dr. Hanna Klaus, M.D., "Fact Sheet: Action, Effectiveness and Medical Side-Effects of Common Methods of Family Planning," in *Crossing the Threshold of Love*, by Mary Shivanandan, pp. 282-283.

[452] Cf. John and Sheila Kippley, *The Art of Natural Family Planning*, (Cincinnati: Couple to Couple League: 1996), p. 12.

[453] Ruth D. Lasseter, "Sensible Sex," in *Why* Humanae Vitae *Was Right: A Reader*, ed. Janet E. Smith, (San Francisco: Ignatius Press, 1993), pp. 484-485. The article first appeared in *Homiletic and Pastoral Review* 92:11 (Aug.-Sept. 1992), pp. 19-31.

prevents implantation of a fertilized ovum in the uterus. When it functions this way, it must be classified as an abortifacient — something causing an abortion. There is still some debate within the medical community as to whether the *primary* action of the IUD is to prevent a newly conceived human life from implanting in the uterus. But it is certain that it does so at least some of the time, and so it must be judged morally as an abortifacient.

What are the effects of IUDs on the unfortunate women who utilize them? There have been so many lawsuits stemming from perforation of the womb, health damage and even death due to infections caused by IUDs that most companies have removed them from the market in the U.S. John Kippley sums up the present situation. "A determined woman can still get an IUD in the United States, but she has to sign a legal document twelve times, releasing the manufacturer from all liability for any problems it may cause her."[454]

C. Sterilization

A highly effective — and permanent — form of artificial contraception is sterilization.[455] Ligation of a woman's fallopian tubes to prevent the sperm and egg from uniting in the tube results in an unplanned pregnancy rate from .4 to 2 percent.[456] What effects do these operations have on women? "The health problems of tubal ligations are so common that doctors have a new phrase: 'post-tubal ligation syndrome.'"[457] One medical study obtained the following results: "The incidence of complications was 22 percent to 37 percent, with symptoms of dysfunctional uterine bleeding, dysmenorrhea [painful periods], dyspareunia [pain during intercourse] and pelvic pain."[458]

The more time that passes after a tubal ligation, the more problems seem to develop. Kippley summarizes the results of another study: "Of 374 patients who were followed for at least 10 years after tubal ligation, 43 percent needed further gynecological treatment and 25 percent had major gynecological surgery [read hysterectomy]."[459]

---

[454] Kippley, *The Art of Natural Family Planning*, p. 11; referring to Alza Corporation, *Progestasert Patient Information* (1987).

[455] It is now possible at times to reverse the effects of both male and female sterilization, but the surgery is difficult and expensive, and positive results cannot be guaranteed. They vary a good deal depending upon the quality of the sterilization operation as well as its after effects.

[456] Dr. Hanna Klaus, M.D., "Fact Sheet: Action, Effectiveness and Medical Side-Effects of Common Methods of Family Planning," in *Crossing the Threshold of Love*, by Mary Shivanandan, pp. 282-283.

[457] Kippley, *The Art of Natural Family Planning*, p. 13.

[458] Joel T. Hargrove and Guy E. Abraham, "Endocrine profile of patients with post-tubal-ligation syndrome," *Journal of Reproductive Medicine* 26:7 (1981), p. 359; cited in Kippley, *The Art of Natural Family Planning*, p. 13.

[459] Kippley, *The Art of Natural Family Planning*, p. 15; referring to M. J. Muldoon, "Gynaecological Illness After Sterilization," *British Medical Journal* (January 8, 1972), pp. 84-85.

The psychological effects of sterilization and its aftermath can be just as devastating for a woman as the health problems. Once again, Ruth Lasseter gives her testimony.

> Rollin was opposed to the ligation, but I had the so-called "band-aid" operation anyway. ("It's my body and my decision," I had parroted.) No one else opposed this surgery at all; quite the opposite, in fact. The very first effect of this, as in an abortion, was relief. That relief didn't last long. Ensuing hormonal imbalance caused a deep, prolonged depression. In fact, as I later learned, my estrogen level dropped to a menopausal level, literally, overnight. I gained a lot of weight in a very short time, another common side effect. My mind was confused; and I was filled with irrational resentment. There was abdominal pain for months after the surgery, probably caused by the nitrous oxide gas that was used to inflate my abdomen for surgery. Periods became so heavy that twice I was hospitalized for excessive hemorrhaging, another common but seldom publicized side-effect. At the age of thirty, I was forced by deteriorating health to have a hysterectomy."[460]

Perhaps men fare better who choose to have a vasectomy, cutting the vas deferens tube to prevent sperm from leaving the scrotum? Medical studies suggest the contrary. Since sperm cannot be released in the normal fashion after a vasectomy, they enter the body by leakage. Once there, an auto-immune response results, with the body reacting to them as foreign bodies. About 50 percent of vasectomized men develop sperm antibodies that can have lasting effects on the immune system.[461]

Two studies published in 1993 in the *Journal of the American Medical Association* demonstrated a clear relationship between vasectomy and prostate cancer. One study showed a 66 to 85 percent greater risk of developing prostate cancer in men who had had vasectomies performed on them. The second study showed a 56 to 106 percent greater risk.[462] Since prostate cancer is the second leading cause of men dying from cancer, the warning is a strong one.

Regarding sterilization, no less an authority than the *British Medical Journal* reiterated the criteria which should govern operations within the medical profession. Surgery should be performed when there is a disease or disorder to be treated. It should not be carried out upon healthy, normally functioning organisms. Neither male nor female fertility constitutes a disease.

---

[460] Lasseter, "Sensible Sex," p. 488.
[461] Kippley, *The Art of Natural Family Planning*, p. 17.
[462] Ibid.; citing Edward Giovannucci, Alberto Ascherio and four others, "A Prospective Cohort Study of Vasectomy and Prostate Cancer in US Men," *JAMA* 269:7 (February 17, 1993), pp. 873 and 878.

It is a sound guiding principle of surgery never to disturb the function of a normal structure except as may be necessary for the effective treatment of a related disorder. Consequently, whereas vasectomy may be appropriate in the treatment of an established urogenital disease to prevent the spread of infection, its performance in a healthy man for a purpose other than for the protection of his own health is difficult to reconcile with the traditions that normally guide clinical judgment.[463]

D. A Revolutionary Development: The Pill

In the 1950s a revolutionary new development occurred in the field of artificial contraceptives: "the Pill." Increased knowledge of the structure and function of female reproductive hormones, especially estrogen and progesterone, made it possible to produce an oral contraceptive that purported to stop ovulation and to be much more effective than any of the barrier methods, without the permanence of sterilization.

Many voices hailed the Pill as one of man's greatest achievements. Ashley Montagu, an anthropologist and sociobiologist, made the following claim in 1969, barely a decade after the Pill came into general use:

> The Pill! The fact that it is referred to so majestically represents something of the measure of importance that is generally attached to this genuinely revolutionary development. For it is a revolutionary development, probably to be ranked among the half dozen or so major innovations in man's two or more million years of history. In its effects I believe that the Pill ranks in importance with the discovery of fire, the creation and employment of tools, the development of hunting, the invention of agriculture, the development of urbanism, scientific medicine, and the release and control of nuclear energy.[464]

1. Is It Effective?

Hormonal contraception is certainly much more effective at preventing pregnancy than any of the barrier methods. The surprise pregnancy rate for the different forms of the Pill, as well as for Depo-Provera injections and the Norplant system, ranges from 1 to 4 percent.[465] It should be noted, however, that when adolescents employ the Pill, the surprise pregnancy rate can be as high as 11 to 15 percent.[466]

---

[463] Editorial, "Sterilization in Man," *British Medical Journal*, 1 (1966), p. 1554, quoted in Kippley, *The Art of Natural Family Planning*, p. 17.

[464] Ashley Montagu, *Sex, Man and Society* (New York: G. P. Putnam's Sons, 1969), p. 13; as cited in Shivanandan, *Crossing the Threshold of Love*, p. 178, footnote 5.

[465] Dr. Hanna Klaus, M.D., "Fact Sheet," in *Crossing the Threshold of Love*, by Mary Shivanandan, pp. 282-283.

[466] Ibid.

2. Is It Safe?

Is the Pill kind to women who use it? The fact that the original combined Pill (synthetic estrogen and progesterone) was later followed by other forms such as the progesterone-only "mini-pill" should already be an indication. The risk of developing blood clots among women who utilize different forms of the Pill (including Depo-Provera and Norplant) is 3 to 11 times greater than among those who do not.[467] Blood clots can cause strokes, heart attacks, pulmonary embolism, or blindness.

John Kippley outlines some of the other health hazards of the Pill. "The risk of fatal heart attacks is approximately twice as great among users of the current low-dose Pill compared to non-users.[468] The risk of a fatal brain hemorrhage is 1.4 times higher among Pill users than among non-users. Among women who smoke and use the Pill, there's a 12-fold increase in fatal heart attacks and a 3.1-fold increase in fatal brain hemorrhage."[469]

If the above facts were not enough to dissuade any woman concerned with her health and well-being from utilizing the Pill, they only represent some of the health hazards of this "major innovation in man's history." A few more possible side effects can be summarized as follows:

> Headaches, migraines, mental depression (even to the point of suicide and/or suicidal tendencies), a decrease or loss of sexual drive, abdominal cramps, bloating, weight gain or loss, and water retention; nausea and vomiting (in about 10 percent of users); symptoms of PMS, vaginitis and vaginal infections, changes in vision (temporary or permanent blindness, and an intolerance to contact lenses); gall bladder disease; and either temporary or permanent infertility, when discontinuing the Pill, in users with previous menstrual irregularities or who began the drug before full maturity."[470]

Simply from a medical point of view, even before taking into account the moral implications of the Pill, the Kippleys sum up their view of the issue. "Quite frankly, we cannot understand why any informed woman would ever take the Pill for birth control. We cannot understand why any husband who loves his wife and understands the health hazards of the Pill would allow his wife to use it if he has anything to say about it."[471]

---

[467] "Demulen," *Physicians' Desk Reference* (1993), p. 2254.

[468] M. Thorogood, J. Mann, M. Murphy, M. Vessey, "Is oral contraceptive use still associated with an increased risk of fatal myocardial infarction? Report of a case-control study," *British Journal of Obstetric Gynecology*, 98 (1991), pp. 1245-1253.

[469] Kippley, *The Art of Natural Family Planning*, p. 8; citing Thorogood, M., Vessey, M., "An epidemiologic survey of cardiovascular disease in women taking oral contraceptives," *American Journal of Obstetric Gynecoly* 163 (1990), pp. 274-281.

[470] Paul Weckenbrock, *The Pill: How does it Work? Is it Safe?* (Cincinnati: Couple to Couple League, 1993), p. 8; cited in Kippley, *The Art of Natural Family Planning*, p. 8.

[471] Kippley, *The Art of Natural Family Planning*, p. 8.

Two new forms of hormonal contraception are the Norplant (a device implanted in a woman's arm) and Depo-Provera (long-lasting injections). Both use the same or similar progestin (a synthetic form of progesterone) that is used by the combination Pill or progesterone only "mini-pill," so both imply the same health hazards. The Norplant tubes, which last three to five years, carry the additional onus of being expensive and difficult to remove, often leaving a woman permanently scarred. Once a Depo-Provera injection has been given, there is no turning back from its effects until the chemicals have been completely metabolized by the body. This takes at least three months. Once the shots are discontinued, an average of 10 months is required before fertility returns.[472]

3. Is It Moral?

The pill is certainly less than kind to the unfortunate women who use it. On the physical level it is harmful to health and well-being. But the pill's most destructive effects on the human person arise from the fact that it is immoral, as are all forms of artificial contraception. Paul VI explains why contraception is intrinsically wrong in *Humanae Vitae*. Contraception violates "the inseparable connection, established by God, which man on his own initiative may not break, between the unitive significance and the procreative significance which are both inherent to the marriage act."[473]

The Pill, Norplant, and Depo-Provera are also immoral for another reason. At least part of the time they function as abortifacients. Though their primary action is to prevent ovulation, at least part of the time ovulation does occur when they are being used. When this happens and fertilization occurs, they also affect the endometrium of the uterus, so that it prevents the fertilized egg from implanting in the womb. A silent abortion takes place. A woman using the Pill does not even know when this early abortion is occurring within her own body.

Some recently developed forms of the Pill, such as the "morning-after pill" or RU-486, are openly touted as abortifacients. Their primary action is to prevent a new human life, already conceived, from implanting in the mother's uterus. On September 28, 2000, the Food and Drug Administration approved marketing RU-486 in the U.S. The abortion pill functions by administering two potent drugs, which frequently produce profuse bleeding, in order to kill a human embryo who is two to five weeks old.[474] How can one not feel concern for a society which seeks new technological advances so that they may be used to silently eliminate innocent human beings before they ever see the light of day?

---

[472] Cf. Kippley, *The Art of Natural Family Planning*, p. 10.
[473] Paul VI, encyclical letter *Humanae Vitae*, 12. Cf. *Catechism of the Catholic Church*, 2336.
[474] Cf. Zenit News Service, September 28, 2000.

III. Is There a Reliable Alternative?
— Natural Family Planning

A married couple is faced with the loving, yet not always easy, task of being responsible parents. At times, for serious reasons, this duty may lead them to decide that they should space the births of new children or even limit the size of their family. Given the immorality of contraceptives and their long list of damaging side effects, where is a married couple to turn? Does a trustworthy alternative exist to artificial contraception?

Thanks to the wonderful ways of God's providence in creating the human person, male and female, a morally honest way for responsible parents to regulate births does exist: Natural Family Planning. The same scientific progress in understanding the hormonal functioning of a woman's fertility cycle that led to contraceptives also made it possible to develop the different methods of natural family planning.

A. The Fertility Cycle

It was not until the late 1920s and early 1930s that the two female hormones of progesterone and estrogen, essential to reproduction, were discovered.[475] Gradually the process of the menstrual cycle and the effects of the hormones on it came to be understood. The hormonal cycle can be explained in a somewhat simplified manner as follows.

Shortly after menstruation, the pituitary gland secretes FSH (follicle stimulating hormone.) FSH stimulates the development of an ovarian follicle and the ovum it contains. The follicle in turn secretes estrogen. Several effects follow from the increased level of estrogen. The inner lining of the uterus (endometrium) builds up, becoming apt for a fertilized egg to be implanted. The cervix secretes a mucus discharge, which changes in character as the estrogen level becomes higher. Body temperature may also fall slightly.

When the estrogen level reaches its high point, it causes the pituitary gland to secrete LH (luteinizing hormone). The LH surge stimulates the ovarian follicle to release the egg in ovulation. After releasing the egg, the follicle turns yellow and becomes known as the corpus luteum (yellow body). It takes on a new function: to secrete the second female hormone — progesterone.

Progesterone has several effects on the fertility cycle. First, it maintains the endometrium at a thick level with a rich blood supply. Second, it suppresses ovulation by communicating to the pituitary gland not to send out FSH. Third, it causes the cervical mucus to thicken. Finally, the woman's resting body temperature also rises due to the higher progesterone level.

---

[475] Shivanandan, *Crossing the Threshold of Love*, pp. 179-180.

If fertilization of the ovum does not occur, after approximately two weeks the corpus luteum ceases to secrete progesterone. This causes the endometrium to be shed in menstruation, the pituitary gland sends out FSH once more, and the cycle begins anew.

If the egg is fertilized after ovulation, about one week later the embryo implants in the endometrium. Very shortly, the placenta of the newly conceived child begins to secrete a hormone called HCG (human chorionic gonadotropin). HCG tells the corpus luteum to continue secreting progesterone until the baby's placenta takes over for the rest of the pregnancy. The continued high level of progesterone maintains the endometrium to support the new life, while continuing to suppress ovulation.[476]

After ovulation, the ovum has a life span of only 8 to 24 hours in which it may become fertilized. It is possible for a second ovulation to occur within 24 hours of the first. This is the case with fraternal twins. The life span of a sperm is no more than 3 to 5 days. That means there are only 5 to 7 days within a woman's cycle during which she is fertile. The question is how to determine precisely this fertile period shortly before and immediately after ovulation in order to avoid or achieve pregnancy.

B. Calendar Rhythm: A First, Ineffective Form of NFP

A first method to determine a woman's fertile period was developed almost simultaneously in the early 1930s by a Japanese doctor, Kyusaku Ogino, and an Austrian gynecologist, Herman Knaus.[477] This method, known as calendar rhythm, did not take into sufficient account irregular cycles that all women have some of the time and some women have most of the time.[478] It simply involved too much guesswork to be an adequate method of family planning.

---

[476] For a more detailed description of the fertility cycle see Kippley, *The Art of Natural Family Planning,* pp. 87-98.

[477] Shivanandan, *Crossing the Threshold of Love,* p. 278.

[478] Ogino's original formula was "10 plus the shortest cycle minus 28 days equals the first fertile day; 17 plus the longest cycle minus 28 days equals the last fertile day." (See Shivanandan, p. 378, note 10.)

Preview

SEVEN "LOVE AND ALL THAT IS OPPOSED TO LOVE":
THE DEVELOPMENT OF NATURAL FAMILY PLANNING AND CONTRACEPTION *(continued)*

III. Is There a Reliable Alternative? — Natural Family Planning *(continued)*
    c. Modern, Effective Methods of NFP
    1. The Sympto-Thermal Method
      -A Noble Sacrifice that Enriches Married Love
    2. The Ovulation or Billings Method
    3. A Little-Known Aspect of NFP: Ecological Breastfeeding

IV. Is Natural Family Planning Really Effective?

V. Does Natural Family Planning Make for Happy Marriages?
    A. Artificial Contraception and Divorce
    B. NFP and Enduring Marriages

VI. Conclusion: "The Word Is Very Near You"

Points to look for

1. What are the three phases of a woman's menstrual-fertility cycle?

2. What are the two signs a woman uses in the Sympto-Thermal Method of NFP to determine the fertile and infertile phases of her cycle?

3. What advantages do the methods of NFP have over artificial contraception on the level of physical and psychological health?

4. Why can NFP be used either to avoid or achieve pregnancy?

5. How much periodic abstinence is required of couples who practice NFP to avoid pregnancy for serious reasons?

6. Why does periodic abstinence not diminish the spontaneity and tenderness of love between husband and wife?

7. How does marital chastity enrich married love?

8. How does the Ovulation Method differ from the Sympto-Thermal Method?

9. What is ecological breastfeeding? How does it differ from cultural breastfeeding?

10. How can ecological breastfeeding be an integral part of natural family planning?

11. What is the effectiveness level of the Sympto-Thermal Method of NFP? What evidence can be cited to confirm this?

12. What statistical evidence can be cited to demonstrate that artificial contraception has been a major contributor to skyrocketing divorce rates in the U.S.?

13. What relationship is there between NFP and lasting marriages? Why?

14. Why can married couples be confident that they will have the strength to practice natural family planning?

C. Modern, Effective Methods of NFP

In the mid-1970s two new, effective methods of natural family planning were developed. These differ from calendar rhythm in that they do not depend upon the average length of cycles. Instead, they offer the possibility of identifying the fertile or infertile phases of a woman's menstrual cycle, regardless of whether that cycle is normal or irregular. The methods do not depend upon the length of the cycle, but instead are based upon the observation of certain symptoms, which invariably occur during the fertile and infertile phases of the cycle. These symptoms are scientifically linked to the hormonal changes that occur during the cycle's different phases.

Unlike artificial forms of contraception, the natural methods of family planning have absolutely no harmful side effects on the couple who practice them. In fact, the opposite is true. Neither are they expensive. All that is needed is a little training, some charts, and a thermometer for one of the methods. Finally, the natural methods are reversible at the will of the couple. They can be used with equal effectiveness either to avoid or to achieve pregnancy.

1. The Sympto-Thermal Method

The first form of natural family planning is known as the Sympto-Thermal method, because it relies on observing symptomatic changes in a woman's cervical mucus and in her basal body temperature (BBT) during the different phases of her cycle. Foremost among the pioneers of this method were a Canadian couple group called SERENA, along with Dr. Joseph Roetzer, whose manual *Family Planning the Natural Way* has become a classic, and John and Sheila Kippley, founders of the Couple to Couple League.[479]

The Sympto-Thermal method is based upon the three phases in a woman's menstrual-fertility cycle:

Phase I = the infertile time before ovulation. It begins on the first day of menstruation.

Phase II = the fertile time before and immediately after ovulation.

Phase III = the infertile time after ovulation. It begins several days after ovulation.

How does the method work? In its simplest form, when a woman detects the first appearance of cervical mucus a few days after menstruation, she realizes that ovulation is soon to occur. She has entered her fertile period, and the couple should begin their period of abstinence from marital relations if they are seeking to avoid pregnancy for serious reasons.

---

[479] Shivanandan, *Crossing the Threshold of Love*, p. 281.

How does the woman know when her fertile period has ended? There are two signs: one positive, and the other negative. Increased levels of progesterone following ovulation cause the woman's resting body temperature to rise noticeably. A positive sign that the fertile period has ended is the upward shift in temperature for at least three days. This symptom is cross-checked by a negative sign: the drying up of the cervical mucus for four days. Once these two signs occur, the woman has entered her infertile period after ovulation, and marital relations will not result in pregnancy.

Since it enables a woman to identify her fertile period, the Sympto-Thermal method can also be used to achieve pregnancy. If a couple is seeking to have children, they will naturally engage in marital relations during the woman's fertile time. Changes in the texture of the cervical mucus within the fertile period help to pinpoint even more precisely which days are the most fertile.

When a couple practices natural family planning to space the births of their children or limit family size, how much abstinence is required of them? Depending on a woman's situation and particular cycle, the period of abstinence can vary from as little as seven to as many as fourteen days. In most cases, it is between eight and ten days.[480]

-A Noble Sacrifice that Enriches Married Love

Naturally, periodic abstinence for married couples is a sacrifice. But it is a noble one, a free oblation that enriches their married love. In no way does marital chastity hinder the spontaneity or tenderness of love between spouses, as countless married couples who practice natural family planning attest. The periods of continence bring husband and wife to discover new ways of manifesting their affection for one another. Wives especially experience the joy of knowing that a kiss or hug from their spouse during a time of abstinence is a simple gesture of love for them as a person, one that seeks no further gratification in return.

As we shall see more fully in Chapter 9, periodic continence also deepens the love expressed by husband and wife during their acts of conjugal union. Periodic abstinence forms the virtue of chastity. Only a person who truly possesses himself through chastity is able to make a sincere gift of himself in love to his spouse in the act of marital union.

2. The Ovulation or Billings Method

Doctors John and Evelyn Billings of Australia were another couple who did pioneering work in the development of modern natural family planning. They were the first to rely exclusively on the mucus sign and to develop rules for its use as a complete method in itself. This form of

---

[480] Kippley, *The Art of Natural Family Planning*, p. 251. In certain infrequent situations the period of abstinence could be more than two weeks.

NFP is officially called the Ovulation Method, but is often popularly referred to as the Billings Method. It has the advantage of being somewhat simpler than the Sympto-Thermal Method, since it relies only upon the mucus sign. Dr. James B. Brown has worked closely with the Billings since the 1940s. A new study, which he released in July of 2000, provides valuable information on the ovulation method and its effectiveness.[481]

Both the Sympto-Thermal and Ovulation methods of natural family planning are being practiced by married couples in many parts of the globe. Dedicated teacher couples go to poor third world countries in order to train spouses there in one of the two methods. With great joy and gratitude couples from these countries learn the methods — ones that impose no economic burden upon them and are in complete harmony with the Christian faith they cherish.

3. A Little-Known Aspect of NFP: Ecological Breastfeeding

Sheila Kippley has proposed "ecological breastfeeding" as an integral part of natural family planning. The term was created by the Kippleys to distinguish the method from "cultural breastfeeding," practiced by many young mothers. Ecological breastfeeding means that the baby gets 100 percent of his liquids, nourishment, and pacification directly from his mother's breasts for the first six months or so.[482] Once the baby begins to take solids at around six months, the mother continues to let him nurse as often as he wants until he weans himself.

Ecological breastfeeding delays the return of the menstrual cycle, and so, of fertility. Studies show that the average delay of menstruation is 14.5 months.[483] The most important factor in delaying the return of fertility is the frequency with which the baby suckles. Frequent nursing is precisely what distinguishes ecological from cultural breastfeeding. The latter is the most common practice among mothers in Western culture. In cultural breastfeeding a mother supplements in the early months with bottles of liquids and baby foods or other solids. She tries to get her baby to nurse on a regular schedule, as would be the case with complete bottle-feeding. Since the single most important factor in delaying the return of fertility is the frequency of nursing, mothers who practice cultural breastfeeding can expect their fertility to return quickly after childbirth.

Ecological breastfeeding is a natural way God has provided to space babies about two years apart. Studies show that mother's milk is much

---

[481] "Studies on Human Reproduction: Ovarian Activity and Fertility and the Billings Ovulation Method," J.B. Brown (July 2000), Ovulation Method Research and Reference Centre of Australia, ISBN 0-908482-12- 4; cf. http://www.woomb.org/bom/science/ovarian.html.
[482] Kippley, *The Art of Natural Family Planning*, p. 324.
[483] Ibid.

more healthy for the young baby than any artificial formula.[484] The amount of time spent nursing at his mother's breast is also extremely beneficial for the emotional security and peace of the baby. In poor third world countries another decisive advantage is that ecological breast-feeding does not impose on the family the economic burden of expensive formulas and baby foods.

Does ecological breastfeeding offer a real alternative to artificial contraception? One citation from a doctoral thesis provides the answer. "A recent survey [not including China] revealed that breastfeeding contributes more to birth regulation worldwide than the sum of all public and private contraceptive programs. The magnitude of the natural effect has been estimated to be at least 36 million couple-years of protection against pregnancy, compared with 27 million couple-years afforded by contraception."[485]

IV. Is Natural Family Planning Really Effective?

After seeing the remarkable advantages natural family planning has over artificial contraception, one lingering doubt could still remain in our minds. Is NFP really effective? Don't couples who practice natural methods usually end up having a child when they least expect one?

The answer to these questions is quite simple: the effectiveness rate of the methods of natural family planning, when the rules are properly followed, has been demonstrated to equal the effectiveness of any form of artificial contraception short of sterilization.

In a chapter of *The Art of Natural Family Planning* on the effectiveness of the Sympto-Thermal Method, Thomas McGovern, M.D. writes: "The reality is that NFP can be used at the 99 percent level of effectiveness by married couples who understand the method and *always* follow the rules."[486] What exactly does "99 percent level of effectiveness" mean? It is shorthand for "a surprise (unintended) pregnancy rate of one per 100 woman-years."[487] That means that one woman out of 100 practicing the Sympto-Thermal Method for one year in the studies became pregnant.

How does the effectiveness of the Sympto-Thermal Method compare with that of the Ovulation or Billings Method? In 1976-1978 the U.S. Department of Health, Education and Welfare conducted a study in Los Angeles to determine the relative effectiveness of these two methods of natural family planning. Among the couples who followed the

---

[484] Cf. David Stewart, Ph.D., *The Five Standards for Safe Childbearing* (Marble Hill, MO: Napsac Reproductions, 1981).

[485] Harry William Taylor, Jr., *Effect of nursing pattern on postpartum anovulatory interval*, doctoral dissertation (Davis: Univ. of California, 1989), p. 4. The survey Taylor quotes: Franz W. Rosa, "Breast feeding: a motive for family planning," *People*, vol. 3 (1976), pp. 10-13.

[486] Thomas W. McGovern, M.D., Chapter 13, More on Effectiveness, in Kippley, *The Art of Natural Family Planning*, p. 139.

[487] Cf. Ibid.

rules for their methods, the investigators found zero unplanned pregnancies in the Sympto-Thermal Method group (a zero percent surprise pregnancy rate) and 6 in the Ovulation Method group (for a 5.7 percent surprise pregnancy rate).[488] More recent and wider-ranging studies, however, confirm that the Ovulation Method has an effectiveness rate of above 99 percent, equivalent to that of the Sympto-Thermal Method, when the rules are correctly followed.[489]

Dr. Thomas Hilgers has developed the Creighton Model, a refined form of the Ovulation Method. At the Pope Paul VI Institute for Human Reproduction in Creighton, Nebraska, he has achieved notable success, not only in fostering the responsible avoidance of pregnancy through NFP, but also in aiding couples to achieve pregnancy.[490]

Still more studies should be undertaken and evaluated to confirm these results on larger control groups in different areas of the world. But it is clear from the research already completed, as well as from the experience of thousands of married couples who have been practicing NFP for many years, that it is a scientifically effective method of family planning — one that is in full harmony with the truth about married love in God's plan of creation and redemption.

V. Does Natural Family Planning Make for Happy Marriages?

A. Artificial Contraception and Divorce

In 1910, when the production, distribution, and sale of contraceptives were illegal in most states thanks to the Comstock Laws, there was one divorce for every 11 marriages in the United States.[491] Then Margaret Sanger began to organize her birth-control and sexual-libertarian campaign. By 1925, the divorce rate had jumped sharply to 1 divorce for every 7 marriages.

The advent of the Pill made "sexual freedom" as easy as swallowing an oral contraceptive. By 1965, 1 out of every 4 marriages ended in divorce. The "sexual revolution" soon swept across the country, leaving broken homes and devastated lives in its wake. In the year 1977 the divorce rate reached the tragic ratio of 1 divorce for every 2 new marriages.

How widespread has the practice of contraception become in a country where 1 of every 2 marriages ends in divorce? By 1990 more

---

[488] Cf. Ibid., p. 149. Details of the study cited can be found in Wade ME, McCarthy P, Braunstein GD, et al., "A randomized prospective study of the use-effectiveness of two methods of natural family planning, *American Journal of Obstetrics and Gynecology* (No. 138, 1980), pp. 1142-1147.

[489] Cf. "The Study of Method and User Effectiveness of the Creighton Model of the Ovulation Method" in the June, 1998 edition of the *Journal of Reproductive Medicine.*

[490] Cf. http://www.mitec.net/~popepaul/Fert_Care1.htm.

[491] The marriage and divorce statistics that follow are taken from the *Statistical Abstract of the United States, 1978.*

than 70 percent of married women in the United States were using contraceptives.[492] Have Catholics fared better than non-Catholics in resisting the contraception campaign? In 1965, 32 percent of married Catholics practiced natural family planning. (In the 1960s that meant the frequently unreliable calendar rhythm method.) By 1988, despite the development of modern, effective methods, a mere 4 percent of Catholic couples practiced NFP.[493] That figure is only slightly higher than the 2 percent of Protestants who practiced various forms of NFP. By 1988 there was no significant difference between the number of Catholics and non-Catholics who practiced contraception.[494] Father Daniel McCaffrey, an expert in the field of natural family planning among Catholics, recently affirmed: "Between 80 to 90 percent of Catholics practice contraception and sterilization."[495] As to the divorce rate among Catholics, it increased to be on a par with the national average at around 50 percent.

Obviously many elements have entered into the heartbreaking rise in the number of divorces in our country. But who can deny, when confronted with such overwhelming empirical evidence, that contraception was a principal factor, if not *the* primary cause? These statistical facts suggest that breaking away from contraception is the best way to combat divorce. Does experience bear out this claim?

B. NFP and Enduring Marriages

No comprehensive statistical studies have yet been completed on the divorce rate among couples who practice natural family planning. But some convincing evidence is available. As of December 11, 1995, the Couple to Couple League had certified 1,098 teaching couples since its origin in 1971. Fifteen of those marriages ended in divorce. That yields a divorce rate of 1.4 percent among this select group. Even tripling the figure as a conjecture to estimate the divorce rate among the larger group of couples practicing NFP yields a divorce rate of 4.2 percent — less than one-tenth of the national divorce rate and the divorce rate among Catholics in general.[496]

A few scientific studies have been done concerning the relationship between NFP and marital satisfaction. In 1977 M. Peter McCusker surveyed 98 couples with a 41-item questionnaire, including nine open-

---

[492] Figures are based on information supplied by the Population Research Institute of Washington, D.C.

[493] Figures are taken from Calvin Goldscheider and William D. Mosher, "Patterns of Contraceptive Use in the United States: The Importance of Religious Factors," *Studies in Family Planning* (1991; 22:2), pp. 102-115, at p. 104. The article cites the Cycle IV of the National Survey of Family Growth (1988).

[494] Ibid.

[495] Father Daniel McCaffrey, Natural Family Planning Outreach. "Combat Training Comes In Handy," in *National Catholic Register*, April 2-8, 2000, Vol. 76, No. 14, p. 16.

[496] John F. Kippley, "Marital Duration and Natural Family Planning," (Cincinnati: CCL, 1995), one page fact sheet.

ended questions to permit maximum freedom for the respondents. "The investigator concluded that fertility awareness methods of natural family planning were perceived as contributing positively to the marital relationship by 98 married couples who had used natural methods for an average of 1.76 years at the time of the study."[497]

In a 1979 study Joseph Tortorici used standardized instruments to measure self-esteem and marital satisfaction among 45 Catholic couples, some of whom practiced NFP, while others employed artificial means of contraception. Tortorici concluded: "1. Catholic couples in this study who are at present using natural methods of conception regulation demonstrate higher levels of self-esteem than do couples, grouped as a whole, who are using other methods. . . . 4. Catholic couples who use natural methods demonstrate higher levels of marital satisfaction than do couples who are using other methods of conception regulation."[498]

Ruth Lasseter gives a moving testimony of what following God's law did for her marriage in the years before she had a tubal ligation. Though she and her husband were Anglicans when they married, a close Catholic friend warned them about the dangers of artificial contraception — one year before *Humanae Vitae* was promulgated. The effective methods of NFP had not yet been developed in the 1960s, so Ruth and her husband, Rollin, made the decision to be open to as many children as God wanted to send them. Their one negative experience with contraceptives after the birth of their first child convinced them to reject artificial contraception for many years. Ruth describes those early years of marriage.

> It is a recognized trend that the older parents grow, the less they remember of unpleasantness and trials in their young families. We are no exception. Our memory of that time is of mad-cap joy, knee-deep in babies and toddlers, six of them, age five and under! That we were sometimes so dead tired that we could barely push through the day is remembered only vaguely.
>
> In truth, I don't think we slept more than a few hours any night for at least seven years, and we were always worried about how we were going to support our family. We were filled with trust in one another and with a sense of purpose, and we drew strength from it; it kept us from being overwhelmed by anxiety and fatigue. There was a sense of divine protection and mystery behind everything that happened in those years.
>
> Because we had chosen obedience to the will of God and had entrusted our fertility, as well as our souls, to one another, we knew

---

[497] M. Peter McCusker, "NFP and the marital relationship: the CUA Study," *International Review of Natural Family Planning*, (1977; 1:4), pp. 331-340, at p. 334.
[498] Joseph Tortorici, "Conception Regulation, self-esteem, and marital satisfaction among Catholic couples: Michigan State University study," *IRNFP*, (1979; III:3), pp. 191-205, at pp. 197-198.

the gift of unconditional love. This was a shared secret between us, given us by Christ, whose presence was constantly felt as a "third" in our marriage. This secret, pondered deeply in my heart and cherished in Rollin's, took the form of enormous confidence about what we were doing. This was not pride, though pride is ever a threat in every human being, but rather a certainty born of deep reverence for an awareness of the presence of Christ's holiness in our marriage.[499]

This mother of six reflects on the paradox of human life and love in light of those difficult, yet happy years: "Suffering and sweetness are indivisible; both are essential. The adventure of faith, lived out in sacramental marriage, is one great, mysterious union of suffering and unconditional love."[500]

VI. Conclusion: "The Word Is Very Near You"

As young couples embark upon the expectant journey of married life, how closely do the horizons stretching out before them resemble the panorama that lay before the people of Israel on their flight to the Promised Land! Artificial contraception and natural family planning lie open as two divergent paths leading to profoundly different destinies. Moses proclaimed to the Chosen People: "I call heaven and earth to witness against you this day, that I have set before you life and death, blessing and curse; therefore choose life, that you and your descendants may live, loving the Lord your God, obeying his voice, and cleaving to him."[501]

Natural family planning is not an easy journey. It entails the self-sacrifice of the cross. But Christ walks along the path with each married couple. He goes before them, taking the heaviest burden of the cross upon himself. The gift of the Holy Spirit that he has won for each man and woman through his redemption gives joy even in the midst of self-denial. Christ's Spirit makes his yoke easy and his burden light.

May the words of Moses to God's people, given new force by the transforming power of Christ's redemption, echo in the hearts and lives of all married couples: "For this commandment which I command you this day is not too hard for you, neither is it far off. It is not in heaven, that you should say, 'Who will go up for us to heaven, and bring it to us, that we may hear it and do it?' Neither is it beyond the sea, that you should say, 'Who will go over the sea for us, and bring it to us, that we may hear it and do it?' But the word is very near you; it is in your mouth and in your heart, so that you can do it."[502]

---

[499] Ruth D. Lasseter, "Sensible Sex," in *Why* Humanae Vitae *Was Right: A Reader,* edited by Janet E. Smith, (San Francisco: Ignatius Press, 1993), pp. 485-486.

[500] Ibid., p. 481.

[501] Dt 30:19-20.

[502] Dt 30:11-14.

EIGHT

Contraception's Ideological Roots: A Compelling Response

Preview

I. Why Is Contraception Flourishing?
   A. Economic Factors
   B. Ideological Roots

II. Origins of the Contraceptive Mentality: Nineteenth Century Malthusianism

III. "What is Man?" Eighteenth Century Rationalist Materialism
   A. *Sapere Aude*: The Enlightenment
   B. From Exaltation to Abasement: A Reductive View of the Human Person
      1. The Elimination of Mystery
      2. The Opposition Between Faith and Reason
      3. The Divorce of Faith and Culture
      4. The Darkening of Reason: Radical Skepticism

IV. The Twentieth Century: Reaping the Bitter Fruits of Enlightened Rationalism
   A. Secular Humanism and Other Destructive "-isms"
   B. "The Pulverization of the Person"

Points to look for

1. How do economic factors explain why artificial contraception is flourishing despite the harmful effects of contraceptives?

2. What factors, even deeper than economic ones, account for the present contraceptive mentality?

3. What is Malthusianism and how did it help give rise to the contraceptive ideology?

4. How is Malthusianism rooted in the rationalist materialism of the Enlightenment?

5. What does the Holy Father mean when he says there is both a moral and an anthropological difference between natural family planning and contraception?

6. What is implied by the motto of the Enlightenment: *sapere aude* (dare to know)?

7. Why does enlightened rationalism have a reductive view of human reason?

8. Why does the Enlightenment's exaltation of human reason lead to the abasement of the human person?

9. What is secular humanism?

10. How is secular humanism a bitter, present-day fruit of rationalism?

11. What can be described as the goal of secular humanism?

12. What is meant by the "pulverization of the person"? How is it a fruit of reductive "-isms"?

I. Why Is Contraception Flourishing?

A. Economic Factors

We have seen the physical and psychological harm contraceptives inflict upon those who use them. There is also overwhelming evidence that the practice of contraception has been one of the most important factors in the tragic rise in the number of divorces. Natural family planning, while it is just as effective a means of regulating births as the Pill and much more so than any of the barrier methods, has absolutely no negative physical or psychological side effects. Rather than weakening marriages, it helps to strengthen them. Yet almost no one speaks of NFP in the public arena and artificial contraception continues to flourish. Why?

Obviously, one key factor is economic. Contraceptives are a multi-billion dollar worldwide business. Once couples learn natural family planning, no pharmaceutical company will receive any financial gain from them. All that a husband and wife need to purchase in order to follow God's plan for married love throughout all their fertile years are a few charts and a thermometer.

B. Ideological Roots

Still, the explanation as to why contraception continues to flourish and to be so vigorously promoted by international agencies in the world today goes much deeper than financial considerations. In the first place, contraception is the easy path for historical man, tainted by sin, to follow. The legitimacy of choosing to walk down the wide, spacious path is also supported by an entire ideological framework. This ideology embraces a specific vision of the human person and human sexuality — one that is irreconcilable with the transcendent mystery that constitutes each human person, created in the image of God and redeemed by Christ.

Where did the ideology that underlies contraception originate? The direct beginnings of the present contraceptive mentality can be traced to nineteenth-century Malthusianism, with its myth of an impending population explosion. But the roots of the contraceptive ideology penetrate even deeper. They are nourished by eighteenth-century Enlightenment rationalism, with its reductive view of the human person as a material, individual member of the human species. In sketching the rise of the contraceptive ideology, it will be possible to discover its fundamental errors.

II. Origins of the Contraceptive Mentality: Nineteenth-Century Malthusianism

All of the countries in Western Europe, along with the United States, Canada, China, Japan, and a host of others are failing to replace their populations. Yet many international agencies continue to employ rhetoric about the threat of overpopulation. When did the idea of a population explosion first arise?

In 1798 Thomas Robert Malthus of England first propounded the notion of overpopulation. His projections of a geometric increase in human population accompanied by a simple arithmetic growth in the food supply led him to envision massive starvation in the future. As a solution, he advocated moral restraint among men and women — delayed marriage, celibacy, and abstinence in marriage — to decrease the number of children being born.[503]

In 1822 Francis Place, a neo-Malthusian, combined the idea of contraception with the population question. By the end of the nineteenth century, a new movement promoting contraception began to grow out of Malthusianism: eugenics. Charles Darwin's cousin, Francis Galton, was the first one to coin the term "eugenics."[504] While Malthusians sought to limit all births, eugenicists sought to improve the human species by limiting births of those considered inferior: the poor, handicapped, or unfit, or those belonging to "lesser" races. It was a simple question of applying Darwin's theory of the survival of the fittest to human beings!

III. "What is Man?" Eighteenth-Century Rationalist Materialism

How is it possible that the contraceptive ideology born of Malthusianism continues to hold sway in so much of the world, despite the crisis of so many countries who are not even replacing their own population? How did it come about that human persons in all of their transcendent reality have been reduced to simple members of the human species, who can be manipulated just like any other species? The answer lies in an even deeper eighteenth-century ideology, out of which Malthusianism itself arose: rationalist materialism.

---

[503] Cf. Mary Shivanandan, *Crossing the Threshold of Love: A New Vision of Marriage* (Washington, D.C.: CUA Press, 1999), p. 184. The projections of Malthus have been repeatedly demonstrated to be false both scientifically and empirically. (The United States alone produces enough food to feed the entire world several times over. All of the people in the world could fit quite comfortably into a rather small portion of Texas.) Still, Malthusian fears of overpopulation continue to hold sway in many circles.

[504] Cf. ibid.

A brief look at the Enlightenment, source of modern rationalism, and its consequences, will reveal just how much is at stake behind present-day efforts to foist contraception upon the peoples of the world. The rationalist concept of man shows John Paul II to be correct when he resoundingly affirms that the difference between contraception and natural family planning is, at its core, an anthropological one. Let us view once again the prophetic text from *Familiaris Consortio* as we begin to explore rationalism's implications.

> In the light of the experience of many couples and of the data provided by the different human sciences, theological reflection is able to perceive *the difference, both anthropological and moral,* between contraception and recourse to the rhythm of the cycle: it is a difference which is much wider and deeper than is usually thought, one which involves two irreconcilable concepts of the human person and of human sexuality.[505]

A. *Sapere Aude*: The Enlightenment

A pervasive movement swept across Europe in the eighteenth century, hailed by its supporters as the "Enlightenment." The rationalism of the Enlightenment exalted human reason to the point of making it the measure of all things. Immanuel Kant's celebrated phrase, *sapere aude* (dare to know), became the motto of the Enlightenment.

Notable scientific advances led to great optimism about the possibilities of the human intellect. Through reason man could liberate himself from a state of infantile dependence. He could attain maturity and true freedom. Unlimited horizons of human development and progress would steadily open.

But the human reason exalted by the Enlightenment was not the same one which had led the early Church Fathers to inculturate the truths of revelation in the fruitful soil of Greek philosophy. It was not the reason that had enabled them to penetrate into the mysteries of the faith, proclaiming Christ "one in being (*homoousios*) with the Father,"[506] and possessing two natures in one person (*prosopon*) in the Incarnation.[507] Nor was it the reason that had led St. Thomas Aquinas, six centuries earlier, to unsurpassed heights in probing the mystery of God and human life with rational understanding: the *Summa Theologiae*.

The Enlightenment acclaimed a reason born of the empirical sciences and their method. It was a reason which reduced all human knowing to facts that could be empirically verified — observed, measured, and quantified. Since all human knowing involved material facts of sense experience, the human person soon came to be viewed in a ma-

---

[505] *FC*, 32.
[506] Council of Nicea I (325): DS 130.
[507] Council of Chalcedon (451): DS 302.

terialistic way. Thinkers such as La Mettrie in France and P.H.D. von Holbach in the Netherlands applied René Descartes' mechanistic explanation of plants and animals to man himself. Man was reduced to a material individual, a type of living robot, who was nothing more than the sum of his parts.

B. From Exaltation to Abasement: A Reductive View of the Human Person

1. The Elimination of Mystery

Tragic consequences have resulted from rationalism's impoverished answer to that timeless question, posed with utter simplicity by the psalmist: "What is man?"[508] Paradoxically, the attempted exaltation of man and his reason to be the measure of all things has led to a cruel abasement of the human person. All at once man is no longer a mystery. The human person can be studied, understood, quantified, and completely determined by reason. It is simply a question of time and the progress of the sciences until this goal will be achieved. By the tenets of rationalist materialism, banished from man's life forever is the wonder at his own being in the hands of God that moved the Psalmist to exclaim:

> Thou dost beset me behind and before
> and layest thy hand upon me.
> Such knowledge is too wonderful for me;
> it is high, I cannot attain it.[509]

2. The Opposition Between Faith and Reason

When mystery is eliminated from man's life, faith must necessarily be cast off as well. The separation between reason and faith avowed by early Enlightenment thinkers quickly developed into an opposition between faith and reason. Faith came to be viewed as nothing more than superstition — the enemy of reason and of all true human progress. A noted historian sums up the attitude of the enlightened rationalist thinkers, or *philosophes*, toward religion.

> The *philosophes* regarded religion, especially Christianity, as fantasy that drew humanity away from the rational world into a realm of hope and belief in a nonexistent life beyond. The spiritual world was not subject to reason or proof and therefore drew scorn from the *philosophes*. Indeed, they contended that organized religion sought to control thought and was therefore anathema to true intellectual freedom."[510]

---

[508] Psalm 8.
[509] Psalm 139:5-6.
[510] Perry M. Rogers, editor, *Aspects of Western Civilization, Problems and Sources in History, Volume II* (Englewood Cliffs: Prentice-Hall, 1988), p. 97.

The opposition between faith and reason introduced by the Enlightenment was a new phenomenon in Western Civilization. Since the early centuries of Christianity, for the first Christian apologists such as St. Justin, martyr, the relationship between faith and reason had generally been a harmonious one. The revelation of divine mysteries, accepted by faith, was seen as the glorious crowning of reason. Faith elevated reason to heights it could not attain on its own. It opened before the human spirit a completely new dimension of the meaning of existence, one that was capable of satisfying the deepest aspirations of the human heart.

3. The Divorce of Faith and Culture

The tragedy begun by falsely opposing faith and reason has continued to be played out in many different acts, even to the present day. Human persons express who they are and strive to give answers to the most essential questions about the meaning of life through *culture*. Ever since the Enlightenment, attempts have been made to construct an entirely secular culture — one that excludes God. Can any person truly discover the answers to his most pressing questions about his purpose in life, the goal and worth of his endeavors and toils, in a culture which denies the One for whom every heart is made? Pope Paul VI has affirmed without hesitation that the fundamental drama of our times is precisely "the split between faith and culture."[511]

To encounter disturbing proof of Paul VI's assertion, it is not necessary to look beyond the boundaries of America itself — a country once founded as a haven for religious freedom, a shining "city on a hill." In the second half of the twentieth century there has been an unparalleled attempt to remove religion from public life in the United States: to take God out of government, out of schools, and out of public institutions. The result of this movement is aptly described by Father Richard John Neuhaus in the title of one of his books: *The Naked Public Square.*

A new tragic episode in this unfolding drama took place during June of the Jubilee Year 2000. It involved a case of student-led prayer before high-school football games in Texas. By a 6-3 vote, the Supreme Court denied student speakers from the Santa Fe Independent School District the right to direct a public pre-game prayer. The ruling was made despite the fact that the speaker was elected by the students and given a choice between delivering a message or an invocation.

"School sponsorship of a religious message is impermissible," Justice John Paul Stevens wrote in the majority opinion, "because it sends the ancillary message to members of the audience who are non-adherents that they are outsiders"[512] and violates the First Amendment. Jus-

---

[511] *Evangelii Nuntiandi*, 20.
[512] As cited in "Supreme Court Overrules Pre-Game Student Prayer," *National Catholic Register*, Vol. 76, No. 26, June 25-July 1, 2000, p. 3.

tice Stevens failed to point out that prohibiting students from praying publicly sends the ancillary message that all those present who believe in God are outsiders. What the Supreme Court decision basically amounts to is denying the right to invoke the name of God in public. Chief Justice William Rehnquist disagreed with the court majority. He said the ruling "bristles with hostility to all things religious in public life."[513]

Little more remains, other than for the highest court in the land to declare America's motto, "In God We Trust," unconstitutional. That could possibly happen, if the American Civil Liberties Union has its way. Also in June of 2000, the ACLU filed a lawsuit against the Shawnee County treasurer in Topeka, Kansas, attempting to force her to remove two posters from the treasurer's office. What is the content of the posters? It is the official national slogan, "In God We Trust." What could be incriminating about posters with the country's motto? The word "God" stands out in reddish letters.[514]

The right to invoke the name of God in the public forum is a basic aspect of religious freedom. On December 7, 1995, in his remarks to the participants of the Becket Fund's Congress on Secularism and Religious Freedom, Pope John Paul II reiterated the Church's position on this crucial issue. He affirmed that not only the well-being of society is at stake, but also the very nature of the human person. How resounding is the final query the Holy Father addresses to those who would remove all vestige of religious expression from the public square!

> If citizens are expected to leave aside their religious convictions when they take part in public life, does this not mean that society not only excludes the contribution of religion to its institutional life, but also promotes a culture which re-defines man as less than what he is?
>
> In particular, there are moral questions at the core of every great public issue. Should citizens whose moral judgments are informed by their religious beliefs be less welcome to express their most deeply held convictions? When that happens, is not democracy itself emptied of real meaning?[515]

4. The Darkening of Reason: Radical Skepticism

When enlightened rationalism cut off reason from the certitude of faith, the consequences were not long in making themselves felt within the realm of the intellect itself. The impoverished reason of the Enlightenment, reduced to knowing empirical facts which could be verified by

---

[513] As cited in Ibid.

[514] Cf. Robert R. Holton, "Is the U.S. Motto Un-American?" in the *National Catholic Register*, Vol. 76, No. 27, July 2-8, 2000, pp. 1 and 7.

[515] As cited in Ibid., p. 7.

sense experience, soon came to realize that it was insufficient unto itself. Reason began to doubt its own ability to understand reality. Before long, radical skepticism was flourishing as a philosophical current.

In our own twentieth century this skepticism has assumed many clever disguises. It has often retreated to a position that on the surface seems less self-contradictory: relativism. The most varied intellectual finery in a myriad of hues and shades is brought out in order to dress up this underlying relativism and make it more presentable. *Pensiero debole* (weak thought), multiculturalism, and diversity studies parade resplendent before our eyes, subtly proclaiming as absolute the truth that all truth, all thought, all culture is relative.

What happens to human persons when transcendent mystery is eliminated from their life and they are viewed as nothing more than material creatures? What consequences ensue when faith is divorced from reason and culture? What effect does it have on peoples' lives when reason itself retreats into disguised skepticism in an endless variety of forms?

The prophetic document of the Second Vatican Council on the Church's role in the modern world, *Gaudium et Spes*, describes in two concise phrases the inevitable abasement of the person which results from the attempt to exalt him above all else. "For without the Creator the creature would disappear. . . . When God is forgotten . . . the creature itself grows unintelligible."[516]

IV. The Twentieth Century: Reaping the Bitter Fruits of Enlightened Rationalism

A. Secular Humanism and Other Destructive "-isms"

Many devastating "-isms" have come to "strut and fret their hour upon the stage" in the twentieth century. Each of these false "-isms" contains an element of truth. That is what makes them so appealing, so seductive. But all of them try to *reduce* the entire reality of the human person to that one aspect of the truth about man which they have discovered. When we are dealing with the transcendent reality that is the human person, an "-ism" that is *reductive* is *destructive*.

Marxist-Leninism gave rise to communism, the Gulags, and the "empire of lies." Nietzscheism led to fascism, with the terrible horror of World War II and the holocaust. Freudianism helped give birth to the sexual revolution and the untold miseries it has inflicted upon countless spouses, families, and young people by degrading the most intimate commitment of human love.

All of these pernicious "-isms" trace their origin, in one way or another, to eighteenth-century rationalism, with its erroneous and reduc-

---

[516] *Gaudium et Spes*, 36.

tive answer to that most fundamental of questions: "What is man?" John Paul II has affirmed that Enlightenment rationalism marked the beginning of a three-hundred year battle against God. What have been the dimensions of this confrontation? According to the Holy Father, it has been a *"struggle against God, the systematic elimination of all that is Christian.* This struggle has to a large degree dominated thought and life in the West for three centuries. *Marxist collectivism is nothing more than a 'cheap version' of this plan.* Today a similar plan is revealing itself in all its danger and, at the same time, in all its faultiness."[517]

To some extent communism, fascism, and even Freudianism have been relegated to "the dust bin of history," as Ronald Reagan once put it. But what is the "similar plan" against God that John Paul II claims is unveiling itself today? The twentieth-century version of enlightened rationalism, thriving still on the threshold of the third millennium despite "all its faultiness," is called *secular humanism.*

According to secular humanism, man is his own end. His present, earthly life constitutes the measure of all reality. Deluded by the reductionism that views empirical facts observed by the senses as the sole true object of knowledge, secular humanists avow nature to be the only thing that is real. The supernatural is wholly excluded. Most vehemently denied is the possibility that any supernatural reality could ever penetrate into the natural realm of this world. Divine revelation in Scripture and organized religions fall under interdict, as does God's providence. The very idea of the Incarnation — God becoming man to enter human history — is simply preposterous.

Man himself must bring about his own salvation through scientific and technological progress, since he is ultimately the source of his own happiness. Cut off from communion with God, the "man" proposed by secular humanism tends to be one of radical individualism rather than a being called to a communion of persons, where he encounters his deepest fulfillment.

What is the goal secular humanism seeks to achieve? George Weigel has described in vivid terms what remains as a goal for democracy once it has lost its moral values. Certainly no proponent of secular humanism would formulate the aspiration of his philosophy with such language. But Weigel's description remains accurate. It can aptly be applied to the ultimate goal that secular humanism strives to attain: "the gratification of the unencumbered, self-constituting, imperial Self."[518]

---

[517] John Paul II, *Crossing the Threshold of Hope* (New York: Alfred A. Knopf, 1994), p. 133.
[518] George Weigel, *Soul of the World* (Grand Rapids: Eerdmans, 1996), p. 127.

B. "The Pulverization of the Person"

During the watershed year of 1968, Karol Wojtyła wrote a letter to his friend, the Jesuit theologian Henri de Lubac. In reflecting upon the sufferings that afflicted humanity, Wojtyła penetrated to their deepest cause. The moral evils of the twentieth century had arisen from false "-isms," reductive ideologies which put forward a spurious metaphysical description of what it meant to be a human person. By eliminating the transcendent dimension of the person, the call to communion with others and with God himself, these destructive ideologies had degraded persons to anonymous individuals, open to manipulation and abuse from every side. Erroneous and partial answers to the question "What is man?" had broken persons to bits, had pulverized them.

As a shepherd prepared to lay down his life for the sheep, Karol Wojtyła succinctly formulated his response to the ravenous ideological wolves seeking to devour mankind. To engage in stubborn debate would have been useless. What was needed was to propose anew the inviolable mystery, the transcendent vocation and destiny of the human person. A compelling vision of mankind's true greatness in Christ, an authentic Christian humanism, would sweep away empty ideologies like dust in the wind. Wojtyła wrote:

> The evil of our times consists in the first place in a kind of degradation, indeed in a pulverization, of the fundamental uniqueness of each human person. This evil is even more of the metaphysical order than of the moral order. To this disintegration planned at times by atheistic ideologies we must oppose, rather than sterile polemics, a kind of 'recapitulation' of the inviolable mystery of the person.[519]

Guided by the Holy Spirit, the Church has vibrantly proclaimed the transcendent, inviolable mystery of the person from the Second Vatican Council, through the pontificates of Paul VI and John Paul II, leading humanity across the threshold of the third millennium. Still, more than a few people have been closed and even hostile to the voice of the Church, as she calls men and women to rise to the heights they can attain through the transforming power of Christ's redemption.

In 1985 John Paul II called an Extraordinary Assembly of the Synod of Bishops to evaluate the fruits of the council and its implementation twenty years later. The synod's *Final Report* ardently affirmed Vatican II as a "grace of God and a gift of the Holy Spirit." The *Report* also noted difficulties in the reception of the council's message. George Weigel sums up well the principal cause in his biography of John Paul II, *Witness to Hope*. It consisted of "an ideologically hardened secularism that

---

[519] Cited in "John Paul II and the Crisis of Humanism," by George Weigel, in *First Things*, December 1999, pp. 31-36, at 32.

was not open to dialogue. This close-mindedness, the *Final Report* stated bluntly, was a manifestation of the 'mystery of iniquity' in our day."[520]

The powers of darkness have maintained their assault upon mankind throughout history, seeking to deceive and destroy humanity. They will continue to do so until Christ returns in glory to establish a new heavens and a new earth. But as we advance along the sometimes uncertain journey through history, there is one unshakeable truth we can be sure of: "The light shines in the darkness, and the darkness has not overcome it."[521]

---

[520] George Weigel, *Witness to Hope*, (New York: HarperCollins, 1999), p. 503.
[521] Jn 1:5.

Preview

EIGHT CONTRACEPTION'S IDEOLOGICAL ROOTS: A COMPELLING RESPONSE *(continued)*

V. A Reply to Rationalist Materialism
   A. Critique
      1. Materialism Refuted
      2. Skepticism Refuted
         a) The Horizons of Reason: Philosophy and the Empirical Sciences
         b) The "Intelligent Design" Movement: Opening the Empirical Sciences to Reason's Horizons
            (1) Specified Complexity: Detecting Intelligent Design Empirically
            (2) Irreducible Complexity: Intelligent Design in Biology — Darwinism Refuted
         c) Skepticism: Self-destruction by Self-contradiction
           -Definition of Objective Truth
           -Skepticism's Unavoidable Self-contradiction
         3) Relativism Refuted

Points to look for

1. Why are the experiences of our own acts of knowing and the free decisions of our will the best evidence to refute materialism?

2. How does the fact that we are capable of knowing universal truths prove that our intellect is spiritual?

3. What is an existential proof that we possess freedom of the will?

4. How does the sense of loss which accompanies the free decisions of our will prove that our will is spiritual?

5. How do the empirical sciences depend upon universal, philosophical principles about the nature of being itself — principles which our reason is able to grasp?

6. What reply could be made to rationalists who affirm that our reason is only capable of knowing empirical, scientific facts and cannot grasp universal principles which describe the nature of being itself?

7. What is the "intelligent design" movement which seeks to overcome materialism within the empirical sciences?

8. What is *complexity* within the empirical sciences?

9. What does it mean for something to be *specified* empirically?

10. How does the criterion of *specified complexity* make it possible to detect intelligent design in the physical universe by means of the empirical sciences?

11. What is *irreducible complexity* in biology? What is *cumulative complexity*?

12. How do irreducibly complex biological systems refute the Darwinian hypothesis of evolution by natural selection?

13. What effect would overcoming rationalist materialism in the sciences have on a total vision of the human person?

14. Why is it so vitally important for people's lives to overcome the skepticism engendered by enlightened rationalism's reductive view of human reason?

15. What is the classic definition of "truth"? What characteristics of truth are implied in this definition?

16. How does skepticism destroy itself in self-contradiction?

17. Why are the many forms of relativism so destructive, even though they appear broad-minded and tolerant on the surface?

18. How is relativism guilty of self-contradiction?

V. A Reply to Rationalist Materialism

We have witnessed and even experienced the devastating consequences of denying the transcendent aspect of the human person, reducing men and women to nothing more than material, individual members of a species. John Paul II advocates as the best remedy to this affliction a compelling re-proposal of the inviolable mystery that is each human person. He has done so in his five-year series of Wednesday audiences on the theology of the body.

In addition to proposing a transcendent vision of the human person, is it possible to refute rationalist materialism on its own terms — to show an inner contradiction within its fundamental principles? If the fallacy and emptiness of this ideological position can be clearly made known, would not many of its adherents — at least those who cling to it in good faith — be moved to seek the true vision of the human person? The basic principles of rationalist materialism are not difficult to disprove. In fact, we have already disproved them by establishing the spiritual nature of our intellect and will.

A. Critique
1. Materialism Refuted

The acts of knowing with our intellect and freely choosing with our will — acts each one of us undertakes every day of our life — are the best evidence against materialism's fallacy. Material things are by nature individual, singular, and limited. Yet we are capable of knowing *universal* truth. We are able to grasp that most universal of all metaphysical principles, one that describes the nature of every being which has ever existed or ever will exist: the principle of non-contradiction. We know as absolutely certain that no thing can ever be and not be at the same time and under the same aspect.

Our neighbors are either proud parents of four boys and two girls or they are not. It is simply impossible for the husband and wife who live next door to both have and not have children. Neither can the pride and joy of our neighbors' oldest son, whom he admiringly calls "Star Ranger," be both a black stallion and a golden retriever. The boy's companion is either one or the other. (Seeing Star Ranger gallop past our living-room window with his master at the reins would be strong evidence for the former.)

Since our intellect is capable of grasping universal truths that can be applied to every single being, it must itself be spiritual — for no material object is capable of performing spiritual acts. (William the chimpanzee will never type out anything remotely resembling Shakespeare's *Hamlet*, no matter how many lessons he is given in English composition or hours he is allowed before a word-processor keyboard.) And since we are persons who possess a spiritual intellect, our nature cannot be simply material, but is necessarily spiritual as well.

Our will is also a spiritual faculty. If it were simply material, then we could not explain our own experience. First of all, we experience the *freedom* of our will in the choices we make. Proof of our freedom is the existential experience of guilt that accompanies doing something we know to be wrong.

Let us suppose that I am a happily married husband and father of five young children. A creditor is unjustly seeking to foreclose upon our house. I do not feel guilty if a tree happens to fall upon his tent during his summer camping expedition, sending him to the hospital and preventing him from following through on the foreclosure. I would feel guilty, however — unless my conscience was significantly deformed — if I had been standing behind that tree, sawing away at the trunk, just before it fell. Why do I feel guilty in the second scenario and not the first, if the results are exactly the same? Because in the second case there is an action I have freely chosen with my will and so am responsible for.

The freedom of our will — the only possible explanation for our experience of guilt when we do something wrong or for the contrary experience of deserving merit when we perform a good act — this freedom proves that our will is spiritual. Our will freely chooses concrete, individual goods only within the spiritual horizon of the universal good. We are open to absolute goodness, to Goodness itself, and we experi-

ence this openness in the sense of loss that accompanies every individual choice we make, no matter how good that choice may be.

Let us suppose that a senior in college, contemplating law school,
begins to discern a call from God to the priesthood. The prayers his
mother has been saying for him for the past twenty-two years of his life,
along with her countless hidden sacrifices, have won for him the grace
to be generous and freely say "yes" to God's call. As a priest he will be
able to help many people experience Christ and gain their eternal salvation. But he will never be able to become a Supreme Court justice, with
the unique opportunity to defend the most basic, inalienable human
right of every person from the moment of conception: the right to life.

A sense of loss accompanies even the noble decision the young man
has made to become a priest. This experience of loss cannot be explained except by the fact that his will is open to universal, absolute
Goodness. Nothing less than the face-to-face experience of this Goodness in heaven is capable of satisfying the most profound aspirations of
our spirit. Then, after that greatest experience of loss, death itself, has
been overcome, and every tear has been wiped away, God will be all in
all.

2. Skepticism Refuted
a) The Horizons of Reason:
Philosophy and the Empirical Sciences

We have seen that materialism cannot stand up to the test of experience. Our intellect and will are both spiritual faculties, which means
that our human nature itself is not only material, but also spiritual. Enlightenment rationalism went astray when it tried to limit the domain of
reason to the empirical sciences: to knowing material, experimentally
observable facts. Our intellect is capable of much more. It is able to
grasp universal truths such as the principle of non-contradiction. In fact,
the empirical sciences themselves depend upon universal, metaphysical
principles.[522] These principles are determined by the very structure of
being, which our reason is able to penetrate.

The scientific method of controlled observation and experimentation leads empirical scientists to formulate by induction new hypotheses in order to explain the observed facts. For example, every time a
given amount of mass is converted into energy under controlled circumstances, the same amount of energy is generated. Repeated experimentation led Einstein to establish by induction the celebrated
formula $E=mc^2$ (Energy = mass multiplied by the speed of light

---

[522] Metaphysics is the philosophical study of being inasmuch as it is being. Metaphysics asks
questions such as the following: What is being? What does it mean to be, to exist? Why is
there being rather than nothing? Are there any properties that are true of all beings which
exist, simply because of the fact that they exist?

squared). From the general formula $E=mc^2$, arrived at through repeated experimentation and induction, other formulas can be reached by direct deduction.[523] Thus, the inductive-deductive cycle of the empirical sciences is born.

The capacity of human reason is not limited, however, to establishing the formulas and hypotheses of the empirical sciences. Nor is it true that empirical knowledge is the only valid form of knowing. In order for the scientific method to even be possible, certain fundamental philosophical principles must be true. These principles can never be established through scientific experimentation, since the very possibility of experimentation being meaningful and leading to reliable results depends upon their truth. Such foundational principles about the nature of reality itself are only accessible directly by reason. These truths represent the domain of philosophy.

We have already considered one of these principles: non-contradiction. If the principle of non-contradiction were not true, absolutely no laws whatsoever would govern the universe. People could neither speak nor think, much less perform scientific experiments with trustworthy results. Existence itself would be meaningless.

A second basic principle of philosophy on which the empirical sciences depend is that of causality. In its simplest formulation, this principle states that for every effect there must be a cause. It is clearly impossible for something to be spontaneously generated out of nothing. While reason itself grasps that the principle of causality is true and universal, admitting of absolutely no exceptions, the empirical sciences cannot establish it. By leaving behind the realm of matter and traveling toward nothingness, we surpass the bounds of the empirical sciences. In that incredibly dense, minute concentration of matter out of which the universe may have exploded during the Big Bang a few billion years ago, the empirical science of physics reaches its limits.

Every scientific experiment performed by physics depends upon the existence of matter, precisely because it is carried out upon matter. So to explain the very first appearance of matter is *ipso facto* beyond the competence of science. Once matter is already there, the empirical sciences can begin to study it. Each scientific experiment also depends upon the validity of the principle of causality; otherwise, it would be possible to obtain the effect of an experiment without its cause — that is, without even performing the experiment itself! If scientific experiments depend upon the principle of causality in order to be possible, they obviously cannot establish the principle's validity.

---

[523] Through inductive reasoning, particular facts or cases are used to arrive at a general conclusion. In the deductive process, a general principle is the starting point for arriving at particular conclusions.

The principles of philosophy upon which the empirical sciences depend are valid, however, and we know that they are valid. We know they are true not through any scientific experiment, but directly, by the capacity of reason itself. We can be absolutely certain that they are true, because if they were not, the sciences would not function, our experience of each day could not be explained, and the universe would be completely meaningless. (To affirm a meaningless universe is patently absurd, since any such affirmation has meaning in itself.)

We have seen that the empirical sciences themselves rest upon reason's capacity to know directly universal, philosophical truths regarding the nature of being itself. So when Enlightenment rationalism attempted to reduce reason's domain to the field of the empirical sciences, it is not surprising that widespread skepticism about reason's ability to know the truth at all quickly ensued. When the foundations of a house are damaged, the entire edifice begins to sway perilously.

b) The "Intelligent Design" Movement:
Opening the Empirical Sciences to Reason's Horizons
(1) Specified Complexity:
Detecting Intelligent Design Empirically

As John Paul II points out in his 1998 encyclical *Fides et Ratio* (Faith and Reason), the natural limitation of reason and the inconstancy of the heart often distort the search for truth.[524] But that is not all. "People can even run from the truth as soon as they glimpse it because they are afraid of its demands."[525] Still, it is heartening to realize that the truth can never be completely suppressed without annihilating man himself. Four centuries before Christ, the Greek philosopher Aristotle began his *Metaphysics* with the timeless phrase, "All men by nature desire to know."[526] Just as all people yearn to know the truth, that same truth continues to reassert itself, even when it is denied.

Within the empirical sciences themselves a vigorous new movement has begun to challenge the legacy of rationalist materialism. It is known as *intelligent design*. This movement recognizes reason's ability to transcend what can be empirically observed. It acknowledges the three basic levels of truth outlined by John Paul II in *Fides et Ratio*: scientific truth, philosophical truth, and religious truth.

> It may help, then, to turn briefly to the different modes of truth. Most of them depend upon immediate evidence or are confirmed by experimentation. This is the mode of truth proper to everyday life and to scientific research. At another level we find philosophi-

---

[524] *Fides et Ratio*, 28.
[525] Ibid.
[526] Aristotle, *Metaphysics*, Chapter 1, as cited in *Aristotle on Man in the Universe*, translated by John H. MacMahon, (New York: Classics Club, 1943), p. 5.

cal truth, attained by means of the speculative powers of the human intellect. Finally, there are religious truths which are to some degree grounded in philosophy, and which we find in the answers which the different religious traditions offer to the ultimate questions.[527]

Once reason is freed from the chains that bind it to empirical reality, the consequences are dramatic — not least of all for the empirical sciences themselves. One of the movement's founders, William Dembski, a mathematician and philosopher, succinctly describes its scope. "Intelligent design is three things: a scientific research program that investigates the effects of intelligent causes; an intellectual movement that challenges Darwinism and its naturalistic legacy; and a way of understanding divine action. Intelligent design therefore intersects science and theology."[528]

The modern empirical sciences experienced their birth pangs at the height of Enlightenment rationalism. Ever since their origin, they have been marked by a pervasive rationalistic legacy: *naturalism*. What does naturalism affirm? That nature, the physical universe, is entirely sufficient unto itself. Within biology, naturalism is translated as Darwinism or neo-Darwinism. It asserts that blind, undirected natural forces have caused the evolution of all the incredibly complex forms of life existing today, including the human species. What is the mechanism responsible for the wonderful development of inert matter into an organism called man — a being who is at once physical and spiritual, capable of reflecting upon his own existence as well as his very acts of knowing, and at the same time able to distinguish between moral good and evil in the hidden sanctuary of his own inner life? All this has taken place through the chance mutation of genes (over a very long period of time, certainly) and natural selection of the fittest members of each species.

Intelligent design looks naturalism squarely in the eye and identifies it for what it truly is: not a mere scientific theory, but an entire world-view with unacknowledged philosophical and even religious presuppositions. In his book *Intelligent Design*, William Dembski sums up well how naturalism not only redefines science and the universe, but also our very humanity.

> Naturalism is an ideology. Its key tenet is the self-sufficiency of nature. Within Western culture its most virulent form is known as scientific naturalism. Scientific naturalism locates the self-sufficiency of nature in the natural laws of science. Accordingly scientific naturalism would have us to understand the entire universe in terms of

---

[527] *Fides et* Ratio, 30. Cf. Second Vatican Ecumenical Council, Declaration on the Relation of the Church to Non-Christian Religions, *Nostra Aetate*, 2.

[528] William B. Dembski, *Intelligent Design: The Bridge Between Science and Theology*, (Downers Grove, Il: InterVarsity Press, 1999), p. 13.

such laws. Thus in particular, since human beings are a part of the universe, who we are and what we do must ultimately be understood in naturalistic terms. This is not to deny our humanity. But it is to reinterpret our humanity as the consequence of brute material processes that were not consciously aiming at us.[529]

What position does God occupy in the naturalistic ideology? He is reduced to a hypothesis for which there is no need. "Naturalism affirms not so much that God does not exist as that God need not exist. It's not that God is dead so much as that God is absent. And because God is absent, intellectual honesty demands that we get about our work without invoking him. This is the received wisdom."[530]

The intelligent design movement counters the "received wisdom" with the hypothesis that more is at work in the universe than blind, undirected forces of nature. It affirms that the experimental sciences can detect an intelligent cause behind certain empirical phenomena in the physical universe — and it establishes a verifiable, scientific criterion for doing so. What is this criterion? "Specified complexity" or equivalently "specified small probability."[531]

"Complexity guarantees that the object in question is not so simple that it can readily be attributed to chance."[532] Biologist Michael J. Behe illustrates the meaning of complexity with an example in his foreword to Dembski's book.[533] If we entered a room and came upon a table with a couple of Scrabble letters that spelled "AN," we would not, simply on that basis, be able to decide whether or not they were purposely arranged that way by an intelligent agent. The probability of obtaining such a short word by chance is not prohibitive.

The probability of seeing some particular long sequence of Scrabble letters, such as "DNEIBFAUMOHRJKISEZL," on the other hand, is quite small — around one in one billion billion billion. This long sequence of letters is *complex*. Still, we would certainly not conclude that the letters were intentionally arranged in that manner, since they are not *specified*: They match no recognizable pattern. But what if the nineteen letters were positioned on the table to spell out "THEGIFTOF SELFINLOVE"? We would certainly conclude that the letters were intentionally arranged that way. The sequence of letters is not only highly improbable, but it also matches an intelligible English phrase, one with a very distinctive meaning. The sequence is a product of intelligent design.

---

[529] William B. Dembski, *Intelligent Design*, pp. 103-104.
[530] Ibid., p. 103.
[531] Ibid., p. 10. For a complete explanation of the criterion see Chapter 5, Reinstating Design within Science, pp. 122-152.
[532] Ibid., p. 17.
[533] Cf. Ibid., p. 10.

Behe sums up specified complexity as a criterion for detecting intelligent design in the universe. "We apprehend design in highly improbable (complex) events that also fit some independently identifiable pattern (specification)."[534]

Are the phenomena that enable us to empirically detect intelligent design in the universe through specified complexity numerous? Yes. They display themselves in vast abundance. A startling empirical fact about the physical universe is the number of times that conditions turn out to be "just right" for human life to develop. Even the slightest variation in any one of these conditions would make the universe completely uninhabitable for human life — and oftentimes for any form of life. Cosmologists refer to these conditions as "anthropic coincidences." What are some of them?

> Anthropic coincidences signify all the prior conditions that need to be precisely satisfied and correlated for human life to be possible. . . . For example, the fundamental forces of nature have to fall within very precise tolerances for the basic constituents of the universe to support life. If the strong nuclear force were slightly stronger, hardly any hydrogen would form because its nuclei would be unstable. If, on the other hand, it were slightly weaker, no elements other than hydrogen could form. Similarly if the force of gravity were slightly stronger, stars would burn out too rapidly to support life on surrounding planets. If, on the other hand, it were slightly weaker, there would not be enough heavy elements with which to build surrounding planets.[535]

There are two possible ways of explaining how all the ingredients needed to produce the universe came together in just the right proportions to support human life: chance and intelligent design. For chance to be a viable contender, the probability of everything coming out "just right" must not be too low. As it turns out, the probability is infinitesimally small. William Dembski cites the physicist Roger Penrose.

> How big was the original phase-space volume . . . that the Creator had to aim for in order to provide a universe compatible with the second law of thermodynamics and with what we now observe? . . . The Creator's aim must have been [precise] to an accuracy of one part in $10^{10^{123}}$. This is an extraordinary figure. One could not possibly even *write the number down* in full, in the ordinary denary notation: It would be a "1" followed by 10^{10} successive "0"s! Even if we were to write a "0" on each separate proton and on each separate neutron in the entire universe — and we could throw in all the

---

[534] Ibid., p. 10.
[535] Ibid., p. 265, referring to Henry Petroski, *Invention by Design: How Engineers Get from Thought to Thing* (Cambridge: Harvard University Press, 1996), p. 30. Petroski is a professor civil engineering as well as a professor of history at Duke University.

other particles as well for good measure — we should fall far short
of writing down the figure needed. [Such is] the precision needed
to set the universe on its course.[536]

(2) Irreducible Complexity: Intelligent Design in Biology — Darwinism Refuted

Within cosmology the very makeup of the universe offers compelling evidence for intelligent design. Another science in which the specified complexity criterion leads to dramatic conclusions is biology.
Darwinism's assertion of blind, undirected evolution through chance
mutation of genes and natural selection of the fittest members in each
species simply fails to hold up under scrutiny.

Biochemist Michael Behe presents a powerful argument for design
within biological systems in his book *Darwin's Black Box*. Central to his
argument is the notion of *irreducible complexity*. "A system is irreducibly
complex if it consists of several interrelated parts so that removing even
one part completely destroys the system's function."[537] An example of
irreducible complexity is a mousetrap. It consists of a platform, a hammer, a spring, a catch, and a holding bar. Remove any one of these five
components and the mousetrap is no longer functional.

Irreducible complexity must be contrasted with *cumulative complexity*. "A system is cumulatively complex if the components of the system
can be arranged sequentially so that the successive removal of components never leads to the complete loss of function."[538] An example of cumulative complexity would be a city. Services and population can be
continually reduced until the city has become a village, without it ever
ceasing in its function as a community.

Darwinism's mechanism of selection and mutation can account for
cumulative complexity, but it fails utterly before irreducibly complex
biological systems. If selection were to act toward a goal (that is, if an intelligent agent were guiding the evolutionary process), it could produce
irreducible complexity. Given the goal of constructing a mousetrap, one
could specify a goal-directed process that first selects a platform, then a
hammer, next a spring, a catch, and a holding bar, and finally puts all of
these components together to produce a functional mousetrap. But Darwinian selection is precisely *natural* selection resulting from blind, undirected forces of nature. Behe explains why natural selection cannot possibly account for irreducibly complex systems.

An irreducibly complex system cannot be produced . . . by slight,
successive modifications of a precursor system, because any pre-

---

[536] Ibid., p. 266, citing Roger Penrose, *The Emperor's New Mind* (New York: Oxford, 1989), p. 344.
[537] Ibid., p. 147, referring to Michael Behe, *Darwin's Black Box* (New York: Free Press, 1996), pp. 39-45.
[538] Ibid.

cursor to an irreducibly complex system that is missing a part is by definition nonfunctional.... Since natural selection can only choose systems that are already working, then if a biological system cannot be produced gradually it would have to arise as an integrated unit, in one fell swoop, for natural selection to have anything to act on.[539]

Are there many examples of irreducibly complex biological systems within living organisms? They are superabundant. Every living cell is like a factory that contains intricately complex protein assemblies, which biologists refer to as "machines" due to the precise coordination of their various parts. Take away any one of these parts, and the machines are completely nonfunctional. Behe elucidates how something as apparently simple as a flagellum on a bacterium is in reality an irreducibly complex system.

The flagellum is a whip-like rotary motor that enables a bacterium to navigate through its environment. The flagellum includes an acid-powered rotary engine, a stator, O-rings, bushings and a drive shaft. The intricate machinery of this molecular motor requires approximately fifty proteins. Yet the absence of any one of these proteins results in the complete loss of motor function.[540]

An objective appraisal of irreducible complexity within the science of biology discredits Darwinian natural selection. Dembski notes one final element that definitively seals the fate of Darwinism. "Moreover, because irreducible complexity occurs at the biochemical level, there is no more fundamental level of biological analysis to which the irreducible complexity of biochemical systems can be referred and at which a Darwinian analysis in terms of selection and mutation can still hope for success."[541]

In conclusion, the emergence of irreducibly complex biological systems simply cannot be accounted for by a gradual process of evolution that is the result of blind, undirected forces of nature. These systems can only come into being as the marvelous work of intelligent design.

What effect will the intelligent-design movement have upon the empirical sciences? The movement is still fledgling, but it offers the promise of overcoming the legacy of rationalist materialism that has confined science itself for generations. Dembski puts it well: "Barring design from science distorts science, making it a mouthpiece for materialism instead of a search for truth."[542]

---

[539] Behe, *Darwin's Black Box*, p. 39, as cited in Dembski, *Intelligent Design*, p. 148.
[540] Dembski, *Intelligent Design*, p. 148, referring to Behe, *Darwin's Black Box*, pp. 69-72.
[541] Dembski, *Intelligent Design*, p. 148.
[542] Ibid., p. 151.

Freeing reason to rise above materialism in the empirical sciences would bring humanity one step closer to a true, transcendent vision of the human person — a total vision that allows room for faith. It would also bring us nearer to restoring reason's confidence in itself, to curing that inexorable malady of our present age: skepticism.

c) Skepticism: Self-destruction by Self-contradiction

In the first letter he wrote after his conversion, St. Augustine spoke of the crisis that plagued his contemporaries. "It seems to me that one must bring men back . . . to the hope of finding the truth."[543] Sixteen centuries later, as mankind crosses the threshold of the third Christian millennium, humanity finds itself in a similar plight — one whose roots lie in the reductive view of reason espoused by Enlightenment rationalism.

During his address to the American bishops on their *ad limina* visit of May 30, 1998, John Paul II echoed St. Augustine's sentiments. The Holy Father affirmed that the greatest contribution which can be made to culture today is to *"restore to that culture the conviction that human beings can grasp the truth of things, and in grasping that truth can know their duties to God, to themselves and their neighbors."*[544] The Holy Father concluded, "On the threshold of a new century and a new millennium, the Church continues to proclaim the capacity of human beings to know the truth and to grow into genuine freedom through their acceptance of that truth."[545]

Each person experiences the vital necessity of encountering an ultimate, absolute truth on which to ground his life. In *Fides et Ratio* the Holy Father eloquently describes this essential aspect of our humanity. "Whether we admit it or not, there comes for everyone a moment when personal existence must be anchored to a truth recognized as final, a truth which confers a certitude no longer open to doubt."[546]

But what response can be made to the pervasive skepticism and its seductive disguises of relativism that are subjecting humanity under their yoke today? Is it possible to convincingly refute the claim that there is no objective, absolute truth? First we must consider an even more fundamental question, the same one Pontius Pilate scornfully asked Christ: "What is truth?" Unlike the Roman procurator, we may pose the question in the confident hope of receiving a convincing answer.

---

[543] St. Augustine, *Ep.* 1,1: PL 33, 61.
[544] John Paul II, *Springtime of Evangelization*, edited by Rev. Thomas D. Williams, L.C. (San Diego: Basilica Press, 1999), p. 82.
[545] Ibid., p. 88.
[546] *FR*, 27.

-Definition of Objective Truth

Both St. Thomas Aquinas and St. Bonaventure have formulated the classic definition of truth. It is the conformity of the mind with objective reality, *"adaequatio rei et intellectus."*[547] Thus, truth cannot be determined by a majority vote. It is not born of consensus.[548] "Every truth — if it is really truth — presents itself as universal, even if it is not the whole truth. If something is true, then it must be true for all people and at all times."[549]

-Skepticism's Unavoidable Self-contradiction

With this clarification regarding the nature of truth, it is not difficult to refute skepticism — a most paradoxical fruit of rationalism's attempt to exalt human reason. What does the skeptic claim? "There is no truth." While no apparent contradiction can be found in the assertion itself, one is there under the surface. For what the skeptic is really affirming is the following: "It is *true* that there is no truth." The skeptic falls into a contradiction between his statement or affirmation, and his very act of asserting it. This form of contradiction is called a "contradiction *in actu exercito."*[550]

Truth is simply inescapable. It cannot be denied. The attempt to deny truth is always a self-contradiction. It destroys itself in the very act of being asserted.

3. Relativism Refuted

Since the skeptic's position is untenable, many have attempted to save themselves from blatant self-contradiction by taking up the alluring standards of relativism. What could be more tolerant, more open-minded, than for each individual and group to hold their own particular truth, while allowing every other group a truth of their own? No one ventures to claim that his own truth is right while another's is wrong — no matter how contradictory the two may be. Certainly no one dreams of presuming to have discovered *the* truth. That would be dogmatism! No. Everyone simply traipses blissfully along, unassumingly content with his or her particular version of truth, sufficient for the pleasures and frights of the day.

At first glance, the underlying relativism that characterizes such trends as multiculturalism and diversity studies appears quite innocuous, even broad-minded and open. Yet a destructive form of intolerance without parallel lurks just below the surface — intolerance toward truth itself. Relativism rejects the very nature of truth as objective and univer-

---

[547] St. Thomas Aquinas, *Summa Theologiae*, I, 16, 1; St. Bonaventure, *Coll. In Hex.*, 3, 8, 1. Cited in *Fides et Ratio* 82. (Literally: the conformity of the thing and the intellect.)

[548] Cf. *Fides et Ratio*, 56.

[549] *FR*, 27.

[550] It is a contradiction in the very fact of the act being exercised or carried out.

sal. Either something is true for all people at all times, or it is false. Multiculturalism notwithstanding, it is sheer nonsense to claim that the principle of causality may be true for Western Civilization, with our Greek philosophical heritage, but may not necessarily be true for the Chinese culture, in which metaphysics is made much more difficult by the fact that no exact term even exists for the word *being*. What self-respecting physicist would maintain that Einstein's theory of relativity is only true for people who possess a modern scientific mentality, so it would not have been true in the era of pre-Newtonian physics?

Not only does relativism violate the objective nature of truth, but it is also guilty of a self-contradiction every bit as blatant as the one committed by skepticism. Since he cannot deny the existence of truth, a relativist does the next best thing and says: "Truth is relative." But the safety of relativism is only apparent. For the relativist surely believes that his position is the correct one. He likewise holds that all are wrong who dogmatically maintain truth to be objective, universal and absolute. But for that to be the case, the relativist's affirmation must be true for everyone. It must be absolutely true. So what the relativist actually asserts is, "It is *absolutely* true that truth is relative."

Once again we discover that truth reaffirms itself in its authentic nature as objective, absolute, and universal, even in the very act which seeks to refute it. Both skepticism and relativism destroy themselves, engulfed by the waves of inescapable self-contradiction.

Preview

EIGHT CONTRACEPTION'S IDEOLOGICAL ROOTS: A COMPELLING RESPONSE *(continued)*

V. A Reply to Rationalist Materialism *(continued)*
    B. John Paul II's Compelling Response: *Fides et Ratio (Faith and Reason)*
        1. Humanity Today: A "Crisis of Meaning"
        2. Why a Crisis? Man is a Being Who Seeks the Truth
        3. To Resolve the Crisis: Restoring Reason's Confidence in Itself
        4. How to Restore Reason's Confidence:
           Healing the Rupture Between Faith and Reason
           a) Allies, Not Antagonists
           b) Two Wings to Rise Toward Truth
        5. To Seek the Truth in Love
           The Truth is a Person: Christ!

Points to look for

1. What have been the fruits of Enlightenment rationalist materialism in the empirical sciences?

2. What has rationalism led to in the field of philosophy?

3. How has rationalist materialism gone beyond the confines of the sciences and philosophy to profoundly affect human life today?

4. What does John Paul II mean by a "crisis of meaning" that humanity faces today?

5. Why does doubt about the possibility of discovering real meaning in life lead to a true crisis, even when people possess enough resources for a comfortable existence?

6. What is the best way to resolve the crisis of skepticism and doubt that burdens humanity today?

7. How can reason's confidence in itself best be restored?

8. Why are faith and reason inextricably intertwined in human life?

9. Why does faith not violate our reason, but rather fulfill it?

10. How does faith serve to strengthen and encourage reason?

11. Why is seeking the truth in human life much more than a mere intellectual undertaking?

12. What is the ultimate truth that we seek in life as persons?

13. Who are the most compelling witnesses to the ultimate truth of human existence? Why?

14. How do the search for truth and the desire to experience love converge in human life?

15. Why can there be no contradiction between the truths of the empirical sciences, the general truths of philosophy, and the truth of the person of Christ?

16. Why does John Paul II feel such an ardent longing for all people to know Christ?

17. How is this longing shared by all holy men and women of our day?

B. John Paul II's Compelling Response: *Fides et Ratio (Faith and Reason)*
1. Humanity Today: A "Crisis of Meaning"

For the past three hundred years, under the domination of Enlightenment rationalism, mankind has been suffering from the trauma of a great divorce: the separation between faith and reason. Far from liberating reason, thrusting it forward upon the path toward adulthood, this unwarranted break has caused the human mind to doubt its own capacity to know the truth about reality and to turn in upon itself.

The paradoxical legacy of the attempts to make reason completely autonomous has affected all areas of human knowing. In the empirical sciences unbridled rationalism has led to naturalism: a materialist view of the universe and of the human person, where nothing is at play other than blind, undirected forces of nature. Those disciplines within the empirical sciences that deal directly with the human person, such as psychology and sociology, more often than not reduce men and women to material individuals who are nothing more than the product of their environment and physiological makeup.

Within philosophy, reason's turning in upon itself has resulted in a focus on the study of human knowing, rather than reflection on being, on reality itself. Even within the philosophy of knowledge, the limitations of human knowing have been stressed, instead of reason's capacity to know the truth. What have been the consequences? They extend far beyond the confines of philosophy itself. Widespread relativism, often translated as a false pluralism, has come to dominate thought today. Ultimately it leads to skepticism and a pragmatic, utilitarian attitude toward life. Men and women often fail to ask the most fundamental questions about the meaning of human existence. John Paul II outlines the disturbing panorama.

> Reason, in its one-sided concern to investigate human subjectivity, seems to have forgotten that men and women are always called to direct their steps towards a truth which transcends them. Sundered from that truth, individuals are at the mercy of caprice, and their state as person ends up being judged by pragmatic criteria based essentially upon experimental data, in the mistaken belief that technology must dominate all. It has happened therefore that reason, rather than voicing the human orientation towards truth, has wilted under the weight of so much knowledge and little by little has lost the capacity to lift its gaze to the heights, not daring to rise to the truth of being. Abandoning the investigation of being, modern philosophical research has concentrated instead upon human knowing. Rather than make use of the human capacity to know the truth, modern philosophy has preferred to accentuate the ways in which this capacity is limited and conditioned.
>
> This has given rise to different forms of agnosticism and relativism which have led philosophical research to lose its way in the shifting sands of widespread skepticism. Recent times have seen the rise to prominence of various doctrines which tend to devalue even the truths which had been judged certain. A legitimate plurality of positions has yielded to an undifferentiated pluralism, based upon the assumption that all positions are equally valid, which is one of today's most widespread symptoms of the lack of confidence in truth. Even certain conceptions of life coming from the East betray this lack of confidence, denying truth its exclusive character and assuming that truth reveals itself equally in different doctrines, even if they contradict one another. On this understanding, everything is reduced to opinion; and there is a sense of being adrift. . . . Hence we see among the men and women of our time, and not just in some philosophers, attitudes of widespread distrust of the human being's great capacity for knowledge. With a false modesty, people rest content with partial and provisional truths, no longer seeking

to ask radical questions about the meaning and ultimate foundation of human, personal and social existence.[551]

Abandoning the quest for ultimate truths and losing the hope of being able to attain them has led humanity to a profound crisis. The Holy Father terms it a "crisis of meaning."[552] He describes in dramatic language its dimensions. "We are faced with the patent inadequacy of perspectives in which the ephemeral is affirmed as a value and the possibility of discovering the real meaning of life is cast into doubt. This is why many people stumble through life to the very edge of the abyss without knowing where they are going."[553]

2. Why a Crisis? Man is a Being Who Seeks the Truth

Why does the loss of confidence in man's ability to know ultimate truths end in turmoil, even though material progress assures most people everything they need for a comfortable life? The reason is that persons strive for truth by what is most intimate in their nature. This search constitutes the very definition of who we are. "One may define the human being, therefore, as *the one who seeks the truth*."[554] The yearning for truth cannot be removed without threatening our very existence as persons. "The thirst for truth is so rooted in the human heart that to be obliged to ignore it would cast our existence into jeopardy."[555]

Nowhere could the threat skepticism poses to our existence be more evident than in one present-day existential current: *nihilism*. This devastating attitude is skepticism's logical conclusion. It entails "the denial of all foundations and the negation of all objective truth."[556] Any hope of encountering meaning in human life is abandoned, since existence itself is viewed to be utterly devoid of meaning.[557] "Nihilism is a denial of the humanity and of the very identity of the human being."[558] Rejecting the truth enslaves mankind to the point of obliterating who we are. Nihilism holds out to humanity a terrible alternative. It leads "either to a destructive will to power or to a solitude without hope."[559] Only truth offers mankind the possibility of real freedom. "Once the truth is denied to human beings, it is pure illusion to try to set them free. Truth and freedom either go together hand in hand or together they perish in misery."[560]

---

[551] *Fides et Ratio*, 5.

[552] *Fides et Ratio*, 81.

[553] *FR*, 6.

[554] *FR*, 28.

[555] *FR*, 29.

[556] *FR*, 90.

[557] Just how pervasive has nihilism become in society today? Thomas Hibbs, acting chair of philosophy at Boston College, provides a penetrating answer to that query in his recent book *Shows About Nothing: Nihilism in Popular Culture from The Exorcist to Seinfeld* (Dallas: Spence, 1999).

[558] *FR*, 90.

[559] Ibid.

[560] Ibid.: cf. *Redemptor Hominis*, 12.

3. To Resolve the Crisis:
Restoring Reason's Confidence in Itself

How can the present "crisis of meaning" that afflicts humanity be resolved? A vital first step is to restore reason's confidence in itself — in its own ability to know the truth. Within the empirical sciences, reason could break the shackles of an oppressive naturalist materialism. In the realm of philosophy, a newly acquired self-confidence would enable reason to once again ask the most fundamental questions about reality. Thus, philosophy would be able to recover anew its *"sapiential dimension* [wisdom dimension] as a search for the ultimate and overarching meaning of life."[561]

To a world burdened under the weight of skepticism and doubt, John Paul II responds with the exhortation of the Greek philosophers: "know yourself."[562] We have seen that a reflection upon who we are as persons, a consideration of the frontiers to which our intellect and will are open, is the best defense against skepticism. Not only do our spiritual faculties of intellect and will reveal the self-contradiction of skepticism, the very fact that human beings strive for truth in the first place would be utterly unintelligible if we were not capable of knowing truth. The Holy Father elucidates this point.

> It is unthinkable that a search so deeply rooted in human nature would be completely vain and useless. The capacity to search for truth and to pose questions itself implies the rudiments of a response. Human beings would not even begin to search for something of which they knew nothing or for something which they thought was wholly beyond them. Only the sense that they can arrive at an answer leads them to take the first step. This is what normally happens in scientific research. When scientists, following their intuition, set out in search of the logical and verifiable explanation of a phenomenon, they are confident from the first that they will find an answer, and they do not give up in the face of setbacks.[563]

4. How to Restore Reason's Confidence —
Healing the Rupture Between Faith and Reason
a) Allies, Not Antagonists

If today reason often assumes the role of Hamlet, tormented by doubt and indecision, how can reason's self-confidence be restored?

---

[561] *FR*, 81. For a compelling analysis of the need for philosophy to recover the dimension of wisdom see Amador-Pedro Barrajón, L.C., "Sapiential Dimension of Philosophy: A Reading of *Fides et Ratio* from the perspective of St. Bonaventure," *Alpha Omega*, (Journal of Philosophy and Theology of Regina Apostolorum Pontifical University), Year II, Number 3, September-December, 1999, pp. 363-375.

[562] *FR*, 1.

[563] *FR*, 29.

Paradoxically, the most effective cure for our present malady is to heal the rupture between reason and faith. For these two most fundamental human realities are not really meant to be antagonists, but rather the closest of allies in enabling us to discover the meaning of life and to travel the sometimes-arduous road toward true fulfillment and happiness.

The Holy Father recognizes that faith and reason possess a mutual autonomy, which must be respected.[564] Yet from within their own fields, they call upon each other, strengthening and enlightening one other, challenging each other to rise to new heights. We have seen that both will and intellect are open to the absolute. So reason brings human persons up to the threshold of faith in the One who is Absolute, inviting us to cross. In its turn, faith in God's Revelation presents reason with many startling truths about reality that it can investigate and make its own. The very notion of "person" itself entered reason's domain of philosophy through faith — the attempts to understand the Trinitarian mystery of three persons in one God and the equally unsearchable mystery of two natures in the one divine person of Christ.

When faith and reason are separated, devastating consequences result for each of them. Reason soon falls into skepticism and becomes trapped within itself, closed to seeking the ultimate meaning of human life. Faith, left on its own, "runs the grave risk of withering into myth or superstition."[565] John Paul II cites St. Augustine on the intimate role reason plays in faith: "To believe is nothing other than to think with assent. . . . Believers are also thinkers: in believing, they think and in thinking, they believe. . . . If faith does not think, it is nothing."[566]

Faith and reason are two fundamental aspects of what it means to be human. They are inextricably intertwined in daily life. Even though we are beings who seek the truth, we actually believe many more truths than we are ever able to verify strictly with our intellect. How many people from North America have actually set foot upon Australia in order to corroborate with their own senses and rational faculties all that has been said of it? Yet who from North America would ever dream of questioning the existence of this continent? Only through faith in others, in the truths which they themselves have discovered and confirmed, can we arrive at new truths ourselves. Faith is so closely linked with reason that *living by belief* also belongs to the definition of who we are as persons.

> There are in the life of a human being many more truths which are simply believed than truths which are acquired by way of personal

---

[564] *FR*, 48.
[565] *FR*, 48.
[566] St. Augustine, *De Praedestinatione Sanctorum*, 2, 5: *PL* 44, 963; cited in *FR*, 79.

verification. Who, for instance, could assess critically the countless scientific findings upon which modern life is based? Who could personally examine the flow of information which comes day after day from all parts of the world and which is generally accepted as true? Who in the end could forge anew the paths of experience and thought which have yielded the treasures of human wisdom and religion? This means that the human being — the one who seeks the truth — is also *the one who lives by belief.* (31)

Faith brings us certitudes that strengthen and encourage reason in its own search for intellectual certainty. Faith is audacious — it gives us the courage to rise above ourselves, to achieve lofty goals. We must strive to renew our faith at the dawn of the third millennium, so that our reason too may be set free. John Paul II exclaims that the daring of faith must be matched "by the boldness of reason."[567]

b) Two Wings to Rise Toward Truth

Since faith involves the whole person, intellect and will, it does not violate our freedom or our reason, but fulfils them.[568] Faith enhances reason. It gives reason courage to explore new fields of mystery and meaning. "It is faith which stirs reason to move beyond all isolation and willingly to run risks so that it may attain whatever is beautiful, good and true. Faith thus becomes the convinced and convincing advocate of reason."[569]

Reason guided and enlightened by faith is not condemned to a perpetual state of immaturity. It is rather "a reason which grows more penetrating and assured because of the support it receives from faith."[570] With tones of wonder John Paul II sums up the relationship between these two fundamental human realities in the very first sentence of *Fides et Ratio.*

Faith and reason are like two wings on which the human spirit rises to the contemplation of truth; and God has placed in the human heart a desire to know the truth — in a word, to know himself — so that, by knowing and loving God, men and women may also come to the fullness of truth about themselves.[571]

5. To Seek the Truth in Love

The first sentence of *Fides et Ratio* reveals a vital dimension of the desire for truth that is written on each person's heart. What we irrepressibly long for is not simply an abstract empirical or philosophical truth, but the truth of who we are as persons. We have been created to

---

[567] Ibid.
[568] *FR*, 13.
[569] *FR*, 56.
[570] *FR*, 106.
[571] *FR, 1*; cf. *Ex* 33:18; *Ps* 27:8-9; 63:2-3; *Jn* 14:8; *1 Jn* 3:2.

be loved and to love — to entrust ourselves to others while making a gift of ourselves in love. Thus our journey towards the fullness of truth involves an interpersonal relationship of trust and self-giving. The Holy Father describes the quest that we undertake with our lives.

> In believing, we entrust ourselves to the knowledge acquired by other people. This suggests an important tension. On the one hand, the knowledge acquired through belief can seem an imperfect form of knowledge, to be perfected gradually through personal accumulation of evidence; on the other hand, belief is often humanly richer than mere evidence, because it involves an interpersonal relationship and brings into play not only a person's capacity to know but also the deeper capacity to entrust oneself to others, to enter into a relationship with them which is intimate and enduring.
>
> It should be stressed that the truths sought in this interpersonal relationship are not primarily empirical or philosophical. Rather, what is sought is *the truth of the person* —what the person is and what the person reveals from deep within. Human perfection, then, consists not simply in acquiring an abstract knowledge of the truth, but in a dynamic relationship of faithful self-giving with others. It is in this faithful self-giving that a person finds a fullness of certainty and security. At the same time, however, knowledge through belief, grounded as it is on trust between persons, is linked to truth: in the act of believing, men and women entrust themselves to the truth which the other declares to them.[572]

Who are the most compelling witnesses to the ultimate truth about human life, about the deepest meaning of our existence? *The martyrs.* Throughout the centuries of Christian history, these heroic men and women have discovered the truth of their own identity in the love Jesus Christ has for them. So intimately have they experienced this love, so ardently have they longed to return it, that they have found strength to conquer the ultimate enigma of human existence: death itself. John Paul II ponders their testimony.

> Any number of examples could be found to demonstrate this; but I think immediately of the martyrs, who are the most authentic witnesses to the truth about existence. The martyrs know that they have found the truth about life in the encounter with Jesus Christ, and nothing and no one could ever take this certainty from them. Neither suffering nor violent death could ever lead them to abandon the truth which they have discovered in the encounter with Christ. This is why to this day the witness of the martyrs continues to arouse such interest, to draw agreement, to win such a hearing and to invite emulation. This is why their word inspires such confidence: from the moment they speak to us of what we perceive deep

---

[572] *FR*, 32.

down as the truth we have sought for so long, the martyrs provide evidence of a love that has no need of lengthy arguments in order to convince. The martyrs stir in us a profound trust because they give voice to what we already feel and they declare what we would like to have the strength to express.[573]

The human person's journey toward truth, one that is undertaken with both reason and faith, leads us beyond the realm of abstract knowledge to entrust ourselves in love to other persons. Examining the Holy Father's summary of this process, we can begin to intimate where this convergence between truth and persons will ultimately lead.

> Step by step, then, we are assembling the terms of the question. It is the nature of the human being to seek the truth. This search looks not only to the attainment of truths which are partial, empirical or scientific; nor is it only in individual acts of decision-making that people seek the true good. Their search looks towards an ulterior truth which would explain the meaning of life. And it is therefore a search which can reach its end only in reaching the absolute.[574] Thanks to the inherent capacities of thought, man is able to encounter and recognize a truth of this kind. Such a truth — vital and necessary as it is for life — is attained not only by way of reason but also through trusting acquiescence to other persons who can guarantee the authenticity and certainty of the truth itself. There is no doubt that the capacity to entrust oneself and one's life to another person and the decision to do so are among the most significant and expressive human acts.[575]

The Truth is a Person: Christ!

The journey toward truth, undertaken in complete sincerity and openness, can only find its fulfillment in the One who is "the Way, and the Truth, and the Life."[576] As the noted theologian, Bishop Rino Fisichella, points out, in the final analysis, the truth is Christological.[577] *Truth is a person: Christ!* It is Christ whom the Psalmist is seeking when he exclaims, "In the night also my heart instructs me."[578] It is Christ whom Job mysteriously foretells in the midst of his suffering, as he cries out, "I know that my Redeemer lives."[579] Christ alone is capable of satisfying the deepest aspirations of the human person for truth and love. Jesus Christ, the Redeemer of Man, is the one for whom every heart is made.

---

[573] Ibid.
[574] Cf. General Audience (October 19, 1983), 1-2: *Insegnamenti* VI, 2 (1983), 814-815.
[575] *FR*, 33.
[576] Jn 14:6.
[577] Cf. Rino Fisichella, "*Fides et Ratio*: L'enciclica che immette nel terzo millennio," in *Alpha Omega*, Year II, Number 1, January-April, 1999, pp. 3-12, at p. 4.
[578] Psalm 16, 7.
[579] Job 19:25.

From all that I have said to this point it emerges that men and women are on a journey of discovery which is humanly unstoppable — a search for the truth and a search for a person to whom they might entrust themselves. Christian faith comes to meet them, offering the concrete possibility of reaching the goal which they seek. Moving beyond the stage of simple believing, Christian faith immerses human beings in the order of grace, which enables them to share in the mystery of Christ, which in turn offers them a true and coherent knowledge of the Triune God. In Jesus Christ, who is the Truth, faith recognizes the ultimate appeal to humanity, an appeal made in order that what we experience as desire and nostalgia may come to its fulfillment.[580]

What harmony and unity are present in human life, clearly visible to the eyes of faith! The truth our intellect seeks and the love our heart and will long to experience all converge in the person of Christ. There can be no conflict between the empirical truths of science, the general truths of philosophy, and the truth of Christ. For it is the same God who through the eternal Word created the universe and our reason, capable of penetrating that universe, who also asks us to believe by faith that he is our Father, revealed through his Son.

This truth, which God reveals to us in Jesus Christ, is not opposed to the truths which philosophy perceives. On the contrary, the two modes of knowledge lead to truth in all its fullness. The unity of truth is a fundamental premise of human reasoning, as the principle of non-contradiction makes clear. Revelation renders this unity certain, showing that the God of creation is also the God of salvation history. It is the one and the same God who establishes and guarantees the intelligibility and reasonableness of the natural order of things upon which scientists confidently depend,[581] and who reveals himself as the Father of our Lord Jesus Christ. This unity of truth, natural and revealed, is embodied in a living and personal way in Christ, as the Apostle reminds us: "Truth is in Jesus" (cf. *Eph* 4:21; *Col* 1:15-20). He is the *eternal Word* in whom all things were created, and he is the *incarnate Word* who in his entire person[582] reveals the Father (cf. *Jn* 1:14, 18). What human reason seeks "without knowing it" (cf. *Acts* 17:23) can be found only through Christ: what is revealed in him is "the full truth" (cf. *Jn* 1:14-16) of everything which was created in him and through him and which therefore in him finds its fulfillment (cf. *Col* 1:17). (FR34)

---

[580] *FR*, 33.
[581] Cf. John Paul II, Address to the Pontifical Academy of Sciences (November 10, 1979): *Insegnamenti*, II, 2 (1979), 1111-1112.
[582] Cf. Second Vatican Ecumenical Council, Dogmatic Constitution on Divine Revelation *Dei Verbum*, 4.

How the Holy Father longs for all people in the world today to discover the fullness of the truth about themselves in the person of Christ! He begins his 1990 encyclical *Redemptoris Missio* (*The Mission of the Redeemer*) with the moving words: "The mission of Christ the Redeemer, which is entrusted to the Church, is still very far from completion. As the second millennium after Christ's coming draws to an end, an overall view of the human race shows that this mission is still only beginning and that we must commit ourselves wholeheartedly to its service."[583]

What pain must John Paul II have experienced when he was forced to write the following lines just a few paragraphs later in that same encyclical: "The number of those who do not know Christ and do not belong to the Church is constantly on the increase. Indeed, since the end of the Council it has almost doubled. When we consider this immense portion of humanity which is loved by the Father and for whom he sent his Son, the urgency of the Church's mission is obvious."[584]

The Pope's sentiments are ardently felt by holy men and women of our day. At an International Youth and Family Encounter in Atlanta, Georgia in November 1998, Father Marcial Maciel was asked the following question: "If God would grant you one wish right now, what would it be?" His response: "My one desire would be that all people who live in this world would know Christ, believe in Christ, love Christ, and live with that immense joy our heart experiences when we are a friend of Christ."

---

[583] *Redemptoris Missio*, 1.
[584] Ibid., 3.

NINE

Contraception's View of Men and Women: Objects To Be Manipulated

Preview

I. The Historical Drama of Contraception Unfolds
    A. The "Great Mystery" is Threatened
    B. Planned Parenthood and a "New Sexual Order"
    C. Contraception: From Secular Ideology to Christian Heresy

II. The Catholic Church Defends the Inviolable Mystery of Married Love
    A. *Casti Connubii*: A Response to the Lambeth Conference
    B. Pius XII: Defending Married Love in the Decade of the Pill
    C. John XXIII: The Beginning of Dissent
    D. *Gaudium et Spes*: Married Love in the Mystery of God's Plan

III. *Humanae Vitae*: The Truth that Sets Married Love Free
    A. A Sign of Contradiction
    B. A New Phenomenon: Widespread Dissent

Points to look for

1. What does John Paul II mean when he declares, "The 'great mystery' is threatened in us and all around us"?

2. What evidence is there that the foundations of the 1960s' "sexual revolution" were laid at the turn of the century?

3. How does Pius XI's 1930 encyclical, *Casti Connubii*, defend the inviolable mystery of married love?

4. How does Pope Pius XII reaffirm the continuous teaching of the Church and of his predecessor on the conjugal union between husband and wife?

5. Where does Pope John XXIII reveal that he was not considering any change in the Church's teaching on the regulation of births?

6. How does Vatican II's Pastoral Constitution on the Church in the Modern World *Gaudium et Spes* lay the foundations for *Humanae Vitae*?

7. What response can be given to the argument in favor of contraception from the "principle of totality"? (Totality states that each individual conjugal act need not be open to life provided the totality of acts in the marriage as a whole are.)

8. Why was Pope Paul VI's encyclical *Humanae Vitae* received with consternation by so many people?

9. What is the reason Pope Paul VI gives in *Humanae Vitae* as to why contraceptive acts are always wrong?

10. Why can it be said that the erroneous moral theory of proportionalism developed in large part as a response to *Humanae Vitae*?

11. How does proportionalism seek to eliminate intrinsically evil acts?

I. The Historical Drama of Contraception Unfolds
A. The "Great Mystery" is Threatened

We have examined materialist rationalism's impoverished concept of the human person. It is a view that seeks to eliminate the transcendent mystery which is present in each person's life. We have pondered some of the tragic consequences that have followed from adopting a rationalist perspective and reflected on how this deficient view may be overcome. To surmount the reductive rationalist outlook is an urgent task. Rationalism has swept like a surging tide across Western civilization, threatening to engulf what is most noble in the human person. John Paul II reveals the drama of the present situation in his 1994 *Letter to Families*:

> Modern rationalism does not tolerate mystery. It does not accept the mystery of man as male and female, nor is it willing to admit that the full truth about man has been revealed in Jesus Christ. In particular, it does not accept the "great mystery" proclaimed in the letter to the Ephesians but radically opposes it. It may well acknowledge, in the context of a vague deism, the possibility, or even the need for a supreme or divine Being. But it firmly rejects the idea of a God who became man in order to save man. For rationalism, it is unthinkable that God should be the Redeemer, much less that he should be *"the bridegroom"* . . . Rationalism provides a radically different way of looking at creation and the meaning of human existence. But once man begins to lose sight of a God who loves him, a God who calls man through Christ to live in him and with him, and once the family no longer has the possibility of sharing in the "great mystery," what is left except the mere temporal dimension of life? Earthly life becomes nothing more than the scenario of a battle for existence, of a desperate search for gain, and financial gain before all else.
>
> The deep-seated roots of the "great mystery," the sacrament of life and love which began with Creation and Redemption and which *has Christ the Bridegroom as its ultimate surety*, have been lost in the

modern way of looking at things. The "great mystery" is threatened in us and all around us."[585]

How have we arrived to the present situation, where the "great mystery" of God's redemptive plan of salvation in Christ and our sharing in that mystery is threatened "in us and all around us"? Rationalism has provided ideological support for undermining the "great mystery" precisely where human life and love meet God's own: the family. The relentless contraception campaign, begun in the nineteenth century, continues unabated to our day. This secular ideology has managed to sweep many Christian churches off the rock of Christ's teaching. Only at the price of prolonged suffering was the Vicar of Christ, in the person of Pope Paul VI, able to stand firm. What were the steps that led up to Pope Paul VI's 1968 encyclical *Humanae Vitae*?

B. Planned Parenthood and a "New Sexual Order"

At the turn of the century, the standard of contraception was taken up by the American Birth Control League, later to be known as Planned Parenthood. Although the "sexual revolution" is generally acknowledged to have erupted during the 1960s, its foundations were already established by the first decades of the twentieth century. John D'Emilio and Estelle Freedman describe the period from 1880 to 1930 as a transition to a "new sexual order."[586] One unexpected statistic confirms the accuracy of their claim. "By the turn of the century, the birth rate among white middle class women had fallen dramatically to two children or less."[587]

The practice of contraception, which ushered in a new "sexual freedom," soon passed beyond the realm of secular environments to enter the domain of purported Christian life. Beginning in 1930, many Christian denominations began to declare that contraception among married couples was morally acceptable in certain circumstances. How does this dramatic development square with the perennial teachings of the Christian faith?

C. Contraception: From Secular Ideology to Christian Heresy

Since the very first centuries of Christianity, the Catholic Church has been unwavering in its condemnation of contraception as an immoral action, since it violates God's plan for human love. John T. Noonan, Jr., has written a definitive study outlining the history of the doctrine of non-contraception.[588]

---

[585] John Paul II, *Letter to Families*, 19.
[586] John D'Emilio and Estelle B. Freedman, *Intimate Matters: A History of Sexuality in America* (New York: Harper & Row, 1988), p. 169.
[587] Mary Shivanandan, *Crossing the Threshold of Love*, p. 195.
[588] John T. Noonan, Jr., *Contraception: A History of Its Treatment by Catholic Theologians and Canonists* (Cambridge, MA: The Belknap Press of Harvard University Press, 1965).

In fact, up until 1930, all Christian churches were unanimous in declaring the immorality of contraception. One event in the public forum in the United States reflects the universality of Christian belief at that time. In 1873, responding to the pressure of a campaign for artificial birth control, an American evangelical reformer, Anthony Comstock, convinced the U.S. Congress to legislate against the manufacture, distribution and sale of contraceptive devices. Most states passed similar legislation, which became known collectively as the Comstock laws.[589] These laws continued to be in effect in several states until the early 1960s.[590] It should be noted that legislators, a majority of whom were Protestant, passed these anti-contraceptive laws for a largely Protestant America.

As late as 1920, the bishops of the Church of England reaffirmed the traditional teaching against unnatural forms of birth control, in response to the agitation of Margaret Sanger and Planned Parenthood. They stressed the importance of conscious self-control for both husband and wife. Then they went on to solemnly declare, in words that would prove prophetic:

> We utter an emphatic warning against the use of unnatural means for the avoidance of conception, together with the grave dangers — physical, moral, and religious — thereby incurred, and against the evil which the extension of such use threatens the race.[591]

Inexplicably, just ten years later, the Anglican Church broke with its own teaching. On August 14, 1930, at the Lambeth Conference, Anglican bishops permitted husband and wife to practice contraception in certain cases. Thus, the Church of England became the first Christian church to accept contraception as morally licit. Unfortunately, many others were soon to walk down the same path. The widespread acceptance and practice of contraception among Christians today, including Catholics, has caused this ideology to assume the dimensions of a genuine present-day heresy.

II. The Catholic Church Defends the Inviolable Mystery of Married Love

A. *Casti Connubii:* A Response to the Lambeth Conference

Pope Pius XI was quick to respond to the threat that the Lambeth decision posed to the sacred and inviolable nature of the self-giving love between husband and wife in each act of marital union. On December 31, 1930, he issued the encyclical *Casti Connubii* (*On Christian Marriage*). Number 20 of the encyclical makes clear that declaring contraception

---

[589] Cf. John F. Kippley, *Sex and the Marriage Covenant*, p. 225.
[590] Cf. Janet E. Smith, "*Humanae Vitae* at Twenty," in *Why* Humanae Vitae *Was Right: A Reader*, ed. Janet E. Smith (San Francisco: Ignatius Press, 1993), p. 503.
[591] Noonan, *Contraception: A History of Its Treatment by Catholic Theologians and Canonists*, p. 427.

morally acceptable is an erroneous departure from the teachings of Christianity. Every marital act must be open to life, or a grave sin is committed.

> Since, therefore, openly departing from the uninterrupted Christian tradition, some recently have judged it possible solemnly to declare another doctrine regarding this question, the Catholic Church, to whom God has entrusted the defense of the integrity and purity of morals . . . in order that she may preserve the chastity of the nuptial union from being defiled . . . proclaims anew: any use whatsoever of matrimony, exercised in such a way that the act is deliberately frustrated in its natural power to generate life is an offense against the law of God and of nature, and those who indulge in such are branded with the guilt of a grave sin."[592]

Pius XI states the reason for this teaching. Since contraceptive acts violate the natural law, whose source is God, they are always wrong in themselves. No good intention of husband or wife could ever change the evil nature of an act that is intrinsically wrong. The Pope affirms: "No reason, however grave, may be put forward by which anything intrinsically against nature may become conformable to nature and morally good."[593]

But *Casti Connubii* is more than a simple response to the Lambeth decision, with a reaffirmation of the Church's traditional teaching on married love. One dramatic passage moves beyond the prior tendency to consider marriage primarily as a contract and opens the doors to a personalist perspective. Theologians will eagerly develop this vision of marriage from the viewpoint of personalism during the following decades. It will find authoritative expression in the Second Vatican Council, in numbers 47-52 of *Gaudium et Spes*. They speak of marriage and the family in clearly personalistic language. Thus, Pope Pius XI first charts the course that the Church will follow to defend the Christian doctrine of married love by vibrantly proclaiming the inviolable mystery of the person that is expressed in the conjugal union between husband and wife.

Pius XI reflects that the molding of husband and wife in their inner sphere (precisely where they are persons) by sharing their lives together is at the heart of marriage:

> This mutual inward molding of husband and wife, this determined effort to perfect each other, can in a very real sense, as the Roman Catechism teaches, be said to be the chief reason and purpose of matrimony, provided matrimony be looked at not in the restricted sense as instituted for the proper conception and education of the

---

[592] Pope Pius XI, encyclical letter *Casti Connubii*, *AAS* 22 (1930), n. 56; *Denzinger-Schönmetzer*, 3717.
[593] *Casti Connubii*, n. 54; *DS*, 3716.

child, but more widely as a blending of life as a whole and the mutual interchange and sharing thereof.[594]

B. Pius XII: Defending Married Love in the Decade of the Pill

The development of the birth control pill in the 1950s, along with more widespread use of the natural calendar rhythm method by Catholic couples, brought the issue of the regulation of births to the fore once again. Pope Pius XII confirmed the Church's constant teaching on the intrinsic immorality of contraception. He did so in a 1951 address to Italian midwives.

> Our predecessor, Pius XI, of happy memory, in his encyclical *Casti Connubii*, December 31, 1930, solemnly proclaimed anew the fundamental law governing the marital act and conjugal relations: that any attempt on the part of married people to deprive this act of its inherent force and to impede the procreation of new life, either in the performance of the act itself or in the course of the development of its natural consequences, is immoral; and no alleged "indication" or need can convert an intrinsically immoral act into a moral and lawful one.[595]

> This precept is as valid today as it was yesterday; and it will be the same tomorrow and always, because it does not imply a precept of the human law but is the expression of a law which is natural and divine.[596]

Pius XII's final statement in the above quotation clearly reveals the inalterable character of this teaching. The Church has no power to alter divine or natural law. It only has authority to change human laws according to new circumstances, when necessary for the good of souls.

In his address Pius XII also reaffirmed that it was morally acceptable for couples to limit marital relations to the wife's infertile periods in order to regulate the births of children, if they did so for "serious reasons" and not from selfish motives. He expressed the hope that medical science would soon perfect the natural method of birth regulation.

C. John XXIII: The Beginning of Dissent

During the reminder of Pius XII's pontificate, the question of artificial birth control appeared to be resolved in the Catholic world. It was not until 1963, the final year of the pontificate of his successor, John XXIII, that a few influential articles appeared in serious theological journals, advocating a change in Church teaching.[597]

---

[594] *Casti Connubii*, n. 24: *DS*, 3707.

[595] Cfr. *AAS*, vol. 22, pp. 559 ff.

[596] Pius XII, "Address to the Italian Catholic Union of Midwives," October 29, 1951 (*AAS* 43:843). Cited in Kippley, *Sex and the Marriage Covenant*, p. 327.

[597] Cf. Janet E. Smith, "*Humanae Vitae* at Twenty," in *Why Humanae Vitae Was Right: A Reader*, p. 503. For a detailed description of these articles see John F. Kippley, *Sex and the Marriage Covenant*, pp. 229-230.

With the opening of the Second Vatican Council, Pope John XXIII had convened a small commission to advise him on these matters. After John's death, Pope Paul VI greatly expanded the commission for the study of population, the family, and births. It eventually grew to nearly sixty members, including three married couples. One of those members was Bishop Karol Wojtyła of Poland. Although he was unable to attend the sessions, denied permission to leave the country by the communist regime, he was instrumental in helping a group of Polish bishops and theologians draft a document concerning the principles of conjugal life that was sent to Pope Paul VI.[598]

Upon the formation of this commission, speculation began that Pope John XXIII might be considering the possibility of changing the Church's teaching on artificial birth control. Was he? John XXIII's landmark encyclical *Mater et Magistra* (Mother and Teacher) "On Recent Developments of the Social Question in the Light of Christian Teaching,"[599] issued one year before the council, reveals his thinking on the matter. The encyclical reaffirms the Church's traditional teaching.

In a section titled "Population Increase and Economic Development," "good Pope John" declares that the arguments about overpopulation — one of the original justifications for contraception — are less than convincing. Nor does he foresee such a problem developing, thanks to the goodness of God's providence.

> Now to tell the truth, the interrelationships on a global scale between the number of births and available resources are such that we can infer grave difficulties in this matter do not arise at present, nor will in the immediate future. The arguments advanced in this connection are so inconclusive and controversial that nothing certain can be drawn from them.
>
> Besides, God in his goodness and wisdom has, on the one hand, provided nature with almost inexhaustible productive capacity; and, on the other hand, has endowed man with such ingenuity that, by using suitable means, he can apply nature's resources to the needs and requirements of existence.[600]

John XXIII then goes on to affirm, as did his predecessors, the categorical immorality of contraception: "Accordingly, that the question posed may be clearly resolved, a course of action is not indeed to be followed whereby, contrary to the moral law laid down by God, procreative function is also violated."[601]

---

[598] "Les Fondaments de la Doctrine de L'Eglise Concernant les Principes de la Vie Conjugale," *Analecta Cracoviensia*, (No. 1, 1969) pp. 194-230.

[599] John XXIII, encyclical letter *Mater et Magistra*, May 15, 1961, N.C.W.C. translation (Boston: St. Paul Editions). The headings and paragraph numbers are from the N.C.W.C. text.

[600] John XIII, encyclical letter *Mater et Magistra*, 188-189.

[601] Ibid., 189.

D. *Gaudium et Spes*:
Married Love in the Mystery of God's Plan

By 1965, the final year of the Second Vatican Council, articles from theologians advocating a change in the Church's teaching on contraception had swelled from a mere trickle to a torrent. As the council fathers outlined a vibrant, personalist vision of married love and the family in *Gaudium et Spes* (The Pastoral Constitution on the Church in the Modern World), Pope Paul VI reserved the specific question of contraception to himself.[602]

The text of *Gaudium et Spes* lends full support to Pope Paul VI's future pronouncement in *Humanae Vitae*. A first important affirmation is that God, the author of marriage, cannot have engendered any conflict between the expressions of married love that unite the spouses and the procreation of children. "The Church wishes to emphasize that there can be no conflict between the divine laws governing the transmission of life and the fostering of authentic married love."[603]

As if in response to many prevailing opinions of the day, which claimed that the intentions of husband and wife for the good of their marriage and family were the ultimate criteria for determining the morality of the conjugal act, *Gaudium et Spes* once again confirms the Church's teaching on the objective criteria that determine the nature of the conjugal act itself. By affirming that these objective criteria require the practice of the virtue of chastity, the document points directly to the essential difference between natural methods of birth regulation and contraception. Finally, it calls on married couples to be faithful to the Church's Magisterium, indicating in a footnote past authoritative statements by the Church condemning contraception.

> When it is a question of harmonizing married love with the responsible transmission of life, it is not enough to take only the good intention and the evaluation of motives into account; the objective criteria must be used, criteria drawn from the nature of the human person and human action, criteria which respect the total meaning of mutual self-giving and human procreation in the context of true love; all this is possible only if the virtue of married chastity is seriously practiced. In questions of birth regulation the sons of the Church, faithful to these principles, are forbidden to use methods disapproved of by the teaching authority of the Church in its interpretation of the divine law.[604]

---

[602] Cf. *Gaudium et Spes*, 51; note 14.

[603] *GS*, 51.

[604] *GS*, 51, referring in the note to Pius XI, encyclical letter *Casti Connubii: AAS* 22 (1930), pp. 559-561; *DS*. 3716-3718; Pius XII, *Allocution to the Congress of Italian Midwives*, Oct. 29, 1951: *AAS* 43 (1951), pp. 835-54; Paul VI, *Allocution to the Cardinals*, June 23, 1964: *AAS* 56 (1964), pp. 581-9.

III. *Humanae Vitae*: The Truth that Sets Married Love Free
A. A Sign of Contradiction

After the council ended, Pope Paul VI's special advisory commission on population, the family, and births continued its deliberations. Members of the commission were unable to arrive at a consensus among themselves. So two reports were drafted for Paul VI. The Majority Report affirmed that it was morally acceptable for married couples to practice contraception under certain circumstances. The Minority Report disagreed, pointing to fundamental flaws in the reasoning of the majority opinion and appealing to the Church's constant teaching on the matter.

Though all the members of the commission were bound to strict secrecy, incredibly, the Majority Report was leaked to the press. The report immediately fueled speculation that the Church was about to change her teaching on contraception. In his analysis of the situation following Vatican II, Ralph McInerny describes what the times were like:

> It is important to understand the atmosphere of those days. Moral theologians of repute, on and off the papal commission, were writing in favor of lifting the ban on artificial contraception. This became, of course, a matter of classroom discussion in Roman Catholic colleges, in seminaries, and beyond. The discussion spilled over into publications of wide circulation. Pastoral care was affected by the expectation that soon the Church would rescind Her prohibition. Couples preparing for marriage could hardly be expected to be guided by a prohibition whose days were numbered.[605]

In seeking to justify its position that artificial contraception could be morally licit, the Majority Report appealed to the principle of totality. They claimed that it wasn't necessary for each and every marriage act to be open to new life, as long as the marriage acts on the whole, in their totality, were open to children. It is not difficult to spot the fallacy in this line of reasoning. It could be applied just as easily to justify committing adultery, as Ruth Lasseter points out:

> By the same formula of totality, extended into marital fidelity, need *every* act of sexual union necessarily be with one's spouse? Couldn't one affirm, by the principle of totality, that if one affirmed marriage *most* of the time, did one have to be faithful to marriage *all* of the time, every single time? The widespread infidelity which followed closely behind the argument for totality in matters of contraception is no accident; in fact, contraception made concupiscence and its justification possible.[606]

---

[605] Ralph M. McInerny, *What Went Wrong with Vatican II*, (Manchester, NH: Sophia Institute Press, 1998), p. 43.

[606] Ruth D. Lasseter, "Sensible Sex," in *Why* Humanae Vitae *Was Right: A Reader*, p. 482.

Pope Paul VI's encyclical *Humanae Vitae,* signed July 25, 1968, was released to the press on July 29. Ralph McInerny remarks that the Pope's message was received "as a surprise — indeed as a bombshell."[607]

U.S. bishops were quick to affirm their support of the Holy Father's teaching, calling upon the faithful entrusted to their pastoral care to follow the guidance of Christ's Vicar. On July 31 Archbishop John F. Deardon of Detroit, president of the National Conference of Catholic Bishops, released the following public statement:

> The sacredness of Christian marriage makes it a special concern of the Church. Its dignity must be carefully safeguarded and its responsibility fulfilled. The recent encyclical letter of Pope Paul VI reflects this concern.
>
> The Holy Father, speaking as the supreme teacher of the Church, has reaffirmed the principles to be followed in forming the Christian conscience of married persons in carrying out their responsibilities.
>
> Recognizing his unique role in the Universal Church, we, the bishops of the Church in the United States, unite with him in calling upon our priests and people to receive with sincerity what he has taught, to study it carefully and to form their consciences in its light.
>
> We are aware of the difficulties this teaching lays upon so many of our conscientious married people, but we must face the reality that struggling to live out the word of God will often entail sacrifice.
>
> In confident trust in the firmness of their faith, in their loyalty to the Holy Father and to his office, and in their reliance on divine help, we ask of them a true Christian response to this teaching.[608]

B. A New Phenomenon: Widespread Dissent

Despite the almost immediate response of the bishops, uniting themselves as teachers and pastors with the successor of Peter, someone else reacted first: dissenting theologians. On July 30, within twenty-four hours of *Humanae Vitae*'s public pronouncement, more than two hundred theologians signed a full-page ad in the *New York Times,* declaring their disagreement with the doctrine of the encyclical. They went even further, asserting that Catholic faithful could at times decide in conscience to disregard the Church's teaching.

> Therefore, as Roman Catholic theologians, conscious of our duty and our limitations, we conclude that spouses may responsibly decide according to their conscience that artificial contraception in

---

[607] Ralph M. McInerny, *What Went Wrong with Vatican II,* p. 41.
[608] "U.S. Bishops Ask Acceptance," *National Catholic Reporter,* August 7, 1968, p. 4.

some circumstances is permissible and indeed necessary to preserve and foster the values and sacredness of marriage.[609]

Twenty-four hours hardly seems a sufficient period to have studied carefully Paul VI's encyclical, as the U.S. bishops urged. Nor did the dissenting theologians' advice to spouses correspond with the bishops' appeal that they form their consciences in the light of *Humanae Vitae's* teachings. It is rather astounding that these theologians should have taken it upon themselves to give direct pastoral advice to married couples contrary to that of the bishops and pope, since the role of pastor, as well as authoritative teacher of the faith, belongs precisely to the bishops in communion with the successor of Peter. The task of theologians is to penetrate more deeply into the truths of the faith. This vital role arises from the inner dynamism of truth itself, and from the nature of love, which always strives to know more intimately the beloved.[610] But the theologian can only fulfill his mission united with the Church's pastors, who have received from the Holy Spirit the charism of authentically teaching the faith.[611] How can the *New York Times* possibly be considered a proper venue for objective theological discussion?

The *New York Times* ad marked the beginning of a new phenomenon: widespread dissent among theologians to the Church's teachings authoritatively proclaimed by the Magisterium. Just what dimensions this dissent came to assume can be perceived by considering one current of thought that sprang up within moral theology in reaction to *Humanae Vitae.*

In explaining why contraception is always immoral, Pope Paul VI reaffirms the Church's constant teaching that contraceptive acts are intrinsically disordered or evil (*intrinsece inhonestum*). Thus, a person can never choose to do them, even if it is for a good intention. For whenever the will chooses something evil, even as a means to a good end, it cannot help but desire the evil it chooses directly, and so the person's will itself becomes infected by evil. Paul VI firmly grounds the prohibition against contraceptive acts on the fact that they are intrinsically wrong.

> In truth, if it is sometimes permissible to tolerate a lesser moral evil in order to avoid a greater evil or to promote a greater good,[612] it is not permissible, not even for the gravest reasons, to do evil so that good may follow therefrom.[613] One may not, in other words, make into the object of a positive act of the will something that is intrinsically disordered and hence unworthy of the human person, even

---

[609] "Text of the Statement by Theologians," *New York Times*, August 31, 1968, p. 16.

[610] Cf. Congregation for the Doctrine of the Faith, Instruction on the Ecclesial Vocation of the Theologian *Donum Veritatis* (May 24, 1990), 7.

[611] Cf. *Donum Veritatis*, 6.

[612] Cf. Pius XII, Allocution to the Fifth National Italian Congress of the Union of Catholic Jurists, Dec. 6, 1953: *AAS* 45 (1953), pp. 798-99.

[613] Cf. Rom 3:8.

when the intention is to safeguard or promote individual, family or social goods. Consequently it is an error to think that a conjugal act which is deliberately made infertile and so is intrinsically wrong [*intrinsece inhonestum*] could be made right by a fertile conjugal life considered as a whole.[614]

Theologians who disagreed with the Church's position on contraception had been unable to sway Paul VI's judgment in writing *Humanae Vitae*. Since the encyclical could no longer be changed, another strategy soon emerged: Change all of moral theology in order to eliminate intrinsically evil acts. *Proportionalism* appeared on the scene as a new moral theory.

What is the chief tenet of proportionalism? In order to determine the moral value of any action, it is necessary to establish a proportion between the good and bad effects resulting from the act. Thus, no action can be judged good or evil in itself, independent of its actual consequences and those intended by the agent who performed it. In other words, intrinsically evil acts — those actions which are always wrong due to their very nature — are suddenly eliminated.

---

[614] *Humanae Vitae*, 14; English translation by Marc Calegari, S.J., (San Francisco: Ignatius Press, 1978), p. 13.

Preview

NINE CONTRACEPTION'S VIEW OF MEN AND WOMEN: OBJECTS TO BE MANIPULATED *(continued)*

III. *Humanae Vitae*: The Truth That Sets Married Love Free *(continued)*
    C. Resisting Erroneous Theology: A Firm Defense of the Human Person
    D. Seeking to Win Over Theologians: "The Bruised Reed He Shall Not Break"
        1. 1989: The *Profession of Faith and Oath of Fidelity*
        2. 1990: The Instruction on the Ecclesial Vocation of the Theologian *Donum Veritatis*
        3. 1998: *Ad Tuendam Fidem* (To Defend the Faith)
    E. *Humanae Vitae*'s Prophecies
        1) Conjugal Infidelity and a Lowering of Morality —
           Especially Among Young People
           -Sex Education, Contraception, and Abortion
        2) Loss of Respect for Women
        3) A Dangerous Weapon in the Hands of Public Authorities

Points to look for

1. What effect would proportionalism have upon the teachings of Christianity?

2. What effect would proportionalism have upon society itself and the fundamental dignity of each human person?

3. How does John Paul II's 1993 encyclical *Veritatis Splendor* defend Christian faith and the inviolable rights of each person against the proportionalist error?

4. In addition to the Creed, what else must theology teachers profess by the 1989 *Profession of Faith and Oath of Fidelity*?

5. What is the principal task of theology according to *Donum Veritatis*?

6. What is essential for theologians to fulfill their task within the community of faith?

7. What does *Donum Veritatis* say about theological dissent?

8. What tragic irony is revealed in the first sentence of John Paul II's 1998 Apostolic Letter *Ad Tuendam Fidem*?

9. What was the purpose of *Ad Tuendam Fidem*?

10. What was Paul VI's first prophecy in *Humanae Vitae* regarding the consequences of legitimizing contraception? What evidence can be cited to show that it sadly has been fulfilled?

11. What was Paul VI's second prophecy? How has it also come true?

12. How does contraception prevent acts of marital union between husband and wife from being a renewal of the sacramental graces of matrimony?

13. Why is it so vitally urgent for married couples and priests to proclaim the truth about natural family planning in God's plan for married love?

14. What was Paul VI's third prophecy? How has it also been fulfilled?

15. Why is it no accident that legitimizing contraception has led to appalling violations of women's rights?

C. Resisting Erroneous Theology: A Firm Defense of the Human Person

Just how far-reaching are the implications of proportionalism? This theory would have created a genuine "brave new world" were it to have won the day. Not a single pillar of the Church's moral teaching would have remained standing. Since the Ten Commandments impose absolute moral obligations due to the nature of the acts themselves, they would have all collapsed. The moral precepts of the New Testament would have encountered a similar fate.

The tremors of the proportionalist earthquake would not have ceased after devastating Christianity. They would have gone on to demolish the foundations of civil society itself. What are the founding principles of American democracy as set forth in the Declaration of Independence? The foundation stones of our free society are each person's inalienable rights to "life, liberty, and the pursuit of happiness." But inalienable rights are nothing other than the flip side of intrinsically evil acts. To violate the Fifth Commandment and directly kill an innocent person is an intrinsically evil act. It is always wrong in itself, regardless of the intention of the one who kills or the consequences, because an innocent person has an inalienable right to life that may never be violated. If there are no such things as intrinsically evil acts, then neither can there exist any inalienable rights, which may never be violated. Society collapses and persons are left defenseless before assaults on their basic human dignity.

When confronted with this panorama, it becomes clear what is riding on *Humanae Vitae*. Not only the sacredness of married love and the family is at stake, but also the very dignity and inalienable rights of each human person, created in the image of God.

John Paul II has perceived the distant horizons with the clarity of prophetic vision that was granted his predecessor. He has guided the bark of Peter on a firm course in resisting these potentially catastrophic theological errors. Under his leadership the Church, *Mater et Magistra* (mother and teacher), has proved herself to be a valiant defender of humanity.

The *Catechism of the Catholic Church*, promulgated in 1992, "contains a complete and systematic exposition of Christian moral teaching."[615] The Holy Father himself admits that this teaching was being threatened by "certain theological positions, encountered even in seminaries and in faculties of theology, with regard to questions of the greatest importance for the Church and for the life of faith of Christians, as well as for the life of society itself."[616]

In 1993 John Paul II issued his landmark encyclical on the foundations of moral theology: *Veritatis Splendor* (*The Splendor of Truth*). In his introduction to the encyclical, the Pope makes clear the drama of the present moment, characterizing it as a "new situation" in the Church's life with regard to the extent and nature of theological dissent.

> In fact, a new situation has come about *within the Christian community itself*, which has experienced the spread of numerous doubts and objections of a human and psychological, social and cultural, religious and even properly theological nature, with regard to the Church's moral teachings. It is no longer a matter of limited and occasional dissent, but of an overall and systematic calling into question of traditional moral doctrine, on the basis of certain anthropological and ethical presuppositions.[617]

John Paul II describes the actual situation as "*a genuine crisis*, since the difficulties which it engenders have most serious implications for the moral life of the faithful and for communion in the Church, as well as for a just and fraternal social life."[618] The Pope also diagnoses what lies at the root of the erroneous moral theories: "the more or less obvi-

---

[615] John Paul II, encyclical letter *Veritatis Splendor*, 5.
[616] *Veritatis Splendor*, 4.
[617] *Veritatis Splendor*, 4.
[618] Ibid., 5.

ous influence of currents of thought which end by detaching human freedom from its essential and constitutive relationship to truth."[619]

We cannot help but hear echoing once more Bishop Karol Wojtyła's resounding words during the Second Vatican Council: "There is no freedom without truth!" *Veritatis Splendor* is one of John Paul II's most crucial encyclicals, precisely because it defends the truth of human dignity, arising from our free moral acts, against the grave assault of proportionalism. After a detailed refutation of proportionalist theories, marked by unassailable logic, the encyclical definitively rejects their central thesis: that it is impossible to qualify acts as morally evil in themselves.

> *One must therefore reject the thesis,* characteristic of teleological and proportionalist theories, *which holds that it is impossible to qualify as morally evil according to its species — its "object" — the deliberate choice of certain kinds of behavior or specific acts, apart from a consideration of the intention for which the choice is made or the totality of the foreseeable consequences of that act for all persons concerned.*[620]

The encyclical also makes clear that such a rejection is not based simply upon philosophical grounds, but is necessary because proportionalist theories violate the truths of the faith as taught by the Church. "Such theories however are not faithful to the Church's teaching, when they believe they can justify, as morally good, deliberate choices of kinds of behavior contrary to the commandments of the divine and natural law. These theories cannot claim to be grounded in the Catholic moral tradition."[621]

John Paul II is quick to add that it is not enough to point out the errors present in false ethical theories like proportionalism. He affirms, "We must first of all show the inviting splendor of that truth which is Jesus Christ himself."[622] Only by uniting with the Holy Father to ardently proclaim the truth of the inviolable mystery that is each human person in Christ, can Christians offer true hope to mankind at the dawn of the third millennium.

D. Seeking to Win Over Theologians: "The Bruised Reed He Shall Not Break"

1. 1989: The *Profession of Faith and Oath of Fidelity*

While firmly defending the truths of Christian faith and life, John Paul II has never ceased in his efforts to seek out theologians at times caught up in the dense thickets of present-day relativistic, libertarian, or reductivist currents of thought. The 1989 *Profession of Faith and Oath of*

---

[619] Ibid., 4.
[620] Ibid., 79.
[621] Ibid., 76.
[622] Ibid., 83.

Fidelity,[623] to be pronounced by all persons who teach theology or assume a task of governing within the Church, was meant to ensure that those being formed in the faith (future theologians among them) would receive the full truth of the Gospel message from their teachers.

In addition to professing the Creed, teachers of theology are asked to affirm their faith in all of the Church's teachings, with the three different levels of assent that correspond to the three ways in which a teaching may be proposed. For the highest level of assent, the oath states: "With firm faith, I also believe everything contained in the word of God, whether written or handed down in Tradition, which the Church either by a solemn judgment or by the ordinary and universal Magisterium sets forth to be believed as divinely revealed."[624]

The second level of assent refers to all that has been definitively proposed by the Church. Theology teachers must swear: "I also firmly accept and hold each and everything definitively proposed by the Church regarding teaching on faith and morals."[625] Finally, teachings proposed by the Church's ordinary Magisterium should also be adhered to. The oath adds: "Moreover I adhere with submission of will and intellect to the teachings which either the Roman Pontiff or the College of Bishops enunciate when they exercise their authentic Magisterium, even if they do not intend to proclaim these teachings by a definitive act."[626]

2. 1990: The Instruction on the Ecclesial Vocation of the Theologian *Donum Veritatis*

Another key effort was made in 1990 to overcome the rift between many theologians and the Church's Magisterium, formed by the pope and the bishops united with him. On May 24 of that year, with John Paul II's full approval, the Congregation for the Doctrine of the Faith issued the Instruction on the Ecclesial Vocation of the Theologian *Donum Veritatis* (The Gift of Truth).[627] The document begins by reflecting on the crucial task of theology, especially today. At the same time, it acknowledges the dangers this science has not always been able to avoid.

In times of great spiritual and cultural change, theology is all the more important. Yet it also is exposed to risks since it must strive to "abide" in the truth (cf. *Jn* 8:31), while at the same time taking into ac-

---

[623] *Profession of Faith and Oath of Fidelity*, Congregation for the Doctrine of the Faith (January 9, 1989): *AAS* 81 (1989).

[624] Cf. Second Vatican Ecumenical Council, Dogmatic Constitution on the Church *Lumen Gentium*, 25; Dogmatic Constitution on Divine Revelation *Dei Verbum*, 5; Congregation for the Doctrine of the Faith, Instruction on the Ecclesial Vocation of the Theologian *Donum Veritatis* (24 May 1990), 15: *AAS* 82 (1990), 1556.

[625] Cf., Congregation for the Doctrine of the Faith, Instruction on the Ecclesial Vocation of the Theologian *Donum Veritatis* (May 24, 1990), 16: *AAS* 82 (1990), 1557.

[626] Cf. Ibid.

[627] Congregation for the Doctrine of the Faith, Instruction on the Ecclesial Vocation of the Theologian *Donum Veritatis* (May 24, 1990), 15: *AAS* 82 (1990).

count the new problems which confront the human spirit. In our century, in particular, during the periods of preparation for and implementation of the Second Vatican Council, theology contributed much to a deeper "understanding of the realities and the words handed on."[628] But it also experienced and continues to experience moments of crisis and tension.[629]

The theologian seeks to penetrate more deeply into the truths of the faith. This vital role arises from the inner dynamism of truth itself, and from the nature of love, which always strives to know more intimately the beloved.[630] But the theologian can only fulfill his mission united with the Church's pastors, who have received from the Holy Spirit the charism of authentically teaching the faith. "His role is to pursue in a particular way an ever deeper understanding of the Word of God found in the inspired Scriptures and handed on by the living Tradition of the Church. He does this in communion with the Magisterium which has been charged with the responsibility of preserving the deposit of faith."[631] Under the guidance of the Church's pastors, theology "aids the People of God in fulfilling the Apostle's command (cf. 1 *Pet* 3:15) to give an accounting for their hope to those who ask it."[632]

Since theology is a fully constituted academic discipline, with its own proper methodology, theologians have a legitimate claim to academic freedom. One important fact must be kept in mind, though. "The freedom proper to theological research is exercised within the Church's faith."[633] That is why "the theologian is called to deepen his own life of faith and continuously unite his scientific research with prayer."[634] Another vital consequence is that "the commitment to theology requires a spiritual effort to grow in virtue and holiness."[635]

After laying down the foundations of the theologian's role within the community of faith, in communion with the Church's Magisterium, *Donum Veritatis* goes on to address the fundamental problem afflicting theology today: *dissent*. In some cases dissenting theologians have gone so far as to practically constitute a "parallel magisterium" within the Church. *Donum Veritatis* acknowledges the reality of this present situation and the harmful consequences which result. "As to the 'parallel magisterium,' it can cause great spiritual harm by opposing itself to the

---

[628] Dogmatic Constitution *Dei Verbum*, 8.
[629] *Donum Veritatis*, 1.
[630] Cf. *Donum Veritatis*, 7.
[631] *Donum Veritatis*, 6.
[632] Ibid., 6.
[633] Ibid., 11.
[634] Ibid., 8. Cf. John Paul II, "Discourse on the occasion of the conferral of the International Paul VI Prize to Hans Urs von Balthasar," June 23, 1984: *Insegnamenti di Giovanni Paolo II*, VII, 1 (1984), pp. 1911-1917.
[635] *Donum Veritatis*, 9.

Magisterium of the Pastors.... This cannot but seriously trouble the People of God and lead to contempt for true authority."[636]

Viewed from this perspective, the drama that has been unfolding since *Humanae Vitae* goes even beyond the sacredness of married love and the family. It is a question of authority within the Church, founded by Christ upon the rock of Peter and his successors. Ralph McInerny gives a personal assessment.

> The vast majority of Catholics have to rely on the credibility of those who give them advice. They have to choose between authorities, not arguments. The dissenting theologians seem almost heedlessly unaware of the anguish that this causes the faithful and the confusion that dissent introduces. To a man, they seem to feel they are alleviating an anguish already felt, but they must see that what they have done is to ask the faithful to accept the word of the dissenters and turn a deaf ear to the word of the Pope and the bishops. For laymen, it is not contraception but authority that is the issue: to whom should laymen turn? To the Pope or to dissenting theologians?[637]

3. 1998: *Ad Tuendam Fidem* (To Defend the Faith)

Donum Veritatis made it clear that dissent — and above all public dissent — from the teachings of the Magisterium was not a legitimate posture for theologians to adopt. It also sought to heal the wounds of division and strengthen theology in its noble task of enabling God's faithful people to give reasons for their hope.[638] The beauty and depth with which *Donum Veritatis* reflected upon the role of theology has made a lasting impression upon many theologians. Its enriching influence will continue to be felt among young men and women who take up the sublime commission of theology in the future.

Despite all the good achieved and still promised by this document, it did not resolve the problem of theological dissent within the Church. Dissent continued to such an extent that in 1998 John Paul II found it necessary to enact a firm disciplinary measure with his Apostolic Letter *Motu Proprio*,[639] *Ad Tuendam Fidem*. By this letter the Pope inscribed penalties into canon law for dissent that violated the 1989 *Profession of Faith and Oath of Fidelity*. The opening sentence of *Ad Tuendam Fidem* reveals the tragic irony of the situation which had developed. John Paul II was forced to defend the faith against theologians — precisely those persons entrusted with the mission of elucidating the faith so that it could be more effectively and ardently transmitted.

---

[636] Ibid., 34.

[637] Ralph McInerny, *What Went Wrong with Vatican II*, p. 92.

[638] Cf. 1 Pet 3:15.

[639] The Latin phrase *motu proprio* refers to something done on one's own initiative. Regarding papal documents, it refers to those written on the Pope's own authority, often to meet a special and urgent need in the Church.

To protect the faith of the Catholic Church against errors arising from certain members of the Christian faithful, especially from among those dedicated to the various disciplines of sacred theology, we, whose principal duty is to confirm the brethren in the faith (*Lk* 22:32), consider it absolutely necessary to add to the existing texts of the *Code of Canon Law* and the *Code of Canons of the Eastern Churches*, new norms which expressly impose the obligation of upholding truths proposed in a definitive way by the Magisterium of the Church, and which also establish related canonical sanctions.[640]

Under John Paul II, the Magisterium has clarified the challenging and vital task of theologians. The needed disciplinary measures have been enacted to safeguard their role. Now the Catholic faithful, thirsting for the truth of the Gospel message in all of its depth and beauty, eagerly await the theologians' response.

E. *Humanae Vitae's* Prophecies

Pope Paul VI made several predictions in *Humanae Vitae* regarding the grave consequences that would follow upon a widespread practice of artificial birth control. At the time they were received with astonishment and even disdain. More than thirty years later, no one can deny that these predictions were really prophecies — each one of which has been tragically fulfilled. Paul VI affirmed that contraception would lead to an increase in marital infidelity, a lowering of morality among young people, and a loss of respect for women by men, who would be free to treat women as mere objects of pleasure.

Upright men can even better convince themselves of the solid grounds on which the teaching of the Church in this field is based, if they care to reflect upon the consequences of methods of artificial birth control. Let them consider, first of all, how wide and easy a road would thus be opened up toward conjugal infidelity and the general lowering of morality. Not much experience is needed in order to know human weakness, and to understand that men — especially the young, who are so vulnerable on this point — have need of encouragement to be faithful to the moral law, so that they must not be offered some easy means of eluding its observance. It is also to be feared that the man, growing used to the employment of anticonceptive practices, may finally lose respect for the woman and, no longer caring for her physical and psychological equilibrium, may come to the point of considering her as a mere instrument of selfish enjoyment, and no longer as his respected and beloved companion.[641]

---

[640] *Ad Tuendam Fidem,* May 28, 1998.
[641] *Humanae Vitae,* 17.

1. Conjugal Infidelity and a Lowering of Morality —
Especially Among Young People

In light of Paul VI's first prophecy, let us review once again the dire statistics on marriage and public morality since the 1960s, which ushered in the widespread use of contraception.

> In what was called 'the demoralization of American society,' a number of statistical indicators came together. In the 30 years 1960-90, while the U.S. population rose by 41 percent, there was a 560 percent increase in violent crime, 200 percent in teenage suicide, 200 percent rise in divorce, over 400 percent rise in illegitimate births, 300 percent rise in children living in single-parent homes — producing *in toto* the significant fact that children formed the fastest-growing segment of the criminal population.[642]

> Up to 1920, the proportion of children born to single women in the United States was less than 3 percent, roughly where it had been throughout the history of the country. . . . By the end of 1994 it [the illegitimacy rate] was 33 percent for the nation as a whole, 25 percent for whites, and 70 percent for blacks. In parts of Washington, capital of the richest nation in the world, it was as high as 90 percent.[643]

Pope Paul VI expressed special concern about the vulnerability of the young. Critics dismissed his worries with indulgent smiles. Are young people suffering today as a result of contraception?

> By age 19, 8 of every 10 males and seven of ten females has had sexual intercourse. Four of 10 teenagers have had at least one pregnancy. . . . Nearly a million and a half abortions occur each year and nearly a third of these (almost 400,000) are obtained by teenagers. . . .

> These figures are chilling; so too is their meaning. It is disturbing that they seem to be self-perpetuating; consider that roughly 80 percent of girls who are mothers at age 15 are daughters of women who had babies when they were teenagers.[644]

-Sex Education, Contraception, and Abortion

It has long been a standard argument by many people who oppose Paul VI's vision that two things were needed to reduce teen-age pregnancy: sexual education and ready access to contraception. Just make contraceptives available to teens and teach them how to use them, and teen pregnancy would be greatly reduced. As a result, abortions among teens would also decline.

---

[642] Paul Johnson, *A History of the American People*, (New York, Harper Collins, 1997), pp. 965-966. The source of these figures is William J. Bennett, *Index of Leading Cultural Indicators* (New York 1993).

[643] Ibid., pp. 971-972. The source of these figures is Charles Murray, "Bad News About Illegitimacy," in *Washington Weekly Standard*, August 5, 1996.

[644] Janet E. Smith, "Paul VI as Prophet," in *Why* Humanae Vitae *Was Right: A Reader*, p. 521.

New research indicates that the opposite is true. More sexual education and contraception have actually made the problem worse. A study published in the August 18, 2000, *British Journal of Medicine* reveals that teens who consult with medical professionals about contraception actually have a *higher* rate of pregnancy than those who don't.

"The study found that 71 percent of 223 teen-age girls who became pregnant had discussed contraception with a health expert in the year before they became pregnant."[645] As to contraception's reducing the number of abortions, "Studies show that over 80 percent of young women who have had abortions are contraceptively experienced."[646]

That more abortions follow from contraception is not at all surprising. Dr. Janet Smith sums things up with unassailable logic.

> Most abortions are the result of unwanted pregnancies, most unwanted pregnancies are the result of sexual relationships outside of marriage, and most sexual relationships outside of marriage are facilitated by the availability of contraception. To turn this "progression" around: contraception leads to more extra-marital sexual intercourse; more extra-marital sexual intercourse leads to more unwanted pregnancies; more unwanted pregnancies lead to more abortions.[647]

2. Loss of Respect for Women

Paul VI warned that contraception would lead the man to consider the woman "as a mere instrument of selfish enjoyment, and no longer as his respected and beloved companion."[648] We have heard Ruth Lasseter's vibrant testimony of the mutual trust she and her husband experienced when practicing natural family planning — the strength they drew from it, the secret presence of Christ as a third partner in their marriage. Then circumstances led Ruth to have a tubal ligation. Side effects from the operation caused her health to deteriorate. At age thirty she was forced to have a hysterectomy. How did things change?

> Thereafter, Rollin and I seldom talked about the operation or what had led up to it. We seldom talked at all. We became very touchy about "slights"; we were impatient and sometimes rude to each other; we were often filled with self-pity. Despite a steady and comfortable income, we quarreled constantly about money. We became stressed and tense. . . . We lost our sense of humor and seemed to bicker over everything. He began to lose respect for me and I for him. Aversion to intimacy began to develop. Life became a horrid burden to us both, each secretly resenting and blaming the other.[649]

---

[645] Brian McGuire, "Sex Education Can Backfire, Says British Study," in the *National Catholic Register*, Vol. 76, No. 36, September 3-9, 2000, p. 1.

[646] Janet E. Smith, "Paul VI as Prophet," in *Why* Humanae Vitae *Was Right: A Reader*, p. 522.

[647] Ibid., p. 523.

[648] *Humanae Vitae*, 17.

[649] *Why* Humanae Vitae *Was Right: A Reader*, p. 488.

In the midst of their difficulties, the Lasseters received another blow. Their Catholic friends, who had warned them about the dangers of artificial contraception, now parents of seven children, were not getting along and were thinking about divorce. What had gone wrong?

> Our friends told us that they had decided that the whole Church was wrong, that it was just a power institution imposing rules on "little people" to spoil their sexual freedom. They renounced their former convictions about the evils of unnatural contraception; they ridiculed themselves for ever having held such convictions. We were embarrassed by their rude jokes; they were insulting to each other; their language had become coarse and vulgar. Both had come to support abortion. They encouraged their children to use contraception themselves. They talked about sex as if they were talking about a tennis match. The final severance came when a newly-launched affair with a female graduate student became a public scandal.[650]

The claim is sometimes made that a celibate Pope cannot truly understand married couples, or know what is best for them. From her own personal experience, Ruth Lasseter ponders the effects contraception has on husbands and wives and on their relationship with their children.

> It is true that women who contracept do feel exploited by their husbands; husbands who resort to condoms feel resentment towards their wives' fertility. Here is another social rift; husbands and wives don't talk about contraceptives either. As our own beloved children grow into puberty, we who are using unnatural contraceptives cannot talk to them about sexual chastity and self-control, even in the face of AIDS and STDs and every sort of promiscuously born disease of soul and body. Even while we are told that we are free at last, we know that we are helpless; we give our children condoms and are silent about chastity; we feel heartbroken, not knowing why.[651]

Mrs. Lasseter dispels the myth that contraception helps foster married love, enabling it to be more tender and spontaneous. In reality, the opposite is true. Love gives way to sensuality and a feeling of being used.

> Under the guise of helping love, artificial contraception cunningly establishes a tyrant in the marriage: The sex act declines from a reaffirming of the whole marriage covenant, true lovemaking, to joint seeking of mutual satisfaction. A subtle shift, but a decisive one, away from God and the covenant of marriage. . . .

---

[650] Ibid., pp. 489-490.
[651] Ibid., p. 477.

The nuptial exchange between man and woman is replaced by a woman's sense, vague and miniscule at first, that she must be "available" to her husband; anxiety develops about "performance" and sensual attractiveness; she may begin to feel used by her spouse. The husband, in an equally subtle way, ceases to delight in his bride and begins to think of her as an object to arouse and satisfy passion. He has a vague sense that something is wrong; he feels restless and unsatisfied. If they try to talk about "what's wrong with us?" it often draws up petty resentments. . . . They just don't seem to be able to come to an understanding over their difficulties. This couple may in every other way be moral and exemplary Christians; it has never occurred to them that artificial contraception could be destroying their marriage covenant and their love.[652]

How tragic are the consequences of failing to trust in God's own creative plan for married love — restored at the price of Christ's blood, shed upon the cross! In the most intimate sphere of their spousal union, Christ asks married couples to take up the cross of self-denial, of periodic continence, so that he may be there present with the transforming power of his redemption.

God has meant each act of conjugal union between husband and wife to be a renewal of the sacrament of marriage — that complete gift of themselves the newlyweds made to one another when they pronounced their marriage vows. Christ desires to renew the sacramental grace of marriage in each act of marital union, pouring out his Holy Spirit upon husband and wife, as the bond of love between them.

But who is the Holy Spirit? How do we invoke him each time we pray the Creed? He is the "Lord and Giver of Life." How can the "Lord and Giver of Life" be present in the conjugal union of husband and wife, when that very marital act is closed to life through contraception? If the Holy Spirit is forced to take flight, where he longs to be most intimately present, married love is not enriched, but begins to erode.

The heartbreaking effects of contraception are clear before our eyes. The evidence of broken marriages and shattered lives is overwhelming. And yet . . .? And yet the vast majority of married couples, Protestants and Catholics alike, continue to view contraception as a positive reality. How is this possible? Ruth Lasseter offers a response.

This tiny thing is so very subtle and slow in its tyrannical effect and usurpation; the small denials that anything is wrong (the unspoken concerns about damage inflicted on bodily health by the contraceptive device, the increased tension in conversation and in everyday life, the uneasy sense of future trouble, the steady growth of mistrust, the general boredom with family life in general and spousal

---

[652] Ibid., p. 479.

sex in particular, the secret fantasies and desires) all go unnoticed until their cumulative effect has destroyed trust and made impossible the very love that the contracepting couple so fervently hoped to preserve. Yet, for most Protestants and a majority of Catholics, artificial birth control continues to be accepted and promoted as an unquestioned good.[653]

Let it not continue to be so! May Catholic couples embrace wholeheartedly the Church's teaching on natural family planning — Christ's truth about the gift of self that sets married love free. May they become witnesses of true spousal love to a world so urgently in need of their testimony. May priests be true shepherds of the faithful entrusted to their care, ardently and courageously proclaiming the truth of God's plan for human love. Pope St. Gregory the Great has stern words for those who keep silence when danger threatens.

> Negligent religious leaders are often afraid to speak freely and say what needs to be said — for fear of losing favor with people. As Truth himself says, they are certainly not guarding their flock with the care expected of a shepherd but are acting like hirelings, because hiding behind a wall of silence is like taking flight at the approach of the wolf.... If, then, the priest neglects his preaching, what sort of a warning cry can he, a dumb herald, give? That is why the Holy Spirit settled upon the first religious leaders in the form of tongues: because those whom he fills he fills with his own eloquence.[654]

3. A Dangerous Weapon in the Hands of Public Authorities

What could be more sacred and reserved to the conscience of husband and wife alone — guided by Christ's teaching through the Church — than their intimate conjugal relations? Paul VI warned that legitimizing contraception would give public authorities the excuse they needed to enter this most personal sphere of married life.

Let it be considered also that a dangerous weapon would thus be placed in the hands of those public authorities who take no heed of moral exigencies. Who could blame a government for applying to the solution of the problems of the community those means acknowledged to be licit for married couples in the solution of a family problem? Who will stop rulers from favoring, from even imposing upon their peoples, if they were to consider it necessary, the method of contraception which they judge to be most efficacious? In such a way men, wishing to avoid individual, family, or social difficulties encountered in the observance of the divine law, would reach the point of placing at the mercy of the in-

---

[653] Ibid., pp. 480-481.
[654] *The Pastoral Rule* of Pope St. Gregory the Great, Book 2, 4, in *The Divine Office*, Week 27 of the Year: Sunday, (London: Collins, 1974), pp. 609-610.

tervention of public authorities the most personal and most reserved sector of conjugal intimacy.[655]

At present, aid to developing countries from the United Nations and other organizations such as the International Monetary Fund and World Bank is almost always tied in to population-control programs that mandate the promotion of artificial contraception. Third World countries' insistent protests against "contraceptive imperialism" bear witness to the terrible fulfillment of *Humanae Vitae*'s third prophecy.

It is no accident that the road of contraception has led to atrocious violations of human rights. The attempt to legitimize contraception arises from deep-seated attitudes about human persons and their relationship to God. At its most profound level, the contraceptive mentality rests upon a view of the human person which is irreconcilable with Christianity. The contraceptive vision of men and women is utterly destructive to basic human dignity. What constitutes the idea of the human person that underlies contraception?

---

[655] *Humanae Vitae*, 17.

Preview

NINE CONTRACEPTION'S VIEW OF MEN AND WOMEN: OBJECTS TO BE MANIPULATED *(continued)*

IV. Behind the Tragic Effects of Contraception: A Flawed Idea of the Human Person
   A. Persons in the Rationalist View: Individual Members of the Human Species
      1. A Fallacious Reduction
      2. Can Persons Be Treated as Numerical Individuals?
   B. Persons and Nature: From Legitimate Dominion to Absolute Autonomy
   C. Persons and Their Bodies: What Lies Hidden Behind Contraception
      1. The Essential Problem in the Responsible Transmission of Life
         a) Persons: Self-Mastery through Virtue
         b) Self-Mastery and the Human Body
         c) The Inner Meaning of the Conjugal Act
      2. The Essential Evil of the Contraceptive Act
      3. Inevitable Effects of Contraception
         a) Sexuality Becomes "Commonplace"
         b) The Person Becomes an Object
   D. Conclusion: The Contraceptive "Order of Things"

Points to look for

1. What three fundamental questions are at stake in the present drama of contraception?
2. What happens when human persons are viewed simply as material individuals of the human species?
3. What is the difference between the order of nature and the biological order? Why does the biological order not exist in reality?

4. Why is it wrong to treat human beings as numerical individuals?

5. Denying the human person's transcendence leads to two opposite errors regarding man's proper relationship to nature. What are they?

6. Why is human fertilization *in vitro* always morally wrong?

7. What lies at the heart of being a person according to John Paul II?

8. How do we grow in self-mastery as persons?

9. What is the essential problem in the responsible transmission of human life?

10. Why can we not claim to apply the dominion we exercise over the forces of nature to our own body?

11. How can it be shown that our body is an intimate part of who we are as persons and that our free, bodily actions possess an inner, personal meaning?

12. How are the two opposing tendencies — towards an absolute dominion over nature on the one hand, and the submission of the person to nature on the other — both inextricably present in contraception?

13. What are the two inner meanings of the conjugal act?

14. What is the essential evil of the contraceptive act?

15. When the procreative meaning of the conjugal act is suppressed through contraception, why is the unitive meaning also eliminated, so that it ceases to be an act of love?

16. Why does sexuality become something "commonplace" due to contraception?

17. How does contraception reduce the person to an object of manipulation?

18. Why is the price of legitimizing contraception too high?

IV. Behind the Tragic Effects of Contraception: A Flawed Idea of the Human Person

All of Paul VI's prophecies on the evils of contraception have sadly been fulfilled. Why does contraception prove so devastating to those who practice it? Three fundamental questions are at stake in the present drama. The first could not possibly be more crucial: "What does it mean to be a person?" The second query arises from the first: "What is the relationship between a person and the forces of nature?" The third issue at play also derives from the first: "What is the relationship between a person and his body?"

We have seen that an ideology built upon rationalist materialism underlies the contraceptive mentality. Within that ideology, a critical flaw can be detected in the response to each of the three fundamental questions. How does rationalism reply to the first query: "What constitutes a person?"

A. Persons in the Rationalist View: Individual Members of the Human Species

1. A Fallacious Reduction

The rationalist ideology, which underlies contraception, reduces persons to nothing more than material, individual members of the human species. Man's transcendence — his capacity to rise above himself and penetrate into the very mystery of God — is ignored. The person's ability to enter into an intimate relationship with the three Persons of the Blessed Trinity, to live in *communion* with them, is denied.

What happens when an ideology deprives man of his transcendence and leaves him stripped and beaten, lying on the roadside? Man "is reduced to a number, an economic statistic, or a racial or ethnic entity."[656] Even formulating the question of responsible parenthood in terms of a "population problem" reveals a hidden reductivist approach toward the person. To speak of human beings in the language of "population" is to strip from them their culture, their society, all that constitutes them as fully human, and reduce them to a mere throng of biological creatures.[657]

Yet the "biological order" as such does not exist in reality. In his book *Love and Responsibility*, Karol Wojtyła distinguishes between the biological order and the order of nature. The latter really does exist. The order of nature "means the totality of the cosmic relationships that arise among really existing entities. It is therefore the order of existence, and the laws which govern it have their foundation in Him, Who is the unfailing source of that existence, in God the Creator."[658]

Persons exist within the order of nature in the unity of their physiological, psychological, and transcendent spiritual dimensions. To focus exclusively upon the physiological or biological aspect of a person can be done only through a mental abstraction, prescinding from the full reality of the person, who exists in the order of nature. "The 'biological order,' as a product of the human intellect, which abstracts its elements from a larger reality, has man for its immediate author."[659] Failure to distinguish adequately between these two orders gives rise to one of the main fallacies behind contraception, as we shall later see.

2. Can Persons Be Treated as Numerical Individuals?

Is it legitimate to prescind from the fullness of who persons are and regard only the biological aspect of their nature in dealing with "popu-

---

[656] Shivanandan, *Crossing the Threshold of Love*, p. 217. Citing Jacques Maritain, *Person and the Common Good*, trans. John J. Fitzgerald (New York: Charles Scribner's Sons, 1947), p. 81.

[657] Cf. Amos H. Hawley, "Population and Society: An Essay on Growth," in *Fertility and Family Planning: A World View*, eds. S. J. Behrman, Leslie Corsa, and Ronald Freedman (Ann Arbor, MI: University of Michigan Press, 1970), pp. 189-209.

[658] Wojtyła, *Love and Responsibility*, p. 57.

[659] Ibid.

lation problems"? That is the prevalent approach adopted by the United Nations and other international agencies in their "population-control" programs. Persons are viewed as numerical individuals in the human species. If high numbers lead to poverty and even starvation, artificial contraception is to be promoted — often imposed as a condition for monetary aid — in order to limit births.

But persons cannot be treated as numbers. In his article "Incommunicability of Persons," the philosopher John F. Crosby explains why.[660] Numbers are described as large or small only by comparison with other numbers. Twelve is large in relation to two, but small in relation to fifty. Persons, on the other hand, are not governed by these numerical laws. "In their material individuality they are subject to numerical quantity, but in the transcendence of their personhood they are not."[661] No single human being can be relativized in the presence of another.

If numbers are to be applied to persons, it would be more fitting to speak of them in terms of infinity, so that one numerical infinity is added to another infinity. "Paradoxically, to add one infinity to another adds infinitely more and yet adds nothing, because each person has a certain 'absoluteness' of being. Because of the transcendent nature of the human being, to subject persons to the laws of finite numerical quantity is to relativize them."[662]

In addition to relativizing persons, treating them as material individuals of a species with no regard for their transcendence also affects the relationship between persons and the world of nature.

B. Persons and Nature:
From Legitimate Dominion to Absolute Autonomy

A partial, reductive idea of what it means to be a person cannot help but lead to an erroneous view about the proper relation between persons and the natural world. The Book of Genesis clearly reveals the dominion man is meant to exercise over nature in God's creative plan. "So God created man in his own image, in the image of God he created him; male and female he created them. And God blessed them, and God said to them, 'Be fruitful and multiply, and fill the earth and subdue it; and have dominion over the fish of the sea and over the birds of the air and over every living thing that moves upon the earth.'"[663]

Denying man's transcendence, his personal relationship with the Creator, leads to a paradoxical contrast. On the one hand, man seeks to extend his legitimate dominion over the created world to one of absolute autonomy. In the biomedical field, scientists claim the right to tech-

---

[660] Cited by Mary Shivanandan in *Crossing the Threshold of Love*, p. 217.
[661] Ibid.
[662] Ibid.
[663] Gn 1:27-28.

nically produce new human life in a laboratory through *in vitro* fertilization. By so doing, they contravene God's creative plan. The Creator has willed that a new human being should always come into existence through an act of self-giving love in the conjugal union between his parents. The inviolable dignity of each human person in the unity of body and spiritual soul is the foundation of this right.[664]

Vatican II defends the claim to a just autonomy in the sciences and social life, but also clarifies the limits of this autonomy. *Gaudium et Spes* reminds us:

> If by the autonomy of earthly affairs we mean that created things and societies themselves enjoy their own laws and values which must be gradually deciphered, put to use, and regulated by men, then it is entirely right to demand that autonomy. Such is not merely required by modern man, but harmonizes also with the will of the Creator. For by the very circumstance of their having been created, all things are endowed with their own stability, truth, goodness, proper laws and order. Man must respect these as he isolates them by the appropriate methods of the individual sciences or arts. Therefore, if methodical investigation within every branch of learning is carried out in a genuinely scientific manner and in accord with moral norms, it never truly conflicts with faith, for earthly matters and the concerns of faith derive from the same God.[665] . . .
>
> But if the expression "the independence of temporal affairs" is taken to mean that created things do not depend on God, and that man can use them without any reference to their Creator, anyone who acknowledges God will see how false such a meaning is. For without the Creator the creature would disappear.[666]

We have seen that denying the human person's transcendence can lead to the claim of absolute dominion over nature, with no regard for man's proper role within God's creative plan. Paradoxically, the opposite extreme is also reached. When persons are viewed as nothing more than members of a species, like any other, man can be perceived as an outsider in the world of nature, due to his ability to reshape it for his own needs. He can even be regarded as nature's enemy. Do not certain radical groups within the environmentalist movement arrive to the point of submitting man to nature, thus reversing God's plan as revealed in the Book of Genesis?

---

[664] Cf. Sacred Congregation for the Doctrine of the Faith, "Instruction on Bioethics, Respect for Human Life *Donum Vitae*" (February 22, 1987), Part II, Interventions Upon Human Procreation.

[665] Cf. First Vatican Council, Dogmatic Constitution on the Catholic Faith *Dei Filius*, Chapter III: Denzinger-Schönmetzer, 3004-3005.

[666] *Gaudium et Spes*, 36.

These two opposing tendencies — toward an absolute dominion over nature on the one hand, and the submission of the person to nature on the other — are both inextricably present in contraception. We will seek to discover how.

C. Persons and Their Bodies: What Lies Hidden Behind Contraception
1. The Essential Problem in the Responsible Transmission of Life
a) Persons: Self-Mastery Through Virtue

Is our relationship with our bodies as persons the same as that which we have with the world of nature? Can we claim to apply the dominion we exercise over the forces of nature to our own body? The answer to these fundamental queries lies at the heart of the Church's teaching on the responsible transmission of human life. If contraception is to be legitimized, then it must be permissible to use technology in order to manipulate and control our own body, just as we may do with nature. Much more is implied in accepting the principle of artificially manipulating our body than first meets the eye.

How we may legitimately treat our body depends first of all upon what it means to be a person. John Paul II holds a much nobler view of persons than does rationalist materialism. Because of our intelligence and freedom, as persons we are beings who possess an *inner life,* a *spiritual life.*[667] One immediate consequence of having an interior life shines forth: we are capable of reflecting upon our actions, of freely choosing how to act. Among all creatures in the physical universe, we alone are able to be *masters of ourselves.*

John Paul II affirms that self-mastery lies at the heart of what it means to be a person.

"Man is precisely a person because he is master of himself and has self-control. Indeed, insofar as he is master of himself he can give himself to the other."[668] Self-mastery does not come automatically, nor are all persons equally masters of themselves. Though we have the inner capacity for self-control through our intelligence and free will, because of our fallen human nature, mastery of ourselves presents itself as a *task to be conquered.*

The more we are masters of ourselves, the more do we achieve fulfillment, the more do we live up to what it means to be a person. How, then, do we grow in self-mastery? First of all, we do so by repeatedly choosing good actions, even when those actions are difficult. In this way

---

[667] *Love and Responsibility,* pp. 22-23.
[668] General Audience of August 22, 1984, in *The Theology of the Body,* p. 398.

we build up *virtues*, habitual and firm dispositions to do good.[669] Virtues "make possible ease, self-mastery, and joy in leading a morally good life. The virtuous man is he who freely practices the good."[670]

Human effort is needed to gain virtues. But human effort alone does not suffice. We can acquire genuine virtues, true freedom, authentic mastery of ourselves, only through the transforming power of Christ's redemption. The grace our Redeemer won for us by his agony and death upon the cross alone can offer the freedom for which we have been set free.[671] As the author of the Book of Wisdom observes, "But I percieved that I would not possess wisdom unless God gave her to me — and it was a mark of insight to know whose gift she was."[672]

b) Self-Mastery and the Human Body

If to be a person means to possess an inner life and be master of one-self, how does that affect our relationship with nature and especially with our own body? Here lies the essential problem in the responsible transmission of human life. John Paul II precisely outlines the question in the light of *Humanae Vitae.*

> The problem consists in maintaining an adequate relationship be-tween what is defined as "domination . . . of the forces of nature" (*HV*, 2), and the "mastery of self" (*HV*, 21) which is indispensable for the human person. Modern man shows a tendency to transfer the methods proper to the former to those of the latter. "Man has made stupendous progress in the domination and rational organi-zation of the forces of nature," we read in the encyclical, "to the point that he is endeavoring to extend this control over every as-pect of his own life — over his body, over his mind and emotions, over his social life, and even over the laws that regulate the trans-mission of life" (*HV*, 2).[673]

Is it legitimate to extend this dominion over the forces of nature to our own body? If our body were an object we possessed, such as a laptop computer, it would be. That is the implicit claim which advo-cates of contraception cannot avoid making: Our body is simply an object, divorced from who we are as persons. Thus, if a particular function of our body, such as its fertility, does not please us, we can apply technical means to suppress it, just as we would erase an un-wanted computer program that is filling up space on the hard drive. Only if our body is a mere object, a biological organism external to us

---

[669] Cf. *CCC*, 1833.
[670] *CCC*, 1804.
[671] Cf. Gal 5:1.
[672] Wis 8:21.
[673] General Audience of August 22, 1984, in *The Theology of the Body,* pp. 396-397.

as persons, can we apply the same criteria of dominion to it that we apply to the forces of nature.

But we are all deeply aware, through everyday experience, of the intimate relationship between our body and who we are as persons. In a certain sense each of us must say: "I *am* my body." I do not simply possess it in the way I might possess any other object, like a new cell phone. When something happens to my body, it happens to *me*. When I lie in bed, moaning softly with the pangs of appendicitis, *I* am the one who is sick, not simply my body — or even a part of my body. If someone spits in my face, he does not merely deposit a small amount of liquid on my cheek, he affects *me* as a person, in the inmost sphere of who I am.

Since the body is an intimate part of who we are as persons, its actions possess an inner, personal meaning. This meaning is especially transcendent in the conjugal union between husband and wife, as the Holy Father points out.

> The human body is not merely an organism of sexual reactions. But it is, at the same time, the means of expressing the entire man, the person, which reveals itself by means of the language of the body. This language has an important interpersonal meaning, especially in reciprocal relationships between man and woman.[674]

When what we freely choose to do is in harmony with the inner meaning our actions possess by their very nature, then we are masters of ourselves. We are living up to what it means to be a person. On the other hand, when we manipulate our body so as to perform a given action, while depriving that action of its intrinsic meaning, we simultaneously commit two opposite faults. In the first place, we reduce our body to a mere object, robbing it of its personalistic character and seeking to exercise a dominion over it that is proper only towards the external forces of nature. In the second place, we lower our dignity as persons by submitting ourselves to bodily impulses, rather than exercising mastery over them — that is, mastery of ourselves — the very essence of what it means to be a person.

Now two fundamental questions present themselves. First, what is the personal, inner meaning of the conjugal act between husband and wife? Second, how does contraception affect that inner meaning?

c) The Inner Meaning of the Conjugal Act

The conjugal act possesses a twofold meaning: As an act of love it unites husband and wife, while at the same time it is structured to generate new lives, the fruit of their loving union. In *Humanae Vitae* Paul VI reaffirms that these two meanings are inseparable, since they are inscribed by God in the very being of man and woman. That is why "each

---

[674] Ibid., p. 397.

and every marriage act *(quilibet matrimonii usus)* must remain open to the transmission of life."[675]

As he reaffirms the foundations for this teaching, Paul VI appeals to men and women to recognize its deeply human character. The humanity of the spouses is diminished through contraception. Only by respecting the intrinsic, twofold meaning of the conjugal act can husband and wife truly love each other as unique, personal subjects. When one of the meanings is suppressed, the spouses do not receive each other's body as expressing an act of self-giving love of the entire person. Rather, the body is reduced, through manipulating the meaning of its acts, to an object of pleasure. When a person's body is treated as an object, so is the person.

> That teaching, often set forth by the magisterium, is founded upon the inseparable connection, willed by God and unable to be broken by man on his own initiative, between the two meanings of the conjugal act: the unitive meaning and the procreative meaning. Indeed, by its intimate structure, the conjugal act, while most closely uniting husband and wife, capacitates them for the generation of new lives, according to laws inscribed in the very being of man and of woman. By safeguarding both these essential aspects, the unitive and the procreative, the conjugal act preserves in its fullness the sense of true mutual love and its ordination toward man's most high calling to parenthood. We believe that the men of our day are particularly capable of seizing the deeply reasonable and human character of this fundamental principle.[676]

2. The Essential Evil of the Contraceptive Act

We have now come to identify what John Paul II terms "the essential evil" of contraception. It consists of separating the unitive meaning of the conjugal act from the procreative meaning.[677] Why can these two intrinsic meanings never be separated? Precisely because "both the one and the other pertain to the intimate truth of the conjugal act."[678]

The claim is made by some that at times during a marriage the unitive aspect may have to take precedence over the procreative aspect for the spouses. What matters most in certain moments of trial or growth is for husband and wife to be united in an act of love through their conjugal union, even though they may have to suppress the procreative meaning of their act, if they are not able to responsibly conceive a child at the time.

---

[675] *Humanae Vitae*, 11.
[676] Ibid., 12.
[677] Cf. General Audience of August 22, 1984, in *The Theology of the Body*, p. 398; *HV*, 12.
[678] Ibid., p. 398.

But loving union is inextricably linked with procreation in the very structure of the conjugal act itself. John Paul II affirms, "The one is activated together with the other and in a certain sense by means of the other."[679] What happens if the procreative meaning is suppressed? Since the conjugal act is one and indivisible, eliminating part of its twofold meaning violates the truth of the entire act. Thus, the unitive dimension is also lost. "Therefore, in such a case the conjugal act, deprived of its interior truth because it is artificially deprived of its procreative capacity, *ceases also to be an act of love.*"[680]

Why does conjugal union cease to be an act of love when deprived of its procreative meaning? Primarily because contraception means telling a lie with the body. In the conjugal embrace, the language of the body is meant to express the complete gift of self between husband and wife. But when contraception alters the nature of the act, the spouses come to say the following to each other with their bodies: "I give myself entirely to you, my whole self, with all that I am — but not my fertility. I accept from you in return the complete gift of yourself, your entire person — but not your fertility."

Contraception falsifies the most intimate union between husband and wife. It turns their complete gift of self to one another into a lie. The bodily union of the conjugal act does not reflect a true communion of persons between husband and wife. John Paul II states the matter clearly.

> It can be said that in the case of an artificial separation of these two aspects, a real bodily union is carried out in the conjugal act, but it does not correspond to the interior truth and to the dignity of personal communion — communion of persons. This communion demands that the language of the body be expressed reciprocally in the integral truth of its meaning. If this truth be lacking, one cannot speak either of the truth of self-mastery, or of the truth of the reciprocal gift and of the reciprocal acceptance of self on the part of the person. Such a violation of the interior order of conjugal union, which is rooted in the very order of the person, constitutes the essential evil of the contraceptive act.[681]

3. Inevitable Effects of Contraception
a) Sexuality Becomes "Commonplace"

What inevitably results from depriving the conjugal act of its inner meaning through contraception? The union between husband and wife becomes nothing more than a bodily act which bestows mutual pleasure. As the Holy Father affirms in *Familiaris Consortio*, human sexuality

---

[679] Ibid.
[680] Ibid. Italics are mine.
[681] Ibid.

is reduced "to the level of something commonplace." The contraceptive mentality "lives it in a reductive and impoverished way, by linking it solely with the body and selfish pleasure."[682]

The personal experience of countless couples who have fallen into contraception bears witness to the truth of John Paul II's words. Ruth Lasseter's testimony resounds as an eloquent warning to husbands and wives. "Under the guise of helping love, artificial contraception cunningly establishes a tyrant in the marriage: The sex act declines from a reaffirming of the whole marriage covenant, true lovemaking, to joint seeking of mutual satisfaction."[683]

One letter to "Dear Abby" expresses in darkly humorous tones a reality that is anything but light: the depersonalization of sexuality through contraception, its reduction to something trivial. "I am a twenty-three year old liberated woman who has been on the pill for two years. It's getting pretty expensive and I think my boyfriend should share half the cost, but I don't know him well enough to discuss money with him."[684]

b) The Person Becomes an Object

Since our person cannot be separated from our body, when the body is treated as an object through contraception, so is the person. This is one of the most devastating effects of contraception. It readily explains why contracepting couples often seem to helplessly watch the breakdown of their relationship.

We have already discovered what is specific to persons as free, conscious subjects: self-mastery, the ability to possess oneself and so freely give oneself to another in love. That is precisely why the method of artificially dominating the forces of nature cannot be applied indiscriminately to the person. We live up to our dignity and grow as persons only when we guide our bodily instincts and emotions with our free will. Every good, freely chosen moral action ennobles our person. It increases our self-mastery, enriches us, makes us capable of loving more.

Contraception reverses things. By eliminating the need for self-mastery, it causes men and women to subordinate their free will to sexual instincts and emotions. Self-mastery, that which constitutes a person as a free, conscious subject, is diminished. The person is degraded, his subjectivity is lessened, and he becomes an object for manipulation. So when couples practice contraception, not only do they treat their spouse as an object, they also treat themselves in the same way. John Paul II concisely expresses these truths.

---

[682] *FC*, 37.
[683] Ruth Lasseter, "Sensible Sex," in *Humanae Vitae: A Reader*, p. 479.
[684] A. Van Buren, *The Best of Dear Abby*, (Kansas City, MO: Andrews and McMeel, 1981), p. 242.

This extension of the sphere of the means of "domination of the forces of nature" menaces the human person for whom the method of "self-mastery" is and remains specific. The mastery of self corresponds to the fundamental constitution of the person; it is indeed a "natural" method. On the contrary, the resort to artificial means destroys the constitutive dimension of the person. It deprives man of the subjectivity proper to him and makes him an object of manipulation.[685]

Does the actual experience of married couples confirm the sad reality of contraception's degrading effects on the human person? Here is one of innumerable testimonies. It is from a wife who started practicing contraception.

I began to resent my husband. For the sake of our sexual relationship, I was required to sacrifice my health . . . I felt as if I were an object and not an equal partner in our marriage . . . He (my husband) came to the marriage bed as he was, while I was still required to alter myself. I was not allowed to give myself freely in our marriage relationship, not to experience fully the physical aspect of our love. It seemed to me like using contraceptives was causing our whole sex life to be focused, not on the union of our two persons, but on avoiding the pregnancy which might result.[686]

D. Conclusion: The Contraceptive "Order of Things"

We have uncovered one erroneous concept of the human person that underlies the contraceptive mentality. It is the rationalist view, which reduces persons to material individual members of the human species. Rationalism denies the transcendent dimension of the person. This dimension results from man's intelligence and free will, which make him a conscious, personal subject. It separates persons from the rest of nature, endowing their free actions with an inner meaning, and enabling them to enter into communion with each other and with God.

One must implicitly accept the rationalist view in order to justify contraception. It is legitimate to apply to human persons the method of dominating the forces of nature by artificial means only if their free actions do not possess a transcendent, intrinsic personal meaning. If the unitive and procreative meanings of the conjugal act are denied, then there is no difficulty in suppressing fertility in the conjugal act through contraception.

In a word, what order of things results from the contraceptive mentality? Human persons are reduced to nothing more than thinking chimpanzees. The conjugal union between husband and wife, deprived of its

---

[685] General Audience of August 22, 1984, in *The Theology of the Body*, p. 397.

[686] "Woman Tells of Contraceptives' Effect on Her Marriage," *CCL Family Foundations*, Sample Newsletter, 1. Cited in Shivanandan, *Crossing the Threshold of Love*, p. 261.

inner meaning, is no longer a unitive act of love, nor a free cooperation with God's creative plan in bringing a new human life into the world. It is simply a pleasurable bodily union that fulfills the sexual urge and serves to propagate the human species. In their conjugal union husband and wife reduce themselves and each other to objects of manipulation.

Is this not too high a price to pay for legitimizing contraception?

TEN

What Lies Hidden Behind Contraception

Preview

I. Cartesian Body-Soul Dualism
   A. *"Cogito"*: A Quest for Certainty
   B. Critique: A "Not-So-Methodical" Doubt
   C. Man: An Embodied Spirit — A Response to Dualism

II. Implicit Biologism
   A. Is *Humanae Vitae* Just for Catholics?
      1. Natural Law: Human Reason Participates in God's Own Understanding
      2. Characteristics of the Natural Moral Law
      3. The Magisterium's Authority Regarding the Natural Law

Points to look for

1. Why must an erroneous body-soul dualism be accepted in order to legitimize contraception?

2. How can a dualistic vision of the person, one that would relegate the body to a mere spatial appendage, be refuted?

3. What led Descartes to his reductive vision of the human person as in essence simply a thinking subject?

4. How does our self-awareness through consciousness differ from our knowledge of all other objects?

5. What is meant by the "turn toward the subject" in modern philosophy, which was initiated by Descartes?

6. Why is it impossible to carry out Descartes' "methodical doubt" in a quest for certainty?

7. Why do the descriptions of man as an "embodied spirit" or an "acting person" define what it means to be human much more accurately than Descartes' "thinking subject"?

8. What is the natural moral law?

9. How can we explain the absolute character of natural law precepts?

10. What are the two fundamental characteristics of natural law precepts?

11. What is the reason for each of these two characteristics?

12. Why does the Church's Magisterium have authority to interpret the precepts of the natural moral law?

I. Cartesian Body-Soul Dualism

The reductivist idea of man stemming from rationalism is not the only erroneous view of the human person that lies hidden behind contraception. Inextricably linked with the rationalist concept is a dualism which separates man's soul from his body in considering who we are as persons. The modern origins of this body-soul dualism trace their way back to the seventeenth-century French philosopher René Descartes.

Descartes has become immortalized for his notorious phrase *"Cogito ergo sum"* (I think; therefore, I am). His attempt to resolve the problem of a self-imposed methodical doubt with these three Latin words brought him, perhaps unintentionally, to regard the person in essence as nothing more than a thinking subject. The physical body came to be a mere spatial appendage of the conscious subject, who was the person. Well and good, but what link could possibly exist between Descartes' seventeenth-century philosophical dualism and the present drama of contraception?

The relationship is quite strong. In order to justify contraception, one must implicitly accept body-soul dualism. Only if what constitutes the human person as such is nothing more than his spiritual soul can contraception be acceptable. In that case the bodily act of conjugal union would not be an expression of the person of husband and wife. It would not possess any intrinsic personal meaning in itself, either unitive or procreative. Its meaning would depend entirely upon the intention of the spouses, who in themselves are spiritual souls, simply making use of their bodies. Thus, the procreative dimension of conjugal union could be suppressed by contraception, without touching the person of the spouses.

We have already pondered the intimate union of our spiritual nature with our body as one of the most inescapable facts of our daily existence. In a real way, as persons we *are* our body. No one would seriously claim that spitting in someone's face is in itself a neutral physical gesture, one which depends exclusively upon the perpetrator's intention in order to acquire meaning. Can it ever be a sign of tenderness and endearment to deliver someone a resounding slap across the cheek with pursed lips and glaring eyes? Could we somehow intend to win another's friendship by shaking a clenched fist in his face?

On the other hand, is it possible for a gentle caress or a kiss to be neutral gestures in themselves? When Judas betrayed Christ in the Garden of Gethsemane, the way he did it was so terrible precisely because he violated the intrinsic meaning of love and fidelity that a kiss embodies in itself. Christ brings to light the deep, personal meaning inherent in our free bodily actions with a single question: "Judas, would you betray the Son of man with a kiss?"[687]

How is it, then, that Descartes came to espouse a dualistic view of the person which so plainly contradicts experience?

A. *"Cogito"*: A Quest for Certainty

Not infrequently in life, ideas we have once held firmly are proven false by later experience or a more deeply pondered reflection. At some point our childhood belief that the good guy invariably triumphs was belied. Just what can we be sure of? How can we attain absolute certainty in our knowledge? Is it possible to construct an edifice of truths which we know to be entirely certain? Descartes surmised that the way to achieve this goal was to put in doubt everything we once held to be true with our intellect. To aid in the task of applying this universal, methodical doubt to all our knowledge, Descartes contrived the literary device of a "malignant demon."

Suppose that a malignant demon were deceiving us about everything we believed to be true, including the existence of the physical world around us and even the reality of our own body. Is there anything about which the demon could not possibly deceive us? Would anything remain that we could still know must necessarily be true? If so, this fundamental certainty would be the one upon which to establish all others.

Descartes encountered this paramount certitude in the direct awareness we have of ourselves as conscious subjects. Perhaps the demon could be deceiving me about the sirloin steak that seems to lie poised upon my plate for lunch, or even about my hand, which looks as though it were gripping a fork and raising a succulent portion to my mouth. He may be leading me to believe that my taste buds are actually savoring the morsel, or that my stomach is experiencing the pleasant receding of hunger pangs. But the demon *cannot* be deceiving me about my own existence in the midst of all of these deceptions. I must necessarily exist in order to be deceived. I am conscious of myself, immediately present to myself as a thinking subject, even in the very act of being deceived. *Cogito ergo sum.* Or, if one prefers, *Decipior ergo sum* (I am deceived, therefore I am!).[688]

Descartes' elucidation of our immediate presence to ourselves as conscious subjects initiated a "turn toward the subject" which has characterized modern philosophy ever since the seventeenth century. By doing so, Descartes contributed toward our understanding of ourselves as

---

[687] Lk 22:48.

[688] It should be noted that the *"ergo"* is actually superfluous in Descartes' famous phrase, since he did not intend for the subject's existence to be deduced as in a syllogism. The person is immediately aware of himself as subject in every conscious act, through what some phenomenologists such as Dr. John Crosby have referred to as "lateral self-presence." This

persons in a way that was valuable, though certainly not new. St. Augustine had already forged similar reflections about our own self-awareness twelve centuries earlier.

Descartes' contribution duly acknowledged, it cannot be denied that the methodical demon which he unleashed has wreaked considerable havoc — its mere apparent reality as a literary device notwithstanding. Descartes brought the conscious subject into the fore. But the body-spirit dualism behind his methodical doubt, along with his idealistic theory of knowing, led to a rationalism that entrapped the subject inside of himself, cut off from the world of objective reality. Philosophy has been struggling ever since to emerge from Cartesian solipsism or the "trap of reflection."[689]

B. Critique: A "Not-So-Methodical" Doubt

If we admit that our immediate, conscious presence to ourselves as thinking subjects is the only thing we can know with certainty, then it proves impossible to ever get outside ourselves as subjects and know the truth about objective reality. Thus, it is a natural step to come to view the spiritual soul alone as the essence of what it means to be a person. Body-soul dualism is a logical result of Descartes' methodical doubt. So one of the best ways to overcome this dualism at its roots is to refute the whole idea of radically doubting all we hold as true.

Descartes attempts to arrive at absolute certainty by doubting everything. His methodical doubt inevitably leads to skepticism. But it is a doubt that in reality cannot be carried out, even as a method. It is simply impossible to doubt everything other than my own existence as a thinking subject, with the hypothesis of a malignant demon who is deceiving me. Why?

There are many things outside of my conscious presence to myself that I must already know in order to attempt the methodical doubt. I must know what truth is and recognize the difference between truth and error, in order to fear being deceived by the demon. I must already

---

terminology distinguishes our immediate consciousness of ourselves from the "frontal presence" of objects in intentional acts of knowing. Naturally, the self can become an object of intentional knowing as well. This occurs in acts of self-reflection, as when we think about ourselves thinking. But here, too, we also possess immediate consciousness of ourselves as the subject performing an act of self-reflection. A brief sketch serves to illustrate.

Intentional act of knowing

Subject ⎯⎯⎯⎯⎯⎯⎯⎯→Object (Object known intentionally)
  ↓
Subject (Subject's conscious presence to himself in the act of knowing)

Subject ⎯⎯⎯⎯⎯⎯⎯⎯→Subject (Subject known intentionally in an act of self-reflection)
  ↓
Subject (Subject's conscious presence to himself in the act of knowing)

[689] Cf. George Weigel, "John Paul II — Preparing the 21st Century," *Crisis*, November 1997, p. 10.

know what reality is, in order to fear being deceived by the demon about whether my body or the surrounding world is real. But if I already know reality and can recognize the difference between it and deception, then Descartes' malignant demon could not have always been deceiving me about it. The malevolent fiend vanishes from the scene in the same puff of literary smoke from which he emerged.

Descartes' failed attempt is simply one more illustration of the fact that it is impossible to deny the ability of our intelligence to know reality. Our intellect's knowledge of the truth reasserts itself in the self-contradiction of every attempt to deny it. To affirm, "We cannot know reality," is equivalent to asserting, "We *really* cannot know reality." In an even more evident formulation, it is the same as declaring, "We cannot know objective truth outside of ourselves." But the person who affirms this proposition is actually saying, "I *know* that we cannot know objective truth." Or, "It is *true* that there is no truth."

C. Man: An Embodied Spirit — A Response to Dualism

We have already pondered in John Paul II's theology of the body the inseparable relationship between our spiritual soul and our physical body in who we are as persons. Only through the body can we catch a glimpse of the spiritual, the inner life of the person. Adam exclaims upon seeing Eve, "This at last is bone of my bones and flesh of my flesh; she shall be called Woman."[690] Christ himself fully reveals God, who is Spirit, by taking upon himself a physical human body. The Evangelist John ponders in wonder this impenetrable mystery: "And the Word became flesh and dwelt among us."[691]

John Paul II's response to rationalistic dualism is a compelling one. The English title of his 1969 philosophical work conveys the essence of the human person. Man is not first and foremost a thinking subject. He should be described instead as *The Acting Person*. What we *think* is not ultimately the final, decisive element in revealing and forging the type of person we are. Rather, it is what we *do*. Our free moral *actions*, which we perform thanks to our body, shape us as persons, while at the same time they reveal what is hidden in the depths of our spirit. When we do what is morally good, we grow in virtue and holiness. We fulfill ourselves as persons. Choosing to do evil makes us sinful. It diminishes who we are.

Man is not a spiritual, thinking subject occupying a physical body. He is an _embodied spirit_. The spiritual and the physical are inextricably intertwined in us. Both together constitute our identity as persons. In his *Letter to Families*, John Paul II sums up the reply to rationalistic dualism.

---

[690] Gn 2:23.
[691] Jn 1:14.

The philosopher who formulated the principle of *"Cogito, ergo sum,"* "I think, therefore I am," also gave the modern concept of man its distinctive dualistic character. It is typical of rationalism to make a radical contrast in man between spirit and body, between body and spirit. But man is a person in the unity of his body and his spirit.[692] The body can never be reduced to mere matter: It is a spiritualized body, just as man's spirit is so closely united to the body that he can be described as an *embodied spirit*. The richest source for knowledge of the body is the Word made flesh. *Christ reveals man to himself.*[693] In a certain sense this statement of the Second Vatican Council is the reply, so long awaited, which the Church has given to modern rationalism.[694]

II. Implicit Biologism
A. Is *Humanae Vitae* Just for Catholics?

When Pope Paul VI declared that each and every marriage act must be open to life, he was reaffirming the Church's constant teaching. But is the truth of *Humanae Vitae* reserved to Catholics alone? Beginning in 1930, nearly all Christian denominations broke away from what had previously been a universal prohibition of contraception. So, may Protestants and non-Christians now practice contraception as an action that is morally acceptable, if they do so with just motives? The answer to this question is a resounding *no*.

Objectively speaking, the truth that the unitive and procreative meanings of the conjugal act may never be separated is morally binding upon all men and women. Why is this so? No one may choose to contracept with a correct conscience because of the foundation upon which the norm rests that every marriage act must be open to life. Paul VI states that *Humanae Vitae*'s teaching is founded "on the natural law, illuminated and enriched by divine revelation."[695] To grasp the far-reaching implications of this apparently simple phrase, we must examine more closely the concept of "natural moral law."

1. Natural Law: Human Reason Participates in God's Own Understanding

What exactly do we mean when we speak about the natural moral law? This question is a crucial one. A misinterpretation of the natural law lies behind the accusation of biologism, which has been leveled against *Humanae Vitae*. John Paul II gives a definition of the natural moral law in his 1993 encyclical *Veritatis Splendor*, citing St. Thomas

---

[692] *"Corpore et anima unus"* [one in body and soul], as the Council so clearly and felicitously stated: *Gaudium et Spes*, 14.
[693] Ibid., 22.
[694] *Letter to Families*, 19.
[695] *Humanae Vitae*, 4.

Aquinas. It is "nothing other than the light of understanding infused in us by God, whereby we understand what must be done and what must be avoided. God gave this light and this law to man at creation."[696]

As persons we are endowed with an innate moral capacity, enabling us to distinguish between good and evil. This capacity is the natural moral law. "The natural law expresses the original moral sense which enables man to discern by reason the good and the evil, the truth and the lie."[697] Thanks to our inner moral capacity, we are able to discover the fundamental precepts that must guide our free decisions. "The natural law states the first and essential precepts which govern the moral life."[698]

A striking feature of the natural law presents itself to our experience. We do not invent its precepts with our own reason. We discern them as existing beyond the realm of subjective opinion, so much so that we feel obliged in conscience to obey them. It is always wrong to directly kill an innocent person. Everyone should honor his father and mother. How can we explain this phenomenon of an obligation that each person's reason discovers, but is not free to alter or amend?

Here we see the sublime dignity with which human persons are endowed through the natural law. Our reason is able to discern absolute moral precepts, which oblige our conscience because it participates in the divine understanding of God himself. The fact that we perceive these precepts as absolute, not subjective or alterable, manifests their origin in the One who is Absolute. *Gaudium et Spes* beautifully expresses the reality of this distinct, unfailing call from God in the hidden silence of our interior.

> In the depths of his conscience, man detects a law which he does not impose upon himself, but which holds him to obedience. Always summoning him to love good and avoid evil, the voice of conscience when necessary speaks to his heart: do this, shun that. For man has in his heart a law written by God; to obey it is the very dignity of man; according to it he will be judged (cf. Rm 2:15-16). Conscience is the most secret core and sanctuary of a man. There he is alone with God, whose voice echoes in his depths.[699]

God, in his wisdom, guides all of creation with loving providence, according to his eternal, divine law. While God cares for creatures who

---

[696] *VS*, 12, citing St. Thomas Aquinas, *In Duo Praecepta Caritatis et in Cecem Legis Praecepta. Prologus: Opuscula Theologica*, 11, no. 1129, Ed. Taurinen (1954), 245; cf. *Summa Theologiae*, 1-11, q. 91, a.2; *Catechism of the Catholic Church*, no. 1955.

[697] *CCC*, 1954.

[698] *CCC*, 1955.

[699] *Gaudium et Spes*, 16; cf. John XXIII, Encyclical Letter *Pacem in Terris* (April 11, 1963): *AAS* 55 (1963), 297.

are not persons externally, through the laws of physical nature, he guides man "from within," through our reason. He allows us to freely and knowingly share in his divine providence. This human sharing in God's eternal law is another expression of what the natural law means. John Paul II sums things up in *Veritatis Splendor.*

> But God provides for man differently from the way in which he provides for beings which are not persons. He cares for man not "from without," through the laws of physical nature, but "from within," through reason, which, by its natural knowledge of God's eternal law, is consequently able to show man the right direction to take in his free actions.[700] In this way God calls man to participate in his own providence, since he desires to guide the world — not only the world of nature but also the world of human persons — through man himself, through man's reasonable and responsible care. The natural law enters here as the human expression of God's eternal law.[701]

What has been said up to now leads us to one final, succinct formulation of the natural moral law. The Holy Father cites St. Thomas Aquinas in number 43 of *Veritatis Splendor*: "This participation of the eternal law in the rational creature is called natural law."[702]

2. Characteristics of the Natural Moral Law

The natural law possesses two fundamental characteristics due to its very nature: Its precepts are *universal* and *immutable*.[703] Pope Leo XIII explains the universality of the natural moral law. "The natural law is written and engraved in the heart of each and every man, since it is none other than human reason itself which commands us to do good and counsels us not to sin."[704]

Leo XIII's teaching is confirmed by the *Catechism*. Since all people possess the same human nature — which includes reason — the same fundamental moral precepts, deriving from that nature, extend to all. "The natural law, present in the heart of each man and established by reason, is universal in its precepts and its authority extends to all men. It expresses the dignity of the person and determines the basis for his fundamental rights and duties."[705]

Perhaps in theory the natural law applies to all people, not just to Catholics or even Christians. But can non-Christians really recognize it in practice? The *Catechism* cites the pagan philosopher Cicero as evi-

---

[700] Cf. *Summa Theologiae*, I-II, q. 90, a. 4, *ad primum*.
[701] *VS*, 43.
[702] *Summa Theologiae*, I-II, q. 91, a. 2.
[703] Cf. *Veritatis Splendor*, 51.
[704] Leo XIII, *Libertas praestantissimum*, 597; cited in *Veritatis Splendor*, 44.
[705] *CCC*, 1956.

dence that all people of good will are called upon in conscience to abide by the precepts of the natural law.

> For there is a true law: right reason. It is in conformity with nature, is diffused among all men and is immutable and eternal; its orders summon to duty; its prohibitions turn away from offence. . . . To replace it with a contrary law is a sacrilege; failure to apply even one of its provisions is forbidden; no one can abrogate it entirely.[706]

Just as the natural law is universal, so too is it immutable. Some of its expressions or formulations may vary throughout history, depending upon changing cultural circumstances. But the basic precepts from which these expressions derive are always valid.[707] This teaching is confirmed by the *Catechism*.

> The natural law is *immutable* and permanent throughout the variations of history;[708] it subsists under the flux of ideas and customs and supports their progress. The rules that express it remain substantially valid. Even when it is rejected in its very principles, it cannot be destroyed or removed from the heart of man. It always rises again in the life of individuals and societies.[709]

If the life of man has changed so dramatically over the centuries, as that life is expressed in society, culture, and even civilization itself, how is it possible for the natural moral law to remain immutable? Even though people have changed in many ways throughout the course of history, what is most fundamental about man remains the same — our common human nature. At the dawn of the third Christian millennium, it is still possible to pick up Homer's *Iliad*, written centuries before Christ's birth, and be moved by the terrible consequences of "the anger of Achilles." The blind poet's tale of Odysseus' quest to regain his homeland, and the heroic fidelity of his wife, Penelope, still strikes a chord in every heart.

Christ's Incarnation provides divine testimony that man's human nature, the foundation of the natural law, hasn't changed over the centuries and will not ever do so. The Word of God became true man in the Incarnation. At the same time, the author of the letter to the Hebrews proclaims: "Jesus Christ is the same yesterday, today, and forever."[710]

3. The Magisterium's Authority Regarding the Natural Law

Pope Paul VI affirms that *Humanae Vitae*'s teaching is founded upon the natural law. But if the natural law applies to all people without ex-

---

[706] Cicero, *Rep.* III, 22, 33.
[707] The principal precepts of the natural law are expressed in the Ten Commandments (cf. CCC, 1955).
[708] Cf. *GS*, 10.
[709] *CCC*, 1958.
[710] Hb 13:8.

ception, and not all people are Catholics or even Christians, under what authority does the Pope claim to interpret the natural law's precepts?

Paul VI invokes one of the most fundamental principles in the life of the Church. Christ has constituted his Church "as the instrument for the salvation of all," "the universal sacrament of salvation."[711] Thus, Christ entrusts the Church's Magisterium with the charism of teaching authoritatively in questions of faith and morals, since both are necessary in order to be saved.

When the rich young man encounters Christ in the Gospel, he reveals that a person's faith must be vital; it must express itself by doing what is morally good in order to win salvation. He asks Christ, "Teacher, what good must I do to have eternal life?" (Mt 19:16) Since it is necessary to fulfill the moral law in order to attain salvation, the Church's Magisterium has the authority to interpret the moral law, including its natural law precepts. Paul VI writes:

> Jesus Christ, when communicating to Peter and to the apostles his divine authority and sending them to teach all nations his commandments,[712] constituted them as guardians and authentic interpreters of all the moral law, not only, that is, of the law of the Gospel, but also of the natural law, which is also an expression of the will of God, the faithful fulfillment of which is equally necessary for salvation.[713]

The constant teaching that the Church has the power to express itself with authority in moral questions, including those related to the natural law, is reaffirmed in the *Catechism*.

> The authority of the Magisterium extends also to the specific precepts of the *natural law*, because their observance, demanded by the Creator, is necessary for salvation. In recalling the prescriptions of the natural law, the Magisterium of the Church exercises an essential part of its prophetic office of proclaiming to men what they truly are and reminding them of what they should be before God.[714]

---

[711] *CCC*, 776; citing *Lumen Gentium*, 9 and 48.
[712] Cf. Mt 28:18-19.
[713] *HV*, 4; cf. Mt 7:21.
[714] Cf. *DH*, 14.

Preview

TEN WHAT LIES HIDDEN BEHIND CONTRACEPTION *(continued)*

II. Implicit Biologism *(continued)*
    B. *"Cogito ergo sum"* and the Alleged Biologism of *Humanae Vitae*
        1. The Accusation: Enslaving Reason and Free Will to Biology
        2. Paul VI: Facing the Charge Squarely
        3. Underlying Errors in the Attack Against *Humanae Vitae*
            a) Body-Soul Dualism and a False Abstraction of the Biological Order
            b) Misinterpretation of the Natural Law
            c) A Profound Irony: The Biologism of *Humanae Vitae's* Critics

III. Selfish Utilitarianism
    A. Pleasure as the Object of Our Free Acts: Utilitarianism's Critical Error
    B. The Utilitarian Principle: Maximize Pleasure and Minimize Pain
    C. Utilitarian Love: "The Harmonizing of Egoisms"
    D. Instrumentalizing the Human Person
    E. Contraception's Manifest Utilitarianism

IV. Conclusion: The Resounding Words of *Familiaris Consortio*

Points to look for

1. Why is *Humanae Vitae* accused of enslaving reason and will to biology?

2. How does an erroneous body-soul dualism underlie the accusation of biologism?

3. What is meant by "the false abstraction of the biological order," which *Humanae Vitae's* critics are guilty of?

4. What is the charge of physicalism or biologism that *Humanae Vitae's* critics level against the natural law?

5. How is the charge of biologism refuted by a true interpretation of the natural law?

6. Why are *Humanae Vitae's* critics guilty of the very biologism with which they seek to stigmatize the encyclical?

7. What is utilitarianism?

8. What evidence can be cited to prove that a utilitarian attitude dominates much of the world today?

9. Why do utilitarians commit a critical error in seeking to make pleasure the principal object of our free acts?

10. Why is the supposed altruism of the utilitarian principle simply an illusion?

11. Why is human love under utilitarianism nothing more than a "harmonizing of egoisms"?

12. How does utilitarianism lead persons to instrumentalize one another?

13. Why is contraception clearly utilitarian in nature?

14. Why is it so important to defend the reality of intrinsically evil acts?

15. What is our best hope for overcoming the contraceptive mentality and fostering true self-giving human love?

B. "*Cogito ergo sum*" and the Alleged Biologism of *Humanae Vitae*

1. The Accusation: Enslaving Reason and Free Will to Biology

Humanae Vitae's teaching that contraceptive acts are intrinsically disordered applies to all men and women as a precept of the natural moral law.[715] So it is not surprising that the encyclical's critics have sought to undermine Paul VI's interpretation of the natural law. Overt "biologism" is the principal charge leveled against *Humanae Vitae*. Paul VI has been accused of demeaning the human person by making husbands and wives subject to the physical, biological laws of reproduction inscribed within the conjugal act.

It is claimed that asking married couples to be dependent upon the biological rhythm of the woman's cycle reverses the hierarchy of what constitutes a person's transcendent dignity. Reason and free will above all embody the "image of God" in the human person. Man has employed his reason to develop artificial contraceptives. Married couples should be free to decide whether or not to regulate biological fertility through the use of contraceptives. We intervene artificially in our own bodies in many other ways, by using medicines, life-support systems, and prosthetics. *Humanae Vitae* makes man's reason and free will slaves of a biological process!

2. Paul VI: Facing the Charge Squarely

Paul VI does not shrink from the opposition being raised, nor pretend it away. He faithfully formulates the charge leveled at the Church's teaching on the responsible transmission of human life in the strongest possible terms.

> To this teaching of the Church on conjugal morals, the objection is made today, as we observed earlier (no. 3), that it is the prerogative of the human intellect to dominate the energies offered by irrational nature and to orientate them toward an end conformable to the good of man. Now, some may ask: in the present case, is it not reasonable in many circumstances to have recourse to artificial birth control if, thereby, we secure the harmony and peace of the family, and better conditions for the education of the children already born?[716]

Since a person's intellect penetrates his or her conscious actions, giving them an inner meaning, Paul VI is entirely in agreement that husbands and wives should fully discern with their intelligence when responsibly planning how many children they can bring up in their fam-

---

[715] *HV*, 14.
[716] *HV*, 16.

ily. But precisely because of the inner meaning of those acts, there is one fundamental condition the spouses may not violate: "The Church is the first to praise and recommend the intervention of intelligence in a work that so closely associates the rational creature with his Creator; but she affirms that this must be done with respect for the order established by God."[717]

Paul VI's succinct phrase, "with respect for the order established by God," implicitly reveals all that is lacking in the concept of the human person which underlies contraception. Although the argument for contraception, propped up by the charge of biologism against *Humanae Vitae*, seems persuasive on the surface, it commits four fundamental errors. First of all, it rests upon an implicit body-soul dualism. Secondly, it erroneously abstracts the biological order from the real order of nature. Thirdly, it misinterprets the true meaning of the natural law. These first three errors lead to an ironic state of affairs: Those supporting contraception are actually guilty of the very biologism with which they seek to stigmatize *Humanae Vitae*.

In simplest terms, these four errors can be reduced to one: legitimizing contraception depends upon a vision of the human person irreconcilable with Christianity and contrary to the person's true dignity. It is a concept of persons and their acts which does not respect the order established by God.

3. Underlying Errors in the Attack Against *Humanae Vitae*
a) Body-Soul Dualism and a False Abstraction of the Biological Order

Let us consider one at a time the errors of those who would justify contraception by accusing *Humanae Vitae* of biologism. In the first place, their implicit concept of the human person cannot help but be a dualistic one. Contraception can be justified only if the act of conjugal union possesses no intrinsic personal or moral meaning in itself. It must be simply a physical or biological act, one which leads to reproduction during the fertile time of the cycle if not artificially rendered infertile.

Persons, reduced in essence to spiritual, thinking subjects, convey meaning to the act of conjugal union entirely by their own mental intentions. If husband and wife intend their conjugal union to be an act of love, then it becomes so, regardless of whether or not contraception is utilized. In *Veritatis Splendor* John Paul II speaks of this position adopted by some moralists: "In their view, man, as a rational being, not only can but actually *must freely determine the meaning* of his behavior."[718]

---

[717] *HV*, 16.
[718] *VS*, 47.

To arrive at such a dualistic vision of the person, a second fundamental error must be committed: The biological order is falsely ab-
stracted from the real order of nature and viewed as if it existed in itself.
Karol Wojtyła points out in *Love and Responsibility*: "The accusation of biologism can only be made if we assume in advance that the sexual urge
in man has only a biological sense."[719] But the sexual urge does not, in
fact, exist on a purely biological plane. It is an aspect of the entire person, who exists as a physiological, psychological, and spiritual unity.

We can consider the biological aspect of the conjugal act, which fulfills the sexual urge, independently of its emotional, personal, and
moral dimensions, only through an act of mental abstraction. To pretend that the act of conjugal union constitutes, in itself, simply a biological fact is to claim that the biological order, a product of mental abstraction, exists in reality. This claim is patently absurd. The conjugal act is
not performed by masculine and feminine biological entities. Husband
and wife, in the fullness of their reality as persons, engage in conjugal
union, with all of the emotional and moral aspects this act possesses in
itself, due to its inner, personal meaning.

John Paul II confirms that this erroneous abstraction of the biological order, when considering human persons and their acts, eventually
leads one to hold to positions contrary to the faith. "*A doctrine which dis-
sociates the moral act from the bodily dimensions of its exercise is contrary to
the teaching of Scripture and Tradition.*"[720] The body-soul dualism underlying the accusation of biologism is also contrary to Church teaching:

> It contradicts the *Church's teachings on the unity of the human person,*
> whose rational soul is *per se et essentialiter* [in itself and essentially]
> the form of his body.[721] The spiritual and immortal soul is the prin-
> ciple of unity of the human being, whereby it exists as a whole —
> *corpore et anima unus* [one in body and soul][722] — as a person. . . . *The
> person, including the body, is completely entrusted to himself, and it is in
> the unity of body and soul that the person is the subject of his own moral
> acts.*[723] . . . In fact, *body and soul are inseparable*: in the person, in the
> willing agent and in the deliberate act *they stand or fall together.*[724]

b) Misinterpretation of the Natural Law

Since the prohibition against contraception rests upon the natural
moral law, a sweeping way to undermine the Church's teaching would
be to take issue with the natural law itself. That is precisely what a num-

---

[719] Wojtyła, *Love and Responsibility*, pp. 294-295 (note 20).

[720] *VS*, 49.

[721] Cf. Ecumenical Council of Vienne, Constitution *Fidei Catholicae*: DS, 902; Fifth Lateran Ecumenical Council, Bull *Apostolici Regiminis*: DS, 1440.

[722] Second Vatican Ecumenical Council, Pastoral Constitution on the Church in the Modern World
Gaudium et Spes, 14.

[723] *VS*, 48.

[724] *VS*, 49.

ber of moral theologians have attempted to do. John Paul II notes in his 1993 encyclical *Veritatis Splendor*: "*Objections of physicalism and naturalism* have been leveled against the traditional conception of *the natural law,* which is accused of presenting as moral laws what are in themselves mere biological laws."[725]

Once again the fundamental accusation against the Church's teaching on the responsible transmission of life is that it submits reason and will to a biological law, elevating what is merely a law of nature to the level of a moral law.

This accusation rests upon such an erroneous interpretation of the natural law that it is difficult not to describe it as a misrepresentation, or even a mere characterization. The *Catechism* states clearly the meaning of the term "*natural*" in "natural law." It does not mean that physical laws of nature or mere natural inclinations assume a moral character in themselves simply because they are natural. The tendency to preserve one's own physical life does not become a moral precept simply because it is a natural inclination. "This law is called 'natural,' not in reference to the nature of irrational beings, but because reason which decrees it properly belongs to human nature."[726]

In other words, our reason, which is part of our nature, recognizes that certain aspects of our bodily and spiritual constitution contain a moral dimension within themselves. They do so not simply because they are related to our physical or biological good, but because they have a direct relationship to our good as persons, in all of the transcendence which being a person implies. John Paul II clarifies this point at some length in *Veritatis Splendor*:

> At this point the true meaning of the natural law can be understood: It refers to man's proper and primordial nature, the "nature of the human person,"[727] which is *the person himself in the unity of soul and body*, in the unity of his spiritual and biological inclinations and of all the other specific characteristics necessary for the pursuit of his end. "The natural moral law expresses and lays down the purposes, rights and duties which are based upon the bodily and spiritual nature of the human person. Therefore this law cannot be thought of as simply a set of norms on the biological level; rather it must be defined as the rational order whereby man is called by the Creator to direct and regulate his life and actions and in particular to make use of his own body."[728]

---

[725] *VS*, 47.

[726] *CCC*, 1955.

[727] Second Vatican Ecumenical Council, Pastoral Constitution on the Church in the Modern World *Gaudium et Spes*, 51.

[728] *VS*, 50; citing Congregation for the Doctrine of the Faith, Instruction on Respect for Human Life in its Origin and on the Dignity of Procreation *Donum Vitae* (February 22, 1987), Introduction, 3: *A.A.S.* 80 (1988), 74; cf. Paul VI, Encyclical Letter *Humanae Vitae* (July 25, 1968), 10: *A.A.S.* 60 (1968), 487-488.

The Holy Father goes on to give a specific example of how reason recognizes a moral duty in the natural inclination to preserve one's own physical life. This obligation is expressed in the natural law precept that prohibits killing an innocent person or committing suicide — a precept also made known to us by divine revelation in the Fifth Commandment. If the natural inclination as such were given the status of a moral law, then it would never be permissible to sacrifice one's own life. This is clearly not the case. Reason is aware that "it can be licit, praiseworthy or even imperative to give up one's own life (cf. Jn 15:13) out of love of neighbor or as a witness to the truth."[729]

How can this be so, if the supreme sacrifice of self directly contradicts the natural tendency to preserve our own life? Reason recognizes that the human person, in all of his transcendence, is much more than a biological reality. Our spiritual nature attains the heights of perfection through this most noble of sacrifices. We truly fulfill ourselves as persons. Our immortal spiritual soul will live eternally in the joy of the self-sacrificing love it has brought to fruition with God's help. Could this authentic interpretation of the natural law possibly be farther away from the charge of physicalism or biologism that its critics have leveled against it?

c) A Profound Irony:
The Biologism of *Humanae Vitae's* Critics

We have seen that those who accuse *Humanae Vitae* of biologism commit three fundamental errors: their critique rests upon a false body-soul dualism; they attribute an independent reality to the biological order, which is nothing more than a mental abstraction; and they blatantly misinterpret the natural law. The ultimate irony of the situation is the following: Due to these deep-seated errors, *Humanae Vitae's* critics are guilty of the very biologism for which they so vociferously rebuke the encyclical.

They would deprive the conjugal act of its intrinsic, personal meaning: the inseparable unitive and procreative significance which the act possesses by its very structure. Doing so divests the conjugal union of its inner human and moral content, reducing it to a mere biological act. This arbitrary and reductive approach to persons and their acts is the real biologism. Karol Wojtyła confirms this fact in *Love and Responsibility*. "It is really this reductionism which deserves to be called 'biologism,' since it allows the biological aspect (which is of course important) to obscure the phenomenon as a whole (*pars pro toto*) [the part for the whole], and absolutize it."[730]

---

[729] *VS*, 50.
[730] Wojtyła, *Love and Responsibility*, p. 295 (note 20).

Paul VI proves himself to be a true defender of the human person by safeguarding the inner, human meaning of the conjugal act. It is precisely because of the inherent, personal meaning of the conjugal union that contraceptive acts are intrinsically wrong, and thus degrade the humanity of persons who engage in them. Speaking about such contraceptive acts, Paul VI declares: "It is not licit, even for the gravest reasons, to do evil so that good may follow therefrom,[731] that is, to make into the object of a positive act of the will something which is intrinsically disordered, and hence unworthy of the human person."[732]

With inspiring courage, Paul VI was willing to become a "sign of contradiction"[733] before the world in order to defend authentic, self-giving married love in the acts in which it is most fully embodied. "In defending conjugal morals in their integral wholeness, the Church knows that she contributes toward the establishment of a truly human civilization; she engages man not to abdicate from his own responsibility in order to rely on technical means; by that very fact she defends the dignity of man and wife."[734]

John Paul II confirms the transcendent value of Paul VI's heroic encyclical. "By rejecting all manipulations of corporeity which alter its human meaning, the Church serves man and shows him the path of true love, the only path on which he can find the true God."[735]

III. Selfish Utilitarianism

No one would dispute the claim that the most important part of a building is the foundation. In the Gospel, Christ himself compares a house anchored upon rock to one built on sand. We have already seen that the attempt to legitimize contraception ascends from the treacherous foundations of an erroneous body-soul dualism and an implicit biologism. There is yet another flawed anthropological and moral theory on which the shaky edifice of contraception is propped up: selfish utilitarianism.

In his 1994 *Letter to Families*, John Paul II affirms that utilitarianism is the dominant form of civilization in much of the world today. He goes on to define what he means by that term: "*Utilitarianism* is a civilization of production and of use, a civilization of things and not of persons, a civilization in which persons are used in the same way as things are used. "[736] The devastating consequences of utilitarianism for the human person are already clear from its very nature. Still, the Holy Father notes some of the specific results it leads to: "In the context of a civilization of

---

[731] Cf. Rm 3:8.
[732] *HV*, 14.
[733] Cf. Lk 2:34; *HV*, 18.
[734] *HV*, 18.
[735] *VS*, 50.
[736] John Paul II, *Letter to Families*, 13.

use, woman can become an object for man, children a hindrance to parents, the family an institution obstructing the freedom of its members."[737]

Does utilitarianism really command the world stage today? Is the value of persons actually measured in many cases by their usefulness, by what they can produce, rather than by who they are? Countless examples could be given to support this allegation. Terminally ill persons are often marginalized, while a campaign flourishes to eliminate them from the scene entirely through euthanasia. Radical feminist groups stridently assert that women can achieve true equality with men and fully realize themselves only by pursuing a career. The word "motherhood" was scarcely mentioned in the final document from the United Nations' 1995 International Conference on Women held in Beijing.

The Holy Father himself cites two examples of a pervasive utilitarian climate. "To be convinced that this is the case, one need only look at *certain sexual education programs* introduced into the schools, often notwithstanding the disagreement and even the protests of many parents; or *pro-abortion tendencies* which vainly try to hide behind the so-called 'right to choose' ('*pro-choice*') on the part of both spouses and in particular on the part of the woman."[738]

How does contraception imply a utilitarian view of the human person? To answer this question we must look more closely at the roots of utilitarianism and the way it unfolds as a moral theory.

A. Pleasure as the Object of Our Free Acts: Utilitarianism's Critical Error

In his analysis of utilitarianism in *Love and Responsibility*, Wojtyła notes that the term itself is derived from the Latin verb *uti* ("to use, to take advantage of") and the adjective *utilis* ("useful").[739] But in utilitarianism a second meaning of "to use" also enters into play — not simply the primary meaning: to employ something as a means to an end. The second meaning of "to use" is related to a sensation which accompanies some of our actions: pleasure.

When a marathon runner drinks a bottle of cold water after having crossed the finish line, he experiences pleasure while quenching his thirst. A father laboriously toiling over a hot charcoal grill during the family picnic is rewarded by the pleasure of consuming a succulent barbecued steak. After an arduous ascent, a mountain climber experiences pleasure as he surveys the breathtaking panorama from the summit. One of the most intense forms of pleasure is that experienced by hus-

---

[737] Ibid.
[738] LF, 13.
[739] Cf. Wojtyła, *Love and Responsibility,* p. 35.

band and wife during their conjugal union. "Pleasure appears in different guises or shades — depending on the emotional-affective experiences with which it is connected. It may be either sensual satisfaction, or emotional contentment, or a profound, a total joy."[740]

We have now ascertained the second meaning of the verb "to use." In this sense it is the equivalent of "to enjoy" and means "to experience pleasure, the pleasure which in slightly different senses is associated both with the activity itself and with the object of the activity."[741] Now a fundamental question presents itself. What is the proper relationship pleasure should have to our freely chosen, human acts?

Wojtyła responds clearly and succinctly: "Pleasure is essentially incidental, contingent, something which may occur in the course of an action."[742] In other words, pleasure should never be sought in itself as the direct end or object of the action. The marathon runner who drinks a bottle of cold water seeks directly to quench his thirst. Pleasure accompanies this act. In the same way, husband and wife strive to give themselves in love to one another in the act of conjugal union. The primary goal of their act is not simply the pleasure they experience.

Many times in the course of our lives we need to forego actions that would bring us pleasure and perform acts which cause a certain degree of pain, if we want to do "the right thing." Pleasure is simply not an adequate criterion for acting rationally, according to our true good as persons. During the twentieth century, more men and women than in any other period of history have made the supreme sacrifice of martyrdom, often suffering excruciating torments, in order to remain faithful to Christ.

Here is where utilitarianism commits its most devastating error. It seeks to pursue pleasure as the direct object or goal of free human acts. Utilitarians do not deny that human persons are meant to do good and avoid evil in their actions. But they obliterate the inner meaning of this most fundamental principle of conscience and the moral life by defining the good as what is useful. In its turn, "the useful is whatever gives pleasure and excludes its opposite, for pleasure is the essential ingredient of human happiness. To be happy, according to the premises of utilitarianism, is to live pleasurably."[743]

B. The Utilitarian Principle: Maximize Pleasure and Minimize Pain

By its nature, pleasure is something individual and subjective. Were utilitarians to state simply that the goal of our actions should be to

---

[740] Ibid., p. 32.
[741] Ibid.
[742] Ibid., p. 36.
[743] Ibid., p. 35.

maximize our own pleasure and minimize our pain, utilitarianism would be recognized by all as a system overtly founded upon selfish egoism. Such a degraded vision of the person is not very appealing to our nobler instincts.

Thus, the utilitarian principle is disguised in order to give it a semblance of altruism. It can be formulated as follows: "The maximum pleasure for the greatest possible number of people — obviously with a minimum of discomfort for the same number."[744]

At first glance this principle might seem appealing. In reality, it is impossible to follow as a criterion for action and its supposed altruism is a mere illusion. Since pleasure by its very nature is incidental, a phenomenon which may accompany an action, we can never be sure ahead of time just how much pleasure our specific acts will bring to us — or even whether they will bring us pleasure at all. "Pleasure and pain are always connected with a concrete action, so that it is not possible to anticipate them precisely, let alone plan for them or, as the utilitarians would have us do, even compute them in advance. Pleasure is, after all, a somewhat elusive thing."[745] In practice, it proves impossible for us to base our decisions about how to act on the pleasure principle.

The apparent magnanimity of seeking to foster the pleasure of others along with my own also breaks down under closer scrutiny. If pleasure is the sole good and unique moral norm, I am obligated to aid someone else in experiencing pleasure only so long as his experience of pleasure also gives me pleasure. The moment it ceases to do so, my obligation toward him disappears. What happens if his pleasure comes to bring me real displeasure? Then I could just as readily proceed to do everything possible to cause him pain under the utilitarian principle.

Wojtyła expresses the inescapable conclusion: "It is crystal clear that if utilitarian principles are followed, a subjective understanding of the good (equating the good with the pleasurable) leads directly, though there may be no conscious intention of this, to egoism."[746]

C. Utilitarian Love: "The Harmonizing of Egoisms"

We have seen earlier that the one foundation for authentic love between two persons, especially husband and wife, must be an objective common good to which both persons submit themselves. Only by seeking an objective good outside of themselves can they rise above subjectivism, and the egoism lying hidden beneath it. If both persons together freely seek the same goal, then they can respect each other as persons —

---

[744] Ibid., p. 36.
[745] Ibid.
[746] Ibid., p. 38.

as ends in themselves. They are united in authentic love: a true personal communion. *"Love is the unification of persons."*[747]

What is the definition of love according to utilitarianism? It is nothing more than the "harmonization of egoisms," a term utilitarians themselves invoke.[748] The communion of persons has been replaced by selfish individualism. Who would be willing to concede that love really exists as an objective reality between two persons or within either one of them, when each merely seeks his own pleasure through the other? Wojtyła unmasks the reality of love's utter degradation that utilitarianism would seek to conceal.

> "Love" in this utilitarian conception is a union of egoisms, which can hold together only on condition that they confront each other with nothing unpleasant, nothing to conflict with their mutual pleasure. Therefore love so understood is self-evidently merely a pretence which has to be carefully cultivated to keep the underlying reality hidden: the reality of egoism, and the greediest kind of egoism at that, exploiting another person to obtain for itself its own "maximum pleasure." In such circumstances the other person is and remains only a means to an end.[749]

D. Instrumentalizing the Human Person

Since the goal of all our actions in utilitarianism is pleasure, other persons are necessarily reduced to a means toward this end. The unavoidable instrumentalization of the human person is the most severe indictment against utilitarianism. But not only do we instrumentalize others by following the pleasure principle, we also treat ourselves in the same way. If we regard others simply as means for our own pleasure, we cannot help but view ourselves as having the same function for them.

> The person — and not only "the other person," but the first person too — sinks to the level of a means, a tool. There is an ineluctable, overwhelming necessity in this: if I treat someone else as a means and tool in relation to myself I cannot help regarding myself in the same light. We have here something like the opposite of the commandment to love.[750]

Utilitarianism does not arrive at a conclusion so degrading to the human person by chance. It too lays its foundations upon a fundamental anthropological error: the failure to take into account both the corporeal and spiritual dimensions of man. By making the pursuit of pleasure morality's primary rule, utilitarianism reduces the person to an ephemeral, physical being. Man's reason is no longer the transcendent faculty

---

[747] Ibid.
[748] Ibid.
[749] Ibid., p. 39.
[750] Ibid., p. 39.

which opens us to the infinite, enabling us to respond to God himself in our free actions. Instead, it becomes reduced to a means for calculating how to obtain the most pleasure, while avoiding pain.

> The utilitarian considers pleasure important in itself, and, with his general view of man, fails to see that he is quite conspicuously an amalgam of matter and spirit, the two complementary factors which together create one personal existence, whose specific nature is due entirely to the soul. To a utilitarian a man is a subject endowed with the ability to think and to feel. His sensibility makes him desirous of pleasure and bids him shun its opposite. The ability to think, to reason, is given to man to enable him to direct his activities to the attainment of a maximum of pleasure with a minimum of discomfort.[751]

E. Contraception's Manifest Utilitarianism

The ethical system of utilitarianism and its anthropological foundation are clearly opposed to the basic dignity of the human person. But what relationship, if any, exists between utilitarianism and contraception? The response: contraception by its very nature is utilitarian.

We have already seen that eliminating the procreative meaning of the conjugal act through contraception also eradicates the unitive meaning, since it deprives the act of its truth. Husband and wife no longer give themselves and receive each other in the truth of their fullness as persons, which includes the capacity to become a father or mother. Their conjugal union, deprived of its inner meaning, is no longer an act of love.

What remains to the conjugal act thus stripped of its intrinsic, personal significance? Nothing is left but the mutual pleasure the spouses experience through their sexual union. The marital act is degraded to a utilitarian function. Husband and wife are instrumentalized by one another. They are reduced to objects, means for each other's pleasure.

IV. Conclusion:
The Resounding Words of *Familiaris Consortio*

The dimensions of what lies hidden behind contraception are truly staggering. In order to legitimize contraceptive acts, one must accept a rationalistic view of man that eliminates human transcendence and true personal communion, reducing persons to individual members of a species. An erroneous body-soul dualism robs free human bodily actions of their intrinsic personal meaning, degrading persons to objects of manipulation. An implicit biologism erroneously abstracts the physiological aspect of conjugal union from its full reality as a meaningful and transcendent act of the entire person.

---

[751] Ibid., p. 35.

In order to justify contraception, the natural law itself must be falsely interpreted in a biological perspective that would eliminate intrinsically evil acts entirely. Where does the eradication of intrinsically evil acts lead mankind? Although the absolute prohibition against committing an act which is wrong in itself is a negative precept, it serves to defend an eminently positive reality. What is the flip side of intrinsically evil acts? It consists of nothing less than the inalienable rights of each human person. If there exist no acts evil in themselves, then neither can there survive any inalienable rights never to be violated. If it is not always wrong to directly kill an innocent person, there no longer exists an inalienable right to life. Not only would the Ten Commandments disappear from the scene, so would the Declaration of Independence, and the very foundation for any legitimate form of government.

Finally, the only moral system which coherently supports contraceptive acts is utilitarianism. Persons are diminished to thinking subjects, whose one goal in life is to eke as much pleasure as they can from each action. Husbands and wives instrumentalize each other in a "love" that is nothing more than a desperate "harmonizing of egoisms."

In light of what lies hidden behind contraception, how powerfully do John Paul II's words in number 32 of *Familiaris Consortio* resound: "Theological reflection is able to perceive *the difference, both anthropological and moral,* between contraception and recourse to the rhythm of the cycle: it is a difference which is much wider and deeper than is usually thought, one which involves two irreconcilable concepts of the human person and of human sexuality."[752]

Are the men and women of the third Christian millennium willing to surrender so much in order to legitimize contraception? The two million young people who gathered together in Rome from all parts of the globe for World Youth Day 2000 suggest that they are not. The resounding cheers with which they responded to the Holy Father's call to be martyrs by standing up against the current confirm that they are not.

May the redeeming power of Christ's sacrifice upon the cross, renewed each time the Mass is celebrated, give every Christian couple the strength they need to live up to the truth of who they are as persons and the beauty of their self-giving love to one another. May Christ's silent presence in the Eucharist instill courage in all who are entrusted with the mission of proclaiming the truth about married love, restored by Christ's redemption to God's original plan for man and woman.

How the words from John Paul II's *Letter to Families* must echo in the hearts and minds of all people who truly love humanity: "The family is placed at the center of the great struggle between good and evil, be-

---

[752] FC, 32.

tween life and death, between love and all that is opposed to love."[753] As we cross the threshold of hope into a new millennium, may the Blessed Virgin Mary's intercession, her silent courage at the foot of Christ's cross, enable each one of us to valiantly defend love and resist all that is opposed to love.

---

[753] *Letter to Families*, 23.

ELEVEN

Natural Family Planning Views Men and Women: Free Personal Subjects in Their Inviolable Mystery

Preview

I. A Transcendent Vision of the Person
   A. Personal Subjects in the Unity of Body and Soul
   B. Freedom and Truth: The Inviolable Mystery of the Person
   C. Man's Capacity for Truth: The Condition of Freedom
   D. Duty: The Highest Manifestation of Freedom

II. True Human Love: Attraction, Affection, or Union of Persons?
   A. Love as Attraction: The Sexual Urge
      1. Sexual Attraction *vs.* Love: Acts of Man and Human Acts
      2. The Sexual Urge and Contraception: Can They Be Reconciled?

Points to look for

1. How does the fact that we are persons in the unity of body and soul affect the inner meaning of the conjugal act?

2. Why is the sexual urge different in human beings than in animals?

3. What is the relationship between freedom and communion among persons?

4. Why is the capacity for truth a necessary condition of freedom?

5. Why is freedom not an end in itself?

6. How does duty most fully display the freedom of the human will?

7. What is the difference between a moral obligation and physical necessity?

8. Why does the attempt to eliminate absolute moral norms lead to the death of freedom?

9. Why is duty the path to genuine freedom?

10. What are the three dimensions of love between man and woman?

11. How does the sexual urge reveal the fundamental dependence of the human condition?

12. How does the sexual urge open the possibility of forging authentic love between a man and a woman?

13. What is the difference between acts of man and human acts?

14. Why is the distinction between acts of man and human acts essential for authentic human love?

15. Why is it false to claim that the sexual urge has a mere biological significance?

16. Why does the nature of the sexual urge preclude contraception?

I. A Transcendent Vision of the Person
A. Personal Subjects in the Unity of Body and Soul

The havoc wrought upon the human person by the false ideologies underlying contraception proves them to be a modern form of barbarianism.[754] John Paul II stands courageously with the pastors of the Church, striving to defend humanity from the new barbarians' onslaught. Against the fierce assaults of demeaning reductivism he has erected a solid bulwark: a transcendent vision of human persons in their inviolable mystery.

This vision underlies the Church's teaching on the responsible transmission of life through natural family planning. It is based upon the unbreakable unity of body and soul in the human person.[755] The spiritual and corporeal unity of the human person endows our free actions with an inner, personal meaning. This objective meaning is expressed through the language of the body. Nowhere does the language of the body convey more eloquently the transcendent truth of the human person than in the self-giving love between husband and wife in their act of conjugal union.

In this act, man and woman hold in their hands, as it were, their entire person — in its physiological, sensual, emotional, and spiritual dimensions. The sensual and emotional pleasure they experience in sexual intercourse is a manifestation of the goodness represented by the spiritual communion of persons their act is meant to embody. The new life their act of intimate union is able to bring into the world reveals human love's creative power. It also makes clear that the spiritual bond between husband and wife opens itself to a still more transcendent communion: that of poor, human creatures with the infinite God who created them.

God himself intervenes directly each time a new human life is conceived in order to endow that unique human being with an immortal

---

[754] Cf. Weigel, *Witness to Hope*, pp. 863-864.

[755] "The unity of soul and body is so profound that one has to consider the soul to be the 'form' of the body: i.e., it is because of its spiritual soul that the body made of matter becomes a living, human body; spirit and matter, in man, are not two natures united, but rather their union forms a single nature" (*CCC*, 365). Cf. Council of Vienne (1312): *DS* 902.

soul.[756] This special intervention by God reveals how husband and wife freely cooperate with divine providence in the Creator's plan for human procreation.[757] It also intimates that their interpersonal communion brings them into communion with God himself. That is precisely why husband and wife experience a deep, inner need to justify their conjugal relations — not only before one another and society, through the institution of marriage — but also before God.[758]

Far from constraining individuals or diminishing their freedom, this inner need to justify sexual relations reveals the true greatness of persons. With human beings it is impossible to speak simply of a natural instinct or sexual urge leading to reproduction, as among other species. The interior life that constitutes the person penetrates all free acts of men and women, making them responsible for how they respond to the sexual urge. That inner life imbues the act of sexual intercourse with intense, personal meaning. The very term "procreation" indicates a conscious participation in God's creative plan, infinitely superior to instinctive sexual reproduction among animals.[759] Wojtyła calls attention to this inescapable dignity, which characterizes every person.

> The true greatness of the human person is manifested in the fact that sexual activity is felt to require such a profound justification. It cannot be otherwise. *Man must reconcile himself to his natural greatness.* It is especially when he enters so deeply into the natural order, immerses himself so to speak in its elemental processes, that *he must not forget that he is a person.* Instinct alone can resolve none of his problems, everything demands decisions from his "interior self," his reason and his sense of responsibility. And this is particularly true of the love to which human kind owes its continual renewal.[760]

B. Freedom and Truth: The Inviolable Mystery of the Person

If the transcendent greatness of persons arises above all from their inner life, is it possible to discover any prevailing traits indelibly in-

---

[756] "The Church teaches that every spiritual soul is created immediately by God — it is not 'produced' by the parents — and also that it is immortal: it does not perish when it separates from the body at death, and it will be reunited with the body at the final Resurrection" (*CCC*, 366). Cf. Pius XII, *Humani Generis*: *DS* 3896; Paul VI, CPG § 8; Lateran Council V (1513): *DS* 1440.

[757] God's direct intervention also reveals the dimensions of the moral evil of *in vitro* fertilization. After a human sperm and ovum are united in a laboratory, a new human being comes into the world outside of an act love between mother and father — the only way in which God has ordained human persons to be conceived. (For a summary of the Thomistic philosophy of the soul as the form of the body which "receives the body in the communion of its own act of being," see Etienne Gilson, *Elements of Christian Philosophy* [New York: Doubleday, 1960] pp. 208-209.)

[758] Cf. Wojtyła, *Love and Responsibility*, pp. 222-224.

[759] The sublime mystery of human procreation, the coming into existence of a new human person with an immortal soul, an eternal destiny, is the subject of more and more theological writing in the Church today.

[760] Wojtyła, *Love and Responsibility*, p. 236.

scribed upon this interior realm? Yes. Psychology discerns two axis points around which our inner existence as persons revolves: freedom and truth.

> Psychology, which is, as its name indicates, the science of the soul, endeavors to lay bare the structure and the foundations of man's inner life. Its investigations serve to confirm that the most significant characteristics of that inner life are the sense of truth and the sense of freedom."[761]

A strong desire for truth is implanted within the breast of every human person. It can never be totally silenced. Though crushed and trampled upon, it will always reemerge to begin anew its ceaseless quest. The silent disintegration of the communist "empire of lies" in the year 1989 offers strong evidence that the longing for truth is one of the most powerful forces within the human person.

The strength of man's search for truth should not come as a surprise. At its deepest core, this search is an expression of the insatiable longing within the heart of each human person for the one who is "the Way, the Truth and the Life" — Jesus Christ. As he stood before Pontius Pilate, in the final moments before the agony of his passion, Jesus proclaimed: "For this I was born, and for this I have come into the world, to bear witness to the truth. Every one who is of the truth hears my voice."[762] John Paul II confirms this deepest meaning of the search for truth when he gives his own definition of what study is ultimately: "Study is an expression of the unquenchable desire for an ever deeper knowledge of God, the source of light and all human truth."[763]

Pursuing the truth in freedom lies at the heart of what it means to be a human person. Wojtyła notes how this spiritual capacity stamps a unique seal upon all our acts: "Freedom and truth, truth and freedom determine the spiritual imprint which marks the various manifestations of human life and human activity. They penetrate the remotest recesses of human action and experience, filling them with a content of which we never meet the slightest trace in the lives of animals."[764]

A fundamental aspect of the free possession of oneself is the ability to enter into personal communion with others. A true interpersonal communion can be achieved only if we freely choose to reveal ourselves, to disclose the secrets of our inner life to others, to give our very self to them. Here all believers encounter a startling reality: God himself has chosen to disclose to mankind through the inspired writings of Sacred Scripture the hidden secrets, the impenetrable mystery, of his inner

---

[761] *Love and Responsibility*, pp. 114-115.
[762] Jn 18:37.
[763] John Paul II, Post-Synodal Apostolic Exhortation *Vita Consecrata*, 98.
[764] Wojtyła, *Love and Responsibility*, p. 116.

Trinitarian life. Even more astoundingly, he has sent his only Son as our redeemer, so that each one of us — poor, insignificant creatures — may enter into personal communion with the Father, the Son, and the Holy Spirit. In *Gaudium et Spes*, the Second Vatican Council reaffirms that this call to communion with God is the deepest foundation of human dignity.

> The root reason for human dignity lies in man's call to communion with God. From the very circumstance of his origin, man is already invited to converse with God. For man would not exist were he not created by God's love and constantly preserved by it, and he cannot live fully according to truth unless he freely acknowledges that love and devotes himself to his Creator.[765]

C. Man's Capacity for Truth: The Condition of Freedom

Just what relationship exists between these two poles of the human person's inner life — freedom and truth? Since the beginning of his pontificate, John Paul II has not ceased to reiterate the vigorous affirmation he made during the Second Vatican Council: "There is no freedom without truth!" It is impossible for us to be free without knowing the truth about who we are as persons. Where do we come from? What is the goal and meaning of our lives? What can we hope for as our final destiny? But even beyond this fact, our ability to know the truth of things themselves is intimately tied to the very structure of freedom. The capacity for truth is a necessary condition of freedom. Why is this so?

When we do our utmost to conquer a beckoning mountain peak during summer vacation, or strive to pull in an elusive trout from crystal-clear waters, we experience these activities as being good. In the midst of the pressures and demands of our daily existence, we may on occasion long wistfully for these moments of sheer bliss. Still, we are able to view this time of respite within the broader perspective of our life and mission. Were the welfare of those we are responsible for to demand it, we could doubtless summon the courage to forego even the idyllic joys of vacation.

The occasion to sacrifice something good for the sake of an even greater good is at once a test of our freedom and a manifestation of the noble heights it is capable of attaining. But this exercise of freedom is possible only because we are able to recognize the truth of things as they are in themselves. We realize that vacations are truly a good for us as persons, and so they attract our will; we are drawn toward them. Yet, at the same time, we recognize the truth that our mission to care for those entrusted to us is a much more transcendent good. So we are able to resist the attraction of the lesser good and freely choose the higher

---

[765] *GS*, 19.

one. Were we not able to recognize the truth of each of these aspects of our life, along with their relationship to one another, we would not be free to choose between them.

Without the ability to discern the truth of individual, partial goods within the ultimate horizon of truth itself, each particular good we encountered in our life would so attract and possess our will that we would be powerless to reject it. We would helplessly indulge in every passing pleasure that came our way. When the first distracted thought about vacations crossed our mind, as we sat diligently before a computer spreadsheet in our office, entire working-hours would then inexorably drift past, while we pined after those delightful moments. Dragged and pulled about by every ephemeral pleasure, we would not actually be free. Karol Wojtyła concisely explains how the ability to know the truth is decisive for the very possibility of freedom.

Truth is a condition of freedom, for if a man can preserve his freedom in relation to the objects which thrust themselves on him in the course of his activity as good and desirable, it is only because he is capable of viewing these goods in the light of truth and so adopting an independent attitude to them. Without this faculty man would inevitably be determined by them: these goods would take possession of him and determine totally the character of his actions and the whole direction of his activity. His ability to discover the truth gives man the possibility of self-determination, of deciding for himself the character and direction of his own actions, and that is what freedom means.[766]

D. Duty: The Highest Manifestation of Freedom

"There is no freedom without truth" is another way of saying that freedom is not an end in itself. Freedom exists for the sake of the truth and finds fulfillment in seeking truth. Since the fundamental truth about human persons is that we have been created to be loved and to love, freedom is *for* love. Freedom is fully realized only when a person freely surrenders himself to love and to the one loved. *"Freedom exists for the sake of love.* If freedom is not used, is not taken advantage of by love, it becomes a negative thing and gives human beings a feeling of emptiness and unfulfillment. Love commits freedom and imbues it with that to which the will is naturally attracted — goodness."[767]

Does this paradoxical conclusion mean that the flower children of the 1960s had it right all along? Is the sexual revolution and "free love" really the answer to humanity's frantic quest for happiness? Exactly the opposite is true. Such abuses in the very use of the term "love" plainly manifest the need to discern the authentic nature of human love, as well as freedom's relationship to that love.

---

[766] Wojtyła, *Love and Responsibility*, p. 115.
[767] Ibid., p. 135.

A crucial step along this journey is to ask ourselves, "What is the highest manifestation of freedom?" "When are we most truly free?" Those entrenched in any one of the many forms of relativism or reductivist secular humanism which dominate culture today would reply that freedom reaches its heights when we are free from all restrictions, from all obligations — in short, when we can do whatever we want.

Against this assessment Wojtyła offers a startling assertion: "It is, indeed, duty that most fully displays the freedom of the human will."[768] How can this be? Existentialist philosophers, proportionalist theologians, and secular humanist pundits have all vociferously fought to abolish duty, precisely in the name of freedom. According to Wojtyła, by their struggle they "deny themselves any real understanding of free will, or at any rate of that which most fully reveals it."[769]

Duty enters into freedom because human persons have a duty to choose the true good.[770] Our will "ought to" follow the true good. There exists a moral obligation to do so. Yet the very word "ought" also implies that we "may" choose not to do so. Our will is free.

But where does this mysterious word "ought" come from anyway? Just what sort of constraint does it lay upon us? Certainly not one of physical necessity. The very possibility of experiencing that I *should* do something depends on my being free to choose not to do it. It would make no sense to say that we all should die some day. We all *will* eventually die by implacable necessity. But we should be a good Samaritan and stop to help a person whose car is stalled along I-40 in the middle of the Arizona desert — although we are free to simply keep on driving past.

The mysterious reality of a necessity which at the same time respects our freedom reveals duty's origin. "Duty always grows out of the contact of the will with some norm."[771] What precisely do we mean when we speak about moral norms? According to St. Thomas Aquinas, a norm is *"regula et mensura humanorum actuum"* (the rule and measure of human actions).[772] When our actions correspond to the norm, they are just and noble. We have chosen the true good. When what we do departs from the norm, we have chosen evil and our conduct is blameworthy.

---

[768] Ibid., p. 119.

[769] Ibid., p. 120.

[770] The Second Vatican Council's Declaration on Religious Freedom *Dignitatis Humanae* states in number 2: "It is in accordance with their dignity as persons — that is, beings endowed with reason and free will and therefore privileged to bear personal responsibility — that all men should be at once impelled by nature and also bound by a moral obligation to seek the truth, especially religious truth. They are also bound to adhere to the truth, once it is known, and to order their whole lives in accord with the demands of truth."

[771] Wojtyła, *Love and Responsibility*, p. 120.

[772] *Summa Theologiae*, I-II, q. 90, a. 1.

Our reason is able to recognize norms, which obligate our conscience, because it is capable of discerning the truth of the objective value of things. We are well aware that we ourselves do not invent moral norms; they are realities independent of us that we discover. A father may prefer to go on vacations rather than put in two weeks of overtime to support his family. He may even try to convince himself that it is the right thing to do — or at least an acceptable form of conduct. But the objective value each of his loved ones embodies continues to reverberate within him each time he is with them or thinks about them. Duty's persistent call resounds in the interior silence of his conscience, and obligates his freedom: "You *should* work during those two weeks to support your family. You *must* do so."

Duty, and the moral norms from which duty arises, reveal the drama at play in every free choice we make. Either we respond to values and decide to do what is objectively good — we choose the road of life — or we allow ourselves to be captivated by the siren of subjective satisfaction — we choose death. The Italian philosopher Rocco Buttiglione describes the drama of freedom.

> Freedom is always a choice between either adhering to that fullness of being and goodness which reason acknowledges, or allowing oneself to be seduced by the fascination of a minor truth and the lesser fullness of being and goodness which is found in the attractiveness of the immediate, sensible, and emotional presence.[773]

What happens if the moral norm is denied in the name of freedom, as many clamorous voices would propose today? We have already seen that denying objective truth leads to the death of freedom. Buttiglione puts it well. "If the choice is not between good and evil, all choices are ultimately the same and choice no longer exists, only self-abandonment to multiple and transitory seductions."[774]

Behind the movement to eliminate objective moral norms — all in the name of liberating men and women — one can hear the whispered voice of the tempter, "You will be like God."[775] To deny absolute moral norms is to reject the Absolute God who is their source. It is to silence his voice within our conscience and turn away from his call to personal communion with him, a communion that can only be achieved through the sometimes-painful cross of our duty.

Yet every time we take up that cross, every time we refuse the insinuations of our subjective passions and choose what is truly, objectively good, we become a little bit more free. Freedom is not achieved by

---

[773] Buttiglione, *Karol Wojtyła: The Thought of the Man Who Became John Paul II*, p. 104.
[774] Ibid., p. 105.
[775] Gn 3:5.

being able to do whatever we want. Freedom reaches fulfillment when we want only to do what we *should* do, because that is what Christ wants for us. When our one, ardent, all-consuming desire is to do God's will at every moment of our lives, then we will begin to know what freedom means. St. Augustine reveals the path to true freedom in a single phrase: "Love and do what you will."[776]

II. True Human Love:
Attraction, Affection, or Union of Persons?

In the musical *Oliver Twist*, the young orphan Oliver begins a plaintive song in the midst of the deprived conditions of the orphanage: "Where is love?" The haunting lyrics, sung by someone who has never in his life experienced tender human affection, make John Paul II's oft-quoted words from his first encyclical penetrate deeply within us: "Man cannot live without love. He remains a being that is incomprehensible for himself, his life is senseless, if love is not revealed to him, if he does not encounter love, if he does not experience it and make it his own, if he does not participate intimately in it."[777]

Though love lies at the heart of the mystery that is each human life, love's essence often seems quite elusive — especially in the case of love between man and woman. There appears to be much disagreement as to what constitutes the inner core of love. Romantic novelists would have us believe that love consists of an emotional and erotic transport which seizes a man and a woman, utterly captivating them under its spell. Most popular songs identify love with "falling in love." So when the blissful feeling of being in love begins to dwindle away, it seems that true love has also fled.

Disagreement about the nature of love is not surprising, since love between man and woman is a complex reality. It encompasses all the spheres that make up the human person: the corporeal or sensual, the affective or emotional, and the realm of reason and free will. In *Love and Responsibility*, Karol Wojtyła assesses each of these aspects of human love. Because of love's multi-dimensional character, it becomes vitally important to *integrate* love. Only if the sensual and affective dimensions of love are integrated with love as a free act of the will, a free giving of oneself and receiving of the other, does love rise to the sphere of the person as such. Only then is it worthy to receive the name of true human love.

Paul VI succinctly describes the characteristics of authentic married love in *Humanae Vitae*. We will begin to ponder, under the guiding hand of Karol Wojtyła, the rich content expressed in a few brief lines.

---

[776] St. Augustine, *In Epist. Joann. Tractatus*, vii, 8: *"Dilige et quod vis fac."*
[777] *Redemptor Hominis*, 10.

This love is first of all fully human, that is to say, of the senses and of the spirit at the same time. It is not, then, a simple transport of instinct and sentiment, but also, and principally, an act of the free will, intended to endure and to grow by means of the joys and sorrows of daily life, in such a way that husband and wife become one only heart and one only soul, and together attain their human perfection.[778]

A. Love as Attraction: The Sexual Urge

As Pope Paul VI notes, one dimension of married love entails the sexual instinct of human persons, who are both body and spirit. The natural attraction between the sexes and the drive of the sexual urge provide the raw material from which mature love between a man and a woman develops. This first stage of human love — love as attraction or desire — reveals a basic aspect of our human condition. Our existence is characterized by a fundamental dependency. Neither are we the source of our own being, nor are we complete in ourselves. A man perceives in a woman (and she in him) a fundamental good for himself that he is lacking.

Sexual attraction and the mutual dependence between men and women point to an even deeper reality, as Rocco Buttiglione makes clear in his study of *Love and Responsibility*. "This discovery of dependency has its definitive and organic expression in the recognition of man's dependence on God. It is God who is the sufficient object of that desire for happiness which draws a man toward a woman and one person toward another."[779]

The sexual values of masculinity and femininity awaken the attraction between a man and a woman. Though sexual values arouse the sexual urge, this urge is naturally directed, not toward these values as such, but toward the individual human being who embodies them. Precisely because the sexual urge is directed toward a concrete member of the opposite sex, it opens the possibility of forging authentic love between persons.

Inevitably, then, the sexual urge in a human being is always in the natural course of things directed towards another human being — this is the normal form which it takes. If it is directed towards the sexual attributes as such this must be recognized as an impoverishment or even a perversion of the urge. . . . It is just because it is directed towards a particular human being that the sexual urge can provide the framework within which, and the basis on which, the possibility of love arises.[780]

---

[778] HV, 9.
[779] Buttiglione, *Karol Wojtyła: The Thought of the Man Who Became John Paul II*, p. 95.
[780] Wojtyła, *Love and Responsibility*, p. 49.

1. Sexual Attraction *vs.* Love: Acts of Man and Human Acts

But this mutual attraction between a man and a woman does not in itself represent love. Here it becomes necessary to distinguish between two fundamental concepts in the philosophy of St. Thomas Aquinas, which form the basis for sexual morality: the act of man (*actus hominis*) and the human act (*actus humanus*). "The act of man is what happens in man without the cooperation of his will or the judgment of reason. It implies merely instinctive reactions. But the human act is what is achieved by man insofar as he is a man,"[781] that is, through the engagement of reason and free will. Jerking our hand away after inadvertently touching a hot stove would be one example of an act of man. St. Joan of Arc's decision to allow herself to be burned at the stake rather than betray the mission she had received from God is a heroic instance of a human act.

How do these two concepts of human acts and acts of man relate to the beginnings of love between a man and a woman in sexual attraction? In itself, sexual attraction is an act of man, because it *happens* in man. The person is not responsible for these reactions as such. But the reactions stemming from the sexual urge form the basis for free human acts. Free will and reason enable persons to guide the sexual urge and make them responsible for their actions in the sexual sphere. "There is in man an innate principle which makes him capable of considered behavior, of self-determination. *Man is by nature capable of rising above instinct in his actions.* And he is capable of such action in the sexual sphere as elsewhere."[782] In sexual attraction,

> "something happens to man, something begins to take place without any initiative on his part, and this internal 'happening' creates as it were a base for definite actions, for considered actions, in which man exercises self-determination, decides for himself about his own actions and takes responsibility for them. This is the point at which human freedom and the sex urge meet."[783]

To sum everything up in one sentence: "Man is not responsible for what *happens* to him in the sphere of sex since he is obviously not himself the cause of it, but he is entirely responsible for what he *does* in this sphere."[784]

Here we see the need for integrating love as attraction by guiding the natural impulses of the sexual urge through free will. Without this integration, the result will be surrender to sensual passions and not authentic human love.

---

[781] Buttiglione, *Karol Wojtyła: The Thought of the Man Who Became John Paul II,* p. 103.
[782] Wojtyła, *Love and Responsibility,* p. 49.
[783] Ibid., pp. 46-47.
[784] Ibid., p. 47.

Love is not . . . merely a biological or even a psycho-physiological crystallization of the sexual urge, but is something fundamentally different from it. For although love grows out of the sexual urge and develops on that basis and in the conditions which the sexual urge creates in the psycho-physiological lives of concrete people, it is nonetheless given its definitive shape by *acts of the will at the level of the person*.[785]

Why are reason and will the determinate factors in authentic personal love, and not the sexual urge or the emotional experience of "falling in love" that accompanies sexual attraction? It is because human persons are not only *subjects* who experience sensual and emotional attraction within themselves. They also have an *objective* nature, which reason recognizes and free will must respect. If the objective nature of the person, encompassing all his or her urges and inclinations, is disregarded, there can be no question of true love. Buttiglione sums it up well.

Sexual attraction and falling in love draw the will toward a decision, by making it appear desirable. However, reason should always decide whether it is right to engage the will in the way in which what is happening directs. Only in such a way is love drawn up into the sphere of the person, and only in such a way can it direct itself not toward those particular qualities which arouse sexual and emotional reactions but toward the value of the other person, which manifests itself through its femininity and masculinity.[786]

2. The Sexual Urge and Contraception: Can They Be Reconciled?

If love is to be authentic, if it is to be directed toward the person as such, the objective truth of both the person and the sexual urge must be respected. What, precisely, is the objective meaning of the sexual urge? "The proper end of the urge, the end *per se*, is something supra-personal, the existence of the species *Homo*, the constant prolongation of its existence."[787] In addition, the sexual urge seeks to unite man and woman in the conjugal act of personal, self-giving love.

It now becomes necessary to conclude that contraception cannot be reconciled with the nature of the sexual urge. The object of the sexual urge is the coming into existence of a new human person. Existence is the most fundamental good, without which no other goods are possible. The new human person is brought into being through an act of love that is meant to encompass all the dimensions of the persons of husband and wife — sensual, emotional, and the personal realm of reason and free

---

[785] Ibid., p. 49.
[786] Buttiglione, *Karol Wojtyła: The Thought of the Man Who Became John Paul II*, p. 104.
[787] Wojtyła, *Love and Responsibility*, p. 49.

will. So it cannot be claimed that the sexual urge has a mere biological function. It is incomparably existential in character. Wojtyła explains why the existential nature of the sexual urge excludes contraception, which would manipulate the urge as if it were an external object to be used.

> If the sexual urge has a merely biological significance it can be re-garded as something to be used. We can agree that it is an object for man to enjoy just like any other object of nature, either animate or inanimate. But if the sexual urge has an existential character, if it is bound up with the very existence of the human person — that first and most basic good — then it must be subject to the principles which are binding in respect of the person. Hence, although the sexual urge is there for man to use, it must never be used in the ab-sence of, or worse still, in a way which contradicts, love for the per-son.[788]

Artificial contraception deprives the sexual urge of its objective end: the procreation of a new human person. It is in direct conflict with the natural purpose of the sexual urge. As Wojtyła affirms, "An outright conflict with that purpose will also perturb and undermine love be-tween persons."[789] Even on a strictly natural plane, without any reli-gious perspective, the prohibition against contraception binds all men and women of good will, since contraception violates the very order of human love. The new child who is born through an act of sexual inter-course is at once an affirmation and a continuation of the love of his par-ents. Wojtyła concludes, "The natural order of human existence is not in conflict with love between persons but in strict harmony with it."[790]

---

[788] Ibid., p. 52.
[789] Ibid., p. 53.
[790] Ibid., pp. 53-54.

Preview

ELEVEN NATURAL FAMILY PLANNING VIEWS MEN AND WOMEN: FREE PERSONAL SUBJECTS IN
    THEIR INVIOLABLE MYSTERY *(continued)*

II. True Human Love: Attraction, Affection, or Union of Persons? *(continued)*
    B. Love as Affection: The Emotions
        1. The Vital Role of Emotions in Life and Love
        2. The Ambivalence of Sentimental Love
        3. The Need to Integrate Love
    C. Love as Goodwill: The Unification of Persons
    D. Betrothed Love: The Gift of Self
        1. The Divine Aspect of Love: To Desire God for the Beloved
        2. Love Put to the Test

Points to look for

1. Why are the emotions so important in human life?

2. Why do the emotions play a vital role in elevating human love above the sensual sphere?

3. Why is sentimental love ambivalent and in itself an inadequate foundation for authentic human love?

4. What is the true base upon which an enduring relationship of married love can be built?

5. What is meant by "integrating" love?

6. What is love as goodwill?

7. How is betrothed love different from all other forms of love?

8. What is the divine aspect of authentic human love?

9. Why is it not always easy to discern whether love between a man and a woman is authentic or whether their relationship is based primarily upon sexual attraction and idealized affection?

10. What are the moments in which married love is most severely put to the test?

B. Love as Affection: The Emotions
1. The Vital Role of Emotions in Life and Love

Love as attraction (*amor complacentia*) or desire (*amor concupiscentia*) does not arise simply from the promptings of the sexual urge on a purely sensual plane. A man and woman's emotions also enter into play, endowing their experience of love with a strong affective content. Though emotions are in themselves sensory, they differ fundamentally from sense impressions. "A sense impression is a reaction to a content, an emotion is a reaction to a value."[791]

Affection performs a vital role in elevating human love above the sensual sphere, since it enables one who is in love to experience more

---

[791] Ibid., p. 103.

readily the value of the other as a person. Affectivity *per se* is important in living an intense and meaningful life, as Buttiglione points out. "The more an individual's affectivity is enriched, the more he will be in full and satisfying contact with the reality around him and the more this reality will seem to be worth loving and living. In affectivity, the values of reality reveal themselves and are lived with immediacy and transport."[792]

Though some sort of "material" image is always necessary to stir up an emotion, emotions can also arise in response to spiritual values. In fact, "When its object is a material value the emotion is shallower, more superficial. When, however, the object of an emotion is a supra-material, or spiritual value, it reaches more deeply into a man's psyche."[793] The emotion of someone from the Twin Cities sitting in the stands as the Minnesota Vikings, behind by four points, march down the field toward the goal-line in the final seconds of the Super Bowl can be quite powerful. But it remains at the surface of who he is as a person. Neither exuberance at a winning touchdown nor dismay at being stopped short of the goal line fundamentally alters the direction of his life. Compare that feeling with the emotion evoked by the following passage:

> On September 8, 1970, Nijole Sadunaite was sitting in a courtroom in Moletai, Lithuania. She was not the accused. A priest friend, Antanas Seskevicius, was being tried for the crime of having taught religion to children. . . . The officials removed all potential witnesses from the room, but made a special show of detaining Sadunaite: she had hired a lawyer from her meager earnings as a factory worker (the only kind of job a regular churchgoer could hold) to defend Father Seskevicius. . . .
>
> Sadunaite was . . . adamant when she was charged with "anti-Soviet agitation and propaganda". . . . [She] even succeeded in turning the tables on her captors, a rare feat in the Soviet Gulag. They accused her of mental illness since she was unrelenting in "slandering" the regime. But when she maintained her self-composure for months, they offered her freedom for just one statement that would incriminate her acquaintances. She replied: "If you gave me eternal youth and all the beautiful things in the world for one statement which would cause some trouble, then those years would turn into hell for me. Even if you kept me in the psychiatric hospital all my life, as long as I knew that no one had suffered on my account, I would go around smiling. A clear conscience is more precious than liberty or life. I do not understand how you, whose conscience is burdened by the spilled blood and tears of so many innocent

---

[792] Buttiglione, *Karol Wojtyła: The Thought of the Man Who Became John Paul II*, p. 100.
[793] Wojtyła, *Love and Responsibility*, p. 103.

people, can sleep at night. I would agree to die a thousand times rather than be free for one second with your conscience." At this retort, Major Vyatautas Pilelis, a notorious KGB agent who was questioning her, "blanched and hung his head."[794]

Four centuries before Nijole Sadunaite was alive to tell her story, a Spanish soldier named Ignatius of Loyola came upon similar accounts of heroism in a "Lives of the Saints" that fell into his hands, as he lay wounded in a hospital. The depth of the emotions stirred up in him, united with God's grace, transformed his superficial and worldly existence. He soon became a man of deep prayer. As Wojtyła notes, "The ability to experience emotions which are at once profound and powerful seems to constitute a particularly important factor in the interior life."[795] By founding the Jesuits and passing on to the Church the legacy of his spiritual exercises, St. Ignatius helped decide the course of Western Civilization.

The vital role of emotions in shaping life also comes into play in the development of love between a man and a woman. Love as emotional affection is necessary in order to elevate the sensual aspect of sexual attraction toward the sphere of the person. "Sensuality in itself is quite blind to the person, and oriented only towards the sexual value connected with 'the body.'"[796] The sentiments or emotions that give rise to affection, on the other hand, display a different inner content than sensuality. Sentimental love expresses itself above all in a desire to be near the person loved, in a longing for intimacy.

> Affection appears to be free from that concupiscence of which sensuality is full. In such an emotional state, though, a different sort of desire is discernible and a different need makes itself felt. This is the desire for nearness, for proximity, and simultaneously for exclusivity or intimacy, a longing to be always together. Sentimental love keeps two people close together, binds them — even if they are physically far apart — to move in each other's orbit.[797]

2. The Ambivalence of Sentimental Love

While emotions help to elevate human love, since they are directed toward the other as a person, and not merely toward his or her sexual qualities, sentimental love is not an adequate foundation for authentic love between husband and wife. Why is this so? Above all, because human persons in the fullness of their reality are both subjects and objects.

---

[794] Robert Royal, *The Catholic Martyrs of the Twentieth Century* (New York: Crossroad, 2000), pp. 243-244); citing Nijole Sadunaite, *A Radiance in the Gulag: The Catholic Witness of Nijole Sadunaite*, trans. Rev. Casmir Pugevicius and Marian Skabeikis (Manassas, Va.: Trinity Communications, 1987), p. 46.

[795] Wojtyła, *Love and Responsibility*, p. 103.

[796] Ibid., p. 108.

[797] Ibid., p. 110.

On the one hand, we are free, conscious subjects, and sentimental love is among the strongest subjective experiences possible. On the other hand, as subjects who are creatures, we do not have the power to create our own nature or that of the person who is loved. We have been endowed with an objective nature at the moment of conception, which must be respected, if we are to attain happiness and fulfillment. Authentic love must be founded upon the objective truth of who the man and the woman are, and also upon the objective truth of their mutual relationship.

Sentimental love, because it is such a subjective experience, tends to idealize the person who is loved. It often focuses more upon the inner emotions kindled by the blissful feeling of "being in love" than upon the actual qualities of the other person. "Thus in the eyes of a person sentimentally committed to another person the value of the beloved object grows enormously — as a rule out of all proportion to his or her real value."[798]

We can see how love as affection is not yet mature. In a certain sense it is still self-centered, turned in upon one's own emotions. What is loved is not so much the other person as he or she really is, but the emotional experience of being in love with an idealized figure who does not exist in reality. Sentimental love thus shows itself to be ambivalent. On the one hand, it desires intimacy with the beloved, but it does not really unite the two as persons, since it feeds itself upon an idealized image of the other. That is why a love based simply upon feelings can easily lead to disillusionment and even hatred, when the bubble of fantasy is burst. Wojtyła reflects on the weakness of love as affection.

> That form of love shows a characteristic ambivalence; it seeks to be near the beloved person, seeks proximity and expressions of tenderness, yet it is remote from the beloved in that it does not depend for its life on that person's true value, but on those values to which the subject clings as to its ideal. This is why sentimental love is very often a cause of disillusionment. . . . The discrepancy between the ideal and the reality often results in sentimental love fading or indeed changing into a feeling of hatred. Hatred in its turn is intrinsically ('by its very nature') unable to discern the values which really exist in the other person.[799]

3. The Need to Integrate Love

We have seen earlier that it is necessary to integrate the sensual desire of sexual attraction if authentic human love is to develop. The same is true for love as affection. What happens if integration fails to occur on either of these two levels?

---

[798] Wojtyła, *Love and Responsibility*, p. 112.
[799] Ibid., p. 113.

If "love" remains just sensuality, just a matter of "sex-appeal," it will not be love at all, but only the utilization of one person by another, or of two persons by each other, while if love remains mere sentiment it will equally be unlike love in the complete sense of the word. For both persons will remain in spite of everything divided from each other, though it may appear that they are very close just because they so eagerly seek proximity.[800]

If neither sexual attraction nor sentimental affection forms a solid foundation for authentic human love, what is the true base upon which an enduring relationship of married love can be built? Genuine love must be directed toward the other person just as he or she really is. It must also seek the good of the other person for his or her own sake. Only man's spiritual faculties of reason and will are capable of perceiving the objective truth of who the other person is and choosing the true good for that person. Freedom and truth alone provide the basis for integrating love, for elevating it to the sphere of the person. Buttiglione sums up well the strengths and limits of affection as an element of human love, along with the need for reason and will to truly direct love toward the person of the beloved.

Affectivity has an extraordinary importance for the moral life. . . . Without affectivity the moral life is thin and gray, and it inevitably turns into moralism. However, affectivity alone is not sufficient. It needs the standard of an objective judgment. Affectivity concentrates our attention on the values which the other provokes in us, rather than on those values which the other really possesses. And this is a weak base for love between persons. Personal love gains its maturity only when it turns itself away from what the other makes me feel, and toward what the other is in himself or herself, considering not this or that particular characteristic of the beloved which exercises a special charm upon us, but the person as such. Sexual attraction, the charm of femininity or masculinity, therefore becomes a path which leads to the emotional perception of the value of the person. Only the value of the person can sustain a stable relationship. The other values of sexuality are wasted away by time and are exposed to the danger of disillusion. But this is not the case for the value of the person, which is of a different ontological quality, one which is stable and in some way infinite. When love develops and reaches the person, then it is forever. This is why the conjugal covenant is indissoluble; it is a covenant of reciprocal giving founded on the recognition of the value of the person.[801]

---

[800] Ibid., pp. 113-114.
[801] Buttiglione, *Karol Wojtyła: The Thought of the Man Who Became John Paul II*, pp. 100-101.

C. Love as Goodwill: The Unification of Persons

When reason and free will move someone beyond the desire for another person as a good for himself, to seek only the good of the other person, we have reached the noblest form of human love: love as goodwill. Here we see confirmed in a special way Wojtyła's assertion: "Love is an activity, a deed which develops the existence of the person to its fullest."[802] Wojtyła describes the characteristics of what St. Thomas Aquinas called *amor benevolentiae* (benevolent love).

> Goodwill is quite free of self-interest, the traces of which are conspicuous in love as desire. *Goodwill is the same as selflessness in love*: not "I long for you as a good" but "I long for your good," "I long for that which is good for you." ... Love as goodwill, *amor benevolentiae*,[803] is, therefore, love in a more unconditional sense than love as desire. It is the purest form of love. Goodwill brings us as close to the "pure essence" of love as it is possible to get. Such love does more than any other to perfect the person who experiences it, bringing both the subject and the object of that love the greatest fulfillment.[804]

Sexual attraction and sentimental affection bring a man and a woman together. They provide the raw material for conjugal love. But only if reason and will integrate them, so that the other person is freely chosen for his or her own sake, does love enter the sphere of the person as such and become genuine human love. Only the will, under reason's guide, can channel the sensual tendency toward a utilitarian enjoyment of the body and overcome the subjective idealization of the emotions, in order to love the other person for his or her own sake, for who he or she really is as a person.

> The love for a person which results from a valid act of choice is concentrated on the value of the person as such and makes us feel emotional love for the person as he or she really is, not for the person of our imagination, but for the real person. We love the person complete with all his or her virtues and faults, and up to a point independently of those virtues and in spite of those faults.[805]

Only in a fully integrated relationship are a man and a woman truly united in all of the dimensions of their person, so that genuine human love is truly achieved. *"Love is the unification of persons."*[806]

D. Betrothed Love: The Gift of Self

Love as goodwill can be found in many different human relationships. It is the basis for authentic friendship, such as that between

---

[802] Wojtyła, *Love and Responsibility*, p. 82.
[803] "Benevolent love."
[804] Wojtyła, *Love and Responsibility*, pp. 83-84.
[805] Wojtyła, *Love and Responsibility*, p. 135.
[806] Ibid., p. 38.

Jonathan and David. The First Book of Samuel relates, "And Jonathan made David swear again by his love for him; for he loved him as he loved his own soul."[807] Authentic conjugal love must be founded upon love as goodwill, but it is a unique form of love that can exist only between husband and wife. What is the specific characteristic of conjugal or betrothed love? *The gift of one's entire self to another.* Not only does this gift of one's whole person affect in a unique way both husband and wife as subjects who love, but it also creates a distinctive form of interpersonal relationship, the basis for the institution of matrimony.

> Betrothed love differs from all the aspects or forms of love analyzed hitherto. Its decisive character is the giving of one's own person (to another). The essence of betrothed love is self-giving, the surrender of one's "I." This is something different from and more than attraction, desire or even goodwill. . . . "To give oneself to another" is something more than merely "desiring what is good" for another — even if as a result of this another "I" becomes as it were my own, as it does in friendship. Betrothed love is something different from and more than all the forms of love so far analyzed, both as it affects the individual subject, the person who loves, and as regards the interpersonal union which it creates. When betrothed love enters into this interpersonal relationship something more than friendship results: Two people give themselves each to the other.[808]

We have now considered the three dimensions of love between a man and a woman: sexual attraction, sentimental affection, and goodwill. We have also discovered how betrothed love differs from all other forms of human love. Our journey has brought us to our goal, making it possible to present a definitive description of authentic married love. "True love, a love that is internally complete, is one in which we choose the person for the sake of the person — that in which a man chooses a woman or a woman chooses a man not just as a sexual 'partner' but as the person on whom to bestow the gift of his or her own life."[809]

This noble vision of married love brings with it an exalted view of sexuality. The opposite is true of the contraceptive mentality, which "reduces human sexuality to the level of something commonplace, since it interprets and lives it in a reductive and impoverished way by linking it solely with the body and with selfish pleasure."[810] In John Paul II's vision of the person, the one which sustains the Church's teaching on natural family planning, sex is something much more splendid. Human sexuality is "truly and fully personal: for sexuality is an enrichment of

---

[807] 1 Sam 20:17.
[808] Wojtyła, *Love and Responsibility*, p. 96.
[809] Ibid, p. 134.
[810] John Paul II, *Familiaris Consortio*, 37.

the whole person — body, emotions and soul — and it manifests its inmost meaning in leading the person to the gift of self in love."[811]

1. The Divine Aspect of Love: To Desire God for the Beloved

Someone who deeply loves another person with a fully integrated, authentic human love desires above all that the other person be happy. To want happiness for someone means wanting unlimited good for that person, since no individual object or person on this earth, no matter how good, is able to satisfy the human heart's longing for happiness. Here, Wojtyła notes, it is possible to detect a divine aspect in human love. Even though many people do not come to recognize or even acknowledge this conclusion, to want happiness for another person really means to desire God for the beloved. "This is, so to speak, the divine aspect of love. In point of fact, to desire 'unlimited' good for another person is really to desire God for that person: He alone is the objective fullness of the good, and only His goodness can fill every man to overflowing."[812]

That genuine human love is touched by a divine element explains its creative power. Not by chance has the Church for centuries invoked the Holy Spirit, the Spirit of love between the Father and the Son, under the title "creating Spirit," in the liturgical hymn, *Veni, Creator Spiritus*.[813] Not only is authentic love able to create goodness and happiness for the beloved, but the one who loves is also born anew under the transforming influence of this highest of all human actions.

> The great moral force of true love lies precisely in this desire for the happiness, for the true good, of another person. This is what makes it possible for a man to be reborn because of love, makes him aware of the riches within him, his spiritual fertility and creativity: I am capable of desiring the good for another person, therefore I am in general capable of desiring the good. True love compels me to believe in my own spiritual powers. Even when I am "bad," if true love awakens in me it bids me seek the true good where the object of my love is concerned. In this way, affirmation of the worth of another person is echoed in the affirmation of the worth of one's person.[814]

2. Love Put to the Test

It is not always easy to discern whether there is authentic love between a man and a woman, or whether their relationship is primarily based upon sexual attraction and idealized affection. This is especially true since we can never consider genuine love to have been achieved once and for all. Love always presents itself as a task. "Love is never

---

[811] Ibid.
[812] Wojtyła, *Love and Responsibility*, p. 138.
[813] "Come, Creating Spirit."
[814] Wojtyła, *Love and Responsibility*, p. 138.

something ready made, something merely 'given' to man and woman; it is always at the same time a 'task' which they are set. Love should be seen as something which in a sense never 'is' but is always only 'becoming,' and what it becomes depends upon the contribution of both persons and the depth of their commitment.[815]

How, then, can a young man and woman who wish to commit their lives to one another in marriage be confident that their love is founded upon a free choice of the other person in goodwill — a love strong enough to endure until they are separated by death itself? Wojtyła reminds us of the one sure measure of love's authenticity: being put to the test. "We must never forget that only when love between human beings is put to the test can its true value be seen."[816] The Psalmist exclaims to the Lord, "If thou triest my heart, if thou visitest me by night, if thou testest me, thou wilt find no wickedness in me."[817]

If a young, engaged couple has been able to make sacrifices and overcome difficulties out of commitment to their relationship, they can feel reasonably secure that they are building their love on a solid foundation. During marriage, this love will be constantly subjected to trial by the daily struggles and tribulations life brings. Still, can it be said that one period of married life puts love to the test more than others? Is there a certain time when the inner value of that love is revealed, when "the secrets of many hearts are brought to light?" Wojtyła answers, "Yes."

> [Love] is put to the test most severely when the sensual and emotional reactions themselves grow weaker, and sexual values as such lose their effect. Nothing then remains except the value of the person, and the inner truth about the love of those concerned comes to light. If their love is a true gift of self, so that they belong to each other, it will not only survive but grow stronger, and sink deeper roots. Whereas if it was never more than a sort of synchronization of sensual and emotional experiences it will lose its *raison d'être* and the persons involved in it will suddenly find themselves in a vacuum.[818]

Another moment in which human love is keenly tested occurs when one of the partners does something wrong. It is precisely then that a love directed toward the other as a person and matured by the test of time reveals its inner strength. When one of the spouses falls, the other does not cease to love him — for he has not lost his value as a person. If anything, love grows more ardent, in a desire to win him back. Christ asks us in the Gospel, "What do you think? If a man has a

---

[815] Wojtyła, *Love and Responsibility*, p. 139.
[816] Ibid., p. 134.
[817] Psalm 17:3.
[818] Wojtyła, *Love and Responsibility*, p. 134.

hundred sheep and one of them has gone astray, does he not leave the ninety-nine on the hills and go in search of the one that went astray?"[819] Wojtyła reverently describes this love which is stronger than human weakness, stronger even than sin.

> The strength of such a love emerges most clearly when the beloved person stumbles, when his or her weaknesses or even sins come into the open. One who truly loves does not then withdraw his love, but loves all the more, loves in full consciousness of the other's shortcomings and faults, and without in the least approving of them. For the person as such never loses his essential value.[820]

[819] Mt 18:12.
[820] Wojtyła, *Love and Responsibility*, p. 135.

Preview

ELEVEN NATURAL FAMILY PLANNING VIEWS MEN AND WOMEN: FREE PERSONAL SUBJECTS IN THEIR INVIOLABLE MYSTERY (*continued*)

III. Chastity: The Indispensable Condition of Love
  A. Continence: Obstacle to Tenderness, Spontaneity, and Affection?
    1. The Accusation
    2. Temperance, Chastity, and Continence: Are They the Same?
  B. Continence: Condition for Authentic Tenderness, Spontaneity and Affection
    1. An Eminently Positive Virtue
    2. A Virtue that Fosters Tenderness and Affection
    3. Spontaneity of the Passions or the Person?
      a) Eros and Ethos: Called to Meet in the Human Heart
      b) Redemption: The Gift and Task of Conquering Spontaneity
    4. Living a True Communion of Persons

Points to look for

1. Why is chastity the indispensable condition of genuine human love?

2. What are the arguments leveled against periodic continence, which claim that it hinders authentic love between husband and wife?

3. What distinction can be made between temperance, chastity, and continence?

4. How does the virtue of chastity enable us to grow as persons?

5. How does NFP differ essentially from contraception with regard to the virtue of chastity?

6. Why is the depicting of continence as a repression of the sexual drive that leads to frustration a mere caricature of this virtue?

7. How does continence make possible the sublimation of the sexual urge — which is the opposite of repression?

8. Why is concupiscence, not continence, the real enemy of true human love?

9. What is tenderness?

10. How does periodic continence foster, rather than hinder, authentic tenderness between husband and wife?

11. How does periodic continence help safeguard the meaning of the act of sexual intercourse itself as an expression of affection between spouses?

12. Why is the accusation made that periodic continence inhibits spontaneity between husband and wife?

13. What two types of spontaneity must be distinguished with regard to married love?

14. What is eros? How does the Platonic concept of eros fit in well with Pope John Paul II's theology of the body?

15. What is ethos?

16. What does John Paul II mean when he affirms that eros and ethos are called to meet in the human heart?

17. Why is the mature spontaneity of the person both a gift and a task to be conquered?

III. Chastity: The Indispensable Condition of Love

We have already seen that the virtue of chastity is indispensable for integrating the sensual and affective dimensions of human love, elevating love to the sphere of the person. Through chastity a person exercises self-mastery over his passions, and his will is able to choose another person for his or her own sake. While sexual attraction provides the raw material for love, if not integrated by the will, it can easily degenerate into carnal concupiscence — the very opposite of love, in which the other person is treated as an object of sensual enjoyment.

Sentimental affection offers some safeguard against concupiscence, since it is directed toward the other as a human being, not toward mere sexual values. Still, the emotions bring with them the danger of idealization, an obstacle to truly loving the other as a person and a potential source of future disillusionment. "Idealization is an evasion of the problem, not an attempt to face and solve it."[821] A firmer foundation for authentic love than the emotions is needed.

"Complete security against carnal concupiscence is something we find only in the profound realism of virtue, and specifically the virtue of chastity."[822] Only someone who is able to exercise dominion over his sexual drive and channel his emotions, someone who possesses himself by means of chastity, is able to make a free gift of his very self and receive the gift of another. There can be no authentic conjugal love, no true unification of persons without chastity. Wojtyła sums up the need for chastity in order to achieve genuine human love.

---

[821] Wojtyła, *Love and Responsibility*, p. 152.
[822] Ibid.

Love cannot remain merely a subjective "situation" in which sensual and emotional energies aroused by the sexual urge make themselves felt. If it does, it cannot rise to the level appropriate to persons, and cannot unite persons. For love to attain its full personal value, and truly to unite a man and a woman, it must be firmly based on the affirmation of the value of the person. From this, it is a simple progression to the whole-hearted desire of the beloved person's good — a good worthy of the person. This is what gives love its character of a "bringer of happiness." Men and women desire love in anticipation of the happiness which it can bring into their lives.[823]

A. Continence:
Obstacle to Tenderness, Spontaneity, and Affection?
1. The Accusation

It is ironic that chastity, the virtue without which love between a man and a woman can never become fully personal and authentic, has come under the most severe attack by the proponents of contraception as being an enemy of love. The expression of chastity in periodic continence, essential for natural family planning, has been particularly assailed.

Margaret Sanger constantly asserted that contraception would bring true freedom to men and women precisely by allowing free reign to passion. Birth control, accompanied by the sweeping away of sexual moral norms, would provide a panacea for most of society's ills. "The moment civilization is wise enough to remove the constraints and prohibitions which now hinder the release of inner energies, most of the larger evils of society will perish of inanition and malnutrition."[824] Mary Shivanandan notes that Sanger did urge women to learn their monthly cycle — but only to make use of the rising tide of desire in their sex lives. She even predicted "nervous collapse" if women should attempt to avoid intercourse during their fertile time.[825]

Many voices less strident than Sanger's, some of them even within Catholic moral theology, have raised heated objections to periodic continence. The accusation runs along the following lines. Married couples who are not in a position to responsibly have children must abstain from sexual intercourse during the wife's fertile period. The need for abstinence inhibits husband and wife from engaging in spontaneous acts of affection and tenderness for one another. These demonstrations of affection could naturally lead to a dangerous intimacy and a desire for conjugal relations that could not be fulfilled. Both partners would thus

---

[823] Wojtyła, *Love and Responsibility*, p. 145.
[824] Sanger, *Pivot of Civilization*, p. 231; cited by Shivanandan, *Crossing the Threshold of Love*, p. 190.
[825] Cf. Shivanandan, *Crossing the Threshold of Love*, p. 189.

become frustrated. Instead of fostering married love, periodic abstinence must lead either to an increased coldness between husband and wife or sexual frustration.

Rocco Buttiglione summarizes well the attempt to clothe these existential objections with the elegant garments of a philosophical and moral stance opposed to chastity.

> If one accedes to a superficial interpretation of chastity it is easy to see it as an obstacle to love. According to this common perception, chastity keeps man constantly within himself while love takes him out of himself; in losing himself in an ecstatic situation, in a certain way, he loses self-control. Chastity, on such a view, would be the virtue which attempts to keep the person locked within a mediocre life, a life which is emptied of vitality and ultimately selfish.[826]

Wojtyła refers to the German phenomenologist philosopher Max Scheler as he notes that our present cultural climate, in giving rise to such objections, is one characterized by a real *resentment* toward the virtue of chastity.[827] Scheler spoke about resentment toward virtue in general among people today.

Just what exactly is resentment and how does it come about? "Resentment arises from an erroneous and distorted sense of values. It is a lack of objectivity in judgment and evaluation, and it has its origin in weakness of will."[828] Since attaining virtue is difficult, a weak will seeks to minimize its importance, even distorting the very meaning of virtue, so that it appears to be something evil. That way the individual can continue along the easy path, acknowledging as good only what is convenient to him and most pleasurable. "Resentment is a feature of the subjective mentality: pleasure takes the place of superior values."[829]

Before attempting to answer the apparently persuasive but actually specious objections to marital chastity, let us examine more closely the basic concepts involved.

2. Temperance, Chastity, and Continence: Are They the Same?

When we speak of temperance, chastity, and continence, are we referring to the same reality, simply with different terms? Though these virtues are related, they are not identical. The cardinal virtue of *temperance* is the most general, and encompasses both chastity and continence.

---

[826] Buttiglione, *Karol Wojtyła: The Thought of the Man Who Became John Paul II*, p. 106.
[827] Wojtyła's knowledge of Scheler's writings is most thorough, since Wojtyła's thesis for his second doctorate, this one in philosophy, was entitled: *An Evaluation of the Possibility of Constructing A Christian Ethics on the Basis of the System of Max Scheler*. Wojtyła's thesis was approved by the Jagiellonian University of Krakow in 1954. It enabled Wojtyła to begin teaching ethics at the Catholic University of Lublin in the fall of 1954.
[828] Wojtyła, *Love and Responsibility*, p. 143.
[829] Ibid., p. 144.

We have seen earlier that St. Thomas divides the emotions of man's sensitive appetite into two groups: the irascible and the concupiscible passions.[830] "Temperance is a virtue which moderates and restrains the concupiscible appetite and chastity is the virtue which moderates and restrains the concupiscible appetite insofar as it directs itself to sexual objects."[831]

The *Catechism* gives a precise definition of temperance, "which seeks to permeate the passions and appetites of the senses with reason."[832] Clearly temperance plays an essential role in what it means to be a person: exercising the capacity for self-possession and self-determination.

> *Temperance* is the moral virtue that moderates the attraction of pleasures and provides balance in the use of created goods. It ensures the will's mastery over instincts and keeps desires within the limits of what is honorable. The temperate person directs the sensitive appetites toward what is good, and maintains a healthy discretion.[833]

Under the general virtue of temperance, and referring directly to self-dominion in the sexual sphere, is *chastity*. Once again we can rely on the *Catechism* for a precise description of this virtue and its vital role in enabling one to live up to the fullness of personal dignity. There can be little doubt that the following two numbers of the *Catechism* have been inspired by John Paul II's personalism.

> Chastity means the successful integration of sexuality within the person and thus the inner unity of man in his bodily and spiritual being. Sexuality, in which man's belonging to the bodily and biological world is expressed, becomes personal and truly human when it is integrated into the relationship of one person to another, in the complete and lifelong mutual gift of a man and a woman.

> The virtue of chastity therefore involves the integrity of the person and the integrality of the gift.[834]

> Chastity includes an *apprenticeship in self-mastery* which is a training in human freedom. The alternative is clear: either man governs his passions and finds peace, or he lets himself be dominated by them and becomes unhappy.[835] "Man's dignity therefore requires him to act out of conscious and free choice, as moved and drawn in a personal way from within, and not by blind impulses in himself or by

---

[830] *Summa Theologiae*, I-II, q. 23, a. 1.

[831] Buttiglione, *Karol Wojtyła: The Thought of the Man Who Became John Paul II*, p. 106; referring to *Summa Theologiae* II-II, q. 143, a. 1.

[832] *CCC*, 2341.

[833] *CCC*, 1809.

[834] *CCC*, 2337.

[835] Cf. Sir 1:22.

mere external constraint. Man gains such dignity when, ridding himself of all slavery to the passions, he presses forward to his goal by freely choosing what is good and, by his diligence and skill, effectively secures for himself the means suited to this end."[836]

All the baptized are called to chastity in following Christ, but there are three different ways of living this virtue, depending on one's particular vocation. "'People should cultivate [chastity] in the way that is suited to their state of life. Some profess virginity or consecrated celibacy which enables them to give themselves to God alone with an undivided heart in a remarkable manner. Others live in the way prescribed for all by the moral law, whether they are married or single.'[837] Married people are called to live conjugal chastity; others practice chastity in continence."[838]

The virtue of *continence* refers to the specific form of living chastity that entails refraining from sexual intercourse. More broadly, it implies the ability to exercise self-dominion over the passions and the sexual urge through the will. John Paul II offers a technical definition. "Continence consists in the capacity to dominate, control and direct drives of a sexual character (concupiscence of the flesh) and their consequences, in the psychosomatic subjectivity of man. Insofar as it is a constant disposition of the will, this capacity merits being called a virtue."[839]

Natural family planning requires married couples to practice chastity under the form of periodic continence. "Pope Paul VI refers to conjugal chastity when he writes that the observance of periodic continence is the form of self-mastery in which conjugal chastity is manifested."[840] Here we see one of the essential differences between NFP and contraception. Artificial birth control eliminates the need for chastity, giving sensuality free reign to dominate the conjugal relations between the spouses. By calling husband and wife to scale the heights of virtue, NFP respects their dignity as persons and challenges them to live up to personhood in its fullness.

B. Continence: Condition for Authentic Tenderness, Spontaneity and Affection
1. An Eminently Positive Virtue

One of the reasons resentment has built up toward the virtue of continence is because it is often portrayed in a negative light. Continence means abstaining from sex, repressing the sexual drive — synonyms for

---

[836] CCC, 2339; citing GS, 17.
[837] Congregation for the Doctrine of the Faith, *Persona humana*, 11.
[838] CCC, 2349.
[839] John Paul II, General Audience of October 24, 1984, in *The Theology of the Body*, p. 408.
[840] John Paul II, General Audience of August 28, 1984, in Ibid., p.400; referring to *Humanae Vitae*, 21.

frustration. This is a very superficial understanding of continence, a mere caricature, as John Paul II explains.

> Continence is not only, and not even principally, the ability to abstain, that is, mastery over the multiple reactions that are interwoven in the mutual influence of masculinity and femininity. Such a role would be defined as negative. But there is also another role (which we can call positive) of self-mastery. It is the ability to direct the respective reactions, both as to their content and their character.[841]

> It is well to recall that the great classics of ethical (and anthropological) thought, both the pre-Christian ones and the Christian ones (St. Thomas Aquinas), see in the virtue of continence not only the capacity to contain bodily and sensual reactions, but even more the capacity to control and guide man's whole sensual and emotive sphere.[842]

> Since continence enables an individual to guide his sensual and emotional realm, this virtue is the path for elevating one's sexuality into the sphere of the person. We personalize our sexual instincts and emotions by sublimating them. "Sublimation is precisely the process through which energy which was initially bound to an inferior value turns toward superior values."[843]

Sublimation, made possible by continence, is the opposite of repression. The sexual urge and emotional attraction are not frustrated, they are purified of concupiscence and egotism, so they may be drawn upward toward the value of the other person as such. "To the degree that the person allows himself to be penetrated by the fascination of objective value, the energy of affectivity and even of sexuality turns toward it."[844]

Thus, the true enemy of love is not continence, but rather concupiscence, which blinds us to the true value of the person in its craving for sensual gratification. By giving us the strength to overcome concupiscence, the virtue of continence makes love possible. "Concupiscence of the flesh itself, insofar as it seeks above all carnal and sensual satisfaction, makes man in a certain sense blind and insensitive to the most profound values that spring from love and which at the same time constitute love in the interior truth that is proper to it."[845]

2. A Virtue that Fosters Tenderness and Affection

We have just pondered the indispensable and eminently positive role of continence in enabling a man and woman to rise to a love that is

---

[841] John Paul II, General Audience of October 31, 1984, in *The Theology of the Body*, p. 412.
[842] John Paul II, General Audience of November 7, 1984, in *The Theology of the Body*, p. 413.
[843] Buttiglione, *Karol Wojtyła: The Thought of the Man Who Became John Paul II*, p. 110.
[844] Ibid.
[845] John Paul II, General Audience of October 24, 1984, in *The Theology of the Body*, p. 409.

truly personal. With this foundation, it becomes apparent how falla-cious is the claim that periodic continence reduces tenderness between husband and wife. What precisely do we mean when we speak of a love that is tender? Wojtyła responds, *"Tenderness is the ability to feel with and for the whole person,* to feel even the most deeply hidden spiritual trem-ors, and always to have in mind the true good of that person."[846]

Since tenderness arises from the sentiments and not from sensuality, it is directed toward another as a human being, and not simply toward the body. Tenderness seeks to be near the other, and entails "an inner ca-pacity for compassion, for sensitive awareness of another person's feel-ings and state of mind."[847] But tenderness is more than this. Its essence lies in "the tendency to make one's own the feelings and mental states of another person."[848]

Far from diminishing marital tenderness, periodic continence strongly fosters it. A certain firmness of the will must always accom-pany manifestations of tenderness; otherwise, they could degenerate into sickly sentimentalism and merely serve to disguise an egotistical desire for sensual or emotional gratification that is not really concerned with the true good of the other person. The self-dominion of continence ensures the sincerity of expressions of tender affection for the other spouse. When sexual intercourse is excluded during times of absti-nence, husband and wife often discover new ways of displaying tender-ness toward one another.

The testimony of one couple confirms this experience. "In sexual ab-stinence we find the challenge to *truly* love one another and care for each other in ways and on levels which without abstinence we would never be challenged to attain."[849] Buttiglione sums up the moral and an-thropological principles which ground this common experience of in-creased tenderness among couples who practice natural family plan-ning.

> The experience of tenderness, which emerges from the integration of the emotional aspects into the personal whole, presupposes con-tinence and initiates the fully human way to live one's sexuality; the emotional and sensual dynamics of the relationship are contextualized within the respect and reciprocal welcoming of man and woman as well as the requirement of recognizing and respect-ing the other as a person and not as a mere object of one's enjoy-ment within the sexual act.[850]

---

[846] Wojtyła, *Love and Responsibility*, p. 207.
[847] Ibid., p. 201.
[848] Ibid.
[849] *Stepping Stones* (Summer 1992): 2; cited by Shivanandan, *Crossing the Threshold of Love*, p. 265.
[850] Buttiglione, *Karol Wojtyła: The Thought of the Man Who Became John Paul II*, pp. 110-111.

Just as continence enhances tenderness between husband and wife by opening them to higher personal values, so too does it enrich their affection for one another. It enables them to perceive more deeply the nuptial meaning of the body in diverse aspects not directly leading to sexual intercourse. During periods of abstinence, the wife especially experiences the joy of receiving spontaneous signs of affection from her husband that she knows are disinterested — just for her as a person. John Paul II describes how conjugal chastity leads the spouses to greater simplicity and a deeper personal intimacy in their relationship.

> In the light of these considerations it is easy to understand that continence is not limited to offering resistance to the concupiscence of the flesh. But through this resistance it is open likewise to those values, more profound and more mature, inherent in the spousal significance of the body in its femininity and masculinity, as well as in the authentic freedom of the gift in the reciprocal relations of the persons.

> Conjugal chastity (and chastity in general) is manifested at first as the capacity to resist the concupiscence of the flesh. It later gradually reveals itself as a singular capacity to perceive, love and practice those meanings of the language of the body which remain altogether unknown to concupiscence itself. Those meanings progressively enrich the marital dialogue of the couple, purifying it, deepening it, and at the same time simplifying it.

> Therefore, that asceticism of continence, which the encyclical speaks of (cf. *HV*, 21), does not impoverish affective manifestations. But rather it makes them spiritually more intense and therefore enriches them.[851]

Besides encouraging fresh signs of affection between husband and wife and enriching their spiritual content, periodic continence also safeguards the unitive meaning of sexual intercourse itself as a singular act of affection. John Paul II refers to *Humanae Vitae*'s teaching: "In keeping with experience and tradition, the encyclical reveals that the conjugal act is also a 'manifestation of affection' (*HV*, 16). But it is a 'manifestation of particular affection' because at the same time it has a potentially procreative meaning."[852]

Periodic continence not only respects the procreative meaning of the conjugal act, but it also ensures that this act will be a truly personal one of mutual self-giving, not merely a surrender to selfish, sensual gratification. One of the ways periodic continence helps husband and wife to achieve this challenging ideal is by building up their personal communion through fostering creative acts of affection that are not simply foreplay to sexual intercourse.

---

[851] John Paul II, General Audience of October 24, 1984, in *The Theology of the Body*, p. 409.
[852] Ibid., p. 410.

The role of conjugal chastity, and still more precisely that of continence, lies not only in protecting the importance and dignity of the conjugal act in relation to its procreative meaning. But it also lies in safeguarding the importance and the dignity proper to the conjugal act as expressive of interpersonal union, revealing to the awareness and the experience of the couple all the other possible manifestations of affection that can express this profound communion of theirs.

It is indeed a matter of not doing harm to the communion of the couple in the case where for just reasons they should abstain from the conjugal act. Still more, this communion — continually being built up, day by day, through suitable affective manifestations — may constitute a vast terrain on which, under suitable conditions, the decision for a morally right conjugal act matures.[853]

3. Spontaneity of the Passions or of the Person?

A final accusation leveled against periodic continence is that it inhibits spontaneity between husband and wife. Both must walk on tiptoes, as it were, treating each other very gingerly during the wife's fertile period, so as to avoid any amorous acts that would spontaneously arise if nature were allowed to take its course.

Here a fundamental question must be posed: Just what do we mean by spontaneity? If we are referring to the spontaneous tendency of the sexual urge to seek gratification in the act of conjugal union, then continence certainly inhibits this sort of spontaneity. If acting spontaneously signifies giving free reign to the natural tendency of carnal concupiscence to seek its own satisfaction in sensual pleasure — treating the body of the other spouse as an object for manipulation — then once again periodic continence definitely impedes spontaneity.

But there exists a far deeper kind of spontaneity — the only type worthy of the human person as such. It arises from the depths of one's inner, personal center. It moves husband and wife to perceive in the other's body the beauty of its nuptial meaning and the value of a person who deserves the gift of one's entire self. This type of spontaneity does not come easily to our fallen human nature. It must be fought for and conquered over the sometimes-bitter protests of concupiscence. This kind of spontaneity can be achieved only when eros and ethos meet in the human heart.

a) *Eros* and *Ethos*: Called to Meet in the Human Heart

In universal literature, the term "eros" carries with it many different shades of meaning. "Erotic" experiences often refer exclusively to those overtly sexual and sensual in character. John Paul II assumes the philo-

---

[853] Ibid., p. 410

sophical content of eros as expounded by the Greek philosopher Plato, contrasting it with the common meaning. "According to Plato, eros represents the interior force that drags man toward everything good, true and beautiful. This attraction indicates, in this case, the intensity of a subjective act of the human spirit. In the common meaning, on the contrary — as also in literature — this attraction seems to be first and foremost of a sensual nature."[854] The Holy Father further clarifies the meaning of eros for Plato in an illuminating footnote.

> According to Plato, man, placed between the world of the senses and the world of Ideas, has the destiny of passing from the first to the second. The world of Ideas, however, is not able by itself to overcome the world of the senses. Only eros, congenital in man, can do that. . . . Eros, in fact, is the guiding of the "sensual" or "sensitive" man toward what is transcendent: the force that directs the soul toward the world of Ideas. In the Symposium, Plato describes the stages of this influence of eros: the latter raises man's soul from the beauty of a single body to that of all bodies, and so to the beauty of knowledge and finally to the very idea of Beauty (cf. *Symposio* 211; *Repubblica* 514).
>
> Eros is neither purely human nor divine: it is something intermediate (*daimonion*) and intermediary. Its principal characteristic is permanent aspiration and desire. Even when it seems to give freely, eros persists as the "desire of possessing." Yet it is different from purely sensual love, being the love that strives toward the sublime. . . .
>
> The aspiration to transcendence is, therefore, a constituent element of the Platonic concept of eros.[855]

We can see how well the Platonic concept of eros fits in with John Paul II's theology of the body. It is precisely man's physical body which reveals the spiritual world and, ultimately, God himself. By perceiving the nuptial meaning of the body, husband and wife are able to elevate their love from the merely sensual plane to a personal and spiritual one. For John Paul II, erotic experiences are not meant to be purely sensual. "Erotic phenomena are those mutual actions and ways of behaving through which man and woman approach each other and unite so as to be one flesh (cf. Gn 2:24)."[856]

Before considering the relationship between eros and ethos, let us review briefly what the Holy Father means by the latter concept. "It embraces in its content the complex spheres of good and evil, depending on human will and subject to the laws of conscience and the sensitivity

---

[854] John Paul II, General Audience of November 5, 1980, in *The Theology of the Body*, p. 169.
[855] Ibid., Footnote 65, pp. 186-187.
[856] Ibid., p. 170.

of the human heart."[857] In other words, *ethos* goes beyond *ethics*, which outlines a set of moral principles or values. Ethos includes these moral principles as embodied not only in the guiding beliefs of a people, but also within their character and sentiments, within their very moral nature as individuals or a group.

What relationship should exist between eros and ethos, between the sphere of sensual attraction and the realm of doing what is right, in the human person redeemed by Christ? Here the splendor of the truth about redeemed man begins to shine forth in all its radiance. If eros means "the interior force that attracts man toward what is good, true, and beautiful,"[858] is it really opposed to ethos, to doing what is right? Only the lust of the flesh, by deforming eros into the pursuit of selfish, sensual gratification, brings it into conflict with ethos.

But Christ has died for us in agony upon the cross and has risen from the dead. The transforming power of his redemption gives us the strength to overcome concupiscence in the hidden depths of our inner desires, in the secret of our heart. That is precisely the appeal that Christ makes in his Sermon on the Mount. "Everyone who looks at a woman lustfully has already committed adultery with her in his heart."[859] Christ's words mean that "in the erotic sphere, eros and ethos do not differ from each other. They are not opposed to each other, but are called to meet in the human heart, and, in this meeting, to bear fruit. What is worthy of the human heart is that the form of what is erotic should be at the same time the form of ethos, that is, of what is ethical."[860]

The fourth Preface for Easter in the *Roman Missal* proclaims:

> "In him a new age has dawned,
> the long reign of sin is ended,
> a broken world has been renewed,
> and man is once again made whole."[861]

It is no wonder that once, when asked to sum up the central content of his entire pontificate, John Paul II replied with a single word: "Redemption!" Nor is it surprising that his first, programmatic encyclical bears the title *Redemptor Hominis* — The Redeemer of Man!

b) Redemption: The Gift and Task of Conquering Spontaneity

By practicing periodic continence, husband and wife can attain true spontaneity, one that promptly recognizes "in what is erotic the nuptial

---

[857] Ibid., p. 169.
[858] Ibid., p. 170.
[859] Mt 5:28.
[860] John Paul II, General Audience of November 5, 1980, in *The Theology of the Body*, p. 171.
[861] *The Roman Missal* (New York: Catholic Book Publishing Co., 1985), p. 421.

meaning of the body and the true dignity of the gift."[862] For them to do so is not easy. True spontaneity arising from the depths of the person and responding to the authentic value of another human being continually presents itself as a task to be conquered. That it is possible to do so is a gift flowing from Christ's redemption.

What happens when the spontaneity of the passions is indulged and the quest for the more arduous spontaneity of the person is abandoned? "The attraction of the senses and the passion of the body may stop at mere lust devoid of ethical value. Then man, male and female, does not experience that fullness of eros, which means the aspiration of the human spirit toward what is true, good and beautiful, so that what is erotic also becomes true, good and beautiful." That is why, the Holy Father concludes, "it is indispensable that ethos should become the constituent form of eros."[863]

How can spouses achieve a full and mature spontaneity in "the relations that spring from the perennial attraction of masculinity and femininity"?[864] The Holy Father answers based on extensive pastoral experience with many married couples: "This spontaneity is the gradual fruit of the discernment of the impulses of one's own heart."[865] To discern these impulses is not always easy, since the "variants and nuances of the internal movements of the heart can, within a certain limit, be confused with one another."[866] Still, the testimony of countless holy men and women proves that the task can be achieved. It is one eminently worthy of the human person.

But discerning one's own interior impulses is only the first step toward achieving a mature spontaneity of the person. The Christian asceticism of self-denial is necessary in order to attain dominion over the flesh's tendency toward lust and rise to the freedom of the gift, to an authentic spontaneity in the truth of love that sets the human heart free.

> It is precisely at the price of self-control that man reaches that deeper and more mature spontaneity with which his heart, mastering his instincts, rediscovers the spiritual beauty of the sign constituted by the human body in its masculinity and femininity. Since this discovery is enhanced in the conscience as conviction, and in the will as guidance both of possible choices and of mere desires, the human heart becomes a participant in another spontaneity, of which "carnal man" knows nothing or very little. There is no doubt

---

[862] John Paul II, General Audience of November 12, 1980, in *The Theology of the Body*, p. 171.
[863] Ibid.
[864] Ibid., p. 172.
[865] Ibid.
[866] Ibid.

that through Christ's words according to Matthew 5:27-28, we are called precisely to such spontaneity.[867]

4. Living a True Communion of Persons

Where does authentic spontaneity, born of self-knowledge and self-mastery through the practice of continence, ultimately lead husband and wife? It makes possible a true communion of persons — a communion that is the fulfillment of the nuptial meaning of the body, and an anticipation of that happiness for which every human heart has been made: communion with the Father, Son, and Holy Spirit forever in heaven.

> As we know from the biblical and theological analyses we have previously done, the human body in its masculinity and femininity is interiorly ordered to the communion of the persons (*communio personarum*). Its spousal meaning consists in this. The spousal meaning of the body has been distorted, almost at its roots, by concupiscence (especially by the concupiscence of the flesh in the sphere of the threefold concupiscence). The virtue of continence in its mature form gradually reveals the pure aspect of the spousal meaning of the body. In this way, continence develops the personal communion of the man and the woman, a communion that cannot be formed and developed in the full truth of its possibilities only on the level of concupiscence. This is precisely what *Humanae Vitae* affirms.[868]

In the splendor of the truth about married love, how pallid seem the objections against chastity, especially in the form of periodic continence, as an obstacle to tenderness, affection, and spontaneity! Buttiglione sums up the matter well. Far from being a hindrance, chastity is an indispensable condition for authentic human love.

> Chastity is therefore opposed to love only if one makes love synonymous with what happens in sensuality and affectivity. If one places the essence of love in freedom and the will, chastity is an indispensable condition of love. . . . It is an essentially different thing to be carried away by passion and to engage oneself by recognizing in the value of the other something which merits true dedication. In the latter case freedom is superseded, but in a deeper sense it is also maintained and achieves its maximum realization.

> If we strictly connect chastity with love we see how mistaken is the belief that chastity consists in a negation of the value of sex and of the body or that it is a negative attitude, such as an obligation to abstain. On the contrary, chastity engages one in a correct appreciation of the value of the body and of sex, which are perceived in

---

[867] Ibid., p. 173.
[868] John Paul II, General Audience of November 7, 1984, in *The Theology of the Body*, p. 414-415.

their truth only insofar as they are related to the person. These values are esteemed and loved as the quality of the person. . . . Moreover, chastity does not require a merely negative attitude. It consists of a fundamental assent to the value of love, from which follows a series of denials, directed to protecting the possibility of a full development of this love.[869]

---

[869] Buttiglione, *Karol Wojtyła: The Thought of the Man Who Became John Paul II*, p. 107.

Preview

Eleven Natural Family Planning Views Men and Women: Free Personal Subjects in their Inviolable Mystery *(continued)*

IV. Contraception *vs.* Natural Family Planning: The Essential Moral Difference
    A. Essential Difference in the Act
        1. The Three Factors of Morality
            a) The Object
            b) The Intention
            c) The Circumstances
        2. Good and Evil Acts
            a) Three to One: It Is Harder to Do Good than to Commit Evil
            b) Intrinsically Evil Acts
        3. Why a Contraceptive Act is Essentially Different from Intercourse Only During the Infertile Periods
    B. Essential Difference in Attitudes
        1. Attitude Toward Procreation: Openness to Life
            a) Chastity Must Be a Moral Virtue, Not Just a Technique
            b) How To Practice Periodic Continence as a Virtue
        2. Attitude Toward One's Spouse: Love and Responsibility
        3. Attitude Toward God: "Respect for the Creator"
V. Conclusion: The Future of Humanity

Points to look for

1. What is the essential anthropological difference between contraception and natural family planning?

2. What are some moral implications of the two fundamentally opposed anthropologies underlying contraception and NFP — especially with regard to the attitudes they engender toward moral virtues?

3. Among all earthly creatures, why are human persons alone capable of performing moral actions?

4. What are the three sources that determine whether an act is morally good or evil?

5. How is the object of a moral act defined?

6. What is the intention of a moral act?

7. What is the relation between the intentions of our acts and holiness?

8. How do the circumstances contribute to the goodness or evil of a moral act?

9. Why does it seem easier to fall into moral evil than to do what is morally good?

10. What is meant by *intrinsically evil acts*? What are some concrete examples?

11. How does contraception violate both the procreative and the unitive meaning of the conjugal act, making the resulting act intrinsically evil?

12. How does contraception change the intention of the spouses in the conjugal act, degrading the act from the level of persons to that of mere sensuality?

13. Why is refraining from sexual intercourse during the wife's fertile periods essentially different from contraception?

14. What are three essential moral attitudes in the virtuous practice of NFP?

15. What is the difference between chastity as a moral virtue and as a technique?

IV. Contraception *vs.* Natural Family Planning: The Essential Moral Difference

We have already pondered the essential anthropological difference between contraception and natural family planning — they are sustained by two irreconcilable views of the human person. The rationalist anthropology underlying contraception treats men and women as numerical, individual members of the human species. The horizon of their life is completely immanent; the most profound and sacred act of love between husband and wife becomes nothing more than an erotic fulfillment of the sexual urge. In the end, persons are reduced to utilitarian objects for manipulation.

The anthropology that gives rise to natural family planning, on the other hand, respects the transcendent dimension of the human person. The inner personal meaning of the conjugal act, in the inseparable connection between procreation and unitive love, expresses the transcendent capacity of husband and wife to enter into personal communion, not only with each other, but also with God.

Various moral implications of these two conflicting anthropologies have also come to light. The contraceptive mentality builds up resentment toward the virtues, especially chastity. By failing to respect the inner personal meaning of the conjugal act, contraception reduces what should be a loving self-surrender to an egotistical utilization of the other spouse for sensual gratification.

In the anthropology that sustains natural family planning, the practice of the virtues, chastity in particular, is vital for attaining the self-mastery that characterizes what it means to be a person. Respect for the procreative and unitive meaning of the conjugal act ensures that it embodies a true self-giving in personal communion. Adherence to the natural law, from which the prohibition against contraception derives, represents obedience and piety toward God, personal author of the natural order of creation.

Some advocates of contraception attempt to claim, however, that there is really no essential moral difference between artificially suppressing procreation in the conjugal act and natural family planning. In both cases the spouses have the same intention: to prevent a child from being born. The two methods simply represent different techniques for achieving the same purpose. In order to refute this claim, it is necessary to examine more closely both the conjugal act itself and the fundamental attitudes which underlie the act in natural family planning as opposed to contraception. This analysis will make it clear that the moral contrast between the two forms of regulating birth could not possibly be starker.

A. Essential Difference in the Act
1. The Three Factors of Morality

Before clarifying the essential moral difference between a contraceptive act and a loving act of conjugal union when spouses practice natural family planning, it would be helpful to make a preliminary consideration. Let us suppose we are hiking through the green hills of Umbria, not far from Assisi, on a sun-drenched spring morning, and we come across a shepherd pasturing his flock. Pleased at the unexpected relief from his solitude, the shepherd begins to tell us about his fine golden collie, who just three days past risked his life defending the sheep against a stray pack of wolves.

We might feel moved to exclaim, "What a courageous dog you have!" We may even call him a very "good" dog. But we certainly would not mean by our expressions that the collie possesses the moral virtue of courage, or that his acts of fending off the wolves were morally good. The ability to perform moral actions is reserved to human persons alone. What is it, precisely, about man that makes him the only moral actor upon the stage of earthly existence? The *Catechism* offers an exact reply. "Freedom makes man a moral subject. When he acts deliberately, man is, so to speak, the *father of his acts*. Human acts, that is, acts that are freely chosen in consequence of a judgment of conscience, can be morally evaluated. They are either good or evil."[870]

Freedom lies at the very heart of the drama that is human life. It makes us responsible for our actions. With each free act we not only change the world around us, we also change who we are as persons. Every time we choose the good, we become a better person; we draw closer to fulfilling our destiny. Each time we choose to act in an evil way, we are diminished as persons. "Thus we are in a certain way our own parents, creating ourselves as we will, by our decisions."[871]

---

[870] *CCC*, 1749.
[871] St. Gregory of Nyssa, *De Vita Moysis*, 11, 2-3: *PG* 44, pp. 327-328; cited in *Veritatis Splendor*, 71.

If freedom causes our actions to be moral, just what is it that determines whether an act is morally good or evil? There are three sources of morality: the object of the act, the intention, and the circumstances. Each must be carefully considered.

a) The Object

"The *object* chosen is a good toward which the will deliberately directs itself. It is the matter of a human act."[872] Of the three factors determining the morality of human acts, the object is the most decisive. "The morality of the human act depends primarily and fundamentally on the 'object' rationally chosen by the deliberate will."[873] In speaking of the object of an act, we are not referring to a material thing or even to an event that is merely physical in nature.

When two male teenage students perpetrated the tragedy at Columbine High School, one of them held a gun to the head of a young girl who was a fellow student and asked whether she was a Christian. After a moment's pause, she answered, "Yes." Then he pulled the trigger. The object of that heroic young woman's act was not simply to physically pronounce the word "yes." It was the freely chosen act of bearing witness to her faith in Christ at the cost of her own life.

Because the object of the act was good, the young woman's will was made good in choosing it, and she was perfected as a person. She became a martyr for her faith. "The object chosen morally specifies the act of the will, insofar as reason recognizes and judges it to be or not to be in conformity with the true good. Objective norms of morality express the rational order of good and evil, attested to by conscience."[874] John Paul II describes the object of a moral act from the perspective of the acting person in his 1993 encyclical *Veritatis Splendor*.

> The object of the act of willing is in fact a freely chosen kind of behavior. To the extent that it is in conformity with the order of reason, it is the cause of the goodness of the will; it perfects us morally, and disposes us to recognize our ultimate end in the perfect good, primordial love. By the object of a given moral act, then, one cannot mean a process or an event of the merely physical order to be assessed on the basis of its ability to bring about a given state of affairs in the outside world. Rather, that object is the proximate end of a deliberate decision which determines the act of willing on the part of the acting person.[875]

---

[872] CCC, 1751.
[873] *Veritatis Splendor*, 78.
[874] CCC, 1751.
[875] *VS*, 78.

b) **The Intention**

"In contrast to the object, the *intention* resides in the acting subject. Because it lies at the voluntary source of an action and determines it by its end, intention is an element essential to the moral evaluation of an action."[876] The fact that the object and the subjective intention constitute the essential elements in evaluating the moral goodness or evil of human acts confirms anew John Paul II's fundamental anthropology. Human persons are at one and the same time free, conscious *subjects* endowed with an *objective* nature to which they must conform their actions in order to attain happiness and fulfillment.

The intention is the end or purpose that our will seeks in performing a given action. It is the goal of the action. The object of the act answers the question, "*What?*" What is the nature of the act I am about to perform? The intention, on the other hand, answers the question, "*Why?*" Why do I want to perform this particular act? What is the goal I hope to achieve? The *Catechism* defines quite thoroughly the intention of an act. "The intention is a movement of the will toward the end: it is concerned with the goal of the activity. It aims at the good anticipated from the action undertaken."[877]

Intentions are vital in determining the effect of an act on the subject who performs it. A single intention is capable of guiding many different actions. In the course of her life, Mother Teresa of Calcutta comforted an untold number of dying persons from every faith and ethnic background. But all of these actions were motivated by one sole intention: Mother Teresa saw Christ suffering in each person and sought to alleviate his agony. Her intention of love for Christ, fruit of supernatural grace, has made her a universally acclaimed saint.

At the same time, a single act may be motivated by several intentions. Christ exhorts us in the Gospel, "And when you pray, you must not be like the hypocrites; for they love to stand and pray in the synagogues and at the street corners, that they may be seen by men. Truly, I say to you, they have their reward. But when you pray, go into your room and shut the door and pray to your Father who is in secret; and your Father who sees in secret will reward you."[878]

Only through asceticism, vigilant examination of our motives, and patient acceptance of the sufferings and purifications God sends us throughout our life can we approach true holiness. Saints are not remote, inaccessible figures. They are simply persons who direct all their acts to God with purity of intention, desiring only to love him and all those whom he has redeemed. Every Christian is called to this holiness,

---

[876] *CCC*, 1752.
[877] Ibid.
[878] Mt 6:5-6.

as the Dogmatic Constitution on the Church *Lumen Gentium* reminds us. "All the faithful, whatever their condition or state, are called by the Lord, each in his own way, to that perfect holiness whereby the Father himself is perfect."[879]

c) The Circumstances

The circumstances which surround a free human action enter as the third factor affecting its moral value. Unlike the object and the intention, circumstances are a secondary element in the morality of an act. In themselves, circumstances can never determine whether an action is morally good or evil. Their effect on a human act is limited to increasing or diminishing its goodness or evil.

> The *circumstances*, including the consequences, are secondary elements of a moral act. They contribute to increasing or diminishing the moral goodness or evil of human acts (for example, the amount of a theft). They can also diminish or increase the agent's responsibility (such as acting out of a fear of death). Circumstances of themselves cannot change the moral quality of acts themselves; they can make neither good nor right an action that is in itself evil.[880]

The good or bad consequences of an action are one particular type of circumstance. The moral theory known as "proportionalism" seeks to give a decisive weight to an action's consequences, asserting that it is impossible to determine whether an action is morally good or evil in itself, without first weighing the proportion between the good and bad consequences following from the act. We have already seen that proportionalism emerged in large part out of opposition to *Humanae Vitae's* teaching.[881] Were this theory to hold sway, it would not only eliminate the Ten Commandments as the basis of Christian moral life, but also all objective norms of conduct, which form the foundation of civil society itself.

We have considered earlier the critique that can be made of proportionalism from the perspective of faith.[882] But this theory can also be refuted by reason alone, since it rests upon an erroneous view of the human act. By considering the consequences of an act as more decisive than the object of the act itself, proportionalism implicitly regards the human act as a physical event occurring in the world. This position ignores the personal, inner nature of human acts as *choices* of freedom, which determine the will, and so shape the very person of the moral subject who chooses them.

---

[879] *Lumen Gentium,* 11.
[880] CCC, 1754.
[881] See pages 224-227.
[882] See page 227.

The German theologian Robert Spaemann ponders a case from World War II that leads him to a decisive critique of the moral vision underlying proportionalism. A sadistic German officer ordered one of the guards in a concentration camp to shoot a twelve-year Jewish girl, with the threat that if the guard did not do so, the officer himself would execute twelve other Jewish prisoners. Following proportionalist logic of weighing the bad and good consequences of his act, the guard shot the girl — and later went mad with guilt.

By making a person responsible for the good of the whole world in each choice, proportionalism ends up taking away the person's responsibility for his own acts. In reality, the guard was only responsible for his own choice of whether or not to shoot the innocent girl, not for the immoral decision the officer would make. Our responsibility as moral subjects is limited to our own free acts. We are responsible for avoiding evil and doing good, not for goodness triumphing in the world.

Ultimately, proportionalism is a moral theory based upon the atheistic premise of an absence of Divine Providence. In fact, God alone can bring about the ultimate victory of good over evil. As Christians, we are called to entrust ourselves into his hands, and strive to respond to his grace, so that good may triumph first of all in our own lives — and through us in the lives of others, as God so ordains.

2. Good and Evil Acts
a) Three to One:
It Is Harder to Do Good than to Commit Evil

Why is it that so often "doing the right thing" seems challenging and arduous? In contrast, we can slip into committing evil actions almost without noticing it. Certainly our fallen human nature is the root cause. But the sources of morality also help account for this phenomenon. For an act to be morally good, the object, the intention, and the circumstances must all be good. But if the object alone is evil, so is the act, regardless of how good the intention and the circumstances might be. If the intention is evil, the act is an evil one for the subject who commits it, even if the object and circumstances are both good.

The *Catechism* sums things up: "A *morally good* act requires the goodness of the object, of the end, and of the circumstances together. An evil end corrupts the action, even if the object is good in itself (such as praying and fasting 'in order to be seen by men')."[883] It is not hard to understand why the author of the Book of Job refers to man's life upon earth as a battle. Still, it is a struggle from which we can be confident of emerging victorious, thanks to Christ's redemption.

---

[883] *CCC*, 1755.

b) **Intrinsically Evil Acts**

Certain acts are always evil, in and of themselves, because of their object — that is, due to the very nature of the act. They are *intrinsically evil*. "The *object of the choice* can by itself vitiate an act in its entirety. There are some concrete acts — such as fornication — that it is always wrong to choose, because choosing them entails a disorder of the will, that is, a moral evil."[884] No matter how good one's intention may be, by choosing such an act the subject's will is made evil, since the will cannot help but desire an act it freely chooses. If by its very nature a given act cannot be ordered to the true good of the person, then choosing that act represents an evil choice by the will.

> Reason attests that there are objects of the human act which are by their nature "incapable of being ordered" to God, because they radically contradict the good of the person made in his image. These are the acts which, in the Church's moral tradition, have been termed "intrinsically evil" (*intrinsece malum*): they are such *always and per se*, in other words, on account of their very object, and quite apart from the ulterior intentions of the one acting and the circumstances.[885]

What are some of these acts that are intrinsically evil, since they always violate the true good of the person? The Second Vatican Council identifies a number of them according to three principal categories: acts which destroy life, harm the integrity of the human person, or offend human dignity.

> Whatever is hostile to life itself, such as any kind of homicide, genocide, abortion, euthanasia and voluntary suicide; whatever violates the integrity of the human person, such as mutilation, physical and mental torture and attempts to coerce the spirit; whatever is offensive to human dignity, such as subhuman living conditions, arbitrary imprisonment, deportation, slavery, prostitution and trafficking in women and children; degrading conditions of work which treat laborers as mere instruments of profit, and not as free responsible persons: all these and the like are a disgrace, and so long as they infect human civilization they contaminate those who inflict them more than those who suffer injustice, and they are a negation of the honor due to the Creator.[886]

In *Humanae Vitae* Pope Paul VI reaffirmed the Church's constant teaching that contraception is among those acts that are always evil due to their very nature.[887] The *Catechism* confirms this fundamental moral truth, contrasting the manner in which periodic continence respects the

---

[884] *CCC*, 1755.
[885] *Veritatis Splendor*, 80.
[886] *Gaudium et Spes*, 27.
[887] Cf. *HV*, 14.

inner meaning of persons and their acts with contraception's violation of them.

> Periodic continence, that is, the methods of birth regulation based on self-observation and the use of infertile periods, are in conformity with the objective criteria of morality.[888] These methods respect the bodies of the spouses, encourage tenderness between them, and favor the education of an authentic freedom. In contrast, "every action which, whether in anticipation of the conjugal act, or in its accomplishment, or in the development of its natural consequences, proposes, whether as an end or as a means, to render procreation impossible"[889] is intrinsically evil.[890]

3. Why a Contraceptive Act is Essentially Different from Intercourse Only During the Infertile Periods

Contraception is intrinsically evil, first of all, because it eliminates the procreative meaning of the conjugal act. The spouses positively exclude that openness to parenthood which must accompany sexual intercourse, since procreation is an essential aspect of the meaning of the act by its very structure. In a contraceptive act of intercourse, the husband does not accept the wife as one who may become a mother, and she does not accept him as one who may become a father. Nor do they give themselves to each other in fullness as persons who may become parents. So it is clear they are not really making an act of self-giving love of their entire person, or receiving the self-surrender of the spouse in completeness as a person. The truth of the act as an expression of self-giving love is also violated. Not only is the procreative meaning suppressed, the act is not truly unitive.

For both of these reasons contraception is intrinsically evil. It violates both the unitive and procreative dimensions of the conjugal act, degrading it from the personal order to the level of mere sensual pleasure.

> Mutual betrothed love demands a union of persons. But the union of persons is not the same as sexual union. This latter is raised to the level of the person only when it is accompanied in the mind and the will by acceptance of the possibility of parenthood. This acceptance is so important, so decisive that without it marital intercourse cannot be said to be a realization of the personal order. Instead of a truly personal union all that is left is a sexual association. . . . Neither in the man nor in the woman can affirmation of the value of the person be divorced from awareness and willing acceptance that he may become a father and she may become a mother. . . .

---

[888] *HV*, 16.
[889] *HV*, 14.
[890] *CCC*, 2370.

If the possibility of parenthood is deliberately excluded from marital relations, the character of the relationship between the partners automatically changes. The change is away from unification in love and in the direction of mutual, or rather, bilateral "enjoyment."[891]

Wojtyła notes how the very nature of sexual intercourse changes as a result of contraception. The object of the contraceptive act is different from the object of the conjugal act when contraception is not practiced. The object of the contraceptive act becomes sensual enjoyment, rather than the complete self-giving of persons. The adherence of the will, the fundamental intention of spouses who contracept, changes due to the intrinsically evil nature of the contraceptive act.

> By definitively precluding the possibility of procreation in the marital act a man and a woman inevitably shift the whole focus of the experience in the direction of sexual pleasure as such. The whole content of the experience is then "enjoyment," whereas it should be an expression of love with pleasure as an incidental accompaniment of the sexual act.

> The very fact of deliberately excluding the possibility of parenthood from marital intercourse makes "enjoyment" the intention of the act.[892]

Now let us consider a married couple who have reached the conclusion that they would not be acting responsibly if they were to conceive a child during a certain period of time. As a result, they decide to practice natural family planning. Through periodic abstinence, they engage in sexual intercourse only during the wife's infertile periods. It is an obvious fallacy to claim that their practice of periodic abstinence to avoid having children is the moral equivalent of contraception, since the intention is the same. The moral philosopher Joseph Boyle is able to make this point in a single sentence. "Refraining from intercourse is not contraceptive intercourse, since it is not intercourse at all."[893]

The intention of spouses who practice natural family planning is essentially different from that of couples who contracept. The husband and wife who practice periodic continence respect both the procreative and unitive meanings of the conjugal act. That is precisely why they refrain from engaging in the act when they judge they cannot responsibly become parents. As Wojtyła notes, "Those who do not desire the consequence must avoid the cause. Since sexual intercourse is the biological cause of conception, spouses who wish to avoid conception must ab-

---

[891] Wojtyła, *Love and Responsibility*, p. 228.
[892] Ibid., pp. 234-235.
[893] Joseph M. Boyle, "Contraception and Natural Family Planning," in *Why Humanae Vitae Was Right: A Reader*, p. 415.

stain from intercourse. From the moral point of view, the principle is absolutely clear."[894]

One final analogy serves to illustrate the essential moral difference between the periodic abstinence of natural family planning and contraception. It is the difference between refraining from speaking the truth, which may be a moral obligation at times, and deliberately telling a lie, which can never be morally justified.

> Just as there are times when the truth should not be spoken, there are times when children should not be conceived. But the act of refraining from speaking differs essentially from the act of internally separating speech from its power truthfully to express and generate judgments in the mind of another. Similarly, the act of refraining from coital activity differs essentially from the act of internally separating coital union from its generative power.[895]

B. Essential Difference in Attitudes

The essential moral difference between contraception and natural family planning on the level of the act of conjugal union brings to light another fundamental contrast between these two methods: Essentially different moral *attitudes* lie behind them. Natural family planning is not simply a technique for preventing children from being born. John Paul II affirms, "It is an attitude which is based on the integral moral maturity of the persons and at the same time completes it."[896] At the heart of this attitude is the living out of chastity in the form of periodic continence, not as a technique, but as a moral virtue. Three vital dispositions are involved in the practice of chastity as a moral virtue. The first of these respects procreation. It consists of openness to life. Love and responsibility toward one's spouse comprise the second fundamental attitude in living chastity as a virtue. Finally, the virtue of chastity entails loving respect toward God, the Creator.

1. Attitude Toward Procreation: Openness to Life

We have seen that if the inner meaning of the conjugal act is to be respected, husband and wife must be open to new life when they engage in the act. They must be open to the possibility of becoming a father or a mother. The accusation is often made that couples who practice periodic continence so as to have sexual intercourse only during the wife's infertile periods are not really open to life, to becoming parents. After all, they are seeking to avoid having children. So, in effect, their attitude is not morally different from that of a couple who contracepts. Wojtyła formulates this objection in very strong terms.

---

[894] Wojtyła, *Love and Responsibility*, p. 239.

[895] Mary R. Joyce, *The Meaning of Contraception* (Liturgical Press: Collegeville, MN 1970), p. 41; cited in Boyle, "Contraception and Natural Family Planning," pp. 415-416.

[896] General Audience of September 5, 1984, in *The Theology of the Body*, p. 403.

If a man and a woman time their periods of continence to coincide with the . . . periods of [in]fertility, and so have sexual intercourse only as and when they expect procreation to be biologically impossible, can it be said that they bring to the marital act that readiness for parenthood, that acceptance of the idea that "I may become a father," "I may become a mother"? . . . After all, they have intercourse in the expectation that they will not become parents: It is precisely for that reason that they have chosen the period during which the woman is supposed to be infertile. Are they, then, not deliberately excluding the possibility of procreation? Why should the natural method be morally superior to artificial methods, since the purpose is the same in each case — to eliminate the possibility of procreation from sexual intercourse?[897]

The basic fallacy underlying this objection is that it takes a utilitarian view of periodic continence, considering it as nothing more than a technique for preventing conception. "Looked at like this, the natural method is just another means to ensure the maximum pleasure, differing from artificial methods only in the direction it takes. But this is where the fundamental error resides."[898] Continence must be practiced as a virtue for natural family planning to be morally acceptable.

a) Chastity Must Be a Moral Virtue, Not Just a Technique

Natural family planning isn't morally good in and of itself, just because a couple follows all of the rules. If husband and wife have no intention of ever forming a family (without some weighty moral reason), if they do not perceive the goodness of children, and so are not open to life, they are not living periodic continence as a moral virtue. Quite the opposite — their behavior is morally evil. Wojtyła affirms, "If periodic continence can be regarded as a 'method' at all, it is a method of regulating conception and not of avoiding a family."[899]

John Paul II clearly confirms the ethical dimension of periodic continence as a virtue in his Wednesday audiences on love and fruitfulness.

Even though the periodicity of continence in this case is applied to the so-called "natural rhythms" *(HV,* 16), the continence itself is a definite and permanent moral attitude. It is a virtue, and therefore the whole line of conduct guided by it acquires a virtuous character. The encyclical emphasizes clearly enough that here it is not merely a matter of a definite technique, but of ethics in the strict sense of the term as the morality of conduct.[900]

---

[897] Wojtyła, *Love and Responsibility,* p. 240.
[898] Ibid.
[899] Ibid., p. 242.
[900] General Audience of August 28, 1984, in *The Theology of the Body,* p. 400.

The possibility of practicing periodic continence as a simple technique, without the proper motives, clearly does exist. Wojtyła notes, "Self-interested, calculating continence awakens doubts. Continence must, like all other virtues, be disinterested, and wholly concerned with 'justice,' not with 'expediency.' Otherwise, there will be no place for it in a genuine love of persons. Continence, unless it is a virtue, is alien to love."[901] Continence must help shape love. "Only then is the 'natural method' congruent with the nature of the person: Its secret lies in the practice of virtue — technique alone is no solution here."[902]

b) How To Practice Periodic Continence as a Virtue

If the essential moral goodness of natural family planning rests upon living continence on the ethical plane, as a virtue, a looming question emerges. How can married couples ensure that they are in fact practicing continence as a moral virtue, concerned with justice, and not simply as a technique for seeking out utilitarian pleasure?

Fundamentally, it is the inner content of the attitude the spouses assume towards continence that is decisive. First of all, husband and wife must believe that abstaining periodically from intercourse does not damage their love. On the contrary, it enriches their mutual self-giving through sacrifice and asceticism, which enables them to possess themselves more fully as persons, in order to give themselves more authentically to one another. "Inherent in the essential character of continence as a virtue is the conviction that *the love of man and woman loses nothing as a result of temporary abstention from erotic experiences, but on the contrary gains*: the personal union takes deeper root, grounded as it is above all in the affirmation of the value of the person and not just in sexual attachment."[903]

Secondly, in their practice of periodic continence, husband and wife must be open to life, to becoming a father or a mother. But that was precisely the objection raised against periodic continence. What is it, precisely, that constitutes openness to life, in one's interior attitude? Wojtyła explains clearly that it is not necessary to positively desire to become a parent during a given period of time in order to be open to life. It is sufficient to accept the possibility that one may become a father or a mother as a result of the conjugal act, and to do nothing deliberate regarding the act itself in order to eliminate that possibility.

As long as a husband and wife do not use artificial means and methods to prevent procreation *in potentia* [in its possibility], so long do they accept in their consciousness and their will the possi-

---

[901] Wojtyła, *Love and Responsibility*, p. 241.
[902] Ibid., pp. 241-242.
[903] Ibid., p. 241.

bility of parenthood ("I may become a father," "I may become a mother"). It is enough that they are willing to accept conception, although in the particular instance they do not "desire" it. It is not necessary for them expressly to desire procreation. . . . For infertility in itself is not incompatible with inner willingness to accept conception, should it occur. It makes no difference that conception may not occur because it is precluded by nature. . . . The attitude just described justifies ("makes just") sexual intercourse between a married couple in their own eyes and before God the Creator."[904]

An example can serve to illustrate the point. St. Thomas More vigorously affirmed on many occasions that he had no desire to become a martyr. But his conduct clearly indicated that he was open to that possibility, should God ordain it for his life. He was unwilling to perform the positive and morally wrong act of acknowledging Henry VIII as head of the Church or accepting the validity of the king's remarriage in order to avoid martyrdom. In the same way, the attitude of a couple who practices periodic continence with openness to life is essentially different from that of a couple who positively suppress procreation through the use of contraception.

2. Attitude Toward One's Spouse: Love and Responsibility

When a couple practices natural family planning, their attitude toward one another as husband and wife is also essentially different than it would be were they to contracept. Periodic continence elevates the act of love to the level of the person. It also fosters an attitude of responsibility towards the other as a person, which in the case of the woman entails her fertility cycle — an integral part of who she is. Wojtyła explains the intrinsic link between responsibility and authentic love.

There exists in love a particular responsibility — the responsibility for a person who is drawn into the closest possible partnership in the life and activity of another, and becomes in a sense the property of whoever benefits from this gift of self. It follows that one also has a responsibility for one's own love: Is it mature and complete enough to justify the enormous trust of another person, the hope that giving oneself will not mean losing one's own "soul," but on the contrary enlarging one's existence — or will it end in disillusionment? Responsibility for love clearly comes down to responsibility for the person, originates it and returns to it. . . .

Love divorced from a feeling of responsibility for the person is a negation of itself, is always and necessarily egoism. *The greater the feeling of responsibility for the person the more true love there is.*[905]

---

[904] Ibid., p. 236.
[905] Ibid., pp. 130-131.

3. Attitude Toward God: "Respect for the Creator"

A third essential Christian attitude that natural family planning fosters is respect for God the Creator. Husband and wife render justice toward God in abiding by his providential plan for the responsible transmission of human life, as that plan is expressed in the natural order. Wojtyła reflects, "It is much easier to understand the power of the natural order (and its constitutive significance for morality, and for the development of the human personality) if we see behind it the personal authority of the Creator."[906]

By respecting the natural law through periodic abstinence, husband and wife cooperate in God's own plan for transmitting life, as Paul VI points out in *Humanae Vitae*. "To make use of the gift of conjugal love while respecting the laws of the generative process means to acknowledge oneself not to be the arbiter of the sources of human life, but rather the minister of the design established by the Creator."[907]

Natural family planning does not imply the submission of transcendent human persons to an impersonal, biological law of nature. Exactly the opposite is true. Husband and wife with their own reason recognize God's plan in the order of nature, in the periodicity of the woman's cycle, and they make it their own. "The true good of the human person consists in the faithful execution of this plan."[908] By obeying the natural law, husband and wife are showing respect and love to the Person who created the order of nature — to God himself. John Paul II elaborates this point, referring to *Humanae Vitae*.

> The morally correct regulation is also called "the *natural* regulation of fertility," which can be explained as conformity to the natural law. By natural law we mean that order of nature in the field of procreation, insofar as it is understood by right reason. This order is the expression of the Creator's plan for man. It is precisely this that the encyclical, together with the whole Tradition of Christian teaching and practice, stresses in a particular way: the virtuous character of the attitude which is expressed in the natural regulation of fertility is determined not so much by fidelity to an impersonal natural law as to the Creator-Person, the Source and Lord of the order which is manifested in such a law.[909]

In practicing natural family planning, husband and wife fulfill the first and greatest of all the commandments. "You shall love the Lord, your God, with all your heart, and with all your soul, and with all your might."[910]

---

[906] Ibid., p. 237.
[907] *HV*, 13.
[908] General Audience of August 28, 1984, in *The Theology of the Body*, p. 401.
[909] Ibid.
[910] Dt 6:4.

V. Conclusion: The Future of Humanity

The essential contrast between contraception and natural family planning is stark. On a moral level they differ essentially, both in the nature of the act itself and in the attitudes which underlie the act. Contraception is intrinsically evil. It degrades the marriage act into a mutual seeking of sensual pleasure and robs human sexuality of its truly personal dimension. Husband and wife convert one another into objects to be manipulated.

Natural family planning, through the practice of continence as a moral virtue, enables both spouses to grow in self-mastery, in possession of themselves as persons. Thus, the conjugal act becomes one of true mutual self-giving on the level of persons. The inner truth of the conjugal act as expressed in the language of the body is fully respected. Periodic continence also fosters the fundamental Christian attitudes of openness to life, love and responsibility toward one's spouse, and justice toward God the Creator, toward his providential plan for human life as revealed in the order of nature.

On an anthropological level, two irreconcilable views of the human person lie behind the two methods. The contraceptive mentality is grounded in a rationalist and utilitarian view of man that eliminates his transcendent dimension. Persons are reduced to individual, material members of the human species. Sexuality becomes sensuality.

Natural family planning rests upon a vision of the human person as created in the image and likeness of God. The spiritual faculties of intellect and will enable persons to transcend their limited, physical existence and enter into a true *communio personarum* with one another and, ultimately, with God himself. True married love entails the integration of the sensual and emotional dimensions of the experience of "falling in love" or "being in love" through the guidance of reason and will. In this way love attains the personal dimension and becomes a true self-giving of persons. The mutual gift of self between husband and wife in conjugal union is an image of the eternal self-giving love of the three persons of the Blessed Trinity.

The starkly opposed fruits of contraception and natural family planning are visible the world over in broken marriages *vs.* enduring ones, dysfunctional households *vs.* families where love and joy radiate to those around them. John Paul II has offered the Church and the world a priceless gift at the dawn of the third Christian millennium: a compelling vision of the transcendent beauty of married love and fruitfulness, developed in his theology of the body.

Will Christians accept this gift? Will society embrace John Paul II's vision? The question is not an incidental one. Everything depends upon the answer. The Holy Father was clearly aware of the crossroads at which mankind now finds itself when he wrote the closing lines of *Familiaris Consortio*: *"The future of humanity passes by way of the family."*[911]

---

[911] *FC*, 86.

TWELVE

"Through Him, With Him, In Him": Responsible Parenthood and the Spirituality of Marriage

Preview

I. Responsible Parenthood: Inseparably Linked to Marriage Spirituality
    A. Responsible Parenthood: General Attitudes
    B. Responsible Parenthood: Specific Questions
        1. Is There an Obligation for Married Persons to Have Children?
        2. Is the Obligation Absolute?
        3. What Are Just Reasons for Limiting Family Size?
        4. Should Parents Have Few Children?

Points to look for

1. How does John Paul II define responsible parenthood?
2. Why is responsible parenthood inseparably linked to marriage spirituality?
3. What are two general attitudes necessary for responsible parenthood?
4. What are the four characteristics of authentic love between husband and wife?
5. How do the demands of genuine married love lead to true inner freedom?
6. Is there an obligation for married persons to have children?
7. Is the obligation to have children absolute?
8. How does God make husband and wife partners in the Divine Providence by which he guides humanity?
9. What are the four general criteria for exercising responsible parenthood by limiting family size?
10. Could there ever exist an obligation for parents to limit births of new children in their family?
11. According to the criteria for responsible parenthood of the good of the parents and the family, does it seem that parents should generally have only one or two children?
12. What do the criteria of the good of the Church and society seem to indicate about family size?

I. Responsible Parenthood:
Inseparably Linked to Marriage Spirituality

When husband and wife live out their married love and their vocation to become father and mother by respecting God's plan for transmitting human life through the conjugal act, they are exercising responsible
parenthood. We have seen that a tremendous drama is at play in the
quest to be trustworthy parents. No man and woman can hope to live
up to this sublime vocation relying on their own strength. Only in union
with Christ, through the love of the Holy Spirit poured into their hearts,
can spouses fulfill God's redemptive design. That is why responsible
parenthood is inseparably linked to the spirituality of marriage.

John Paul II reaffirms the meaning of responsible parenthood and
its intrinsic bond with marriage spirituality. "We call that fatherhood
and that motherhood responsible which correspond to the personal dignity of the couple as parents, to the truth of their person and of the conjugal act. Hence arises the close and direct relationship that links this dimension with the whole spirituality of marriage."[912]

Marriage spirituality is founded upon an intimate, personal relationship with Christ. The Redeemer of Man ardently desires to make
visible, to incarnate, his steadfast love for each human being through
the enduring faithfulness of husband and wife. The Father's merciful
love, stronger than sin and death, is made present in every act of mutual
forgiveness between spouses. The Holy Spirit, "the Lord and Giver of
Life," renews the face of the earth in each son and daughter that parents
lovingly bring into the world.

Openness to the gifts of the Holy Spirit and union with Christ
through the sacraments and prayer constitute the very heart of marriage
spirituality. But before reflecting upon these aspects of the spiritual life
which make it possible for husband and wife to fulfill their transcendent vocation, we must ask ourselves what precisely is implied by responsible parenthood. We first need to consider the general attitudes of
an authentic father and mother, and then address some specific questions about the meaning of responsible parenthood.

A. Responsible Parenthood: General Attitudes

To exercise responsibly the call to be ministers of God's plan in creating new human beings with an eternal destiny, parents must above all
respect the integral meaning of the conjugal act. "Responsible fatherhood and motherhood means the spiritual appraisal — conforming to

---

[912] John Paul II, General Audience of October 31, 1984 in *The Theology of the Body*, p. 411.

truth — of the conjugal act in the knowledge and in the will of both spouses. In this manifestation of affection, after considering the interior and external circumstances, especially the biological ones, they express their mature readiness for fatherhood and motherhood."[913] When husband and wife are faithful to the intrinsic meaning of the language of the body in the conjugal act, not only do they deepen their mutual love and personal communion, they also enter into communion with God himself. By openness to being a father or a mother, each spouse truly becomes a "minister of the design established by the Creator."[914] God bends down, as it were, and surrenders his creative omnipotence to husband and wife, becoming a partner with them in their loving gift of self to one another — through that gift bringing a new human life into existence.

God's humble trust in husband and wife brings to light a second basic attitude of responsible parenthood: openness to life. Married couples are called to recognize the precious gift that is each son or daughter. They must be open to receiving such a gift from God, "the Father, from whom every family in heaven and on earth is named."[915] John Paul II highlights *Humanae Vitae*'s teaching on this aspect of married love. "The encyclical underlines that a right and lawful regulation of fertility demands above all from husband and wife a definite family and procreative attitude. That is to say, it requires 'that they acquire and possess solid convictions about the true values of life and of the family' (*HV*, 21)."[916]

By respecting the integral meaning of the conjugal act and being always open to life, spouses guarantee the authenticity of their love. Their gift of self to one another realizes the four characteristics of genuine married love. The love of husband and wife by its very nature must be fully human or personal, total, exclusive and faithful until death, and open to fertility.[917]

These demands of love, though difficult for fallen human nature, do not confine or impoverish man and woman. Exactly the opposite is true. As married couples strive to live up to these lofty demands, with the strength of God's grace and merciful forgiveness, they become more and more free. For inner freedom is precisely the ability to choose behavior that conforms to truth and love.[918]

---

[913] John Paul II, General Audience of November 21, 1984 in Ibid., p. 418.

[914] *Humanae Vitae*, 13.

[915] Ephesians 3: 14-15.

[916] John Paul II, General Audience of August 28, 1984, in *The Theology of the Body*, p. 399.

[917] Cf. *HV*, 9, *FC*, 13 and 50, *CCC*, 1643-1644.

[918] Cf. Elzbieta Wójcik, "Natural Regulation of Conception and Contraception," in *Why* Humanae Vitae *Was Right: A Reader*, p. 438.

Who can forget the moving testimony of heroic inner freedom displayed by the mother Eleni Gatzoyiannis from Greece? Eleni lived by her deep religious convictions and love for her family, but professed no political creed. So when her village was "liberated" by the Communists in the late 1940s during the Greek Civil War, she did not disobey. When they took the food from the villagers to give to the soldiers, she got by with what she could find. When they forced one of her daughters to fight in the army for a cause she did not understand and made Eleni herself work day after day at hard labor, all in the name of freedom, she did not defy them. But when they said she must give up her children so that they could be raised as Communists behind the Iron Curtain, she would go no further.

Eleni arranged for her children to escape from Greece to their father in America. She was charged with treason, tortured and sentenced to the firing squad. As Eleni stood before her executioners, ready to die, she raised her arms in a victorious gesture of self-sacrifice and cried out, "My children!"

Eleni's supreme act of love achieved much more than the freedom it won for her children. In 1987 President Ronald Reagan cited on national television the book *Eleni*, written by her son, as a source of inspiration in his efforts to seek an arms agreement with Soviet leader Mikhail Gorbachev. Reagan told the world: "[Eleni's] final cry was not a curse on her killers, but an invocation of what she died for, a declaration of love. How that cry echoes down through the centuries — a cry for all children of the world, a cry for peace, for a world of love and understanding."

B. Responsible Parenthood: Specific Questions
1. Is There an Obligation for Married Persons to Have Children?

The sacrifice of living out responsible parenthood yields abundant fruits. The rich harvest of graces extends far beyond one's own family, to sustain Christ's mystical body. Now we must reflect on what is specifically entailed by the basic attitudes of responsible parents. A first question immediately arises. "Is there an obligation for husband and wife to have children?"

The fundamental answer to this query can only be, "Yes." As Canon Law states, referring to *Gaudium et Spes*: "The matrimonial covenant, by which a man and a woman establish between themselves a partnership of the whole of life, is by its nature ordered toward the good of the spouses and the procreation and education of offspring."[919] If a man and

---

[919] *CIC*, 1055; cf. *GS*, 48; *CCC*, 1601.

a woman seek to marry but intend never to have children, they are going against the very nature of marriage itself.

In our age, marked by the feverish pursuit of freedom, the word "obligation" reverberates with negative overtones. But the obligation for a husband and wife to seek to have children, to become *parents*, is not an onerous burden imposed on them from without. It is a duty that springs from the very depths of who they are as persons. To become father and mother is the fulfillment of their self-giving, spousal love in the gift of a son or daughter, granted them by the Father of the whole human family.

As the years pass, bestowing their measure of delight, suffering, and fatigue, parents contemplate their children's mysterious journey toward adulthood. Which father or mother does not exclaim with St. Paul: "For what is our hope or joy or crown of boasting before our Lord Jesus at his coming? Is it not you?"[920]

2. Is the Obligation Absolute?

Still, the obligation for married persons to have children is certainly not absolute. Why is this so? As Wojtyła notes, the explanation is to be found in the fullness of meaning that matrimony possesses. "The inner and essential *raison d'être* of marriage is not simply eventual transformation into a family but above all the creation of a lasting personal union between a man and a woman based on love."[921] The Second Vatican Council eloquently affirms this teaching on the nature of marriage.

> Marriage to be sure is not instituted solely for procreation; rather, its very nature as an unbreakable compact between persons, and the welfare of the children, both demand that the mutual love of the spouses be embodied in a rightly ordered manner, that it grow and ripen. Therefore, marriage persists as a whole manner and communion of life, and maintains its value and indissolubility, even when despite the often intense desire of the couple, offspring are lacking.[922]

In his command to Adam and Eve, "Be fruitful and multiply,"[923] God does not imply that husband and wife are to simply "let the children come," giving birth to as many offspring as they are physically capable of engendering. Instead, God has submitted his divine plan for increasing the human family to the moral conscience of spouses, to their free and rational decision, to their loving exercise of responsible parenthood.[924] God has made husband and wife partners in the Divine Providence by which he guides humanity.[925]

---

[920] 1 Th 2:19.
[921] Wojtyła, *Love and Responsibility*, p. 218.
[922] *GS*, 50.
[923] Gn 1:28.
[924] Cf. *HV*, 13, 16.
[925] Cf. *GS*, 50.

There may be serious reasons for married persons not to have children during a given period of time. In exceptional cases, these reasons may extend to not having children at all. What matters first and foremost are the motives underlying the decision of parents to limit the number of children in their family. Husband and wife must form their moral conscience according to objective criteria, so that their decision is not based on subjective or selfish reasons. John Paul II notes the general criteria outlined by Pope Paul VI: "As regards the immediate motivation, *Humanae Vitae* requires that 'there exist reasonable grounds for spacing births, arising from the physical or psychological condition of husband or wife, or from external circumstances. . . .' (*HV*, 16)."[926]

3. What Are Just Reasons for Limiting Family Size?

It is clear that, for some married persons, responsible parenthood could entail limiting the size of their family. Echoing number 50 of *Gaudium et Spes*, Pope Paul VI indicates four general criteria by which parents should allow their conscience to be guided. "The responsible exercise of parenthood implies, therefore, that husband and wife recognize fully their own duties towards God, towards themselves, towards the family and towards society, in a correct hierarchy of values."[927]

As they seek to apply these four principles, striving to discern God's will for their lives through diligent prayer and the guidance of trusted pastors, parents may conclude that they should limit new children to be born into their family. But we may go a step further and ask ourselves whether there could ever exist an *obligation* for parents to limit births? In other words, are there times when it would be morally irresponsible not to practice natural family planning in order to limit family size? The answer, affirms Wojtyła, is, "Yes."

> From the point of view of the family, *periodic continence as a method of regulating conception is permissible in so far as it does not conflict with a sincere disposition to procreate.* There are, however, circumstances in which this disposition itself demands renunciation of procreation, and any further increase in the size of the family would be incompatible with parental duty. A man and a woman moved by true concern for the good of their family and a mature sense of responsibility for the birth, maintenance and upbringing of their children, will then limit intercourse, and abstain from it in periods in which this might result in another pregnancy undesirable in the particular conditions of their married and family life.[928]

---

[926] John Paul II, General Audience of August 28, 1984, in *The Theology of the Body*, p. 400.
[927] *HV*, 10.
[928] Wojtyła, *Love and Responsibility*, p. 243.

4. Should Parents Have Few Children?

So at times the exercise of responsible parenthood will lead parents to limit the size of their family, and could even entail a moral obligation to do so. But we could ask ourselves another question on this front. Generally speaking, should parents have few children? Should they perhaps plan on only one or two? *Gaudium et Spes* provides an initial response.

> Thus, trusting in divine Providence and refining the spirit of sacrifice,[929] married Christians glorify the Creator and strive toward fulfillment in Christ when with a generous human and Christian sense of responsibility they acquit themselves of the duty to procreate. Among the couples who fulfill their God-given task in this way, those merit special mention who with a gallant heart and with wise and common deliberation, undertake to bring up suitably even a relatively large family.[930]

The four general principles outlined by Pope Paul VI provide parents with a trustworthy guide for discernment. Let us consider each of these criteria individually. In which direction does parents' duty to God lead them? We have already pondered St. Irenaeus' ringing phrase, *"Gloria Dei vivens homo."*[931] God's love is expansive by its very nature. Our Father in heaven longs for children who can experience his love.

The Second Vatican Council points out that parents' duty to God includes their responsibility toward Christ's Church.[932] Who can doubt that one of the most urgent needs of the Church today is for priests? At present 13 percent of parishes in the U.S. do not have a pastor — and that figure will increase dramatically in the years to come. In many countries of Latin and South America priests are confronted with the humanly impossible task of ministering to the needs of 10,000 to 30,000 faithful in their parishes.

A very significant relationship exists between family size and priestly vocations. Father Paul Marx, founder of Human Life International, has spoken at seminaries all around the world. At the end of his talks he would invariably ask the seminarians present to indicate by a show of hands the size of the family in which they were raised. In every country the results were the same. An overwhelming majority of seminarians came from families with four or more children.

---

[929] Cf. John XXIII, prayer delivered on Oct. 11, 1962, at the beginning of the council: *AAS* 54 (1962), p. 792.

[930] *GS*, 50; referring to Constitution on the Sacred Liturgy, n. 123: *AAS* 56 (1964), p. 131; Paul VI, discourse to the artists of Rome: *AAS* 56 (1964), pp. 439-442.

[931] For man to be alive is the glory of God.

[932] Cf. *GS*, 50.

The second criterion to guide married persons in discerning the number of children is their own objective good as parents and spouses. Here, too, *Gaudium et Spes* provides a vibrant declaration, in a point often pondered by John Paul II. "Children are really the supreme gift of marriage and contribute very substantially to the welfare of their parents."[933] Who can put into words the secret, inner joy of father and mother as they gaze upon their children, "like olive branches" around their table?[934] What greater comfort could be offered to parents in old age by the God who said, "It is not good that the man should be alone,"[935] than the loving presence of their children, now strong and mature adults?

What does the third criterion of discernment reveal to parents — the good of the family, the good of the children themselves? John Paul II spoke movingly about this question on the Mall in Washington, D.C., during his first pastoral visit to the U.S. in 1979.

> Decisions about the number of children and the sacrifices to be made for them must not be taken only with a view to adding to comfort and preserving a peaceful existence. Reflecting upon this matter before God, with the graces drawn from the sacrament, and guided by the teaching of the Church, parents will remind themselves that it is certainly less serious to deny their children certain comforts or material advantages than to deprive them of the presence of brothers and sisters, who could help them to grow in humanity and to realize the beauty of life at all its ages and in all its variety.[936]

In *Love and Responsibility*, Karol Wojtyła reflects on the importance of the family as a *community* for the good and the formation of the children. He agrees with the notion that one or two children do not yet constitute a true community among themselves — they are simply one or two children. Parents know well the difference made by the arrival of the third child, the new types of relationships that began to develop among brothers and sisters, the increased challenges for siblings to grow in generosity and self-giving.

> The family is an institution created by procreation within the framework of marriage. It is a natural community, directly dependent on the parents for its existence and functioning. The parents create the family as a complement to and extension of their love. To create a family means to create a community, since the family is a social unit or else it is not a family. To be a community it must have a certain size. This is most obvious in the context of education. For

---

[933] *GS*, 50.
[934] Cf. Psalm 128.
[935] Gn 2:18.
[936] John Paul II, "Let Us Celebrate Life," (homily, Oct. 7, 1979), in *U.S.A.: The Message of Justice, Peace and Love* (Boston: St. Paul Editions, 1979), pp. 281-282.

the family is an educational institution within the framework of which the personality of a new human being is formed. If it is to be correctly formed it is very important that this human being should not be alone, but surrounded by a natural community. We are sometimes told that it is easier to bring up several children together than an only child, and also that two children are not a community — they are only two children. It is the role of the parents to direct their children's upbringing, but under their direction the children educate themselves, because they develop within the framework of a community of children, a collective of siblings.[937]

What need be said about the fourth criterion of discernment — the good of society? Not a single country in Europe, and neither the United States nor Canada, is replacing its population. The family, the most basic and vital cell of society, in the large majority of countries in the world today, is failing even to ensure the physical continuation of society itself. Here resounds yet one more voice calling out for generous parents!

[937] Wojtyła, *Love and Responsibility*, pp. 242-243.

Preview

Twelve "Through Him, With Him, In Him":
    Responsible Parenthood and the Spirituality of Marriage *(continued)*

II. The Strength to Live Responsible Parenthood: Marriage Spirituality
    A. Fundamental Element: The Gifts of the Holy Spirit
        1. Love Poured Out
        2. The Gift of Piety
        3. Contraception: The Antithesis of Conjugal Spirituality
    B. Prayer and the Sacraments
        1. "Lord, Teach Us to Pray"
        2. The Eucharist and the Sacrament of Reconciliation:
            Love that Knows No Bounds
    C. Marriage Spirituality: A Summary

Points to look for

1. What is the only perspective from which the question, "Is responsible parenthood possible?" can be answered?
2. What is the fundamental element of marriage spirituality?
3. What is the relation between the gifts of the Holy Spirit and conjugal chastity?
4. What is the special role that the gift of piety plays in married love?
5. Why does contraception represent the antithesis of marriage spirituality?
6. What are the two most effective means for married couples to deepen in their relationship with the Holy Spirit?
7. Why does the *Catechism* describe prayer as a "battle"?

8. What are the rewards of winning the battle of prayer?
9. What role do the sacraments of the Eucharist and Reconciliation play in living out marriage spirituality?
10. Why does marriage spirituality, and married love, ultimately lead to Christ?

II. The Strength to Live Responsible Parenthood: Marriage Spirituality

No one denies that living out responsible parenthood is a challenge — at times a difficult one. Pope Paul VI speaks of ascetical practices, of the effort needed to gain self-mastery.[938] John Paul II asks directly, "Is this effort possible?"[939] Can the moral law, recalled and confirmed by *Humanae* Vitae, really be lived in practice?

From a merely human perspective, the answer remains in doubt. But this decisive question brings us to the heart of the Gospel mystery. It unveils the profound transformation wrought in humanity by Christ's redemptive mission. It opens transcendent horizons to be conquered — the new man and woman, recreated in Christ. Only from within the perspective of the spiritual life, of new life in the Holy Spirit, can this question be answered. That is why John Paul II affirms: "It constitutes one of the most essential questions (and currently also one of the most urgent ones) in the sphere of the spirituality of marriage."[940]

In turning our gaze upon the new spiritual life opened to us by Christ, we discover that following him faithfully does not depend primarily on our own efforts. It is given to us as a gift, one that comes from the Holy Spirit, Christ's "first gift to those who believe."[941] In its very foundations, marriage spirituality rests upon the gifts of the Holy Spirit. Prayer and the sacraments are the indispensable means for fostering the life of the Holy Spirit within us. In such simple terms, John Paul II outlines the spirituality of marriage.

A. Fundamental Element: The Gifts of the Holy Spirit
1. Love Poured Out

How the perspective of living out the vocation to be responsible parents changes with the arrival of the Holy Spirit, the "comforter," "the sweet guest of the soul"! What was once a heavy burden becomes light. What seemed an obstacle to happiness is transformed into a source of joy. Even in moments of difficulty or trial, under the promptings of the Holy Spirit, parents are aware that they too are children and can cry out,

---

[938] Cf. *HV*, 21.
[939] John Paul II, General Audience of October 31, 1984, in *The Theology of the Body*, p. 411.
[940] Ibid.
[941] *Roman Missal*, Eucharistic Prayer IV.

"Abba, Father!" With the Psalmist they can repeat, "But I have calmed and quieted my soul, like a child quieted at its mother's breast."[942]

The love of the Holy Spirit, the foundation of marriage spirituality, is intimately related to the virtue of chastity. John Paul II points out this relationship.

> In the light of *Humanae Vitae*, the fundamental element of the spirituality of married life is the love poured out into the hearts of the couple as a gift of the Holy Spirit (cf. Rom 5:5). In the sacrament the couple receive this gift along with a special consecration. Love is united to conjugal chastity, which, manifesting itself as continence, brings about the interior order of married life.[943]

Through the action of the Holy Spirit, conjugal chastity is not simply a moral virtue attained by human effort. It is a gift of grace, one that makes true love between spouses possible. The *Catechism* confirms this new dimension chastity acquires through Christ's redemption. "Chastity is a moral virtue. It is also a gift from God, a *grace*, a fruit of spiritual effort.[944] The Holy Spirit enables one whom the water of Baptism has regenerated to imitate the purity of Christ."[945]

It is the Holy Spirit who enables husband and wife to integrate the sensual and affective dimensions of their married love, elevating that love into the sphere of persons. He who is the "fire of love," uniting the Father and the Son for all eternity, also enables man and woman to give themselves to one another in a true communion of persons. The Holy Father comments on this beautiful reality.

> Those two who, according to the oldest expression in the Bible, "become one body" (Gn 2:24), cannot bring about this union on the proper level of persons *(communio personarum)* except through the powers coming from the spirit, and precisely from the Holy Spirit who purifies, enlivens, strengthens, and perfects the powers of the human spirit. "It is the Spirit that gives life; the flesh is useless" (Jn 6:63).[946]

2. The Gift of Piety

Among the seven gifts of the Holy Spirit, one in particular plays a vital role in married love: the gift of piety. "In the spiritual life of married couples the gifts of the Holy Spirit are at work, especially the gift of piety, that is, the gift of respect for what is a work of God."[947] Since piety engenders a filial reverence for all the works that come from

---

[942] Psalm 131.
[943] John Paul II, General Audience of November 14, 1984, in *The Theology of the Body*, p. 415.
[944] Cf. Gal 5:22.
[945] *CCC*, 2345; cf. 1 Jn 3:3.
[946] John Paul II, General Audience of November 14, 1984, in *The Theology of the Body*, pp. 415-416.
[947] John Paul II, General Audience of November 21, 1984, in *The Theology of the Body*, p. 417.

God the Father, between spouses this gift creates a special respect for the conjugal act, in the procreative and unitive dimensions bestowed on it by God. Through the gift of piety, spouses are able to live marital chastity as the heart of the spirituality of marriage. The Holy Father expands upon this point.

> Chastity means to live in the order of the heart. . . . Therefore, chastity lies at the center of the spirituality of marriage, not only as a moral virtue (formed by love), but likewise as a virtue connected with the gifts of the Holy Spirit — above all, the gift of respect for what comes from God *(donum pietatis)*.[948] This gift is in the mind of the author of the Ephesians when he exhorts married couples to "defer to one another out of reverence for Christ" (Eph 5:21). So the interior order of married life, which enables the manifestations of affection to develop according to their right proportion and meaning, is a fruit not only of the virtue which the couple practice, but also of the gifts of the Holy Spirit which they cooperate with. . . .

> This gift [of piety] sustains and develops in the married couple a particular sensitivity to everything in their vocation and life that bears the sign of the mystery of creation and redemption — a sensitivity to everything that is a created reflection of God's wisdom and love. Therefore that gift seems to introduce the man and woman to a specially profound respect for the two inseparable meanings of the conjugal act, which the encyclical speaks of in relation to the sacrament of marriage *(HV,* 12). Respect for the two meanings of the conjugal act can develop fully only on the basis of a profound reference to the personal dignity of what in the human person is intrinsic to masculinity and femininity, and inseparably in reference to the personal dignity of the new life which can result from the conjugal union of the man and the woman.[949]

The gift of love poured out into the hearts of married couples by the Holy Spirit, especially through the gift of piety, enables them to live conjugal chastity in the personal gift of self. Thus, the Church's teaching on natural family planning forms an integral part of the spirituality of marriage, as the Holy Father confirms.

> The whole practice of the upright regulation of fertility, so closely linked to responsible fatherhood and motherhood, forms part of the Christian spirituality of married life and family life. Only by living "in the Spirit" can it become interiorly true and authentic.[950]

3. Contraception: The Antithesis of Conjugal Spirituality

The spirituality of marriage provides the strength for married couples to live responsible parenthood through the exercise of chastity

---

[948] "The gift of piety."
[949] John Paul II, General Audience of November 14, 1984, in *The Theology of the Body,* p. 416.
[950] Ibid., p. 417.

Catherina/

≪ _7pm_ ≫

9:30

220-8144
Martin

in natural family planning. It offers them hope that this ideal can be attained through new life in the Holy Spirit and the gift of piety. What, then, represents the most direct antithesis to authentic marriage spirituality? Without doubt it is a way of thinking which condones and even promotes contraception. "Therefore, the antithesis of conjugal spirituality is constituted, in a certain sense, by the subjective lack of this understanding which is linked to contraceptive practice and mentality."[951]

The contraceptive mentality fails to recognize in the unitive and procreative meanings of the conjugal act the loving Providence of God the Father. By eliminating the need for periodic continence, it undermines the virtue of chastity, without which spousal love cannot rise to the level of true, personal self-giving. Finally, the contraceptive mentality leads to a loss of respect for life itself, in absolute opposition to the gift of piety. As if in agony the world today cries out for the transforming action of the Holy Spirit. How ardently do men and women long for the inner experience of Christ's love, which no one except the Paraclete can bestow! Only if the contraceptive mentality is overcome through an authentic spirituality of marriage can the Holy Spirit once again renew the face of the earth.

B. Prayer and the Sacraments

If the love of the Holy Spirit poured out, his gift of piety, are at the heart of marriage spirituality, a spontaneous question arises. "How can husband and wife deepen in their relationship with the Holy Spirit?" No means are more effective than prayer and the sacraments. John Paul II confirms this crucial point, commenting on *Humanae Vitae*.

> If *Humanae Vitae* exhorts married couples to "unremitting prayer" and to the sacramental life (saying: ". . . let them drink deep of grace and charity from that unfailing fount which is the Eucharist"; "humble and persevering, they must have recourse to the mercy of God, abundantly bestowed in the Sacrament of Penance" — *HV*, 25), it does so insofar as it is mindful of the Spirit who "gives life" (2 Cor 3:6).[952]

1. "Lord, Teach Us to Pray"

In a single sentence the *Catechism* expresses the vital need for prayer, not only in the life of married couples, but for every Christian. "*We pray as we live, because we live as we pray.*"[953]

Prayer is not easy. More often than not it is a battle.[954] Everyone who seeks to develop a true life of prayer will experience dryness and dis-

---

[951] John Paul II, General Audience of November 21, 1984, in Ibid., p. 417.
[952] John Paul II, General Audience of November 14, 1984, in Ibid., p. 416.
[953] *CCC*, 2725. Italics are mine.
[954] Cf. *CCC*, "The Battle of Prayer," 2725-2745.

tractions, periods when God appears to be distant, when he seems not even to be listening — much less answering our prayers.

But each of the stages we pass through in our life of prayer is part of God's pedagogy for us, part of his loving plan to purify and strengthen us, to strip us of our secret self-love and the desire for emotional consolations, to "feel ourselves holy."

When we pray, we are always in the presence of our Father who knows all of our needs even before we ask him. We are united with Christ, our Redeemer, whose unfathomable love for us moved him to sweat drops of blood in Gethsemane, to die in agony upon the cross, to remain at our side until the end of time, hidden and silent in the Eucharist. The Holy Spirit, Christ's "first gift to those who believe," is working in our souls, enlightening us, speaking silently, strengthening us, setting ablaze in our hearts a burning love for Christ and an ardent desire to make him known.

No happiness in life can be compared to those moments when God allows us to experience him in prayer, to catch a glimpse of his face, to feel his gaze of love rest upon us as it did upon the rich young man of the Gospel. These moments are a brief foretaste of the joy that will be ours forever in heaven. How we need to make our own each time we come before God in prayer the words of the apostles, "Lord, teach us to pray!"[955]

2. The Eucharist and the Sacrament of Reconciliation: Love that Knows No Bounds

"Lo, I am with you always, to the close of the age."[956] To what inconceivable lengths was Christ willing to go in order to keep his final promise to us before his Ascension! The one in whom "we live and move and have our being,"[957] remains humbly present, silent, unobtrusive, in every tabernacle — just as he came into the world almost unnoticed under the night stars at Bethlehem.

How could it not be true that kneeling before him in the Eucharist will change our lives? The woman in the Gospel who suffered from a hemorrhage said to herself, "If only touch his garment, I shall be made well."[958] We are able not only to touch the hem of Christ's garment, we can remain in his presence in our visits to the Eucharist. We can receive him into our hearts in communion. Married couples who live united to Christ in the Eucharist receive an incomparable grace for the deepening of their own personal communion. Christ's faithful company in this sacrament is a pledge of their fidelity to one another.

---

[955] Lk 11:1; cf. John Paul II, Apostolic Letter *Novo Millennio Ineunte*, (January 6, 2001), 32.
[956] Mt 28:20.
[957] Acts 17:28.
[958] Mt 9:21.

"Then Peter came up and said to him, 'Lord, how often shall my brother sin against me, and I forgive him? As many as seven times?' Jesus said to him, 'I do not say to you seven times, but seventy times seven.'"[959] Is not Christ the first one to fulfill his own command to forgive without limits each time we approach him in the Sacrament of Reconciliation?

The experience of Christ's pardon — discreet and without reserve — the personal encounter with the Father's merciful love in this sacrament, engenders within us a profound gratitude. But it also moves us to forgive others, no matter what the cost. The Sacrament of Reconciliation is a source of mutual forgiveness between husband and wife, and among all members of the family.

C. Marriage Spirituality: A Summary

Through persevering prayer, sustained by Christ's grace in the Sacraments of the Eucharist and Reconciliation, spouses are able to live as a reality in their lives the spirituality of marriage. John Paul II recapitulates the principal lines of this spirituality. It is centered upon the love of the Holy Spirit, manifested in a particular way through the gift of piety. This gift enables couples to respect the integral meaning of the conjugal act, living out the language of the body in truth, as they give their very selves to one another.

> The attitude of respect for the work of God, which the Spirit stirs up in the couple, has an enormous significance for those affectionate manifestations. This is because side by side with it there is the capacity for deep satisfaction, admiration, disinterested attention to the visible and at the same time the invisible beauty of femininity and masculinity, and finally a deep appreciation of the disinterested gift of the other.

> All this determines the spiritual identification of what is male or female, of what is corporeal and at the same time personal. From this spiritual identification the awareness emerges of the union through the body, in safeguarding the interior freedom of the gift. Through the affectionate manifestations the couple help each other remain faithful to the union. At the same time these manifestations protect in each of them that deep-rooted peace which is in a certain sense the interior resonance of chastity guided by the gift of respect for what God creates.

> This gift involves a profound and universal attention to the person in one's masculinity and femininity, thus creating the interior climate suitable for personal communion. That procreation which we describe as responsible, rightly matures only in this climate of the personal communion of the couple. . . .

---

[959] Mt 18:21-22.

Humanae Vitae enables us to trace an outline of conjugal spirituality. This is the human and supernatural climate which considers the "biological" order and, at the same time, is formed on the basis of chastity sustained by the gift of piety. The interior harmony of marriage is formed in this climate, in respect for what the encyclical calls "the twofold significance of the conjugal act" (*HV*, 12). This harmony means that the couple live together in the interior truth of the language of the body. *Humanae Vitae* proclaims that the connection between this truth and love is inseparable.[960]

On the sun-drenched morning of August 20, 2000, John Paul II, filled with emotion, gazed out at more than two million young people who had come on pilgrimage from every corner of the globe for World Youth Day of the Jubilee Year 2000. During his homily, the Holy Father pondered St. Peter's exclamation in the Gospel of John: "Lord, to whom shall we go? You have the words of eternal life."[961] The Pope reflected with his captivated audience on the decisions they faced — choices that would shape their destiny. "It is important to realize that among the many questions surfacing in your minds, the decisive ones are not about 'what.' The basic question is 'who': 'Who' am I to go to, 'who' am I to follow, 'to whom' should I entrust my life?"[962]

The Holy Father spoke about that great act of trust, which is love, and the call to marry. He revealed to those eager young men and women the guiding principle of marriage spirituality. Married love, as sincere as it may be, must lead to Christ. For no human person will ever be able to fully satisfy our hearts that have been made for him.

> You are thinking about love and the choices it entails, and I imagine that you agree: What is really important in life is the choice of the person who will share it with you. But be careful! Every human person has inevitable limits: Even in the most successful of marriages there is always a certain amount of disappointment. . . . Only Jesus of Nazareth, the Son of God and of Mary, the eternal Word of the Father born two thousand years ago at Bethlehem in Judea, is capable of satisfying the deepest aspirations of the human heart.[963]

---

[960] John Paul II, General Audience of November 21, 1984, in *The Theology of the Body*, pp. 418-419.
[961] Jn 6:68.
[962] Papal Homily at World Youth Day Closing Mass, August 20, 2000, Number 3.
[963] Ibid.

CONCLUSION:

Evangelizing the Family in the Third Christian Millennium

I. At a Crossroads
A. Rome and Europe During the Jubilee Year

As the sun rises upon the third Christian millennium, humanity stands at a dramatic crossroads. The Jubilee Year 2000 has unleashed torrents of graces that have touched the lives of millions of people from every nation and culture. Vivid images inspiring hope for the future are fresh in our memory: Two million young people flooding every piazza and church in Rome, making it for a few days the youngest city in the world. Those same young people kneeling at hundreds of movable confessionals lining the entire Circus Maximus in order to receive the Sacrament of Reconciliation. Parents and children exultant with joy in St. Peter's Square in the presence of John Paul II, their unswerving advocate, during the Jubilee Day of Families.

Still, other events took place in the year 2000 that gave clear evidence of those forces "backed by very powerful resources ... [which] seem to aim at the breakdown of the family."[964] A new survey released in England at the end of November showed that 44 percent of all adults in the United Kingdom have no religious affiliation. The figure rises to 66 percent among young adults aged 18 to 24.[965] A few months earlier, Peter Brierley, the leading expert on church attendance in Britain, had suggested that Christian life would be all but dead in 40 years, with less than 0.5 percent of the population attending a church service.[966]

In November the Netherlands achieved the dubious distinction of becoming the first country to approve euthanasia throughout the land.[967] Also during the month of November, Germany took the lead in social advancement by approving a law that recognizes the equivalent of homosexual marriages. Neighboring France saw its Supreme Court rule that it is better not to be born than to be born with a handicap. The

---

[964] John Paul II, *Letter to Families*, 4.
[965] Zenit News Service, November 28, 2000.
[966] Ibid.
[967] Ibid.

345

legal decision established that Nicolas Perruche, 17, who was born deaf, partly blind, and mentally retarded in 1983, should be compensated for his birth because the doctors didn't advise his parents to abort him.[968]

B. Across the Atlantic: The Battle for America's Soul

On the other side of the Atlantic, the presidential election in the United States saw Vice President Al Gore, an ardent supporter of abortion on demand and homosexual unions, confront Governor George W. Bush of Texas, who declared that he would seek to foster a culture of life, and that he strongly believed marriage to be between a man and a woman. In one of the closest presidential races in U.S. history, election day came and went, but no one knew the winner.

The attention of the entire world came to focus on the state of Florida, where Al Gore contested Bush's razor-thin popular-vote victory, which would have given him the presidency. A wrenching month of recounts and legal battles ensued. Finally, the U.S. Supreme Court ruled that the recounts gave the victory to Bush, under the established Constitutional procedures of Florida's election system. The date on which the Supreme Court reached its decision? December 12, the Feast of Our Lady of Guadalupe, patroness of the Americas — the only apparition of the Blessed Virgin where she appears carrying the unborn Child Jesus in her womb.

On November 15, in the midst of the recount saga, an op-ed column appeared in the *Wall Street Journal* entitled, "What Divides America." It was written by Francis Fukuyama, professor of public policy at George Mason University. Fukuyama first acknowledged the self-evident: The election results revealed "a sharply divided country." Then came the crucial question: "But what are Americans sharply divided over?"

According to the professor of public policy, they were not divided over "foreign policy, management of the economy, crime, welfare or other traditional issues that used to separate left and right." So, just what is it, then, that divides America? "The real issues in American politics have become *cultural ones* that can only indirectly be addressed through politics and public policy."[969]

Cultural issues are what divide America? In the *Wall Street Journal* we can perceive distant echoes of *Centesimus Annus* and John Paul II's unshakable conviction: The driving force which shapes history is not politics or economics or military might. It is culture. And what, according to Fukuyama, is the one dominant cultural issue presently dividing America? His response seems almost as if it could have been taken from one of John Paul II's pastoral letters to U.S. Bishops.

---

[968] Ibid., November 19, 2000.
[969] Italics are mine.

The single most important social change to have taken place in the United States over the past 40 years concerns sex and the social role of women, and it is from this single source that virtually all of the 'culture wars' stem. Uncomfortable as it may be to acknowledge this fact, the breakdown of the nuclear family, reflected in rising divorce rates, illegitimacy and cohabitation in place of marriage, stems from two sources: the movement of women into the paid labor force, and the separation of sex from reproduction thanks to birth control and abortion.[970]

Francis Fukuyama's essay represents strong confirmation from a secular source that the battle for America's soul, as well as for the soul of Europe, is being waged in the very heart of the family. How can victory be attained in this most crucial of all conflicts? There is an urgent need to *evangelize* the family, so that families in turn may become evangelizers — leaven that transforms society and culture around them.

II. Families: Evangelizers Impelled by Love
A. Pope Paul VI: The Family's Evangelizing Mission

In his Apostolic Exhortation *Evangelii Nuntiandi*, Pope Paul VI beautifully describes how the family is a central *locus* of evangelization. "The family, like the Church, ought to be a place where the Gospel is transmitted and from which the Gospel radiates. In a family which is conscious of this mission, all the members evangelize and are evangelized. The parents not only communicate the Gospel to their children, but from their children they can themselves receive the same Gospel as deeply lived by them."[971]

What is the foundation for evangelizing the family and for the family in turn to become evangelizers? It can be none other than the experience of Christ's love, his intimate, penetrating love for each member of the family — a love for which no occasion is too small or insignificant to manifest itself. Moved by this experience, the family will begin to appreciate Christ's love for all those who still do not know him, or who are acquainted with him only vaguely. An irrepressible desire to share their experience of love with others will be born within the family. Paul VI reflects on this indispensable aspect of evangelization.

> The work of evangelization presupposes in the evangelizer an ever-increasing love for those whom he is evangelizing. That model evangelizer, the Apostle Paul, wrote these words to the Thessalonians, and they are a program for us all: "With such yearning love we chose to impart to you not only the gospel of God but our very

---

[970] Francis Fukuyama, "What Divides America," *Wall Street Journal* (November 15, 2000), Volume CCXXXVI, Section A, p. 26.
[971] Pope Paul VI, Apostolic Exhortation *Evangelii Nuntiandi* (December 8, 1975), 71.

selves, so dear had you become to us."[972] What is this love? It is much more than that of a teacher; it is the love of a father; and again, it is the love of a mother.[973] It is this love that the Lord expects from every preacher of the Gospel, from every builder of the Church.[974]

If the urgency of love converts families into evangelizers, perseverance in this often arduous task can only be assured by maintaining fervor of spirit, by continually renewing an intimate, personal contact with Christ in prayer, the Eucharist, and the Sacrament of Reconciliation. This point brings us to a brief aside. Some persons would seek to portray Pope Paul VI as a twentieth-century Hamlet, melancholy and brooding, continuously oppressed by the burden of the papacy. The Pope's shining words on spiritual fervor belie this attempted caricature of his person. As Christ himself assures us, "from the fullness of the heart the mouth speaks."[975]

> Let us therefore preserve our fervor of spirit. Let us preserve the delightful and comforting joy of evangelizing, even when it is in tears that we must sow. May it mean for us — as it did for John the Baptist, for Peter and Paul, for the other apostles and for a multitude of splendid evangelizers all through the Church's history — an interior enthusiasm that nobody and nothing can quench. May it be the great joy of our consecrated lives. And may the world of our time, which is searching, sometimes with anguish, sometimes with hope, be enabled to receive the Good News not from evangelizers who are dejected, discouraged, impatient or anxious, but from ministers of the Gospel whose lives glow with fervor, who have first received the joy of Christ, and who are willing to risk their lives so that the kingdom may be proclaimed and the Church established in the midst of the world.[976]

B. Pope John Paul II: Encountering Christ the Evangelizer
1. Who Is the Christ of John Paul II?
After his address to the United Nations on October 5, 1995, John Paul II remarked to a Vatican official, "Well, I did it."

"Did what, Your Holiness?" came the reply.

"I told them that Christ is our only motive. He is why we do what we do."

Who is this Christ, who prompts families to proclaim the Gospel, who gave Pope Paul VI a radiant, inner joy, who has enabled John Paul

---

[972] 1 Thess 2:8; cf. Phil 1:8.
[973] Cf. 1 Thess 2:7-11; 1 Cor 4:15; Gal 4:19.
[974] Ibid., 79.
[975] Lk 6:45.
[976] Ibid., 80.

II to become and achieve what is far beyond the human capacity of any person? Where can we find this Christ? Obviously, he is present in the Gospels. There we discover the One who is the same "yesterday, and to-day, and forever."[977] But throughout the two millennia of her history, the Church has also been enriched in her understanding of Christ by the "Christology of the saints" — by the vibrant interpretation of Jesus the saints have given in their splendid personal existence.[978]

Some notable examples are the poor and joyous Christ of St. Francis of Assisi, Christ the king and master of St. Ignatius of Loyola, Christ the educator of St. John Bosco. So the question could be raised, "Who is the Christ of John Paul II?"

Any simple formulation risks being reductive. The Christ of John Paul II is Trinitarian. He reveals the Father, "rich in mercy," and conveys the gift of the Holy Spirit. He is a Marian Christ: the Mother of the Re-deemer provides the surest way to him. He is an anthropological Christ, the One who "reveals man to himself."[979] John Paul II's Christ is also ecclesiological and Eucharistic.

Still, the claim could be made that one aspect of the person of Christ resounds throughout the Holy Father's writings with compelling force. Has not John Paul II transmitted to men and women today *Christ the Evangelizer, on fire with zeal for souls*? Do not the Pope's uplifted arms, which would embrace all of the millions of people in the crowds if it were possible, reveal that burning love of the Redeemer, "who desires all men to be saved and to come to the knowledge of the truth?"[980] Does not John Paul II's gaze reflect the light in Christ's eyes as he called the first Galilean fishermen to be his apostles?

Time and again, to men and women of all ages, nations and cul-tures, but especially to families and young people, the Holy Father has repeated Christ's challenge, "Go into all the world and preach the Gos-pel to the whole creation."[981] He did so at Cherry Creek Park during World Youth Day in Denver in 1993, with words that galvanized the hundreds of thousands of young people gathered for the Eucharistic Celebration. "Do not be afraid to go out on the streets and into public places, like the first Apostles who preached Christ and the Good News of salvation in the squares of cities, towns and villages. This is no time to be ashamed of the Gospel (cf. Rom 1:16). It is time to preach it from the rooftops (cf. Mt 10:27)."[982]

---

[977] Hb 13:8.

[978] Cf. *Jesus Christ, Word of the Father: the Savior of the World*, prepared by the Theological-Histori-cal Commission for the Great Jubilee of the Year 2000 (New York: Crossroad, 1997), p. 53.

[979] *Redemptor Hominis*, 10.

[980] 1 Tim 2:4.

[981] Mk 16:15.

[982] Papal homily during the Mass at Cherry Creek Park, August 15, 1993, in *Messages of Pope John Paul II to the Youth of the World* (Baltimore: Little Sisters of the Poor, 1993), p. 43.

2. Have We Encountered the Christ of John Paul II?

"I came to cast fire upon the earth, and would that it were kindled already!"[983] These words of Christ as he faces his passion reveal who he is in the depths of his being. Persons who truly encounter Christ cannot but feel enkindling in their own hearts the flame of his love for those he came to save. This fire has impelled Christ's Vicar to travel "to the ends of the earth" and spend his life with superhuman heedlessness, making known the unfathomable depths of Christ's love for his people.

Have we, too, encountered the Christ of John Paul II? Do we seek to encounter him? One person who has done so is Father Marcial Maciel. His words reflect the supreme authenticity of this encounter.

> To me, it was always perfectly clear that anyone who knows Christ must make him known to others. Whoever has received the torch of the faith must pass it on to those around him, for faith in Christ is a treasure we must share with joy. Apostolic spirit is a need, spring-ing from within, to communicate an experience that gives meaning to your own life. . . .

> The great field of the world stretches out before our eyes, and it is ready for harvest. Others have sowed and watered it with their blood. Our task is to go and gather the fruits of the seed that God himself has sowed in souls. The world awaits us because it awaits Christ. It awaits the Good News from our lips. We cannot silence the voice of Christ, who sends us into the world. We cannot remain idle doing nothing,[984] staring into the sky, like the apostles on As-cension Day, while the Kingdom demands urgent action. There is no time to lose. We have to set out. Today. Here. Now.[985]

3. God's Only Plan

As we strive to respond to the challenge of evangelization, crossing the threshold of hope into the third Christian millennium, the horizons that open before us are both promising and daunting. The panorama of the world is much like the one Christ contemplated at his Ascension. A story often recounted among Orthodox Christians describes the scene.

> After Easter, when Christ was at the point of going up to heaven, he looked down on earth and saw it submerged in darkness, with the exception of a few small lights that illuminated the city of Jerusa-lem. In the process of his Ascension, he came across the angel Gabriel, who was accustomed to going on terrestrial missions. The divine messenger asked him: "What are those little lights?" "They

---

[983] Lk 12:49.
[984] Cf. Mt 20:6.
[985] Letter of Father Marcial Maciel to all members of the Regnum Christi Movement, *Apostles of the New Evangelization*, November 21, 1993, Solemnity of Christ the King (Hamden, CT: CIF, 1995), pp. 2, 30.

are the apostles seated around my mother. My plan is that, once I return to heaven, I will send them the Holy Spirit so that these little fires become a great fire that inflames the whole earth with love." The angel replied intrepidly: "And, what will you do if the plan doesn't work?" After a moment of silence, the Lord replied: "I don't have any other plan!"[986]

Was Christ not a bit reckless? Did he not confide too much in these men, all of whom had abandoned him under the shadow of the cross? Does not John Paul II also trust families and young people too much? Is his confidence in humanity and hope for the future not excessive, given the cruelty of our past "century of tears"?

Even after the apostles had experienced the joy of Christ's resurrection, they huddled together in fear behind locked doors. Were these the ones, together with Mary and the women who had stood steadfast at the foot of the cross, who would carry out the Savior's plan of salvation in history? In our present day, when one out of every two marriages ends in divorce, will families really carry out a New Evangelization?

Christ knew each of his chosen apostles well — better than they knew themselves. He was fully aware that his salvific plan for humanity far surpassed anything they could ever accomplish. But Christ also knew that he had won for these apostles the gift of the Holy Spirit by his Incarnation, by the drops of blood he sweat in Gethsemane, the crown of thorns he wore, and the agonizing death he suffered upon the cross.

Father Marcial Maciel describes how the Holy Spirit changed the lives of the first apostles — the same Holy Spirit who can transform us into Christ's witnesses at the dawn of the third millennium.

> What we say of Paul could be said of the other apostles. Once they overcame their initial fear they abandoned the policy of "closed doors" to go out into the world and preach Christ. They had a powerful ally — a power that came from on high and to whom we must also turn: the Holy Spirit. Before Pentecost the apostles saw the risen Lord with their own eyes, and they ate and drank with him. Yet the specter of the cross still casts its shadow over their spirits and paralyzes them. They believe in the resurrection and they delight in being with the Master again. Nonetheless, they do not dare to open the doors and go out and bear witness. They need a higher force. They gather in prayer with Mary to seek strength. And, all of a sudden, they are granted the great gift of the Holy Spirit. These irresolute and timid men then break the barriers of fear and burst into the squares speaking about Christ. In reality the Holy Spirit is

---

[986] From the homily of Cardinal Roger Etchegaray for the opening of the Holy Door of the Basilica of St. Paul Outside-the-Walls in Rome, January 25, 2000, as cited by the Zenit News Service.

the true agent of our apostolic endeavors. It is he who helps us to overcome our unfounded worries, our reluctance, the fear we have of giving ourselves, and our human respect. He gives us the grace to leave behind apostolic plans that are no longer effective. He opens new paths where everything seemed blocked. It is he who gives an apostle ardor to preach the Gospel, he who guarantees victory, he who opens hearts to Christ's grace. With the power of the Holy Spirit, these men set out for distant lands, bearing in their hands the cross as their only treasure, the Gospel on their lips as their only wisdom, and in their hearts Christ as their one and supreme love.[987]

III. To Set the World Ablaze

In the inscrutable mystery of God's eternal Providence, each one of us has been called to live at a critical juncture in mankind's history. We have crossed the threshold of hope, led by the man who has brought new confidence to a humanity tempted to despair of itself.

For more than two decades as Pope, John Paul II has not ceased to proclaim the one person who is the true source of hope for all peoples: Christ, the Redeemer of Man. The transforming power of Christ's redemption, the merciful love of the Father he has revealed, the life-giving gift of the Holy Spirit he has won for us — in the Trinity alone rests mankind's hope for the future.

John Paul II believes that through Christ's redeeming power Christian unity can be achieved in the third millennium. He believes that the Church's evangelizing mission *ad gentes* can become a reality on the continent of Asia. He looks with hope upon the unprecedented growth of Christianity in Africa. He believes that the New Evangelization can restore the soul of Europe and America.

But these seeds of hope will grow into a thriving plant, able to provide shelter for the human spirit, only through the renewal of the family. If the most vital cell of society, the domestic Church, is evangelized and becomes an irresistible source of evangelization, then the tears of the twentieth century will truly have prepared the ground for a new springtime of humanity.

John Paul II does not stand alone. Countless mothers and fathers are responding to his appeal. They are strengthening their own families by deepening their life of prayer, their personal relationship with Christ, and transmitting their faith to their children. They are penetrating into the rich treasures of the Church's teaching on marriage and the family through study circles, evening classes, and distance-learning programs.

---

[987] Letter of Father Marcial Maciel to all members of the Regnum Christi Movement, *Apostles of the New Evangelization*, pp. 7-8.

They are forming movements to promote and defend the family, not just among others like themselves, but in the halls of legislatures and the meeting rooms of the United Nations.

Priests and theologians are beginning to light the fuse on the "time bomb" that is John Paul II's theology of the body. More and more married couples are giving vibrant testimony that responsible parenthood through natural family planning is within the grasp of all husbands and wives who are willing to die to themselves so that they and their families may have life.

In a myriad of forms the Holy Spirit is acting, at times perhaps imperceptibly, on occasion with almost unprecedented vigor and force. The Paraclete is coming to humanity's defense by reinvigorating Christian families. Will each one of us respond to his call in our own lives?

On the morning of August 20, 2001, upon the hill of Tor Vergata, just outside Rome, John Paul II celebrated the closing Mass of World Youth Day. His young audience listened in rapt attention to the words of his homily, responding to the most demanding phrases with cheers and applause. As he reached the end of what that occasion permitted him to say, the Holy Father swept a loving gaze across the two million young men and women from every continent gathered on the hills before him.

Many among them would one day become mothers and fathers. Others would consecrate their lives to Christ in virginity for the Kingdom of Heaven. Future priests were there, seated upon the grass. Among the congregation were future politicians and journalists and university professors who would help shape a culture of life.

The Holy Father addressed a final, farewell challenge to that multitude of young people enveloping the Roman hillsides. Who can doubt that he has spoken time and again in his heart those very same words to every Christian family? "From Rome, from the City of Peter and Paul, the Pope follows you with affection and, paraphrasing St. Catherine of Siena, reminds you: 'If you are what you should be, you will set the whole world ablaze!'"

SELECT BIBLIOGRAPHY

Works by Karol Wojtyła

The Acting Person. Trans. Andrzej Potocki. Ed. A. Tymieniecka. *Analecta Husserliana* 10; Dordrecht, Holland: Reidel Publishing Company, 1979.

Collected Plays and Writings on Theater. Trans. Boleslaw Taborski. Berkeley: University of California Press, 1987.

Easter Vigil and Other Poems. Trans. Jerzy Peterkiewicz. New York: Random House, 1979.

Educazione all'amore. (An anthology of Wojtyła's writings.) Trans. Elzbierta Cywiak and Vladyslav [sic] Kujawski. Rome: Edizioni Logos, 1978.

Faith According to St. John of the Cross. Trans. Jordan Aumann, O.P. San Francisco: Ignatius Press, 1981.

The Jeweler's Shop. Trans. Boleslaw Taborski. New York: Random House, 1980.

"La verità dell'enciclica Humanae Vitae.*"* In *L'Osservatore Romano* 109 (January 5, 1969): I, 2.

Love and Responsibility. Trans. H.T. Willetts. New York: Farrar, Straus, and Giroux, 1981.

Sign of Contradiction. New York: The Seabury Press, 1979.

Sources of Renewal: The Implementation of the Second Vatican Council. Trans. P.S. Falla. San Francisco: Harper and Row, 1980.

Works by Pope John Paul II

Ad Limina Addresses: The Addresses of His Holiness Pope John Paul II to the Bishops of the United States During Their Ad Limina *Visits, March 5-December 9, 1988.* Washington, D.C.: United States Catholic Conference, 1989.

Crossing the Threshold of Hope. Ed. Vittorio Messori. New York: Alfred A. Knopf, 1994.

The Encyclicals of John Paul II, edited with introductions by J. Michael Miller, C.S.B. Huntington, IN: Our Sunday Visitor Publishing, 1996.

Gift and Mystery: On The Fiftieth Anniversary of My Priestly Ordination, New York: Doubleday, 1996.

God, Father and Creator: A Catechesis on the Creed. Vol. 1. Boston: Pauline Books and Media, 1996.

Insegnamenti di Giovanni Paolo II. 18 vols. Vatican City: Libreria Editrice Vaticana.

Jesus, Son and Savior: A Catechesis on the Creed. Vol. 2. Boston: Pauline Books and Media, 1996.

John Paul II Speaks to Youth at World Youth Day. San Francisco/Washington, D.C.: Ignatius Press/Catholic News Service, 1993.

Letters to My Brother Priests: Holy Thursday (1979-1994). Ed. James P. Socias. Princeton/Chicago: Scepter Publishers/Midwest Theological Forum, 1994.

The Post-Synodal Apostolic Exhortations of John Paul II. Ed. with introductions by J. Michael Miller, C.S.B. Huntington, IN: Our Sunday Visitor Publishing, 1998.

Prayers and Devotions from Pope John Paul II. Ed. Bishop Peter Canisius Johannes van Lierde, O.S.A. Trans. Firman O'Sullivan. New York: Viking, 1984.

The Pope Speaks to the American Church: John Paul II's Homilies, Speeches, and Letters to Catholics in the United States. Prepared by Cambridge Center for the Study of Faith and Culture. Eds. R. Malone and S. DiGiovanni. San Francisco: Harper Collins, 1992.

Priesthood in the Third Millennium: Addresses of Pope John Paul II, 1993. Princeton/Chicago: Scepter Publishers/Midwest Theological Forum, 1994.

The Social Teaching of John Paul II: The True Dimensions of Development Today, Texts of John Paul II (August 1979-February 1982). Vatican City: Tipografia Poliglotta Vaticana, 1982.

The Spirit, Giver of Life and Love: A Catechesis on the Creed. Vol. 3. Boston: Pauline Books and Media, 1996.

Springtime of Evangelization. Ed. Thomas D. Williams, L.C. San Diego: Basilica Press, 1999.

The Theology of the Body: Human Love in the Divine Plan. Boston, MA: Pauline Books and Media, 1997.

Encyclicals

Redemptor Hominis (The Redeemer of Man) 1979.

Dives in Misericordia (On the Mercy of God) 1980.

Laborem Exercens (On Human Work) 1981.

Slavorum Apostoli (The Apostles to the Slavs) 1985.

Dominum et Vivificantem (The Holy Spirit in the Life of the Church and the World) 1986.

Redemptoris Mater (Mother of the Redeemer) 1987.

Sollicitudo Rei Socialis (On Social Concern)1987.

Redemptoris Missio (Mission of the Redeemer) 1990.

Centesimus Annus (On the Hundredth Anniversary of *Rerum Novarum*) 1991.

Veritatis Splendor (The Splendor of Truth) 1993.

Evangelium Vitae (The Gospel of Life) 1995.

Ut Unum Sint (On Commitment to Ecumenism) 1995.

Fides et Ratio (Faith and Reason) 1998.

Post-Synodal Apostolic Exhortations

Catechesi Tradendae (Catechesis in Our Time) 1979.

Familiaris Consortio (The Role of the Christian Family in the Modern World) 1981.

Reconciliatio et Poenitentia (On Reconciliation and Penance in the Mission of the Church Today) 1984.

Christifideles Laici (Lay Members of Christ's Faithful People) 1988.

Pastores Dabo Vobis (I Will Give You Shepherds) 1992.

Ecclesia in Africa (The Church in Africa) 1995.

Vita Consecrata (Consecrated Life) 1996.

Ecclesia in America (The Church in America) 1999.

Ecclesia in Asia (The Church in Asia) 2000.

Apostolic Constitutions

Sapientia Christiana ("Christian Wisdom," On Ecclesiastical Universities and Faculties) 1979.

Sacrae Disciplinae Leges (On the New Code of Canon Law) 1983.

Divinus Perfectionis Magister[988] (Master of Divine Perfection) 1983.

Pastor Bonus[989] (The Good Shepherd) 1988.

Ex Corde Ecclesiae ("From the Heart of the Church," Apostolic Constitution on Catholic Universities) 1990.

---

[988] This apostolic constitution modified the process for determining sainthood.
[989] *Pastor Bonus* reformed the structures of the Roman Curia.

Fidei Depositum[990] (The Deposit of Faith) 1992.

Universi Dominici Gregis[991] (The Shepherd of the Lord's Whole Flock) 1996.

Apostolic Letters

Dominicae Cenae (Mystery and Worship of the Eucharist) 1980.

Egregiae Virtutis[992] (Men of Extraordinary Virtue) 1980.

Redemptionis Anno[993] (In the Year of the Redemption) 1984.

Redemptionis Donum (To Men and Women Religious on their Consecration in the Light of the Mystery of the Redemption) 1984.

To the Youth of the World 1985.

Euntes in Mundum Universum[994] (Going Out into the Whole World) 1988.

Ecclesia Dei[995] (The Church of God) 1988.

Mulieris Dignitatem (On the Dignity and Vocation of Women) 1988.

On the Fiftieth Anniversary of the Beginning of the Second World War 1989.

Ordinatio Sacerdotalis (On Reserving Priestly Ordination to Men Alone) 1994.

Tertio Millennio Adveniente ("The Coming Third Millennium," On

Preparation for the Jubilee of the Year 2000) 1994.

Orientale Lumen[996] (Light of the East) 1995.

For the Fourth Centenary of the Union of Brest 1995.

Ad Tuendam Fidem[997] (In Protecting the Faith) 1998.

Dies Domini (The Day of the Lord) 1998.

Apostolos Suos[998] (His Apostles)1998.

---

[990] *Fidei Depositum* promulgated the *Catechism of the Catholic Church.*

[991] This apostolic constitution modified the process for electing the pope.

[992] By this letter John Paul II named Sts. Cyril and Methodius, the first evangelists of the Slavic peoples, as co-patrons of Europe along with St. Benedict, the founder of Western monasticism.

[993] In this letter, written to Catholics living in Jerusalem, John Paul proposed a "special Statute internationally guaranteed" to preserve "the unique and sacred character" of the Holy City.

[994] The Holy Father wrote this letter to commemorate the millennium of Christianity in Rus'.

[995] This letter, written after Archbishop's Lefebvre's schismatic ordination of three bishops, created a commission to reconcile those members of the Lefebvrist movement who did not wish to follow the archbishop into schism.

[996] This letter was written to mark the centenary of Pope Leo XIII's Apostolic Letter *Orientalium Dignitas* "in which he sought to safeguard the significance of the Eastern traditions for the whole Church" (OL, 1).

[997] This letter establishes penalties in Canon Law for violating the 1989 Profession of Faith and Oath of Fidelity.

[998] This letter deals with the teaching authority and pastoral role of national conferences of bishops.

Letters and Messages

For the Sixth Centenary of the Death of St. Catherine of Siena 1980.

To Leonid Brezhnev 1980.

For the Fifth Centenary of the Birth of Martin Luther 1983.

Salvifici Doloris (On the Christian Meaning of Human Suffering) 1984.

To Mikhail Gorbachev 1988.

To George Bush and Saddam Hussein 1991.

Letter to Families 1994.

Letter to Children 1994.

Letter to Women 1995.

Encyclicals of Other Popes

Leo XIII. *Arcanum*: Encyclical of Pope Leo XIII on Christian Marriage, February 10, 1880. In *The Papal Encyclicals 1878-1903*. Ed. Claudia Carlen. Wilmington, NC: McGrath, 1986, pp. 29-40.

Pius XI. *Casti Connubii*: Encyclical Letter of Pope Pius XI on Christian Marriage, December 31, 1930. Official Vatican Text edition. Boston: St. Paul Books and Media, n.d.

John XXIII. Encyclical Letter *Mater et Magistra* (Mother and Teacher). May 15, 1961.

N.C.W.C. translation, Boston: St. Paul Editions, 1961.

Paul VI. Encyclical Letter *Humanae Vitae* (On Human Life). July 25, 1968. Official Vatican Text edition. Boston: St. Paul Books and Media, n.d.

Church Documents

Catechism of the Catholic Church. The second English edition, which incorporates the modifications from the *Editio Typica*, Rome-Washington, D.C.: Libreria Editrice Vaticana-U.S.C.C., 1997) Rome-Washington, D.C.: Libreria Editrice Vaticana, 2000.

Congregation for the Doctrine of the Faith:
— Declaration on Procured Abortion, November 18, 1974.
— Declaration on Certain Questions Concerning Sexual Ethics *Persona Humana*, December 29, 1975.
— Declaration on Euthanasia, May 5, 1980.
— Instruction on Certain Aspects of the "Theology of Liberation," August 6, 1984.
— Instruction on Christian Freedom and Liberation: The Truth Makes Us Free *Libertatis Conscientia*, March 22, 1986.
— On the Pastoral Care of Homosexual Persons, October 1, 1986.
— Instruction on Bioethics, Respect for Human Life *Donum Vitae*, February 22, 1987.

— Profession of Faith and Oath of Fidelity, January 9, 1989.

— Some Aspects of Christian Meditation, October 15, 1989.

— Instruction on the Ecclesial Vocation of the Theologian *Donum Veritatis*, May 24, 1990.

— Non-Discrimination against Homosexual Persons, May 30, 1992.

Congregation for Catholic Education:

— Educational Guidance in Human Love, November 1, 1983.

— Religious Dimension of Education in a Catholic School, April 7, 1988.

Pontifical Council for the Family:

— The Truth and Meaning of Human Sexuality, December 8, 1995.

— Preparation for the Sacrament of Marriage, May 13, 1996.

— The Pastoral Care of the Divorced and Remarried, January 26, 1997.

Books

Accattoli, Luigi. *Man of the Millennium: John Paul II*. Trans. Jordan Aumann, O.P. Boston: Pauline Books and Media, 2000.

Ashley, Benedict. *Theologies of the Body: Humanist and Christian*. Braintree, MA: Pope John XXIII Center, 1985.

Augustine, *Confessions*, translated by John K. Ryan, New York: Doubleday Image Books, 1960.

Aumann, Jordan. *Spiritual Theology*. London: Sheed and Ward, 1980.

Beabout, Gregory R., editor. *A Celebration of the Thought of John Paul II*. St. Louis: St. Louis University Press, 1998.

Bennett, William J. *Index of Leading Cultural Indicators*. New York: 1993.

Billings, John. *The Ovulation Method*. Melbourne, Australia: Advocate Press Pty, 1983.

Blanshard, Brand. *Four Reasonable Men*. Middletown, CT: Wesleyan University Press, 1984.

Boniecki, Rev. Adam, M.I.C. *The Making of the Pope of the Millennium: Kalendarium of the Life of Karol Wojtyła*. Trans. Irena and Thaddeus Mirecki et al. Stockbridge, MA: Marian Press, 2000.

Buttiglione, Rocco. *Karol Wojtyła: The Thought of the Man Who Became John Paul II*. Trans. Paolo Guietti and Francesca Murphy. Grand Rapids, MI: Eerdmans, 1997.

Caffarra, Carlo. *Living in Christ: Fundamental Principles of Catholic Moral Teaching*. Trans. Christopher Ruff. San Francisco: Ignatius Press, 1987.

Dawson, Christopher. *Christianity in East and West*. Ed. John J. Mulloy. La Salle, IL: Sherwood Sugden and Company Publishers, 1981 (original edition: 1959).

— *Christianity and the New Age*. Sophia Institute Press, 1988 (original edition: 1931).

D'Emilio, John, and Freedman, Estelle B. *Intimate Matters: A History of Sexuality in America*. New York: Harper & Row, 1988.

De Finance, Joseph, SJ. *An Ethical Inquiry*. Rome: Editrice Pontificia Università Gregoriana, 1991.

— *Conoscenza Dell'Essere: Trattato di Ontologia*. Roma: Editrice Pontificia Università Gregoriana, 1998.

De Haro, Ramón García, *Marriage and Family in the Documents of the Magisterium*. Trans. William E. May. San Francisco: Ignatius Press, 1993.

Dembski, William B. *Intelligent Design: The Bridge Between Science and Theology*, Downers Grove, IL: InterVarsity Press, 1999.

DiNoia, J.A., O.P., and Romanus Cessario, O.P., eds. *Veritatis Splendor and the Renewal of Moral Theology*. Huntington, IN: Our Sunday Visitor Publishing Division, 1994.

Drogin, Elasah. *Margaret Sanger: Father of Modern Society*. New Hope, KY: CUL Press Publications, 1989.

Dulles, Avery. *The Splendor of Faith: The Theological Vision of Pope John Paul II*. New York: Crossroad, 1999.

Finnis, John. *Natural Law and Natural Rights*. Oxford: Oxford Univ. Press, 1980.

— *Fundamentals of Ethics*. Washington, D.C.: Georgetown University Press, 1983.

— *Moral Absolute: Tradition, Revision and Truth*. Washington, D.C.: Catholic University of America Press, 1991.

Frossard, André. *Portrait of John Paul II*. San Francisco: Ignatius Press, 1990.

— and Pope John Paul II. *Be Not Afraid!* New York: St. Martin's Press, 1984.

Grisez, Germain. *The Way of the Lord Jesus. Volume 1: Christian Moral Principles*. Chicago: Franciscan Herald Press, 1983.

— *The Way of the Lord Jesus. Volume 2: Living a Christian Life*. Chicago: Franciscan Press, 1993.

— *The Way of the Lord Jesus. Volume 3: Difficult Moral Questions*. Chicago: Franciscan Press, 1997.

— and Russell Shaw. *Beyond the New Morality: The Responsibilities of Freedom.* 2ⁿᵈ Revised Edition. Notre Dame: University of Notre Dame Press, 1980.

— and Russell Shaw. *Fulfillment in Christ: A Summary of Christian Moral Principles.* Notre Dame: University of Notre Dame Press, 1991.

Grondelski, John. "Fruitfulness as an Essential Dimension of Acts of Conjugal Love: An Interpretive Study of the Pre-Pontifical Thought of John Paul II." Ph.D. Diss.: Fordham University, 1985. Available through University Mircrofilms International, Ann Arbor, MI, #86-12858.

Hogan, Richard M., S.J. and John M. Levoir. *Covenant of Love.* San Francisco: Ignatius Press, 1992 (First edition: Doubleday, 1985).

Johnson, Paul. *A History of the American People.* New York: HarperCollins, 1997.

Kasun, J., *The War against Population: The Economics and Ideology of Population Control.* San Francisco: Ignatius Press, 1988.

Kippley, John F. *Sex and Marriage Covenant: A Basis for Morality.* Cincinnati, OH: The Couple to Couple League, 1991.

— and Sheila Kippley. *The Art of Natural Family Planning*, 4ᵗʰ edition. Cincinnati: Couple to Couple League, 1997.

Krapiec, Mieczyław A., O.P. *I-Man: An Outline of Philosophical Anthropology.* New Britain, CT: Mariel Publications, 1983.

Lawler, Rev. Ronald D., *The Christian Personalism of John Paul II.* Chicago: Franciscan Herald Press, 1982.

Lawler, Rev. Ronald D., Joseph Boyle and William May. *Catholic Sexual Ethics.* 2ⁿᵈ Edition. Huntington, IN: Our Sunday Visitor, 1998.

Lucas Lucas, Rev. Ramón, L.C. *L'Uomo: Spirito Incarnato.* Rome: Edizioni Paoline, 1993. Spanish edition: *El hombre espíritu encarnado: Compendio de filosofía del hombre.* Trans. Ramón Lucas Lucas. Madrid: Atenas, 1995.

— Ed. *Veritatis Splendor: Testo integrale con commento filosofico-teologico.* Milan, 1994.

— Ed. *Comentario Interdisciplinar a la "Evangelium Vitae."* Madrid: Biblioteca de Autores Cristianos (BAC), 1996.

— *Antropologia e problemi bioetici.* Rome: San Paolo, 2001.

MacIntyre, Alasdair. *After Virtue.* Notre Dame, IN: University of Notre Dame Press, 1981.

— *Three Rival Versions of Moral Inquiry.* London: Duckworth, 1990.

Maritain, Jaques. *The Rights of Man and Natural Law*. San Francisco: Ignatius Press, 1986.
— *The Person and the Common Good*. Trans. John J. Fitzgerald. New York: Charles Scribner's Sons, 1947.

Martin, Ralph and Peter Williamson. *John Paul II and the New Evangelization*. San Francisco: Ignatius Press, 1995.

Masters, William H., and Virginia E. Johnson. *Homosexuality in Perspective*. Boston: Brown and Company, 1979.

May, William. *Marriage: The Rock on Which the Family Is Built*. San Francisco: Ignatius Press, 1995.

McInerny, Ralph M. *What Went Wrong with Vatican II*. Manchester, NH: Sophia Institute Press, 1998.

Melina, Rev. Livio. *Morale: Tra Crisi e Rinnovamento*. Milan: Ares, 1993.

Michener, James. *Poland*. New York: Fawcett Crest, 1983.

Miller, J. Michael, CSB. *The Shepherd and the Rock: Origins, Development and Mission of the Papacy*. Huntington, IN: Our Sunday Visitor Publishing, 1995.
— *The Encyclicals of John Paul II*. Edited with introductions by J. Michael Miller, CSB. Huntington, IN: Our Sunday Visitor Publishing, 1996.

Muncy, Mitchell S., editor. *The End of Democracy? The Judicial Usurpation of Politics*. (The Celebrated *First Things* Debate). Dallas: Spence, 1997.
— *The End of Democracy? II — A Crisis of Legitimacy*. Dallas: Spence, 1999.

Neuhaus, Richard John. *Appointment in Rome, The Church in America Awakening*. New York: Herder and Herder, Crossroad, 1999.
— *The Catholic Moment: The Paradox of the Church in the Postmodern World*. San Francisco: Harper and Row, 1987.
— *The Naked Public Square*. Grand Rapids, MI: Eerdmans, 1984.

Noonan, John T. *Contraception: A History of Its Treatment by Catholic Theologians and Canonists*, Cambridge, MA: The Belknap Press of Harvard University Press, 1965.

Pinckaers, Servais, O.P. *The Sources of Christian Ethics*. Trans. Sr. Mary Thomas Noble, O.P. Washington, D.C.: Catholic University of America Press and Edinburgh, Scotland: T&T Clark Ltd., 1995.

Poupard, Paul. *The Church and Culture: Challenge and Confrontation, Inculturation and Evangelization*. Trans. Rev. John H. Miller, CSC. St. Louis, MO: Central Bureau, 1989. Original French edition: *L'Eglise au defie des cultures*, Paris: Desclee, 1989.

Ratzinger, Joseph, and Vittorio Messori. *The Ratzinger Report: An Exclusive Interview on the State of the Church*. San Francisco: Ignatius Press, 1995.

Ratzinger, Joseph, and Peter Seewald. *Salt of the Earth: The Church at the End of the Millennium*. San Francisco: Ignatius Press, 1997.

Rogers, Perry M., editor. *Aspects of Western Civilization, Problems and Sources in History*. Englewood Cliffs: Prentice-Hall, 1988.

Roof, Wade Clark. *A Generation of Seekers: The Spiritual Journeys of the Baby Boom Generation*. San Francisco: HarperCollins Publishers, 1993.

Royal, Robert. *The Catholic Martyrs of the Twentieth Century*. New York: Crossroad, 2000.

Saward, John. *Christ Is the Answer: The Christ-Centered Teaching of Pope John Paul II*. New York: Alba House, 1995.

Schall, J. *The Church, the State, and Society in the Thought of John Paul II*. Chicago: Trans. Boleslaw Taborski. Franciscan Herald Press, 1982.

Schmitz, Kenneth L. *At the Center of the Human Drama: The Philosophical Anthropology of Karol Wojtyła/Pope John Paul II*. Washington, DC: Catholic University of America Press, 1993.

Shivanandan, Mary. *Crossing the Threshold of Love: A New Vision of Marriage*. Washington, DC: Catholic University of America Press, 1999.

Smith, Janet E. *Why* Humanae Vitae *Was Right: A Reader*. San Francisco: Ignatius Press, 1993.

Sorokin, Pitirim. *The American Sex Revolution*. Boston: Porter Sargent Publishers, 1956.

Spaemann, Robert. *Concetti morali fondamentali*. Casale Monferrato: Piemme, 1993.

St. John of the Cross. *The Collected Works of St. John of the Cross*. Trans. Kieran Kavanaugh, OCD, and Otilio Rodriguez, OCD. Washington, D.C.: ICS Publications, 1979.

Sullivan, Francis A. *Magisterium: Teaching Authority in the Catholic Church*. New York: Paulist Press, 1983.

Van Straaten, Werenfried O. Praem. *Where God Weeps*. Netherlands: Oostpriesterhulp, 1970.

Von Hildebrand, Dietrich. *Ethics*. Chicago: Franciscan Herald Press, 1953.
— *Marriage : The Mystery of Faithful Love*. Manchester, NH: Sophia Institute Press, 1991. (First English edition 1942)

Weigel, George. *Witness to Hope.* New York: HarperCollins, 1999.

— *Soul of the World.* Grand Rapids, MI: Eerdmans, 1996.

— *The Final Revolution: The Resistance Church and the Collapse of Communism.* New York: Oxford University Press, 1992.

— and Robert Royal. *Building the Free Society: Democracy, Capitalism and Catholic Social Teaching.* Grand Rapids, MI: Eerdmans, 1993.

Williams, George Huntston. *The Mind of John Paul II.* New York: The Seabury Press, 1981.

— *The Contours of Church and State in the Thought of John Paul II.* Waco, TX: Baylor University, 1983.

Williams, Thomas, L.C. *Building on Solid Ground: Authentic Christian Values and How to Attain Them.* New York: Alba House, 1995.

Woznicki, Rev. Andrew Nicholas. *A Christian Humanism: Karol Wojtyła's Existential Personalism.* New Britain, CT: Mariel Publications, 1980.

— *The Dignity of Man as Person: Essays on the Christian Humanism of John Paul II.* San Francisco: The Society of Christ, 1987.

Zimmerman, Anthony, Francois Guy, and Dionigi Tettamanzi, eds. *Natural Family Planning: Nature's Way, God's Way.* Milwaukee: De Rance Foundation, 1980.

****

Articles

Anderson, Carl. "The Role of the Family in the Conversion of Culture." In *Communio*, 421, Winter 1994, pp. 765-775.

Ashley, Benedict, O.P. and Albert Moraczewski, O.P. "Cloning, Aquinas, and the Embryonic Person." In *The National Catholic Bioethics Quarterly.* Brighton, MA: The National Catholic Bioethics Center (formerly Pope John XXIII Center). Vol. 1, No. 2, Summer 2001, pp. 189-201.

Barrajón, Pedro, L.C. "Sapiential Dimension of Philosophy: A Reading of *Fides et Ratio* from the Perspective of St. Bonaventure." In *Alpha Omega*, Journal of Philosophy and Theology of the Regina Apostolorum Pontifical University of Rome, Year II, Number 3, September-December, 1999, pp. 363-375.

Bernstein, Carl. "John Paul II and the Fall of Communism." In *A Celebration of the Thought of John Paul II*, pp. 134-135.

Bishops' Committee for Pro-Life Activities. *National Standards of the National Conference of Catholic Bishops' Diocesan Development Program for Natural Family Planning.* Washington, D.C.: United States Catholic Conference, USCC, 1990.

Borkman, Thomasina J., and Mary Shivanandan. "The Impact of Selected Aspects of Natural Family Planning on the Couple Relationship." In *International Review of Natural Family Planning*, 8, 1, 1984, pp. 58-66.

Cantu, Yvette. "Recovery Change and Homosexuality: What the Experts Have to Say," at www.frc.org/issues in depth/homosexual culture.

Caffarra, Carlo. "Introduzione Generale: Verità ed ethos del amore umano." In *Uomo e donna lo creò*. Rome: Città Nuova, 1985.

Colson, Charles. "Striving Side by Side for the Gospel in a Post-Christian Culture." In *John Paul II and the New Evangelization*, pp. 269-285.

Crosby, John F. "The Incommunicability of Human Persons." In *The Thomist*, 57, 3, July, 1993, pp. 403-442.

Daniels, Matthew. "Vermont Legislature Threatens Marriage." In *National Catholic Register*, Vol. 76, No. 11, March 12-18, 2000, pp. 1, 15.

Dulles, Avery. "John Paul II and the New Evangelization: What Does It Mean?" In *Pope John Paul II and the New Evangelization*, pp. 25-39.

Ford, Norman, S.D.B. "The Human Embryo as Person in Catholic Teaching." In *The National Catholic Bioethics Quarterly*. Brighton, MA: The National Catholic Bioethics Center (formerly Pope John XXIII Center). Vol. 1, No. 2, Summer 2001, pp. 155-160.

Grondelski, John. "The Social Thought of Karol Wojtyła/Pope John Paul II: A Bibliographical Essay." In *Social Thought* 13 (Spring/Summer 1987), nos. 2/3: pp. 151-167.

Knight, Robert. "How Domestic Partnerships and 'Gay Marriage' Threaten the Family." At www.frc.org/ issues in depth/homosexual culture.

Lejeune, Jerome. "Genetica, etica e manipolazioni." In *Medicina e Morale* 3, 1985, pp. 565-576.

Lobato, Abelardo. "La persona en el pensamiento de Karol Wojtyła." In *Angelicum*, 56, 1979, pp. 165-210.

Maciel, Marcial, L.C., Letter to Members of Regnum Christi Movement, "The Home: School of Evangelization." Hamden, CT: CIF, 1995.

Martin, Francis. "Feminist Hermeneutics: An Overview (Part One)." In *Communio*, 18, Summer 1991, pp. 144-163.
— "Feminist Hermeneutics: An Overview (Part Two)." In *Communio*, 18, Fall 1991, pp. 398-424.

Neuhaus, Richard John. "The Anatomy of a Controversy." In *The End of Democracy?* pp. 175-267.

Rhonheimer, Martin. "Contraception, Sexual Behaviour, and Natural Law: Philosophical Foundation of the Norm of Humanae Vitae." In

Pontificio Istituto Giovanni Paolo II: *Humanae Vitae: vent'anni dopo*. Milan: Ares, 1989, pp. 73115.

Schindler, David L. "Catholic Theology, Gender, and the Future of Western Civilization." In *Communio*, 20, Summer 1993, pp. 200-239.

Schmitz, Kenneth L. "The Geography of the Human Person." In *Communio*, 13, Spring 1986, pp. 27-48.

Scola, Angelo. "L'Imago Dei e la sessualità umana: A proposito di una tesi originale della *Mulieris Dignitatem*." In *Anthropotes* 8, 1 June 1992, pp. 61-73.

Seifert, Josef. "Karol Cardinal Wojtyła (Pope John Paul II) as Philosopher and the Cracow/Lublin School of Philosophy." In *Aletheia* 2 (1981): pp. 130-199.

Styczen, Tadeusz. "L'antropologia della *Familiaris Consortio*." In *Anthropotes*, IX, 1, 1993, pp. 7-42.

Tettamanzi, Dionigi. "La sessualità umana: prospettive antropologiche, etiche e pedagogiche." In *Medicina e Morale* 2 (1984), pp. 129154.

Weigel, George. "John Paul II — Preparing the Twenty-first Century." In *Crisis*, November, 1997, pp. 6-14.
— "Prepared to Lead: The Education of Karol Wojtyła." In *Crisis*, October, 1998, pp. 12-17.
— "John Paul II and the Crisis of Humanism." In *First Things*, December 1999, pp. 31-36.

Williams, Thomas, L.C. " The Power of a Father's Strong Faith." In *National Catholic Register*, January 3, 2000, Vol. 76, No. 5, p. 9.

Wolicka, Elzbieta. "Participation in Community: Wojtyła's Social Anthropology." Trans. Alice Manterys. In *Communio* 8 (Summer 1981): pp. 108-118.

Audiocassettes
"Pandora's Pillbox: Learn to Debunk the Myths of Contraception." The Gift Foundation, Carpentersville, IL 1999.

Smith, Janet. "Contraception: Why Not?"

West, Christopher. "Naked without Shame: Sex and the Christian Mystery — Reflections on Pope John Paul II's Theology of the Body." The Gift Foundation, Carpentersville, IL, 2000.

To the Glory of God through the Kingdom of Christ

Index of Names

A

Abzug, Bella 40
Adam 79-83, 86-89, 130-133, 149,
    161, 255, 333
Aquinas, St. Thomas 64, 68, 71,
    113, 131, 182, 201, 257, 258,
    281, 285, 293, 303
Aristotle 194
Augustine, St. 67, 74, 124, 200,
    207, 254, 283

B

Behe, Michael J. 196-199
Billings, Dr. John and Evelyn 171-
    172
Bonaventure, St. 201, 206
Bonhoffer, Dietrich 10
Bornestein, Kate 40
Brown, Dr. James B. 172
Butler, Judith 45
Buttiglione, Rocco 53, 282, 284,
    300

C

Chesterton, G.K. 9, 27
Cicero 35, 258
Comstock, Anthony 216
Crosby, John F. 240, 253

D

Daniels, Matt 30
Darwin, Charles 181
de Lubac, Henri xxi, xxii, 188
Deardon, Archbishop John F. 222

Dembski, William 195, 197
D'Emilio, John 215
Descartes, René 183, 252-255
de Tocqueville, Alexis 9, 15
Drogin, Elasah 21

E

Engels, Frederick 43, 44
Ettelbrick, Paula 23
Eve 79-83, 86-89, 130-133, 149,
    161, 255, 333

F

Firestone, Shulamith 44
Fisichella, Bishop Rino 210
Freedman 215
Freud, Sigmund 9, 44, 95, 96

G

Galton, Francis 181

H

Hilgers, Dr. Thomas 174
Hitler, Adolph 7, 9
Horowitz, David 45
Hunt, Mary 39

I

Ignatius of Loyola, St. 290, 349
Inherst, Sean 158

J

John of the Cross, Saint 146-148

John Paul II xvii-xx, xxii-xxx, 3-7,
13, 14, 19, 38, 43, 46, 47, 49,
51-53, 59-61, 64, 75, 77-82, 84,
86, 87, 90, 91, 95, 97, 98, 102,
104, 105-109, 111, 114, 115,
117, 118, 120, 122-133, 135,
138-145, 147, 149, 151-153,
157-159, 182, 185, 187, 188,
190, 194, 200, 202-204, 206-
209, 211-215, 224-231, 238,
242, 243, 245-247, 254-256,
258, 263-265, 267, 273, 276,
278, 279, 282-286, 289, 292,
294, 298, 300-311, 314, 315,
321, 322, 325-327, 329-331,
334-336, 338, 339, 341, 343-
353
John XXIII 219
Johnson, Paul 5
Justin, St. 184

K

Kant, Immanuel 57
Kippley, John, Shiela 162, 165, 170,
172
Kissling, Frances 39
Klaus, M.D., Dr. Hanna 161
Knaus, Herman 168
Knight, Robert H. 23, 27

L

La Mettrie 183
Lasseter, Ruth 161, 163, 176, 221,
233-235, 247

M

Maciel, Father Marciel 8, 9, 106,
121, 125, 212, 350, 351
Malthus, Thomas 160, 181
Mark, St. (Gospel of) 140
Marx, Karl 43, 95
Marx, Fr. Paul 335
Matthew, St. (Gospel of) 96-98,
108, 118, 140, 310

McCaffrey, Father Daniel 175
McCusker, M. Peter 175
McGovern, M.D., Thomas 173
McInerny, Ralph 221, 222, 230
Minh, Ho-Chi 43
Montagu, Ashley 164
More, St. Thomas 324

N

Neuhaus, Fr. Richard John xxv, 4,
109, 184
Newman, John Henry 9
Nietzsche, Friedrich 9, 95, 96
Noonan, Jr., John, T. 215, 216

O

Ogino, Kyusaku 168
O'Hair, Madalyn Murray 9
O'Leary, Dale 45

P

Pascal, Blaise 9
Paul, St. 27, 28, 60, 96, 98, 99, 100,
101, 103, 105, 108, 109, 111,
112, 124, 125, 127, 128, 132,
133, 134, 135, 136, 333, 351
Paul VI, Pope xxii, 13, 22, 52, 53,
118, 159, 160, 166, 174, 184,
188, 215, 219, 220, 221, 222,
223, 224, 231, 232, 233, 236,
238, 244, 245, 256, 259, 260,
262, 263, 267, 283, 284, 302,
318, 325, 334, 335, 338, 347,
348
Penrose, Roger 197, 198
Pius XI 216, 217, 218
Pius XII xiii, 213, 218
Place, Francis 181
Plato 109, 307
Pontius Pilate 200, 278

R

Ratzinger, Cardinal Joseph 45, 46
Reagan, Ronald 187, 332

Rehnquist, Chief Justice William
185
Ricoeur, Paul 95
Roetzer, Joseph 170

S

Sadik, Nafis 39
Sadunaite, Nijole 289-290
Sanger, Margaret 20, 21, 174, 216,
299
Scheler, Max 300
Shivanandan, Mary 161
Signorile, Michaelangelo 22, 23
Sorokin, Pitirim 27
Spaemann, Robert 317
Stalin, Joseph 9
Stevens, Justice John Paul 184, 185
Stoddard, Thomas 23

T

Teresa of Calcutta, Mother 315
Tortorici, Joseph 176

V

van Straaten, Father Werenfried 10
Vitz, Dr. Paul 9, 10
von Holbach, P.H.D. 183

W

Weigel, George 187
West, Christopher 145
Wilberforce, Samuel 9
Wojtyła, Karol 53, 54, 55, 74, 188,
219, 227, 239, 264, 266, 280,
283, 300, 304, 336

Index of Topics

A

Abortion 21, 22, 38, 41, 42, 145,
   162, 163, 166, 232, 233, 234,
   318, 346, 347
Abstinence 170, 171, 181, 299, 300,
   304, 305, 320, 321, 325
Act(s)
— circumstances of 316-317
— conjugal 84, 97, 145, 160, 220,
   224, 238, 244, 245, 246, 248,
   256, 262, 264, 266, 267, 272,
   305, 306, 312, 313, 319, 320,
   321, 323, 326, 330, 331, 340,
   341, 343, 344, procreative
   meaning of, 238, 272, 305, 319
— contraceptive 217, 223, 245-246,
   262, 267, 272, 273, 313, 319-
   320
— human 79, 223, 233, 282, 283,
   288, 291, 294, 297, 307, 325,
   326, 330, 332
— intention of 315-316
— intrinsically evil 224, 225, 273,
   318-319
— marital 84, 217, 218, 235, 272,
   320, 322
— moral 218, 227, 247, 255, 264
— morality of 313-319
— object of 56, 314
— of man 285-286
Ad Tuendam Fidem 230-231
Adultery 87, 95, 97, 118, 142
Affection
— and conjugal act 331
— and continence 171, 310
— and interior order of married life
   340
— and love 283, 288-306
Affectivity 289, 292, 303, 310
Alliance for Marriage 30
American Birth Control League 19,
   20, 215
American Civil Liberties Union
   (ACLU) 185
American Psychiatric Association
   30, 32, 33, 34
American Psychological Association
   (and homosexuality) 30-32, 35
Anglican Church 216
Appetite, sense 64-72
Asceticism 305, 309, 315, 323

B

Becket Fund 185
Billings Method (of NFP) 171-174
Biologism 256, 262-264, 266, 267,
   272
Birth Control
— and breakdown in public morality
   347
— and Christian Churches before
   1930 216
— and Margaret Sanger 20, 299
— and Popes 218-222, 231, 262
— and public authorities 236
— and U.N. 41-42, 45-46
— methods of 160-166
— vs. NFP 302
Birth Control Review 20
Birth regulation 118, 173, 218, 220,
   319

Body
— dignity of 103-104
— divinization of 112
— in heaven 109-115
— language of 142-146, 150-153,
    244, 246, 276, 305, 326, 331,
    343, 344
— masculinity and femininity of
    141, 310
— nuptial meaning of 81, 82, 83-
    85, 86, 88, 89, 98, 99, 102, 107,
    114, 115, 120-121, 123, 305,
    307, 310
— spiritualization of 111
— spousal meaning of 138, 310
— theology of xxii, xxiii, xxiv,
    xxvii, 4, 59, 64, 79, 81, 83, 108,
    147, 158, 159, 190, 255, 307,
    326, 353
— reveals divine mysteries 81
— reveals man 81-82
— redemption of 96-101
Breastfeeding, Ecological 172, 173
Body-Soul Dualism 252-256, 263-
    264
British Medical Journal 163

C

Cairo Conference 39
Calendar Rhythm Method (of NFP)
    175, 218
Casti Connubii 216-218
Categorical imperative 57
Catholics for a Free Choice 39
Celibacy
— and marriage 118, 122, 124, 126
— call to 115, 119, 123
— inner meaning of 117, 119
— superior (to marriage) 124-125
— why chosen 121-122
Centesimus Annus 346
Chastity
— and celibacy 115, 124-126
— and continence 299-306,
— and teenagers 234

— as moral virtue 312, 321-323,
    339-341, 343
— as purity 101
— condition for love 298-299, 310-
    311
— conjugal 302, 305, 306, 339, 340
— marital 171, 217, 220, 312
— homosexual persons called to 36
Children
— and birth rate 215
— and chastity 234
— and conjugal life 152-153
— and homosexual adoption 24, 31
— and society today 36, 37, 232
— duty of parents to educate 12-13
— in civilization which uses persons
    268
— in Marxist view 43-44
— importance of families to __
    4-11, 13-14, 18, 347
— number of in family 167, 181,
    262, 334-337
— openness to 321-322, 333
— procreation of 220
— regulating births of 218, 262,
    320, 333
— reflection of God's love 52
— threatened by breakdown of
    families 19, 232
Church of England 216
Civil rights 22, 25, 30, 35
— and homosexuality
— legislation 31
Communion of persons *(Communio
    personarum)* 6, 52, 80, 82,
    107, 310, 326, 339
Communism 186, 187
Community 6, 7, 8, 12, 14, 36, 39,
    41, 122, 136, 162, 198, 225,
    226, 229, 236, 336
— of the family 3, 6, 7
Comstock Laws 174, 216
Concupiscence 88, 89, 90, 100, 104,
    138, 221, 290, 298, 302, 303,
    305, 306, 308, 310
Confessions (of St. Augustine) 67

Congregation for the Doctrine of
 the Faith 45, 228
Conjugal
— act see Act, conjugal
— union
— unitive meaning 245, 312
Continence 119, 120-124, 171,
 235, 299-310, 318-324, 326,
 334, 339, 341
— as a virtue 323-324
— periodic 171, 235, 299, 302,
 304, 305, 306, 308, 310,
 318-327, 334, 341
Contraception
— and flawed idea of the human
 person 238-249, 263-264,
 267-272
— and language of the body 145
— and Margaret Sanger 21-22
— and natural law 256
— and "new genders" 41
— and meaning of sexual urge
 286-287
— Church teaching on 216-222
— definition of 160
— effects of 158-159, 161, 165-
 166, 231-237, 246-249
— essentially different from NFP
 312-327, 340-341
— historical development 214-
 216
— intrinsically evil 245-246,
 267
— methods of 160-164
— vs. NFP 170-177, 272-274,
 302, 312-327, 340-341
— why flourishing 180-181
Contraceptive act(s) (see Act,
 contraceptive)
Contraceptive mentality 159,
 180, 181, 237, 238, 247,
 248, 294, 312, 326, 341
— origins of 159, 181
"Conversion" therapy 32
Couple to Couple League 170,
 175

Covenant
— conjugal 7, 292
— of love 12, 142
— of Yahweh 144
Creighton Model (of NFP) 174
Crossing the Threshold of Love
 161
Culture of Life 145, 146, 346,
 353

D

Darwinism 195, 198, 199
Deconstructionism 44-45
Depo-Provera 164, 165, 166
*Diagnostic and Statistical
 Manual of Mental Disor-
 ders, The* 33
Dialectic of Sex, The 44
Dignity
— human 28, 47, 226, 227, 237,
 279, 318
— of the body 94, 103
Dissent 218, 222, 223, 226, 229,
 230
Diversity training 29
Divine Providence 258, 277,
 317, 333, 335
Divorce 5, 18, 26, 118, 174, 175,
 180, 232, 234, 347, 351
Domestic Church xxvi, 5, 8, 14,
 36, 352
"Domestic Partnerships" 22-24,
 27, 29, 30
Donum Veritatis 228-230

E

Ecclesia domestica (see Domestic Church)
Ecological breastfeeding 172,
 173
Emotions (also see Passions) 64,
 65, 69-74, 90, 91, 243, 247,
 288, 293, 295, 298, 301, 303
— concupiscible 70
— irascible 70

— should obey reason 67, 71-73
Enlightenment 160, 180-187, 192, 194, 195, 200, 203
Ephesians, Letter to the 127, 128, 129, 132, 214
Equality 46, 58
— between men and women 37, 39, 40, 42, 45, 268
Eucharist 12, 13, 71, 112, 113, 122, 131, 273, 341-343, 348
Eugenics 20, 181
— movement 20
Euthanasia 145, 268, 318, 345
Evangelii Nuntiandi 347

F

Faith
— and reason 183, 184, 194, 202, 203, 206, 207, 208, 357
Familiaris Consortio 5, 8, 18, 19, 182, 246, 272, 273, 327
Family
— and future of humanity 4
— and society 7
— as community 7-8
— as domestic Church 14-15
— communion of persons 6, 52, 80, 310, 326, 339
— "first society" 6-7
— kingly role 14
— priestly role 12-14
— prophetic role 8-11
— renewal of 352
— size 171, 334, 335
— society's first and most vital cell 5-6
Family Research Council 23, 27
Fatherhood 19, 84, 330, 331, 340
Fathers 9, 10, 14, 22, 66, 352, 353
Femininity 45, 82-85, 89, 97, 99, 103, 123, 138, 141-144, 149, 150, 152, 284, 286, 292, 303, 305, 309, 310, 340, 343
Feminism
— and Deconstructionism 44

— and Marxism, Neo-Marxism 43-44
— liberal (and goals) 42
— radical (and goals) 38, 39, 42-45
Feminist agenda 40
Fertility 44, 145, 163, 166-168, 170, 172, 176, 234, 243, 246, 248, 262, 295, 322, 324, 325, 331, 340
— cycle 167-170, 324
Fides et Ratio xix, 194, 200, 203, 208
First Amendment 34, 184
Freedom
— academic 35, 229
— and faith 208
— and periodic continence 319
— and personalistic norm 57
— and the Enlightenment 182, 183
— and morality of acts 314, 316
— and utilitarianism 268, 277-283
— based on truth 47, 200, 205, 227, 279
— causes responsibility 55
— □condition for gift of self 83
— condition for love 83, 310
— demands choices and renuncia-tion 67
— from sin 28
— human 227, 285, 301
— inner 36, 98, 301, 331-332
— lost by sin 89-90
— makes us persons 54, 242
— of the gift 83, 89, 90, 102, 112, 126, 138, 140, 150-151, 309, 343
— of conscience 57
— of the Holy Spirit 104-106
— of the will 191
— religious 184, 185
— true meaning of 100-102
— won for us by the Redemption 243
Friendship 39, 129, 293, 294

G

Gaudium et Spes 4, 186, 217, 220, 241, 257, 279, 332, 334, 335, 336
"Gay Marriage" 22, 23, 24
Gender 31, 32, 33, 38-42, 45, 46
— contract 40
— fluidity 40
—perspective at the U.N. 37, 38, 40, 41
— redefining 40
— roles 40
Gender Agenda: Redefining Equality, The 39
Genesis, Book of 26, 43, 52, 79-84, 87, 88, 107, 133, 240, 241
Gift
— betrothed love 293
— freedom a condition for 83
— of self, sincere, only way to find self 59
— law of the 52, 59, 82, 94, 101, 107
Goodwill 288, 293, 294, 296
Gratissimam Sane 6, 7
Guilt 72, 73, 202, 217, 263, 266, 317

H

Heart
— battlefield between love and lust 90-91
— Christ appeals to 95, 98
— correct attitude toward 95-96
Homosexual movement (see also Civil Rights) 17-36, 345, 346
Human Life International 335
Human Rights 37, 38, 41, 47, 237
Humanae Vitae
— and alleged biologism 262-267
— and openness to life 331
— and responsible transmission of human life 243-245, 325, 334
— called for total vision of man (correct anthropology) 53, 118
— contraception intrinsically wrong 166, 318
— definition of contraception 160
— describes authentic married love 283-284
— history of 221-227
— John Paul II's reflections on 147-153, 305, 310
— prophecies of 231-237
— teachings founded on natural law 256
— teachings practical and possible 338-344
Humanism 179-188, 281
Hysterectomy 162-163, 233

I

In vitro fertilization 241, 277
Incarnation 61, 81, 96, 103, 112, 182, 187, 259, 351
Innocence, original 81, 82, 85, 87, 89, 104, 105, 107
Instruction on the Ecclesial Vocation of the Theologian (see *Donum Veritatis*)
Intention, purity of 315-316
Integrity 41, 109, 111, 217, 301, 318
Intellect
— spiritual faculty 66, 191
— rational 66, 68
— practical function 66
— speculative function 66
Intelligent Design 194-199
Intelligent design (theory)
— irreducible complexity 198-199
Intercourse, sexual 74, 141, 232, 233, 276, 277, 287, 298, 299, 302, 304, 305, 312, 319, 320, 321, 322, 324
International Monetary Fund 19, 39, 237
International Planned Parenthood Federation 20, 38

International Year of the Family 6
International Youth and Family
    Encounter 212
Intra-Uterine Device (IUD) 161,
    162

J

*Just the Facts About Sexual Orienta-
tion and Youth* 32, 34

L

Lambda Legal Defense and Educa-
    tion Fund 23
Lambeth Conference 216
Law of the gift 52, 59, 82, 94, 101,
    107
Letter to Families 6, 158, 214, 255,
    256, 267, 273
Love
— and lust 90-91
— authentic 74, 101, 150, 151, 270,
    271, 276, 284, 290, 291, 295,
    297, 298, 324
— betrothed 293, 294, 319
— chastity as condition for 298-299
— conjugal love 118, 123, 124,
    144, 145, 293, 294, 298, 325
— dimensions of 283, 294
— essence of 73, 310
— married 53, 59, 78, 85, 118, 123,
    147, 151, 153, 158, 161, 171,
    174, 180, 216, 216-236, 267,
    273, 283, 284, 292, 294, 300,
    310, 326, 330, 331, 339, 344
— objective dimension of 151-152
— redeemed 152-153
— reveals person 149-150
— self-giving xxiii, 52, 78, 83, 84,
    107, 110, 122, 126, 130, 132,
    137-139, 145, 146, 151, 161,
    216, 241, 245, 273, 276, 286,
    319, 326
— sensual 307
— sentimental 290, 291
— spousal

— true 102, 147, 220, 234, 247,
    267, 283, 286, 294, 295, 324,
    339
— unitive 271, 312
Love and Responsibility xxiii, 53,
    239, 264, 266, 268, 283, 284,
    336
Lust 44, 87-93, 95-106, 107, 151,
    308, 309
— source of shame 88

M

Magisterium 124, 220, 223, 228,
    229, 230, 231, 245, 259, 260
Malthusianism 159, 179, 180, 181
Man
— eschatological 78, 107-108, 118
—historical 78, 86-106, 107, 138,
    180
— original 78, 79, 106
— original solitude 79
— original unity 79-80
— original nakedness 80-81
*Margaret Sanger: Father of Modern
    Society* 21, 361
Marriage
— as analogy and mystery 128-130
— as a permanent commitment 24
— Christian xxiv, 12, 133, 136,
    137, 140, 222
— indissolubility of 118
— matter and form of 140-142
— nature of 51, 140, 333
— sacrament of 137, 138, 235, 340
— spirituality 329-344
— undermined by homosexual
    agenda 22-24
Masculinity 82-85, 89, 97, 99, 103,
    123, 138, 141-144, 149, 152,
    284, 286, 292, 303, 305, 309,
    310, 340, 343
Mater et Magistra 219
Materialism 160, 181-183, 199,
    200, 203, 206, 238, 242
— refuted 190-192

Maternity 46, 120, 121, 123, 124
Matrimony 12, 74, 119, 127, 135,
    137, 140, 141, 142, 144, 145,
    152, 217, 225, 294, 333
Medical Aspects of Human Sexuality
    33
Modesty, sexual 91-92
Morality 27, 220, 224, 231, 232,
    271, 285, 313-319, 322, 325
Motherhood 40, 46, 84, 268, 330,
    331, 340
Mothers 13, 19, 20, 22, 161, 172,
    232, 352, 353

N

Naked Public Square, The 184, 363
Naked Without Shame 81
Nakedness, original 80-82
National Association for Research
    and Therapy of Homosexuality
    33
National Center for Lesbian Rights
    23
National Conference of Catholic
    Bishops 222
National Education Association 32,
    35
Natural Family Planning (NFP)
— and divorce 174-177
— and fertility cycle 167-168
— and spirituality of marriage 340-
    344
— effectiveness 173-174
— effect on marriage 174-177
— fosters trust 235
— increases tenderness between
    spouses 304
— is possible with grace 353
— just reasons for 334
— methods 167, 169, 170-173, 174,
    176
— requires periodic continence 299,
    302
— vs. contraception 157-177, 182,
    312-327
Naturalism 195-196, 203, 265

Natural Law 256-260, 264-266
Naziism 96
Neo-Malthusian 160, 181
New World Order 45-46
Nietzscheism 186
Nihilism 205
Non-governmental organizations
    (NGOs) 38
Norplant 164, 165, 166

O

Openness to life 321, 323, 324, 326,
    331
Overpopulation 160, 181, 219
Ovulation Method (see Billings
    Method)

P

Parenthood 123, 245, 319, 320, 322,
    324, 337
— responsible 78, 239, 329, 330,
    331, 332, 333, 334, 335, 337,
    338, 340, 353
Passion(s)
— concupiscible 69-71, 301
— irascible 70-71, 301
Person(s)
— and rational faculties 64-69
— and shame 92-93
— are responsible 55, 318
— as object 88-89, 247-248
— defense of 225-227
— definition of 54
— endowed with intellect and will
—□inescapable dependence viii, 51,
    55
— mystery of the 277
— rationalist view of 239
— reductive view of 47, 96, 179,
    180, 183, 190, 200
— total vision of human ___ 107,
    118, 127, 190
— transcendent greatness 277
— uniqueness 54-55

— using __ 56-57
— vision of the xiv, 251, 264, 270, 275, 276, 294
Personalistic norm 56-58
Physicalism 265-266
Pill, The 159, 164-166, 174, 180, 218, 247
— health hazards 165-166
Pivot of Civilization 20, 21
Planned Parenthood 19-22, 38, 215-216
Pope Paul VI Institute for Human Reproduction 174
Population
— explosion 180-181
— increase 219
PrepComs (U.N.) 38
Procreation
— an end of marriage 7, 59, 220, 332
— attitude towards 321-322
— basis of marriage 24
— circumstances in which to avoid 334
— cooperation in divine plan 277
— creates family 336
— given up in celibacy 119
— linked with unitive meaning of marriage 246, 312
— meaning of body and__ 83-84
— meaning of man and woman beyond __ 110-111, 114
— morality of methods of avoiding 313-327
— no conflict between unitive and procreative meaning of marital act 220
— not only end of marriage 333
— nuptial meaning of body and __ 83-84
— objective end of sexual urge 287
— physical vs. spiritual 124
— unlawful to impede in conjugal act 160, 218
Profession of Faith and Oath of Fidelity 227-228, 230

Proportionalism 224, 225, 227, 316, 317
Purity 81, 82, 83, 101-105, 315

R

Rationalist materialism 160, 181-186, 190, 194, 199, 202, 238, 242
Reason
— and emotions 71-75
— and faith 183-186
— restoration of confidence in 206-208
Reconciliation, Sacrament of 12, 13, 342-343, 348
Redemption
— and language of the body 144
— confers new dimension to chastity 339
— continence as participation in 120-121
— creates the new man 61, 107, 132
— gives strength in the struggle against sin 317
— gives strength to fulfill God's original plan for marriage 119, 273
— helps to reconquer spontaneity 308-310
— marriage as embodiment of 128, 340
— of the body 96-106, 109-111, 126, 137, 140
— opened heaven 108
— opposed by society 27
— redefined by homosexual activists 25
— source of the Church's sacramentality 131-133, 137-139
— "the great mystery" 214-215
— transforming power of 188, 235, 243, 308
— of the body 96-99, 104, 105, 109, 126, 137, 140

Redemptor Hominis 60, 104, 308
Reductionism 281
Relativism 186, 200, 201-202, 204, 281
"Reparative therapy" 32
Repression 303
Responsibility 8, 9, 21, 55, 74, 138, 146, 222, 229, 277, 285, 316, 317, 321, 324, 326, 334, 335
Rights
— inalienable 41, 55, 225, 226, 273
— human 38, 41, 47, 237
— reproductive 41, 42
— women's 225
Rhythm Method, see Calendar Rhythm Method (of NFP)
Roe v. Wade 19, 21, 29
RU-486 166

S

Same-sex
— marriage 23
— partnerships 22-25
— partners, supported by corporations and universities 23, 29
Secular humanism 186-187, 281
Self-control 89, 94, 100, 101, 216, 234, 242, 300, 309
Self-mastery 36, 101, 242-244, 246, 247, 248, 298, 301, 302, 303, 310, 312, 326, 338
SERENA 170
Sex education 19, 232-233
Sexual attraction 284-297, 298
Sexual urge 96, 97, 249, 264, 277, 284-288, 299, 302, 303, 306, 312
— sublimation of 303
Sexual revolution xxii, xxiii, xxiv, 27, 54, 96, 174, 186, 215, 280
Shame 81, 82, 83
— and nature of person 92-93
— appearance of 87-88
— lust source of 88
— meaning of 91-92

Sin, original 26, 105
Single-parent home 5, 18, 232
Skepticism
— radical 185, 186
— refuted 192-194
— self-destructive 200-201
Solitude, original 79, 80, 85
Song of Songs 73, 74, 147-152
"Spiritual Canticle" 146-148
Spontaneity 171, 299, 302, 306, 308-310
Sterilization 21, 41, 42, 162-164, 173, 175
Supreme Court 24, 29, 30, 184, 185, 345, 346
Sympto-Thermal Method 170-174
Synod of Bishops on the Family 5

T

Temperance 65, 69, 101, 300, 301
Ten Commandments 225, 273, 316
Tobit, Book of 146, 147, 151, 152, 370
Totality, principle of 221
Trinity xxiii, xxvii, 52, 80, 107, 108, 112, 113, 114, 118, 129, 130, 132, 239, 326, 352
Truth
— absolute 200, 202
— definition of objective 201
— is a Person 210
— objective 200, 201, 205, 255, 282, 286, 291, 292
— philosophical 194
— religious 194, 281
— scientific 194

U

United Nations
— 1995 International Conference on Women (Beijing) 38, 39, 40, 41, 45, 46, 268
— and gender issues 38-42
— and our response as Christians 46-47

— International Conference on
    Population and Development
    (Cairo) 38, 39, 41, 46
— Millennium Summit 45
Unity
— of soul and body 265, 276-277
— original 79-80
Universal Declaration of Human
    Rights 38, 47
U.N. (see United Nations)
U.S.
— Department of Health, Education
    and Welfare 173
Utilitarianism 267-272

V

Value
— of body 105, 310
— of other as person 74, 91, 286,
    303
— of sex 310
— spiritual 289
Values clarification 19
Vasectomy 163, 164
Veritatis Splendor 226, 227, 256,
    258, 263, 265, 314
Virginity (also see Celibacy)
— definitive realization of nuptial
    meaning of body 114-115
— inner meaning of vocation to
    118-126, 302
Vocation xx, xxviii, 19, 78, 79, 113,
    118-126, 127-128, 137, 143,
    146, 151, 159, 188, 228, 302,
    330, 332, 335, 338, 340

W

Will
— and emotions 71-75
— free
— human 138, 281, 307
Witness to Hope xxvi, 188
Women-Church Convergence 39
Women's Alliance for Theology,
    Ethics and Ritual (WATER) 39

Women's Empowerment 46
Women's Environmental and
    Development Organization
    (WEDO) 38
World Bank 19, 39, 237